solutions@s

Hack proofing your wireless
network.

With more than 1,500,000 co   d Cisco
study guides in print, we con   ve the
information needs of our rea   .

Readers like yourself have been telling us they want an internet based service that would extend and enhance the value of our books. Based on
reader feedback and our own strategic   n we   o site
that we hope will exceed your expe   s.

Solutions@syngress.com is an interactive treasure trove of useful information focusing on our book topics and related technologies. The site
offers the following features:

- One-year warranty against content obsolescence due to vendor
  product upgrades. You can access online updates for any affected
  chapters.

- "Ask the Author" customer query forms that enable you to post
  questions to our authors and editors.

- Exclusive monthly mailings in which our experts provide answers to
  reader queries and clear explanations of complex material.

- Regularly updated links to sites specially selected by our editors for
  readers desiring additional reliable information on key topics.

Best of all, the book you're now holding is your key to this amazing site.
Just go to **www.syngress.com/solutions**, and keep this book handy when
you register to verify your purchase.

Thank you for giving us the opportunity to serve your needs. And be sure
to let us know if there's anything else we can do to help you get the
maximum value from your investment. We're listening.

www.syngress.com/solutions

HACK PROOFING
YOUR WIRELESS NETWORK

Christian Barnes

Tony Bautts

Donald Lloyd

Eric Ouellet

Jeffrey Posluns

David M. Zendzian

Neal O'Farrell   Technical Editor

SYNGRESS®

KEY	SERIAL NUMBER
001	QJG4TY7UT5
002	KKLRT5W3E4
003	PMERL3SD6N
004	AGD34B3BH2
005	NLU8EVYN7H
006	ZFG4RN38R4
007	CWBV22YH6T
008	9PB9RGB7MR
009	R3N5M4PVS5
010	GW2EH22WF8

PUBLISHED BY
Syngress Publishing, Inc.
800 Hingham Street
Rockland, MA 02370

Hack Proofing Your Wireless Network

Printed in the United States of America

1 2 3 4 5 6 7 8 9 0

ISBN: 1-928994-59-8

Technical Editor: Neal O'Farrell
Technical Reviewer: Jeffrey Posluns
Acquisitions Editor: Catherine B. Nolan
Developmental Editor: Kate Glennon

Cover Designer: Michael Kavish
Page Layout and Art by: Shannon Tozier
Copy Editor: Michael McGee
Indexer: Ed Rush

Distributed by Publishers Group West in the United States and Jaguar Book Group in Canada.

Acknowledgments

We would like to acknowledge the following people for their kindness and support in making this book possible.

Ralph Troupe, Rhonda St. John, and the team at Callisma for their invaluable insight into the challenges of designing, deploying and supporting world-class enterprise networks.

Karen Cross, Lance Tilford, Meaghan Cunningham, Kim Wylie, Harry Kirchner, Kevin Votel, Kent Anderson, and Frida Yara of Publishers Group West for sharing their incredible marketing experience and expertise.

Jacquie Shanahan and AnnHelen Lindeholm of Elsevier Science for making certain that our vision remains worldwide in scope.

Annabel Dent of Harcourt Australia for all her help.

David Buckland, Wendi Wong, Marie Chieng, Lucy Chong, Leslie Lim, Audrey Gan, and Joseph Chan of Transquest Publishers for the enthusiasm with which they receive our books.

Kwon Sung June at Acorn Publishing for his support.

Ethan Atkin at Cranbury International for his help in expanding the Syngress program.

Jackie Gross, Gayle Voycey, Alexia Penny, Anik Robitaille, Craig Siddall, Darlene Morrow, Iolanda Miller, Jane Mackay, and Marie Skelly at Jackie Gross & Associates for all their help and enthusiasm representing our product in Canada.

Lois Fraser, Connie McMenemy, Shannon Russell and the rest of the great folks at Jaguar Book Group for their help with distribution of Syngress books in Canada.

Contributors

Donald Lloyd (CCNA, CCSE, CCSA), co-author of *Designing a Wireless Network* (Syngress Publishing, ISBN: 1-928994-45-8), is a Senior Consultant at Lucent Worldwide Services (Enhanced Services and Sales) and a Regional Leader for their Fixed Wireless Practice. His specialties include network security architecture and wireless network design, as well as the implementation of Juniper routers. Donald's background includes a successful career with International Network Services, and now Lucent Technologies. Besides "unwiring" corporate offices, Donald has spent considerable time designing and deploying secure wireless networks in remote oil and gas fields. These networks not only carry voice and data traffic, but also help energy companies monitor the pipelines that carry these commodities.

David M. Zendzian is CEO and High Programmer with DMZ Services, Inc. He provides senior IT and security solutions to single person startups and multi-national corporations "anywhere the Net touches." His specialties include large- and small-scale IT and security designs, deployments, infrastructure audits, and complete managed support. David's background includes positions with Wells Fargo Bank as a Security Consultant where he developed and evaluated platform-specific security standards, assisted with identification of security risks to applications, and designed bank interconnectivity projects that required firewalls, VPNs, and other security devices. He was also a founding partner in one of the first Internet service providers of South Carolina and founder of the first wireless ISP in the Carolinas, Air Internet.

David is an active Debian Linux developer who maintains packages for network audio streaming (icecast, liveice) and the PGP Public Keyserver (pks). He has provided patches to several projects, most notably to the Carnegie Mellon Simple Authentication and Security Layer (SASL). David studied computer science at the oldest municipal college in America, The College of Charleston in Charleston, SC. He currently lives in the San Francisco area with his wife, Dana. David would like to thank

Change and N8 for providing support and critical commentary needed to finish this work.

Eric Ouellet (CISSP) is a Senior Partner with Secure Systems Design Group, a network design and security consultancy based in Ottawa, Ontario, Canada. He specializes in the implementation of networks and security infrastructures from both a design and a hands-on perspective. Over his career, he has been responsible for designing, installing, and troubleshooting WANs using CISCO, Nortel, and Alcatel equipment, configured to support voice, data, and video conferencing services over terrestrial, satellite relay, wireless, and trusted communication links. Eric has also been responsible for designing some of the leading Public Key Infrastructure deployments currently in use and for devising operational policy and procedures to meet the Electronic Signature Act (E-Sign) and the Health Insurance Portability and Accountability Act (HIPAA). He has provided his services to financial, commercial, government, and military customers including US Federal Government, Canadian Federal Government, and NATO. He regularly speaks at leading security conferences and teaches networking and CISSP classes. He is currently working on two upcoming titles with Syngress Publishing, *Building a Cisco Wireless LAN* (ISBN: 1-928994-58-X) and *Sniffer Network Optimization and Troubleshooting Handbook* (ISBN: 1-931836-57-4). Eric would like to acknowledge the understanding and support of his family and friends during the writing of this book, and "The Boys" for being who they are.

Christian Barnes (CCNP, CCDA, MCSE, MCP+I, CNA, A+) is a member of the Consulting Staff at Lucent Worldwide Services (Enhanced Services and Sales). He is a contributing author to *Designing a Wireless Network* (Syngress Publishing, ISBN: 1-928994-45-8) and he currently provides technical consultation to clients in the South Central Region for Lucent Technologies. His areas of expertise include Cisco routers and switches, wide area network architecture, troubleshooting and optimization, network security, wireless access, and Microsoft NT and 2000 networking design and support. Chris has worked with clients such as Birch Telecom, Williams Energy, and the Cerner Corporation.

Randy Hiser is a Senior Network Engineer for Sprint's Research, Architecture and Design Group, with design responsibilities for home distribution and DSL self-installation services for Sprint's Integrated On Demand Network. He is knowledgeable in the area of multimedia services and emerging technologies, has installed and operated fixed wireless MMDS facilities in the Middle East, and has patented network communication device identification in a communication network for Sprint. He lives with his wife, Deborah, and their children, Erin, Ryan, Megan, Jesse, and Emily, in Overland Park, KS.

Andy McCullough (BSEE, CCNA, CCDA) has been in network consulting for over seven years. He is currently a Distinguished Member of the Consulting Staff at Lucent Worldwide Services (Enhanced Services and Sales). Andy has done architecture and design work for several global customers of Lucent Technologies including Level 3 Communications, Sprint, MCI/WorldCom, the London Stock Exchange, and British Telecom. His areas of expertise include network architecture and design, IP routing and switching, and IP multicast. Prior to working for Lucent, Andy ran a consulting company and a regional ISP.

Andy is co-author of *Building Cisco Remote Access Networks* (Syngress Publishing, ISBN: 1-928994-13-X). He is also an Assistant Professor at a community college in Overland Park, KS, where he teaches networking classes.

Tony Bautts is a Senior Security Consultant with Astech Consulting. He currently provides security advice and architecture for clients in the San Francisco Bay area. His specialties include intrusion detection systems, firewall design and integration, post-intrusion forensics, bastion hosting, and secure infrastructure design. Tony's security experience has led him to work with Fortune 500 companies in the United States as well as two years of security consulting in Japan. He is also involved with the BerkeleyWireless.net project, which is working to build neighborhood wireless networks for residents of Berkeley, CA.

Jeffrey A. Wheat (Lucent WaveLAN Wireless Certification, FORE ATM Certification) is a Principal Member of the Consulting Staff at Lucent Worldwide Services. He currently provides strategic direction and architectural design to Lucent Service Provider and Large Enterprise customers. He is an ATM and Testing Methodology Subject Matter Expert within Lucent, and his specialties include convergence architectures and wireless architectures. Jeff's background with Lucent includes design engagements with Metricom, Sprint ION, Sprint PCS, Raytheon, and Marathon Oil. Prior to his employment with Lucent, Jeff spent 11 years working for the U.S. Intelligence Agencies as a network architect and systems engineer. Jeff graduated from the University of Kansas in 1986 with a bachelor's of Science degree in Computer Science and currently resides in Kansas City with his wife, Gabrielle, and their two children, Madison and Brandon.

Technical Editor

Neal O'Farrell is founder and CEO of security training firm Hackademia Inc., where he oversees the development of more than 30 Web-based security training courses. Neal is a panel expert and regular columnist on SearchSecurity.com and was recently elected Chair of the first Cybercrime on Wall Street Conference. He has written more than one hundred articles and three books, appearing in publications as diverse as *Business Week*, *Information Week*, *NetWorker*, and *Wireless Design News*. With a career in information security that spans nearly two decades, Neal was recently described by the Institute for International Research as one of the world's top 20 security experts. Neal got his first taste of wireless security in the mid-1980s when he was asked by the Irish government to develop a security system for the nation's fledgling cellular network.

In 1989 he co-hosted with IBM one of Europe's first network security conferences, and later helped Nokia incorporate security into their first generation of cellular telephones. As the head of the European crypto firm Intrepid, Neal leads the development of some of the world's most advanced voice, data, and fax encryption systems, including MilCode, a European rival of the U.S. government's Secure Telephone Unit (STU 3).

Technical Reviewer

Jeffrey Posluns (CISA, CISSP, CCNP, SSCP, GSEC) is an information security specialist with over eight years of specialized experience in security methodologies, audits, and controls. He has extensive expertise in the analysis of hacker tools and techniques, intrusion detection, security policies, and incident response procedures.

Jeffrey has held the position of Chief Technology Officer of SecureOps for the past three years, where he has the responsibility of bringing technical vision and strategy to the company, overseeing the development and implementation of all technological initiatives, and being a key resource in the research and development of new practices, methodologies, procedures, and information assets. Jeffrey is a regular speaker at industry conferences organized by such groups as the Information Systems Audit and Control Association (ISACA) and the Association of Certified Fraud Examiners (ACFE). He also speaks regularly for, and participates in, various panels and working groups promoting information security awareness with the Canadian IT, government, and law enforcement industries.

Contents

Answers to Your Wireless Questions

Q: Will i-Mode be available in North America or Europe?

A: Although i-Mode parent NTT DoCoMo has ownership stakes in several North American and European cellular operators, it is not expected that i-Mode, as it currently exists, will be offered in these markets. This is primarily due to the limited 9.6 Kbps access rates.

Tools & Traps…

Clear-text Authentication

An example of a brute-force password dictionary generator that can produce a brute-force dictionary from specific character sets can be found at www.dmzs.com/tools/files. Other brute force crackers, including POP, Telnet, FTP, Web and others, can be found at http://packetstormsecurity.com/crackers.

Chapter 3 Wireless Network Architecture and Design

Fixed Wireless Technologies

In a fixed wireless network, both transmitter and receiver are at fixed locations, as opposed to mobile. The network uses utility power (AC). It can be point-to-point or point-to-multipoint, and may use licensed or unlicensed spectrums.

Chapter 4 Common Attacks and Vulnerabilities   201

Notes from the Underground…

Lucent Gateways broadcast SSID in clear on encrypted networks

It has been announced (www.securiteam.com/securitynews/5ZP0I154UG.html) that the Lucent Gateway allows an attacker an easy way to join a closed network.

Lucent has defined an option to configure the wireless network as "closed." This option requires that to associate with the wireless network a client must know and present the SSID of the network. Even if the network is protected by WEP, part of the broadcast messages the gateway transmits in cleartext includes the SSID. All an attacker need do is sniff the network to acquire the SSID, they are then able to associate with the network.

Guidelines for Analyzing Threats

- Identify assets
- Identify the method of accessing these valuables from an authorized perspective
- Identify the likelihood that someone other than an authorized user can access valuables
- Identify potential damages
- Identify the cost to replace, fix, or track the loss
- Identify security countermeasures
- Identify the cost in implementation of the countermeasures
- Compare costs of securing the resource versus cost of damage control

Chapter 6 Circumventing Security Measures   299

War Driving

War driving has become the common term given for people who drive around with wireless equipment looking for other wireless networks. This term gets its history from "war-dialing" – the age old practice of having your computer dial every phone number within a certain range to see if a computer would pick up.

Chapter 7 Monitoring and Intrusion Detection   327

Defensive Monitoring Considerations

- Define your wireless network boundaries, and monitor to know if they're being exceeded

- Limit signal strength to contain your network.

- Make a list of all authorized wireless Access Points (APs) in your environment. Knowing what is supposed to be there can help you immediately identify rogue APs.

Chapter 8 Auditing   **363**

Auditing Activities

Wireless network audits consist of several stages where different resources or tools are needed to perform a specific activity. These activities generally fall into six categories:

- Audit Planning

- Audit Information Gathering

- Audit Information Analysis and Report Generation

- Audit Report Presentation

- Post-Audit Review

- Next Steps

Implementing an Ultra Secure WLAN

❧

- Make sure that your AP allows you to change ESSID, passwords and supports 128-bit WEP.

- Find an AP that supports the "closed network" functionality.

- Be certain that the AP you buy supports flash upgrades.

- Isolate the AP and regulate access from its network into your internal network.

- Conduct audits of your network using NetStumbler or other wireless scanning tools to make sure that others aren't enabling unauthorized APs.

- Update security policy to reflect the dangers of an unsecured wireless network.

Foreword

The simple way to make a wireless system or device more secure is to put it into a faraday cage. Unfortunately, while this strategy leaves you with a device that is unreachable by attackers, it also leaves you with a device that is almost completely useless.

Traditionally, someone had to be sitting in front of your computer to read your documents, see your e-mail, and mess with your settings. Today, however, someone can be sitting in the office next door, a few floors up or down, or even in the next building, and have the same abilities as if he were in front of your computer. Advancements in wireless communications have allowed for great increases in productivity and ease of use, but have brought with them many additional risks to the systems and information being used.

Are you using an 802.11 or Bluetooth device on your computer? Are you using a PDA to communicate with other systems or to get onto the Internet? Are you using a cellular phone to initiate a network connection back to your office? Have you just set up the latest wireless gateway at home so you can walk around with your notebook? Are you planning on implementing a wireless solution in your office? Simply put, there is now a greater security risk to your information. Someone could more easily read your financial data, look at your saved documents, or browse your e-mails. The advances in ease of use with wireless systems come at a cost—they must go hand in hand with advances in information security. You will now have to deal with issues like: network identification and encryption keys; making your wireless network invisible to people passing close enough to see it; and making sure that nothing and no one, other than your defined list of devices, systems, or people, are able to use your wireless resources.

People are naturally disinclined to consider security. Security and cost, or security and ease of use, are often at odds in the workplace, and many other items tend to be given a comparatively higher business priority. It is for these reasons that one must *anticipate* security when considering any new implementation, generate a clear and well-defined business case, and allow the security processes to be properly and efficiently managed throughout their lifecycles.

There is no way to make your systems 100 percent secure, but what you can do is learn about what hackers and crackers can do to you, learn how to protect yourself from them, learn how to catch them in the act of attacking your computer or other wireless device, and learn how to make it difficult enough for them that they will move on to easier targets.

The intent of this book is to provide perspective and relevant information with respect to wireless communications to people in all areas of business analysis and information technology, whether they are preparing a business case for a wireless project, are IS/IT specialists planning for a new wireless implementation, security neophytes expanding a home network to include wireless access, reacting to an attack on their network, or being proactive in security measures.

If you don't have to time to read and understand all of the chapters describing the complex facets of information security as they are applied to wireless technologies, you can simply follow the instructions on planning and implementing a wireless network, along with the security aspects surrounding it. You will benefit from the hands-on descriptions of hardening and securing your wireless networks and devices, allowing you to rest easy knowing that no one will compromise your information or take advantage of your systems without your knowledge.

—*Jeffrey Posluns, CISA, CISSP, SSCP, CCNP*

Chapter 1

The Wireless Challenge

Solutions in this chapter:

- Wireless Technology Overview
- Understanding the Promise of Wireless
- Understanding the Benefits of Wireless
- Facing the Reality of Wireless Today
- Examining the Wireless Standards

☑ Summary

☑ Solutions Fast Track

☑ Frequently Asked Questions

Introduction

When the concept of a network without wires was first suggested more than two decades ago, it sparked the imagination of scientists, product vendors, and users around the globe eager for the convenience and flexibility of a free roaming connection. Unfortunately, as the variety of wireless solutions began to emerge, anticipation turned to disappointment. The first wave of solutions proved inadequate for the networking, portability, and security needs of a changing IT environment.

While this has largely continued to be the case throughout the 1990s with most cell-based and office local area network (LAN)-based wireless technology deployments, great strides have been made specifically over the last two years to address the fundamental concerns impeding the full acceptance of wireless networking in the mainstream of corporate IT departments and the small office.

In this chapter, you will learn about the technology that is available today for wireless data networking and what tomorrow's wireless technologies have to offer. We will cover office LAN wireless solutions including 802.11, its subgroups (802.11b, 802.11a, 802.11g) and HomeRF, cellular-based wireless data solutions including the Wireless Application Protocol (WAP) and i-Mode and the network infrastructures supporting them (in particular 2G, 2.5G, and 3G), and finally, 802.15 Personal Area Network (PAN) solutions such as Bluetooth. In addition, we will review some of the new standards being developed to create wireless metropolitan area networks (WMANs) and other wireless data transmission solutions that are being proposed for commercial application.

In conjunction with the review of the technologies behind wireless, we will also cover the main security concerns specifically impacting cellular-based office LAN and PAN wireless deployments. In doing so, we will review the major security concerns you can expect to read about in later chapters, and will discuss some of the efforts being made to minimize their impact.

After completing this chapter, you will have gained a solid understanding of wireless technologies and their associated security risks. It is our hope that we provide you with an appreciation of how wireless networking technologies will impact our work and home lives, and that security will have to play an important role in wireless deployments. Let's get started!

Wireless Technology Overview

Wireless technologies today come in several forms and offer a multitude of solutions applicable to generally one of two wireless networking camps:

- Cellular-based wireless data solutions
- Wireless LAN (WLAN) solutions

Defining Cellular-based Wireless

Cellular-based wireless data solutions are solutions that use the existing cell phone and pager communications networks to transmit data. Data can be categorized into many forms, including traditional corporate communications such as e-mail, directory information exchange and basic information transfers, peer-to-peer communications such as messaging services, and information lookups such as navigational information, and news and variety, amongst others.

Some cellular-based wireless data network solutions only support one-way communications. While technically they fall into the category of cellular-based data solutions, we will not include them in the discussions proposed in this book. Instead, we will focus on the cellular-based solutions that provide, at minimum, two-way data communications. Furthermore, in this book, we will only discuss solutions that can support a basic security overlay.

Defining the Wireless LAN

Wireless LAN solutions are solutions that provide wireless connectivity over a limited coverage area. The coverage area generally consists of between 10 and 100 meters (30–300 feet) from a base station or Access Point (AP). These solutions provide the capabilities necessary to support the two-way data communications of typical corporate or home desktop computers with other network resources.

The data streams in this case generally consist of remote application access and file transfers. Wireless LAN solutions provide a means for wireless nodes to interface with hard-wired LAN resources. This results in the creation of hybrid networks where hard-wired nodes and wireless nodes may interact with each other.

The Convergence of Wireless Technologies

While for the time being, the two classifications hold generally true, many new vendor product offerings planned for introduction over the next year will begin to blur the lines between cellular-based wireless devices and wireless LAN-based devices. These include cell phones, high-end pagers, and cell-enabled personal digital assistants (PDAs), which also provide personal area network connectivity to local devices using wireless LAN technologies such as Bluetooth.

This trend will only continue to accelerate. With the evolution of more powerful and compact wireless network components supporting greater access speeds and communications capabilities, and the increased versatility of PDAs and other portable information appliances, consumers will continue to demand more tightly integrated communication environments that provide seamless application support across their hard-wired and wireless information resources.

Trends and Statistics

At this point in our wireless technology review, it is worthwhile to take a closer look at some of the emerging wireless data trends and usage statistics. The picture that begins to emerge is quite interesting.

Initially, the big trend that becomes readily apparent is that support for convergence within devices will be the norm over the next two years. While the majority of cellular-based wireless traffic today mainly consists of voice, it is estimated that by the end of 2003 nearly 35 to 40 percent of cellular-based wireless traffic will be data.

- By 2005, 50 percent of Fortune 100 companies will have deployed wireless LANs (0.7 probability). (Source: Gartner Group)
- By 2010, the majority of Fortune 2000 companies will have deployed wireless LANs (0.6 probability). (Source: Gartner Group)

Figure 1.1 shows the projected number of wireless Internet users in 2005.

Figure 1.1 Projected Number of Wireless Internet Users in 2005 (Source: Yankee Group)

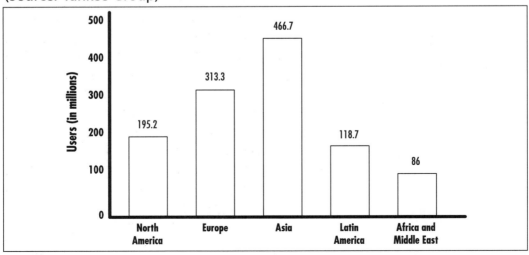

Increasing Use of Information Appliances

While users on the move are leading the push for the integration of wireless devices, a recent trend in the availability of *information appliances* is beginning to have an impact on the wireless industry at large and will soon be one of the leading platforms for wireless data communications.

Information appliances are single purpose devices that are portable, easy to use and provide a specific set of capabilities relevant to their function. Examples of devices currently shipping include PDAs, MP3 players, e-books, and DVD players. Information appliance shipments over this year will outnumber PC shipments. (See Figure 1.2.)

Figure 1.2 Projected PC and Information Appliance Shipments (Source: IDC Report 1998)

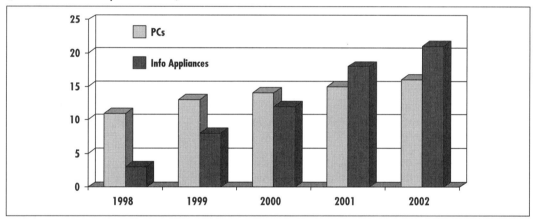

This trend will continue for the foreseeable future. As new features and the level of functionalities incorporated within information appliances increase, so will their market share of the information technology deployment landscape. In the end, the full value of these devices will only be realized when wireless networking capabilities are fully integrated within the information appliances.

As the information appliance and wireless networking integration occurs, end users will be provided with the ability to obtain and manipulate content on demand. Content will range from existing textual data (such as books and news) to full-blown multimedia (such as audio, video and interactive media files). Access to content will be provided using both local (or proximity-based) wireless networking technologies and cellular-based wireless networking technologies. Content will be available from traditional external sources such as content servers and Web servers located on the Internet, and from proximity or locally accessed sources such as shopping malls, airports, office buildings, and other public places.

The Future of Wireless, circa 2005

Think of a nice sunny morning. The year is 2005 and you are about to go on a business trip in a foreign city. You have your trusty universal integrated two-way voice, data, and video multimedia PDA by your side.

Using references to your personal digital identification module stored in your PDA, your travel agent registered all of your travel arrangements, including your flights, car, and a room at your favorite hotel. Now that the preparations are made, let's take a look at how this day might unfold.

Using your wireless PDA, you bring up the local taxi service, and call up and request a car to pick you up from home. The taxi arrives and drives you to the airport. You authenticate to the electronic payment module on your PDA using integrated writing analysis software and charge the cost of the trip to your corporate account. The payment transaction between the cab, your PDA, and your bank is encrypted and digitally signed. A confirmation of payment is recorded for expense billing and audit review at a later date.

You walk up to the self-service check-in counter for frequent flyers. The proximity wireless network in your PDA becomes active and your PDA authenticates you at the counter. An encrypted session is set up. Your flight information is displayed on the check-in counter screen and you are prompted to sign a confirmation on your PDA. Boarding passes and self-tacking baggage tags are printed. You affix the tags to your bags and deposit them on the checked baggage belt. As they disappear behind the wall, you receive confirmation on your PDA that your bags have been checked. As your session with the check-in counter is terminated, a new session is established with airport information control. From now until the time you board the plane, you will be able to obtain the latest information on flight schedules, gate information, baggage information, airport layout, restaurants, shopping and other airport services.

Your flight arrives at its destination and you make your way to baggage claim. A new session has been established with the local airport information control. Based on your ticketing information, it tells you where your bags are currently, where you will be able to pick them up and their estimated time of availability. An airport map is conveniently made available for your use along with information on local services.

You collect your bags and hop on the local car rental agency bus. In transit to the car lot, you preselect your car and sign the rental agreement. The car keys are downloaded to your PDA. To save time, you preconfigure your PDA to open the trunk and unlock the doors when you are within a few feet. You have a few extra minutes left and you use them to check your voice and video messages from your PDA. One of the video messages has a large format graphics file attached. You make a note to view that message when you get to the hotel.

You arrive at the car, the trunk opens and the doors unlock. You store your bags and select the hotel information on your PDA. The in-car display and GPS directional system provides you with directions to the hotel. You prepay the tolls and a confirmation of payment is recorded for expense billing and use at the automated toll. You'll be able to drive to the hotel using the express lane. Your PDA will take care of passing on the prepayment when you get to the tool booth.

You arrive at the hotel and leave the car with the valet. They will take care of carrying your heavy bags up to your room. As you make your way through the lobby, your PDA authenticates your reservation and provides you with your room assignment. You conditionally sign for the room, and the keys are downloaded to your PDA. As you arrive at the door of your room, the door unlocks and you enter. You verify the room is as you asked for and click Accept Room on your PDA.

You make a video call on your PDA to your in-town associates and make reservations for four at a local restaurant for dinner. You download the wine list and menu and make a selection for appetizers. Your PDA reminds you that you still have an unviewed video message.

Now that you are all checked in and in your room, you'll have some time to view it. You bring up the video message with a large format graphic file on your PDA and display it on the in-room TV. It's video highlights of the after-school soccer league game. Your daughter scored the winning goal.

While at first, many of the elements in our "day in the life" may appear to be from the realm of science fiction, by the time you complete this chapter, you will realize that they are not as far-fetched as they may appear. Surprisingly, the technologies and standards exist today to make all of this real.

Let's take a look at what wireless has in store for us.

Understanding the Promise of Wireless

At this point it might be a worthwhile exercise to do a quick historical review of data networking and telephony to get a clearer understanding of where the technology is heading.

As we all know, in the beginning, computers lived in glass houses. At that time, these machines were more like objects to be admired for their technical complexity and problem-solving abilities than as useful day-to-day tools. The fact that they even existed was the stuff of legend, and great pains were taken to keep access to them, and even knowledge of them in some cases, restricted to only a privileged few.

Throughout the sixties and most of the seventies, computing resources remained in the central computing complex. The machines of that period were bulky and difficult to use. Networking was in its infancy and few protocols existed to support the sharing of data.

When the personal computer revolution took hold in the late seventies and early eighties, the demystification of computing resources brought in an unprecedented era of access. New applications were devised in the realms of business, communications and entertainment. A novel trend had emerged: computing technologies were being brought to the users, instead of the users being taken to the computers. As these resources became more compact and more powerful, computing visionaries began to dream about a future where anyone could access a computer at anytime, from anywhere.

The computing folks were not the only ones to share that dream. A similar desire was being manifested within the telephone industry. Users had begun to demand portable telephone services and more extensive telephone coverage in remote or limited access environments where traditional physical line-based services were not viable.

Throughout the late eighties and nineties, a number of wireless telephone solutions began to appear in the market place. By this time, traditional computing had become a user of wired telephone services for network dial-in access, Bulletin Board Services, and other data communications. Laptop computers had become available and the marriage of wireless networking and portable computing had finally arrived. Or so it seemed.

It was a difficult time. Networking standards were evolving at breakneck speeds to address the ever-changing data computing needs of the corporate and scientific users. New applications were being developed that were more powerful and complex, and which required an ever increasing availability of bandwidth. All the while, new security standards were unfolding to address the shift from the glasshouse computing concept to a fully distributed computing model.

Few of these new standards were fully adaptable to meet the demands of wireless networking users. If we take into account all of the data networking standards being defined at that time and factor in the hardware limitations of the day, it's little wonder why wireless never reached the masses. Many of the portable data transceivers and cell phones being offered were very bulky and provided too low of a throughput to make them effective platforms for remote computing.

Wireless networking was an idea too early for the technology and data communication standards available then. The ideal of a completely untethered network would have to wait.

So where are we in terms of wireless networking today? Networking and application standards began to coalesce and are more wireless networking friendly than ever. Special classes of standards have been established to meet the demands of wireless networking. On the technological side, breakthroughs in micro-electronics have manifested themselves in the form of higher density fabrics with lower power requirements. Real-world workable wireless networking solutions have begun to emerge and are now within reach of most corporate and home consumers.

As it would be expected, the original appeal of wireless networking is just as desirable today as it was 10 or 20 years ago. Today's wireless solutions offer us flexibility, performance, and proven solutions that promise increased productivity and potential reductions of long-term capital and management costs associated with network deployments.

Soon wireless will be used in almost every context. Its presence will become universally accepted and implicitly trusted. In many ways, integrated wireless networking technologies will represent a revolution in the way people interact and communicate with each other and with data stores, not unlike the early days of telegraph and Morse code.

This next step will be larger than any other previous evolution in communications. We will have to take care and ensure that our new friend is up to all of the challenges we hope to send its way and that we provide opportunities for it to grow and evolve so that it can meet our needs long into the future.

Wireless Networking

With 3G cellular-based wireless networks, wireless LANs, wireless personal area networks, and broadband wireless services becoming available in most locations over the next few years, new applications and classes of services will be created to meet the networking needs of both business and consumers.

Wireless Networking Applications for Business

Wireless networking applications that provide solutions for business use consist of four major categories:

- Corporate Communications
- Customer Service
- Telemetry
- Field Service

Corporate Communications

Wireless networking solutions for the corporate environment revolves primarily around the remote access of data stores and application servers. With over 38 million Americans working full or part-time from home, new broadcast technologies and peer-to-peer interactive applications are beginning to play more significant roles. The overall application solution set available over wireless consists of three elements:

- Mobile messaging
- Mobile office/corporate groupware
- Telepresence

Mobile messaging involves the extension of an internal corporate messaging network environment to a remote user over a wireless network connection. A typical application includes the use of third-party solutions to extend electronic mail to wireless users. Using wireless-enabled PDAs, two-way pagers, and smart cell phones, users can be kept up-to-date with their corporate e-mail inbox and can provide brief responses to urgent or pressing issues.

The Short Message System (SMS), used to send and receive instant short text messages, is also an effective means used by the corporate user to keep up to date with the latest news and other developments. While the service is predominantly used to obtain information from text information media, it can also be used for two-way text messaging with other users.

Lastly, with the full integration of unified messaging around the world, the mobile wireless user will finally have a true remote presence. Multimedia functions will be incorporated to support both real-time and messaging requirements of users.

In Figure 1.3, we can see that a universal address supporting roaming will provide unprecedented mobility. When this occurs, corporate users will have a single point of contact. Communications will be directed to their localized point of presence, wherever that may be.

Figure 1.3 Single Point of Contact for 3G-enabled Devices

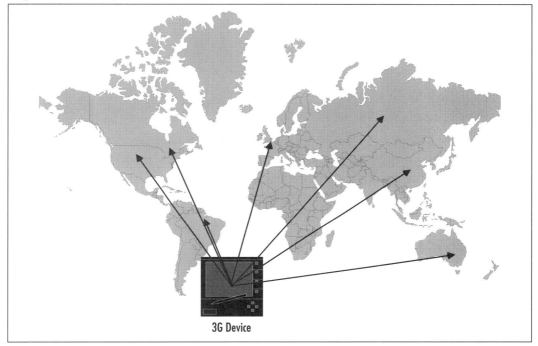

The second area in the wireless corporate communications solution set involves *mobile office and corporate groupware*. Figure 1.4 demonstrates the concept of the roaming wireless desktop. Mobile office and corporate groupware applications over wireless provide internal corporate network resources to the remote user over a wireless network connection. The most dominant applications in this area include corporate database servers, application servers, information and news servers, directory services, travel and expense services, file synchronizations, intranet server browsing, and file transfers.

Telepresence over wireless provides an avenue for increased collaborative networking. Figure 1.5 illustrates the premise of telepresence, that of providing a localized presence to a remote user. Two-way videoconferencing and Webcasts are examples of telepresence.

Figure 1.4 Wireless Mobile Office

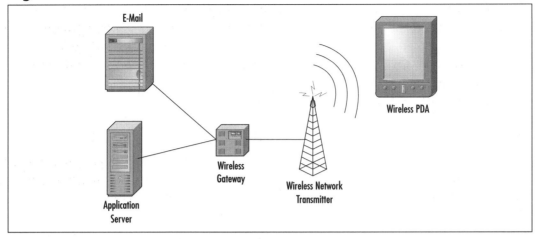

Figure 1.5 Telepresence

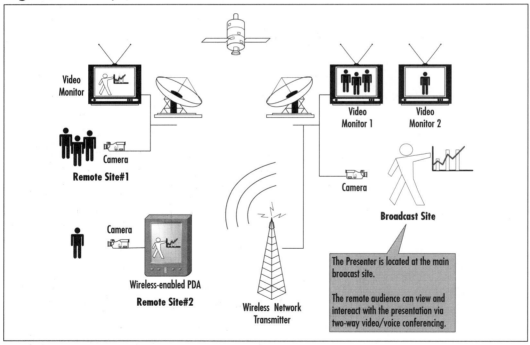

Customer Service

Customer service wireless applications offer added convenience and timeliness to consumers. Customer service agents can provide the same rich capabilities to their remote customers as those working at corporate counters.

Some of the leading applications for wireless customer service include rental car returns, airport check-in, conference attendance verification, accident claim registration, deliveries, and opinion surveys.

Telemetry

Telemetry involves obtaining data and status information from equipment and resources that are located in remote or infrequently visited areas. Transmissions generally occur at regularly scheduled intervals and do not require interaction with the end device.

Wireless telemetry provides opportunities to monitor resources that cannot be cabled or tethered easily or where a localized telephone line is either unavailable or too costly. In these scenarios, wireless networking can be used to obtain status information on devices that are out of reach of conventional communications.

Telemetry is generally categorized into two main areas of support:

- Remote monitoring and control
- Traffic and telematics

Remote monitoring and control involves the communications of state information to a centralized management resource.

An example of monitoring would be that of vending and ticketing machines. These devices would be capable of reporting on their state, activity, and inventory controls over a given period. They would also provide diagnostics and error conditions. In this scenario, the local vendor would have reliable and current information on the levels of stock, sales numbers, and customer preferences.

In the healthcare industry, wireless monitoring agents and sensors can replace the cumbersome cabled heart, blood pressure, and other monitors. Up-to-the-second information could be transmitted to the central nurse desk for real-time analysis instead of a local device, thereby reducing equipment costs and increasing the level of patient care.

The second element of wireless telemetry involves *traffic and telematics*. When adapted to support wireless networking, remote monitoring can now occur on devices that cannot be easily cabled for dial-up access. Examples of these include transportation equipment, road usage, and parking meters.

In the case of transport equipment, sensors located within the tires of a tractor-trailer rig can provide vehicle information such as weight, tire pressure, load balance, and so on. This information can be gathered, stored, transmitted, and verified at truck weigh stations along a route.

In scenarios where traffic densities on roads and highways are a concern, remote wireless traffic sensors can provide up-to-the-minute information for road segments to the centralized monitoring station where alternate traffic routing can be assigned.

Parking metering may never be the same when wireless technologies are integrated. In this application, an intelligent parking meter can assess if a parking spot is being used and if the parking fees have been paid. In the event that a vehicle is present and the parking fees have run out, it can send an alert to the central office where appropriate action can be taken. Areas with higher percentages of unpaid use could be determined and assigned to ticketing agents for review.

Field Service

While field service applications share similarities with some applications of telematics, it is different in that it extends the level of communications between devices to include two-way query/response type interactions. Some implementations support elementary troubleshooting diagnostics while others support full diagnostics, management, and control functions.

As with wireless telemetry, wireless service provides opportunities to monitor and troubleshoot resources that cannot be cabled or connected easily or where a localized telephone line is either unavailable or too costly.

In these scenarios, diagnostic information can be obtained prior to a site visit and can be verified. System checks and reset triggers can be sent remotely. When onsite repair visits are required, field personnel can obtain faulty equipment lists and obtain only the required replacement component. This can save on overall field travel, replacement equipment costs, and time spent diagnosing and servicing equipment.

Wireless Networking Applications for Consumers

Consumers are primarily interested in wireless networking to access remote resources, obtain information, personal entertainment, travel information updates, mobile messaging, e-commerce, and Internet access.

Consumer products and applications supporting 3G cellular-based units will have the added ability to offer context-specific information based on the location of the end user. This will include navigation information and context specific purchases, translation services, safety services, tracking services of equipment, and personal location monitoring services used in health care and law enforcement.

A new motto for the 3G industry might be "the right service at the right time."

Information and Entertainment

Information and entertainment have always been the leading factors in the deployment of new technologies. Wireless terminals will provide the means of interacting person-to-machine and person-to-person independent of location and time. New developments in streaming media will further the use of wireless terminals for news, sports, games, video, and multimedia downloads.

Travel Information Updates

Wireless equipment will be able to determine the location of any user within an area of less than ten meters, depending on environmental constraints such as tall buildings, mountains, and so on. This new functionality will provide the ability to offer context- and time-sensitive services to 3G users. Examples of this will include traffic and navigation information, service locations, and time-based special offers or incentives.

Mobile Messaging

For consumers, wireless Mobile Messaging provides the extension of home messaging systems, including voice, e-mail, fax, and others through a single point of contact. Multimedia functions will be incorporated to support real-time communications and messaging requirements of users.

E-commerce

While traditional e-commerce applications such as online banking, interactive shopping, and electronic ticketing will continue, a new wave of multimedia based e-commerce with context sensitivity will emerge. Music and full video downloads, gaming and other services will be offered.

Internet Access

Internet access will be available on personal wireless devices supporting traditional Web browsing and information portal downloads along with new streaming media applications and intelligent search agents.

Understanding the Benefits of Wireless

Wireless networking will provide a new era of data connectivity unmatched by cabled networks. Increases in the speed of deployment, access to data and scalability mean that the needs of specific user communities can be addressed in ways that were unavailable to network architects a few years ago.

New streams of end user applications and services are being developed to provide businesses and consumers alike with advanced data access and manipulation. The main benefits of wireless integration will fall primarily into five major categories:

- Convenience
- Affordability
- Speed
- Aesthetics
- Productivity

Convenience

First and foremost in the minds of IT professionals, business leaders, and end consumers when discussing wireless networking is the aspect of convenience. This basic benefit more or less outweighs all other benefits combined in terms of user interest in wireless, and is predominantly the main reason for their deployments. Convenience can be broken down into three areas of interest:

- Flexibility
- Roaming
- Mobility

Flexibility

Wireless technologies provide the greatest flexibility of design, integration, and deployment of any networking solution available. With only transceivers to install in the local station and a wireless hub or AP to be configured for local access, it is simple to retrofit wireless networking within existing structures or create access services where traditional networking infrastructures are not capable of addressing.

With traditional networking infrastructures, a physical path is needed between the access concentrator and each of the end users of the network. This means that a wire line needs to be created from one end of the network to the other, for users to communicate with each other (whether they be workstations or servers).

Wired access drops are generally static in location, in that the access is provided from a specified point that cannot easily be moved from one physical location to another. This also implies that if an existing access drop is in use, other users must wait their turn to gain access to the network if the next closest available drop is not conveniently located.

Existing environments may not always be new installation friendly. Many older buildings, houses and apartments do not provide facilities for installing new cabling. In these environments, building contractors and engineers may need to get involved to devise ways of running new cabling systems. When existing cable-run facilities are available, they do not always offer the most optimum path between existing LAN resources and new users. Security concerns also need to be addressed if a common wiring closet or riser is to be shared with other tenants. As such, the cost involved in installing new cabling can be prohibitive in terms of time, materials, or installation costs.

Another factor involving the installation of new cabling is loss of revenue due to the unavailability of facilities during the installation itself. Hotel chains, convention centers, and airports stand to lose revenues during a cable installation retrofit project if a section of the building needs to be closed off to customer access for safety reasons during the installation.

Intangible costs need to be explored as well when investigating the installation of new cable runs. These include customer dissatisfaction and loss of customer goodwill during and after the retrofit project itself.

With wireless networking, all that is required to create a new network is radio wave access between end nodes and/or between an end node and a wireless AP hub within the vicinity of the end nodes.

Radio waves can travel through walls, floors, and windows. This physical property of the transmission medium gives network architects the flexibility to design networks and install wireless APs where best needed. This means that a wireless AP, when properly placed, can be used to support multiple user environments at the same time.

An example of this in a wireless LAN configuration would consist of locating a wireless AP on the inside part of an eastern-facing exterior wall on the second floor of an office building. This one wireless AP could simultaneously service the needs of a group of users on the eastern corner of the first floor, second floor, and third floor along with those on the terrace located outside the first floor eastern corner. In this configuration, access is provided to users located on different floors inside and outside the building with a minimal commitment in terms of equipment and resources.

Another example or a wireless LAN configuration would consist of providing networking access within a large public area such as a library. In this scenario, properly placed APs could provide network coverage of the entire floor area without impacting the day-to-day use of the facilities. In addition, the APs could be located in an area of the library that has restricted access and is physically secure from daily activities.

While these examples represent mostly wireless LAN technologies, similar scenarios will be valid for cellular-based wireless networking in two years or so. Even greater deployment solutions will be available since the network will be accessible in any locality where the cell network is available.

This brings us to the wireless networking concept of a wireless network access zone.

Roaming

A *wireless network access zone* is an area of wireless network coverage. Compared to traditional wire-based networks, a wireless user is not required to be located at a specific spot to gain access to the network. A user can gain access to the wireless network provided they are within the area of wireless coverage where the radio signal transmissions to and from the AP are of enough strength to support communications, and they are granted access by the wireless AP. Figure 1.6 illustrates the concept of wireless access.

It is also possible to organize multiple APs to provide a single contiguous area of coverage extending well beyond the coverage zone of any single wireless AP. See Figure 1.7 and Figure 1.8. In this scenario, a user is only required to be within radio range of any wireless AP that is part of the network to obtain access.

An extension of this concept is that of the roaming user. With the always-on connectivity provided by wireless LANs, a roaming user is one that has the capability of:

- Physically roaming from one location to another within the wireless access zone
- Logically roaming a session from one wireless AP to another

Figure 1.6 Wireless Access

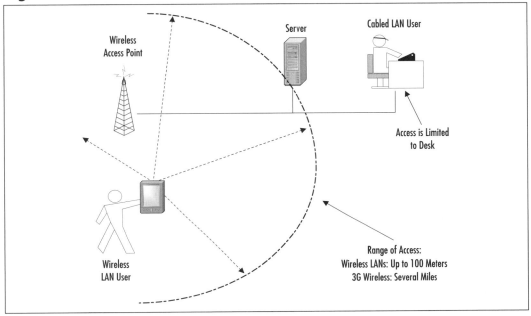

Figure 1.7 Roaming Between Access Points

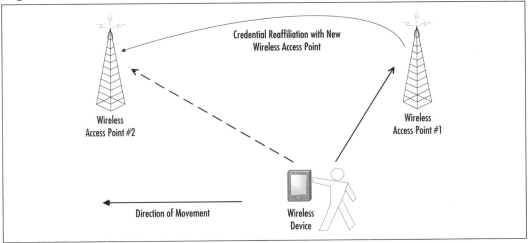

Figure 1.8 Linked Wireless Access Zones

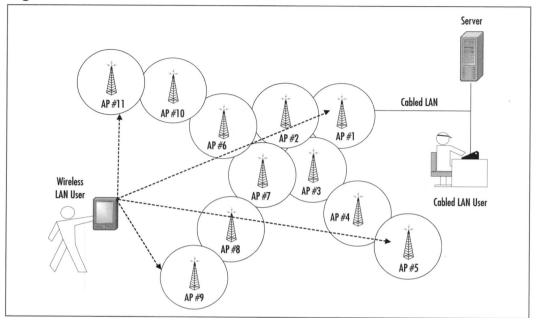

When discussing physical roaming, we would include both the movement of a user within a single AP's wireless network access zone or within the combined network access zones for all the APs that are part of this network.

When discussing logical roaming we refer to the transference of a networking session from one wireless AP to another without the need for any user interaction during the session reassociation process. When a user moves from one wireless AP's area of coverage to another AP's area of coverage, the user's transmission signal strength is assessed. As the signal reaches a threshold, the user credentials are carried over from the old "home base" AP to the new "home base" AP using a session token or other transparent authentication scheme.

This combination of physical and logical roaming allows users to keep data sessions active as they move freely around the area of coverage. This is of great benefit to users who require maintaining a data session with networked resources as they move about a building or facility.

An example of this would be an internal technical service agent. In their day-to-day activities, these agents may be called upon to service end stations where access to technical troubleshooting databases, call tickets, and other support resources may be required. By having access to these services over the wireless network, the technician can move from one call ticket to another without being forced to reconnect to the wire line network as they move about. Another benefit to maintaining an always-on session is that they could provide live updates to the ticketing databases or order replacement supplies at the time of service.

Next, we take a look at a senior manager who is attending a status meeting in a conference room where a limited number of data ports will be available to access e-mail, databases, and other information stores. If this manager had access to wireless networking capabilities on their laptop, they could maintain a connection to the same services they have available at their local desktop. Real-time reports with up to the minute metrics on business activities and critical information flows could be more efficient and timely. The road to the top might actually be a little simpler.

As we mentioned earlier, the lack of wire lines provides the network architect with the ability to design networking solutions that are available anytime and anywhere through always-on connectivity. As can be noted in the previous examples, any networking solution using traditional wire line media would hit a hard limitation when exposed to the same requirements of access coverage. The costs in cabling materials alone would preclude any such contemplation.

Mobility

The last concept dealing with convenience is that of mobility. This benefit alone is often the biggest factor in making organizations decide to go for a wireless-based networking solution.

In traditional wire-line networking environments, once a cabling infrastructure is set in place, rarely does it move with a tenant when they leave to a new facility or area of a building. Cabling installations are considered part of the cost of the move and are essentially tossed out.

With a wireless networking environment, the wireless APs can be unplugged from the electrical outlet and re-deployed in the new facility. Very few cables, if any, are left behind as a going-away present to the building owner. This allows the network architects to reuse networking equipment as required to address the networking realities of each environment.

For example, it is possible to move part or all of a network from one functional area to another, or from one building to another. It facilitates the job of IT managers who are constantly faced with network resource rationalizations and optimizations such as the decommissioning of access ports, or the moving of equipment and personnel from one area to another.

Affordability

With the continuing trend of cheaper, faster, and higher performance hardware available every six months or so, wireless networking has finally reached a price point which makes it a competitively priced solution on equipment and installation costs alone versus wire-line networking.

For wireless LANs, the cost is currently between $125 and $200 for a wireless adapter card, and in the $1500 to $2000 range for 11 Mbps enterprise scale solutions. The number of APs required to provide coverage of a given area can vary.

Home and small office wireless users requiring 2 Mbps have solutions in the $80 to $120 per port range, and those requiring 11 Mbps have solutions in the $140 to $180 per port price range. These costs include wireless networking cards and wireless APs.

While wireless LAN hardware costs can be slightly more than that of cabled LANs, the cost of installation and support of wireless LANs is lower. Wireless LANs can simplify day-to-day user administration and maintenance such as moves, thereby lowering the downtime and network administration costs.

Cellular-based networking solutions are coming down in price as well. Cell phones equipped with basic data networking features are available between $100 and $500, and cellular-adapters for PDAs range from $300 to $600. Cellular plans with data networking are available from service providers for nominal network and data transfer charges above basic voice plans.

The advent of consumer grade equipment is creating a volume of manufacturing for the main wireless components used in both commercial and consumer products. This in turn will drive the manufacturing cost down and product prices will continue to fall. We can see from Figure 1.9 that over the next two years, the cost of wireless networking solutions will become less than traditional wire-based networking.

Speed

When discussing any networking technology, the issue of access speeds and data throughputs is generally the most import factors in deciding which technology to implement. While each of the standards and technologies encompassing these deployments will be covered in greater detail over the next sections, it is important to take a quick note of some of these now.

Figure 1.9 Wireless Cost Trends

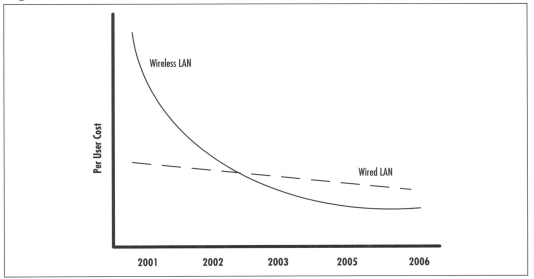

With previous wireless networking, be it cellular-based or wireless LAN, access speeds were rarely considered a benefit. Today the landscape has changed and technologies are quickly providing new means of communicating content rich information to remote users.

With cellular-based wireless technologies, several standards and networking technologies currently coexist for data communications. These are generally categorized into 2G, 2.5G, or 3G wireless network deployments. The majority of existing cellular-based wireless network deployments are using 2G or 2.5G networking technologies. While there are variances in access speeds based on the underlying signaling technology used, they generally range from 8 kbps to roughly 144 kbps. This level of access is sufficient for basic corporate and consumer mobile communications, telemetry, and field service.

With the transition to 3G cellular-based wireless network deployments, network access speeds will bump up to 384 kbps before reaching a proposed access speed of 2 Mbps when complete. With a 2 Mbps access rate, cellular-based wireless networks can support fully unified messaging, rich multimedia, and true telepresence.

Wireless LANs propose the most drastic increase in wireless data networking performance. Standards such as 802.11 are subdivided into evolutionary components with increased access speeds through the 802.11b, 802.11a, and 802.11g series, while HomeRF and others provide a basic scheme for access and technology transitions for increased speeds.

All in all, wireless LANs currently support speeds ranging from 1.6 Mbps to 11 Mbps. Evolutions are planned for technology and signaling schemes that will support access speeds up to 50 Mbps and beyond.

Aesthetics

One of the most underplayed notions in wireless networking is the aspect of aesthetics and safety. With few, if any, cables tethering devices and APs to networks, aesthetics are a welcome benefit to both organizations and end users.

With the size and footprint of wireless APs being no larger than small bookshelf speakers, they can be easily integrated within the most demanding of environments. Due to the radio nature of the transmission medium, APs can even be hidden behind walls or within locked storage.

With personal area network technologies, users can reduce or completely eliminate the local tangle of device interconnections. With these technologies, local devices can create wireless interconnections between themselves. Monitors, printers, scanners and other external devices can be placed where most appropriate without the limitations of cable length and cable access.

As a net result, desk, office, and networking closet cabling clutter can be reduced, thereby greatly increasing the overall safety of workplace and home.

Productivity

The net result of the increased level of flexibility, mobility, and convenience provided through wireless networking is increased productivity. Networked resources can become accessible from any location, thus providing the ability to design and integrate environments where users and services can be colocated where best suited.

Time can be spent working with data instead of being spent traveling to the data store. Wireless networking can provide opportunities for higher level of service and productivity unmatched through cabled networking.

Facing the Reality of Wireless Today

Wireless networking technologies are rapidly being deployed around the globe. While wireless networking is becoming a mainstream data communications technology, it is still mired in controversy. Many organizations are facing challenges over which technology to choose, the level of integration with regards to existing security functionality, privacy issues, and gaining a solid understanding of the gap between the promise and the reality of wireless.

As such, wireless network deployments still have major hurdles to overcome before they can be effectively deployed in all environments. Large corporations may have the advantage of budgets and equipment to allow them to effectively solve the shortcomings of the technology or an implementation, but they, like smaller organizations, home offices, or residential users, must continue to be vigilant.

Standards Conflicts

While a great deal of effort is being placed on developing standards for wireless networking both on the cellular-based networks and wireless LANs, there still exists a number of interim and competing standards which cause interoperability issues.

Specifically, issues over the use of radio frequency bands, frequency modulation techniques, types of security, and the mode of data communications still exist. Further complicating things, is the fact that radio frequency ranges may not be available for use within all parts of the world.

On the wireless LAN front, the war is still raging. Many of the wireless technologies today operate over the unlicensed Industrial, Scientific and Medical (ISM) bands where other devices can freely operate.

When it comes to wireless LAN-specific standards, there is an array of proposed and interim solutions being developed. The IEEE alone has three standards streams addressing wireless networking. Furthermore, technologies being developed under the auspice of the 802.11 streams are not necessarily compatible between generations or between competing technologies such as HomeRF and 802.15 networks based on Bluetooth.

Standards disputes are also occurring over the types of services that should, could, or might be implemented over wireless LANs and the definition of applicable quality of service standards for voice, data, and streaming multimedia. While there are plans in place for the convergence of some of these standards, there are no plans to develop an all-encompassing standard. Many issues still remain regarding frequency support, access speeds, and signaling techniques.

Existing wireless LAN standards include:

- IEEE 802.15 (wireless personal area networks)
- HomeRF

- IEEE 802.11 (wireless local area networks)
- IEEE 802.16 (wireless metropolitan area networks)

Figure 1.10 provides an overview of the wireless access range for each of these technologies.

Figure 1.10 Wireless Access Range

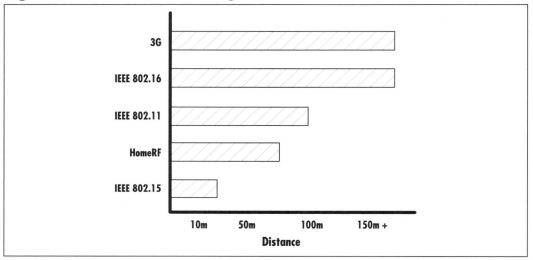

In the case of cellular-based networks, a number of interim technology standards classified as 2G, 2.5G, and 3G are adding confusion to an already complex wireless landscape. Technologies being developed under a category do not necessarily provide the entire capability set of that classification, nor are they necessarily compatible with competing technologies.

The 3G wireless networking groups are working diligently to create a mechanism for the convergence or support of competing radio technologies. While this should resolve many of the issues when 3G technologies are widely deployed and available beyond 2004, we are left to a string of interim solutions that are limited in terms of interoperability.

Lastly, amendments and changes regarding the use of specific radio technologies and frequencies for both wireless LANs and cellular networking are being proposed to governing bodies. While these should assist in providing new avenues for merging wireless deployment solutions, it will be several years before the results of these changes are fully understood.

Commercial Conflicts

Standards provide a good basis for eventually reigning in the various wireless factions on most technical fronts, but there still remain a number of issues regarding the interpretation and implementation of standards by vendors.

Some vendors are choosing to implement selected subsets of features and functions that are least likely to change over the evolution of the various communication protocols, security definitions, and hardware specification standards while others are choosing to implement the full gamut of available options. This situation results in incompatibility between systems sharing the same base standards.

Market Adoption Challenges

While wireless networks are being deployed within many organizations, said deployment may not have been to the extent the wireless industry expected. In many cases over the last year, wireless deployments have been scaled back or have remained within the confines of test equipment labs due to issues over standards interoperability, security features, and deployment architecture.

For many organizations which understand the technology and are comfortable with the security work-arounds, the main adoption challenge is that of technology upgrades. Technology standards are till in a state of flux and are constantly evolving. New technologies are being developed with the enhanced capabilities of networks and devices that in some cases do not interoperate with previous generations. Organizations planning massive deployments are choosing to wait for the technology to stabilize.

In some cases, manufacturers themselves are also reluctant to introduce new products. With the product cycle requiring upwards of one year to develop and market equipment that is destined to be obsolete before it hits shelves, it's easy to understand.

The Limitations of "Radio"

Using radio technology to establish networks is generally categorized as a benefit, but it can also add a new level of complexity for the network architect in designing the network.

The basis of radio technology is that of the circular propagation of waves of radio energy over the air. This general fact implies that waves can travel in any direction, up or down and side to side. Radio waves can go through walls and may bounce off more solid objects. The wave effect of radio transmissions can create interference patterns rendering the reception of signals difficult.

Because radio waves can go through walls, network architects sometimes get a false sense of security when it comes to deploying this technology. They must learn to see their environment from the perspective of unbounded radio.

Wireless LAN technologies typically use Spread Spectrum-based wireless communications schemes. Spread Spectrum was originally devised for military communications during World War II. It provides a means of using noise-like carrier waves and expanding the information contained within a signal so that it is spread over a larger bandwidth than the original signal.

While spreading the signal over a larger bandwidth requires an increase in data rates when compared to standard point-to-point communications, it provides enhanced resistance to jamming signals, has a low interceptability and detection profile, and provides a means for ranging or determining the distance the transmission will travel.

While these benefits could be viewed as a priority primarily within military communications they are easily translated to valid commercial values including signal security, signal integrity, and predictable operation. Another value of Spread Spectrum technology is that it provides a means for enhancing data throughout the radio spectrum.

Depending on the vendor or solution being used, one of two forms of Spread Spectrum technologies are used:

- FHSS (Frequency Hopping Spread Spectrum)
- DSSS (Direct Sequence Spread Spectrum)

Frequency Hopping Spread Spectrum

Frequency Hopping Spread Spectrum (FHSS) is one of two types of spread spectrum technologies. In FHSS, the frequency of the carrier signal is rapidly switched from one frequency to another in predetermined pseudorandom patterns using fast-setting frequency synthesizers. The pseudorandom pattern or code is initially agreed to and kept synchronized by both the end station and the AP. As we can see from Figure 1.11, this forms the basis of a communications channel.

Over time, the signal data energy is spread over a wide band of frequencies. This technique reduces interference due to the fact that a specific frequency is used only for a small fraction of time. Provided the transmitter and receiver remain synchronized over time, a channel can be established and maintained. Receivers that are not synchronized to this communication perceive the transmission as occasional short-duration noise.

Figure 1.11 Frequency Hopping Spread Spectrum

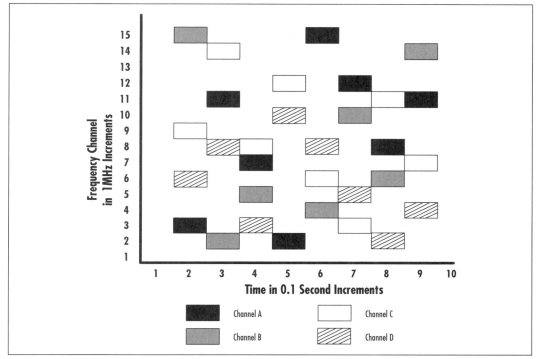

Direct Sequence Spread Spectrum

In Direct Sequence Spread Spectrum (DSSS), the digital data signal is inserted in a higher data rate chipping code according to a predetermined spreading ratio. The chipping code is a bit sequence generally consisting of a redundant bit pattern that incorporates the original bit pattern. Figure 1.12 is a simplification of how a statistical technique is used to create the chipping code abstraction from the original bit sequence.

This technique reduces interference due to the fact that if the original data pattern is compromised, the data can be recovered based on the remainder of the chipping code. The longer the chipping code, the more likely it is that the original data can be recovered. Long chipping codes had the drawback of requiring more bandwidth.

Figure 1.12 Direct Sequence Spread Spectrum

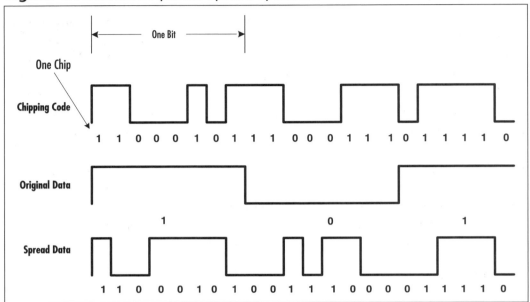

Radio Range and Coverage

When discussing wireless technologies, several aspects of radio must be considered, including: range, coverage, attenuation, and direction. While, in general, these factors are the function of product designs, they must be incorporated within a wireless design plan.

Care must be taken to understand the specific transmit power and receiver sensitivity of wireless nodes and APs/transmitter towers. Wireless transmitters have limitations in terms of how powerful or "loud" a signal can be. Wireless LAN systems, for example, use transmitters that are significantly less powerful than cell phones.

Radio signals can fade rapidly over distance. This, along with other factors impacting the path and propagation of a wireless signal such as walls, floors, ceilings, metal reinforcements, and equipment generating radio noise can limit how far a signal will travel.

Use of Antennas

The use of external and third-party antennas can increase the range of a network deployment as well its overall sensitivity to interference. In general terms, the coverage area of a wireless network AP can be "shaped" using directional and omni-directional antennas.

Omnidirectional antennas provide donut-shaped coverage. High "gain" omni-directional antennas can assist in flattening and stretching the coverage area. Directional antennas are used to focus the radio frequency in a particular direction and generally have a dispersion pattern that emanates outward from a point.

With extended cellular-based wireless network coverage in over 90 percent of urban markets within North America, Europe, and Asia, today's radio transceivers can use less power and leverage advances in signaling techniques. For most users, gone are the days of bulky and awkward external antennas seen on the first cell phones of 15 years ago.

The same level of deployment coverage is being developed on the wireless LAN front. Given wireless AP coverage within both enterprise and home is fast approaching transparent ubiquitous access, lower and lower power radio transceivers are required to establish and maintain a connection.

Interference and Coexistence

Despite the many advances in radio transmission and signaling technologies, even the best planned wireless deployments can be scuttled by other technologies that are generally considered a benign part of everyday life.

Radio frequencies can go through solid objects. When wireless devices are within the proximity of other wireless devices, say on adjacent floors or in rooms next to each other, radio interference can occur causing the degradation of signals. While most wireless technologies provide error-checking mechanisms to thwart such occurrences, their degree of effectiveness can vary based on environment.

With most wireless LAN products operating within the unlicensed Industrial Scientific and Medical (ISM) 2.4GHz to 2.483GHz band along with other products such as cordless telephones, baby monitors, and wireless speaker and headphone systems, interference can occur from devices competing within this crowded bandwidth.

This band will likely get more crowded. There are a number of propositions for new devices to operate within this band. One of them includes allowing lighting devices in the 2.45GHz band. These devices use magnetrons as sources of radio frequency energy to excite the light emitting material.

Microwave ovens can be another source of interference for wireless LANs within the home. While most wireless LAN products provide means to counteract this interference, they are not foolproof.

Wireless LAN technologies are proposed for other Unlicensed National Information Infrastructure and ISM bands, including the 5.15GHz to 5.35GHz band and the 5.725GHz to 5.875GHz band. These bands also present their own sets of challenges and competing emissions for other wireless equipment.

The Limitations of Wireless Security

Cellular-based networks and wireless LANs experience similar challenges when faced with the problem of security. While security standards and certifying bodies are making great strides in educating those deploying networks on the security risks of deploying new technologies, issues still remain over how security is to be applied and audited.

Sound security policies and implementation guidelines need to be devised, maintained, and updated to meet the changing requirements of the organizations and the individuals using the systems.

The issue of fraud is, by far, one of the farthest reaching for the wireless service provider, corporation, and individual. Fraud occurs in many forms but is generally categorized as the unauthorized and/or illegal use of a resource. A resource could consist of a cellular telephone, wireless network, or even airtime.

To gain a better understanding of the scope fraud has on our lives, as well as how we should secure our networks, it helps to review some glaring fraud statistics:

- **Identity theft** According to the Federal Bureau of Investigation, there are 350,000 to 500,000 instances of identity theft each year. (Source: Congressional Press Release, September 12, 2000)

- **International credit card fraud** The Association for Payment Clearing Services (APACS) recently found that counterfeit [credit card] fraud grew *by 89 per cent* last year, and card-not-present fraud committed over the Internet, telephone, or fax grew by a staggering *117 percent*. (Source: M2 PRESSWIRE, September 11, 2000)

- **Communications fraud** A National Fraud Center study revised in November of 2000, estimated communications fraud at *over 1 billion dollars*. Subscriber fraud is estimated to reach $473 million by 2002. (Source: International Data Corporation)

- **Corporate fraud** The same National Fraud Center study estimated corporate fraud including intellectual property and pirated software totaling more than 622 billion dollars.

Some of the biggest issues currently plaguing wireless deployments include the flip side of convenience and security. For example, most wireless devices are small and convenient. This fact also makes them susceptible to being easily lost or stolen. Database updates containing the lists of valid and invalid wireless device serial numbers can take between 48 and 72 hours to come into effect and be propagated to the rest of the network. This cannot easily be remedied.

Other issues include insider attacks, where someone working for the service provider or company deploying the wireless network can obtain secret information on the use of keys and other sensitive information. This can lead to the cloning of wireless devices without knowledge of genuine users or service providers.

Wireless networks are also susceptible to *man-in-the-middle* attacks where malicious users can logically situate themselves between a source and a target, and effectively appear to be a "real" base station while in fact relaying information both ways. With this type of attack, the malicious user is not required to physically be located directly adjacent to the users, or within the "secured" area of the building or facility. Provided they are within radio range, this attack can be initiated with success.

Lastly, with wireless technology deployments being so new to most users and even network administrators, the use of "trust" relationships and other social engineering attacks can lead malicious users to obtain secret keys, passwords, and other sensitive information to gain access to or even destroy information.

Unfortunately, the threat is not limited to these forms of attacks. With the advent of more powerful and feature-rich devices on the horizon, a new breed of wireless security vulnerabilities will soon be plaguing the wireless deployments. The availability of more intelligent devices introduces new options for attacking:

Advanced wireless devices will possess greater intelligence, greater processing capabilities and will ultimately become susceptible to malicious code the way PCs have become vulnerable to attack by viruses, Trojans, and worms over the last 15 years. These, in turn, can be used as the launching pad for creating complex and timed client-to-client and distributed client-to-network attacks. Increased processing power can also lead to real-time brute force attacks.

A host of cheap enhanced radio transceivers will spawn more sophisticated tools for the attackers. These will include interception attacks, insertion attacks, wireless channel flood attacks, denial of service attacks, and signal jamming attacks.

One source of attacks that should not be understated results from the relative complexity involved in the deployment and lockdown of wireless resources. To many, wireless technologies will provide new alternatives for networking that were unavailable before. Many will rush to implement these solutions without spending time to understand all of the possible threats and security precautions that should be taken to mitigate them. As a result, misconfigurations will likely result in the downfall of security within many wireless environments.

When addressing the main issues in security, organizations and individuals resort to *identification* and *authentication*. Identification is the process whereby a network recognizes a user's identity. Identification usually comes in the form of a user ID or Personal Identification Number (PIN).

Authentication is the process whereby the network verifies the claimed identity of a user for authorized use. Credentials, databases, and validation systems are employed to provide users with their list of usage privileges.

As with all Identification and Authentication mechanisms, wireless networks need to balance complexity, user friendliness, effectiveness, reliability, and timeliness with performance requirements and costs.

Cellular-based Wireless Networks and WAP

WAP stands for Wireless Application Protocol. It was originally designed as a specification for presenting and interacting with information on cellular-based wireless devices. It uses the Wireless Markup Language (WML), which is similar to the Hypertext Markup Language (HTML) but is actually an Extended Markup Language (XML) application that allows for variables. WAP provides a means to interface between wireless carriers and the TCP/IP-based Internet.

One of the biggest issues facing the deployment of WAP, stems from the fact that it is still an incomplete standard. Updates to this standard occur regularly, generally every six months, and as such, WAP is often considered a "moving target."

Another source of contention is over the use of the WAP gateway. Currently, cellular-based wireless devices do not possess the processing capabilities or rendering ability to display large content files. To address this issue, the WAP protocol proposes the use of intermediary gateways that can translate Internet information in standard HTML to WML.

The WAP gateway is also used for the encryption and decryption of secure data. The WAP standard proposes that an encrypted session be established between the WAP gateway and the wireless device as well as between the WAP gateway and the Internet content provider. This implies that the information in transit within the WAP gateway is unencrypted and susceptible to attack. This vulnerability is commonly referred to as the "Gap in WAP." As a result of this gap, a turf war has erupted regarding the ownership of the WAP gateway. Some wireless service providers argue that the WAP gateway belongs on their network and are trying to force subscribers to use their wireless gateways. Content providers hold a different opinion claiming concerns over privacy. In the end, the heart of the debate revolves around customer loyalty.

Lastly, other cellular-based wireless networking providers, like NTT DoCoMo with their i-Mode wireless data network solution, are successfully developing competitors to WAP.

Wireless LAN Networks and WEP

WEP is the abbreviation for Wireless Equivalency Protocol. In the IEEE P802.11 draft standard, WEP is defined as providing protection to authorized users from "casual eavesdropping." As such, it provides the means for encrypting the wireless network connection between the mobile unit and the base station. As it currently stands, use of data encryption over the link introduces performance degradations.

To perform the encryption, WEP currently relies on the use of cryptographic key management outside the protocol. That is, administrators and users must manually and securely distribute cryptographic keys prior to establishing an encrypted session. Furthermore, cryptographic keys must also be updated manually when a key expires. This can cause additional confusion when deploying wireless LANs using WEP security.

WEP secured wireless sessions can be configured with the following settings:

- No encryption
- 40-bit encryption
- 64-bit encryption
- 128-bit encryption

Although 128-bit encryption is more effective in creating a security boundary protecting users against casual attacks than 40-bit encryption, both key strengths are subject to WEP's known security flaws.

The most criticized security flaw is that of the weakness of the method used for choosing the Initialization Vector (IV) used in creating the WEP encryption session key. The IV is a 24-bit field sent along with the message. Having such a small space of initialization vectors nearly guarantees the reuse of the same key stream.

Using inexpensive off-the-shelf components and freeware applications, dictionary and statistical attacks can be very successful against WEP with just one day's worth of traffic. This leads to the possibility of real-time decryption of communications traffic between the wireless node and the AP.

Other security concerns include:

- **Passive Attacks** Decryption of encrypted traffic based on statistical analysis
- **Active Network Attacks** Injection of new traffic from an unauthorized wireless node

To address some of these concerns, WEP implements a CRC–32 checksum. The issue with this is not the checksum itself, but rather how WEP implements the checksum. WEP checksums are linear, which means that it is possible to compute the bit difference of two CRCs based on the bit difference of the messages over which they are taken

A secondary function of WEP is that of preventing unauthorized access to the wireless LAN. While not explicitly defined in the standard, it is frequently considered to be a feature of WEP, thus resulting in a false sense of confidence over the security of the wireless network implementation.

Damage & Defense...

Wireless Security Challenges

Going wireless increases the risk factors geometrically! The following list outlines the industry's current security posture, and what it should be aiming for.

1. General Security

Currently, the majority of devices employ weak user authentication. The existing premise is often that possession of the wireless device implies right of access. Even when passwords are implemented, they are limited and offer little protection.

What is required is for the wireless devices to adopt the application of more stringent security policies. Possession cannot, by itself, delineate a trust relationship with its user. Passwords are often regarded in the wired world as being barely adequate security. With wireless devices that are often shared, or that interact with external networks, passwords will not be enough to provide a trusted security overlay across all wireless devices.

A new policy of enforcing two-factor authentication needs to be adopted. This implies the use of something that a user has in their

Continued

possession and something that they know. This combination is the only effective means of providing authentication. Wireless devices can easily support PIN or biometric plus crypto-personalized identity modules.

2. Need for Encryption

There has been an early recognition of the need for wireless encryption of data. These efforts have been primarily focused on addressing privacy issues of transmissions between a user and the AP only. Encryption for privacy is present in WAP, WEP, and most other wireless security solutions. Typically, encryption capabilities have been incorporated within operating systems or within the firmware of the wireless devices.

Many wireless infrastructure encryption methods have proven to be weak or ineffective against serious attacks ad will be relegated to obsolescence.

A mechanism needs to be established that supports complete end-to-end encryption of all data transactions and voice communications.

3. Need for Signatures

While a focus has been placed on providing increased data access speeds, little attention has been paid to ensuring communications are not tampered with or retransmitted. Encryption provides a layer of abstraction from the original data but does not ensure the integrity of the data. While checksum sequences can be used on the network layer to ensure communications are successfully transmitted and received, they do not provide the end user with assurances that the data is still in its original state.

Digital signatures providing clientside data signing is required to ensure the integrity of the data. While full-scale Public Key Infrastructures (PKI) are being piloted, there are few wireless networks deploying PKIs. Wireless PKI protocols and interoperability models are still being developed and still need to be tested for legal and regulatory enforcement.

Wireless deployments will need to adopt optimized client PKI signing and signature verification that is interoperable between wireless network operators and enterprise PKIs. Business-to-business and expanded user trust relationships need to be established to facilitate wireless PKI deployments and to address issues over multiple user PKI credential management, including the use of multiple PKI keys, access to content providers, interaction of PKI identity modules, and lastly, issues over key management (that is, the issuance, control, removal, and update of keys).

Continued

4. Overall Security Position

With existing wireless networks, security is provided by either using WAP gateways architectures that actually compromise the integrity and security of communications or by using WEP which proposes variable security implementations. At this time, wireless end-to-end security back to server-hosted applications can only be provided using third party applications or using proprietary solutions that are not necessarily compatible. In turn, even newer competing technologies are being developed to address existing challenges, thereby creating even more confusion.

The wireless industry needs to create a standard that will support complete end-to-end encryption of all data transactions that is common and interoperable with existing IP standards and protocols.

Examining the Wireless Standards

With an ever-growing list of wireless standards being developed for wireless networking, it may be difficult at times to understand where each of these fit and what capabilities they offer. While there is little doubt that 3G, 802.11, and Bluetooth are the most important, and possibly some of the most controversial standards in wireless networking, the story does not end there.

In the case of 3G and 802.11, we're really not referring to specific standards but rather classes or families of standards. 802.11 alone is made up of over ten working groups, each investigating different aspects of technology, security, and implementation guidelines.

Let's take a look at some of the actual wireless standards.

Cellular-based Wireless Networks

Cellular-based wireless networks are networks that provide wireless access through new or existing cellular telephone technologies. Because cellular wireless networking technologies provide coverage over a large geographic area, they are sometimes referred to as wide area network technologies. The reference should not be confused with wired networking technologies providing the long haul of data called wide area networks.

Typically, cellular-based solutions address the access requirements of devices that are generally over 100 meters away from an AP or transmission tower.

Examples of hardware devices that currently integrate to cellular-based networking include data-ready telephones, two-way pagers, and cellular network-enabled PDAs. These devices use the wireless cellular network as their physical media and rely on higher-level protocols to define the type of data access and functionality they support.

Examples of the most widely used protocols supporting cellular-based wireless networking include WAP and i-Mode.

Communications Technologies

Cellular-based wireless data communication technologies exist under several forms and are generally categorized into groups supporting one of three sets of functionalities:

- 2G Circuit Switched Cellular Wireless Networks
- 2.5G Packed Data Overlay Cellular Wireless Networks
- 3G Packet Switched Cellular Wireless Networks

The majority of currently deployed cellular-based networks are 2G or second generation wireless technologies. They carry the data stream over the empty spaces contained in the voice stream using adapted signaling techniques.

As the transition from 2G to 2.5G and 3G occurs, many service providers are choosing to implement transition or overlapping technologies. This provides them with the ability to support the existing user base while opening the door to new service offerings for those willing to buy new technology. This generally is an effective way to address customer loyalty issues, but comes at the cost of supporting the simultaneous deployment of several types of networks.

When the migration to 3G technology is finally completed, a pure IP packet switched network will provide the communication protocol for both voice and data. In 3G networks, data is no longer streamed over the voice signal. In fact, the opposite is true. Using Voice over IP (VoIP) protocols and Quality of Service (QoS) standards, voice becomes an application being transported over the network, just like data.

2G Circuit Switched

2G is the generic term used for the second generation of cellular-based wireless communications networks. 2G is an evolution from the first generation AMPS (Advanced Mobile Phone Service) network in North America and GSM networks in Europe.

2G cellular networks support basic voice, text, and bi-directional data communications and launch the concept of interactive media over a cellular connection.

Existing 2G networks provide a data throughput in the 9.6 Kbps range. A number of underlying wireless network technologies and architectures are considered part of the second generation of cellular networks. These include:

- CDMA
- TDMA
- CDPD
- GSM

CDMA

Code Division Multiple Access (CDMA) is also referred to as CDMAone. CDMA is a digital transmission technology that uses the Direct Sequence form of Spread Spectrum (DSSS)-based wireless communications scheme originally devised for military communications during World War II.

Spread Spectrum technology provides a means of using noise-like carrier waves and expanding the information contained within a signal so that it is spread over a larger bandwidth than the original signal.

While spreading the signal over a larger bandwidth requires an increase in data rates when compared to standard point-to-point communications, it provides enhanced resistance to jamming signals, has a low interceptability and detection profile, and provides a means for ranging or determining the distance the transmission will travel. While these benefits could be viewed as a priority primarily within military communications, they are easily translated to valid commercial values including signal security, signal integrity, and predictable operation. Another value of Spread Spectrum technology is that it provides a means for enhancing the radio spectrum use.

In Direct Sequence Spread Spectrum, the data signal is inserted in a higher data rate chipping code according to a predetermined spreading ratio. The chipping code or bit sequence generally consists of a redundant bit pattern that incorporates the original bit pattern. This technique reduces interference in that if the original data pattern is compromised, the data can be recovered based on the remainder of the chipping code.

With Code Division Multiple Access, the DSSS frequency is divided up using pseudorandom codes or keys instead of assigning specific radio frequencies to specific channels. Since each channel or subscriber is assigned a specific code, communications can be carried over the entire available DSSS spectrum. These codes provide the basis for the digital transmission of radio signals between the mobile unit and the base units in CDMA networks. Subscriber equipment that is assigned a code only responds to communications using that code. CDMA networks have been implemented in the 800MHz and 1900MHz frequencies.

Variants of the basic CDMA technology include CDMA2000 and WCDMA. CDMA2000 and WCDMA are technological extensions of the CDMA transmission signaling and backbone technologies that provide 2.5G and 3G wireless networking functionality. We will review CDMA200 and WCDMA further in the next sections.

TDMA

Time Division Multiple Access (TDMA) is a digital transmission technology that uses the principle of dividing a radio frequency signal into specific time slots. Another way of way of looking at it is that TDMA provides a means to time-share a radio signal.

Each TDMA radio frequency is divided into six unique time slots. The time slots are assigned in pairs to provide full-duplex communications, thus supporting three independent communications. Alternating time slots over several frequencies are combined to provide a full channel.

TDMA relies on the digitization of signals for effective use. Each sample is subdivided and transmitted at specific time intervals over an assigned channel. TDMA networks have been implemented in the 800MHz and 1900MHz frequencies. TDMA provides the access technology for GSM.

CDPD

Cellular Digital Packet Data (CDPD) is a packet switching technology originally devised in the early 1990s to provide full-duplex data transmissions over the Advanced Mobile Phone Service (AMPS) North American 800MHz cellular phone frequency. It is a digital layered technology that establishes a means for making use of unused cellular channels and short blank spaces between calls to provide theoretical throughput of 19.2 Kbps. Actual throughput figures in the 9.6 Kbps range are typical for most deployments.

The CDPD technology specification, supports IP and the Connectionless Network Protocol (CLNP) to provide users with access to the Internet and other packet switched networks. When using CDPD, users are not required to maintain an open active session with the network resource they are accessing to transmit or receive data. Packets are tagged with a unique identifier alerting the CDPD device that a packet is intended for it. This provides an efficient means of sharing network bandwidth between many users.

CDPD works well over wireless networks experiencing typical use, but performance issues arise when voice usage goes up and the network becomes more congested. When this happens, fewer channels are available for use and data throughput may be affected. As a result many CDPD wireless carriers have elected to provide a dedicated channel specifically for data communication uses, thus ensuring a minimum data throughput during high use and emergency situations.

The security of data communications between the handset and the service provider is ensured using RSA RC-4 encryption.

GSM

Global System for Mobile Communications (GSM) was originally developed in the early 1980s as a standard for cellular mobile communications in Europe using Time Division Multiple Access (TDMA) transmission methods. Through the 1990s, it has evolved into a wireless networking architecture supporting voice and data services such as SMS.

GSM provides a standardized access to the network and establishes the framework for roaming. This means that subscribers can be contacted using the same number anywhere on the GSM network, including internationally. Currently, the GSM service provides 9.6 Kbps data throughput at the 800MHz, 900MHz, and 1900MHz frequencies and is available in over 170 countries. GSM satellite service extends access to areas where ground-based coverage is not available.

2.5G Packet Data Overlay

2.5G wireless networks are an evolution to the 2G networks and a transition point to providing support for 3G functionality. The main technology transition in 2.5G networks is that of introducing Packet Data on top of existing voice services. The 2.5G Packet Data layer provides support for data rates ranging from 100 Kbps to 384 Kbps.

GPRS

General Packet Radio Service (GPRS) is an enhancement to existing GSM- and TDMA-based networks. GPRS implements new packet data wireless network access nodes and upgrades existing wireless network access nodes to provide a routing path for packet data between the wireless user and the gateway node. The gateway node provides connectivity to external packet data networks such as the Internet.

GPRS provides data communications using IP with access rates ranging from 115 Kbps up to 170 Kbps and supports "always-on" connectivity. This provides users with the ability to remain permanently connected and enabled to applications such as e-mail, the Internet, and others. The benefit of GPRS is that the users do not have to pay for always-on connectivity per se, but rather only when sending or receiving data. GPRS provides support for defined QoS specifications, as well as a tunneling protocol called GTP (GRPS Tunneling Protocol) that creates a secure connection over IP by encapsulating encrypted data in an IP packet. Security protocols are used to lock down devices and sessions.

Wireless Service providers who have implemented GPRS can transition their network to carry EDGE and WCDMA traffic.

GPRS/EDGE

GPRS/EDGE is a transitionary state between existing GPRS networks and 3G EDGE-based networks. EDGE is the acronym for Enhanced Data Rates for Global Evolution. Service providers can deploy a combination of the two wireless network technologies to support both existing users and users wishing to purchase new EDGE equipment.

With the addition of the EDGE overlay over existing GPRS networks, current GPRS users are provided with an increase in data throughput rates. Data throughput is increased to 384 Kbps from the 115 Kbps to 170 Kbps typically provided by GPRS alone.

Existing security capabilities of GPRS remain unchanged.

1xRTT

1xRTT is commonly referred to as CDMA2000 Phase One or IMT-CDMA Multi-Carrier 1x. It represents the first stage in bringing existing CDMA wireless radio transmission technology (RTT) up to full 3G capabilities.

1xRTT supports packet data and voice communications up to 144 Kbps or higher in fixed environments. A second release of 1xRTT is being planned which will address increased data rates peaking up to 614 Kbps.

3G Integrated Multimedia Networks

3G wireless technologies refer to the third generation of wireless networks expected in 2004. While similar in basic application to 2.5G wireless networks in terms of voice, text, and data services, it is designed specifically to provide multimedia entertainment to enhanced wireless terminals. 3G-enabled terminals will tend towards a video friendly form factor.

It is expected that the lead end user of 3G wireless networks will be the consumer. 3G will provide the wireless network providers with added capacity that will create a revolution for multimedia content over mobile devices. See Figure 1.13 for an illustration of the improved data download time as the technology has evolved.

Figure 1.13 Data Download Times for 2G, 2.5G, and 3G Networks

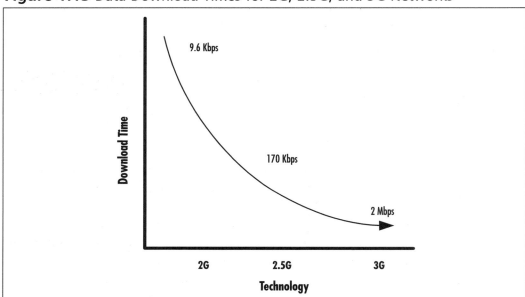

Internet access, entertainment media, and enhanced audio programming are some of the consumer applications expected to flourish with the advent of 3G. With new mobile devices supporting increased data processing capabilities, greater storage, and longer battery life, and wireless networks able to provide high data capabilities in most markets, the traditional wire line telephone and data network connection will likely be replaced with 3G data-ready access terminals.

3G will provide three generalized data networking throughputs to meet the specific needs of mobile users:

- **High Mobility** High Mobility use is intended for generalized roaming outside urban areas in which the users are traveling at speeds in excess of 120 kilometers per hour. This category of use will provide the end user with up to 144 kbps of data throughput.

- **Full Mobility** Full Mobility use is intended for generalized roaming within urban areas in which the user is traveling at speeds below 120 kilometers per hour. This category of use will provide the end user with up to 384 kbps of data throughput.

- **Limited Mobility** Limited Mobility use is intended for limited roaming or near stationary users traveling at 10 kilometers per hour or less. This category of use will provide the end user with up to 2 Mbps of data throughput when indoors and stationary.

The 3G standardization efforts are represented by several groups, including:

- **IMT-2000** International Mobile Telecommunications 2000. This International Telecommunications Union initiative is tasked with standardizing radio access to the terrestrial and satellite-based global telecommunications infrastructure supporting fixed and mobile telephone users.

- **3GPP** The 3GPP (Third Party Partnership Project) is tasked with developing open, globally accepted technical specifications for UMTS networks.

- **3GPP2** The 3GPP2 (Third Party Partnership Project 2) is tasked with developing open, globally accepted technical specifications for CDMA2000 networks.

UMTS

Universal Mobile Telephone System (UMTS) has been defined by the ITU and is referred to as IMT-2000. It is a broadband-based technology that supports voice and data and is predominantly intended for the evolution of GSM networks. UMTS provides access speeds of up to 2 Mbps using IP.

In Europe and Japan, terrestrial UMTS will be implemented with the paired 1920MHz to 1980MHz and 2110MHz to 2170MHz bands while satellite UMTS will be implemented using the 1980MHz to 2010MHz and 2170MHz to 2200MHz bands. In North America, UMTS will most likely be implemented within the PCS, WCS, and UHF TV bands.

UMTS uses smart cards, referred to as Subscriber Identity Modules (SIM), to provide user authentication, session encryption, digital signatures, and non-repudiation.

EDGE

Enhanced Data rates for Global Evolution (EDGE) provides an evolution upgrade for GSM and TDMA-based networks to support full 3G capabilities. It provides a modulation scheme that enhances the efficiency of radio transmissions. EDGE provides data throughputs of up to 3 to 4 times that of GPRS or 384 Kbps.

3xRTT

3xRTT is commonly referred to as CDMA2000 Phase Two or IMT-CDMA Multi-Carrier 3x. It represents the second and last stage in evolving CDMA wireless radio transmission technology (RTT) to full 3G capabilities. 3xRTT supports multiple channel sizes and provides multimedia, data, and voice communications up to 2 Mbps.

From a service providers' perspective, 3xRTT shares the same baseband radio components as 1xRTT. As such, 3xRTT is an evolution of the 1xRTT networks. It is the core technology used to deploy UMTS.

Wireless LAN Networks

Wireless LAN technologies provide the networking and physical layers of a traditional LAN using radio frequencies. Wireless LAN nodes generally transmit and receive digital data to and from common wireless APs.

Wireless APs are the central hubs of a wireless network and are typically connected to a cabled LAN. This network connection allows wireless LAN users to access the cabled LAN server resources such as e-mail servers, application servers, intranets, and the Internet.

A scheme also exists where wireless nodes can set up direct communications to other wireless nodes. This can be enabled or disabled at the discretion of systems administrators through configuration of the wireless network software. Peer-to-peer networking is generally viewed as a security concern in that a nonauthorized user could potentially initiate a peer-to-peer session with a valid user, thus creating a security compromise.

Depending on the vendor or solution being used, one of two forms of Spread Spectrum technologies are used within wireless LAN implementations:

- FHSS
- DSSS

There are four commercial wireless LAN solutions available:

- 802.11 WLAN

- HomeRF

- 802.15 WPAN, based on Bluetooth

- 802.16 WMAN

802.11 WLAN

The IEEE 802.11 wireless LAN standard began in 1989 and was originally intended to provide a wireless equivalent to Ethernet (the 802.11 Protocol Stack is shown in Figure 1.14). As such, it has developed a succession of robust enterprise grade solutions that in some cases meet or exceed the demands of the enterprise network.

Figure 1.14 The IEEE 802.11 Protocol Stack

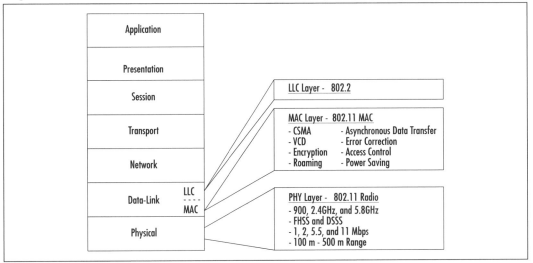

IEEE 802.11 wireless LAN networks are designed to provide wireless connectivity to a range of roughly 300 feet from the base. The lead application being shared over the wireless LAN is data. Provisions are being made to accommodate audio, video, and other forms of streaming multimedia.

The IEEE 802.11 wireless LAN specification generally provides for the following:

- Wireless connectivity of traditional LAN devices such as workstations, servers, printers, and so on

- A common standardized Media Access Control layer (MAC)

  - Similar to 802.3 Ethernet (CMSA/CA)

  - Supports TCP/IP, UDP/IP, IPX, NETBEUI, and so on

  - Virtual Collision Detection (VCD) option

  - Error correction and access control using positive acknowledgment of packets and retransmission

  - Encrypted communications using WEP encryption

  - Roaming

  - Power-saving schemes when equipment is not active

  - Interfaces to Operating System drivers

- Physical Layer which can vary on implementation

  - Supports three radio frequency Spread Spectrum technologies (FHSS, DSSS, and HRDSS) and one infrared technique

  - Specifies which of these techniques can be used within North America, Japan, and Europe

  - Support for 2.4GHz and 5GHz ISM bands

  - Support for access speeds of 1Mbps, 2Mbps, 5.5Mbps, and 11Mbps with additional speeds available in future releases of the standard

- Basic multivendor interoperability

IEEE 802.11 Task Groups

The IEEE 802.11 initiative is very active and now comprises some 11 task groups responsible for addressing specific issues relating to physical layer optimizations, MAC layer enhancements, security definitions, and vendor interoperability. The tasks groups are as follows:

- **IEEE 802.11b** The scope of this working group was to develop a standard of higher data rate throughput using the 2.4GHz band. The working group has completed its work and a standard has been published under the standards amendment IEEE Standard 802.11b-1999.

The commercially available wireless LAN products formed using the 802.11 specification are based on the 802.11a standard. Wireless LANs built to the 802.11a specification can support throughput rates up to 11Mbps.

- **IEEE 802.11b cor1** The scope of this working group project is to correct deficiencies in the MIB definition of 802.11b. The MIB defined in IEEE Standard 802.11b-1999 is not a compileable and interoperable MIB. This project is ongoing.

- **IEEE 802.11a** The scope of this task group was to develop a new physical layer specification for use in the Unlicensed National Information Infrastructure bands NII band. Wireless LAN technologies are proposed for other ISM bands, including the 5.15GHz to 5.35GHz band and the 5.725GHz to 5.875 GHz band.

  The task group has completed its work and a standard has been published under the standards amendment IEEE Standard 802-11: 1999 (E)/Amd 1: 2000 (ISO/IEC) (IEEE Std. 802.11a-1999 Edition). Wireless LAN products based on the 802.11a will be commercially available in 2002.

- **IEEE 802.11c** The scope of this task group was to develop an internal sublayer service within the existing standard to support bridge operations with the IEEE 802.11 MAC layer. The group completed its work in cooperation with the IEEE 802.1 task group. The specification has been incorporated within the IEEE 802.11d standard.

- **IEEE 802.11d** The scope of this task group is to define the physical layer requirements for channelization, hopping patterns, new values for current MIB attributes, and other requirements. This task group will also address the issue of defining the operations or the IEEE 802.11 standard based equipment within countries that were not included in the original IEEE 802.11 standard.

  The activities of the IEEE 802.11d task group are ongoing.

- **IEEE 802.11e** The scope of this task group is to enhance the 802.11 Medium Access Control (MAC), provide classes of service, improve and manage QoS, and enhance security and authentication mechanisms.

  They plan to consider efficiency enhancements in the areas of the Distributed Coordination Function (DCF) and Point Coordination Function (PCF). It is expected by the working group that performance will increase when these enhancements are combined with the new physical specifications of 802.11a and 802.11b.

They expect that as a result of the performance increases, new services such as the transport of voice, audio and video, videoconferencing, media stream distribution, and mobile and nomadic access applications will become applicable to the 802.11 standard.

While enhanced security applications were originally intended to be developed by this working group, they were moved to the IEEE 802.11i task group in May of 2001.

The activities of the IEEE 802.11e task group are ongoing.

- **IEEE 802.11f** The scope of this task group is to develop recommended practices for an Inter-AP Protocol (IAPP). This protocol is intended to provide the necessary capabilities to support AP interoperability between multiple vendors using a Distribution System supporting IEEE P802.11 wireless LAN links.

  The IAPP will be based on IEEE 802 LAN components supporting an IETF IP environment. The activities of the IEEE 802.11f task group are ongoing.

- **IEEE 802.11g** The scope of this task group is to develop higher speed physical specification extensions to the 802.11b standard that remain compatible with the IEEE 802.11 MAC.

  The maximum data rate targeted by this working group is 20 Mbps and will apply to fixed stationary wireless LAN network components and internetwork infrastructures. The activities of the IEEE 802.11f task group are ongoing.

- **IEEE 802.11h** The scope of this task group is to enhance the 802.11 MAC standard 802.11a physical layer supplement that supports the 5GHz band. It also plans to provide indoor and outdoor channel selection for 5GHz license exempt bands in Europe and improve spectrum and transmission power management. The activities of the IEEE 802.11h task group are ongoing.

- **IEEE 802.11i** The scope of this task group is to enhance the 802.11 MAC to support additional security and authentication mechanisms. The activities of the IEEE 802.11i task group are ongoing.

- **IEEE 802.11j**

The IEEE 802.11b Standard

The IEEE 802.11b standard was the first wireless LAN standard to be defined and commercially adopted by equipment manufacturers. It provides data access rates up to 11 Mbps using a variant of DSSS over the 2.4GHz band. Three channels are defined.

The 802.11 general MAC layer provides for capabilities that are similar to 802.3 Ethernet (CMSA/CA). CSMA/CA assures a fair and controlled access to the medium with error correction and access control using positive acknowledgment of packets and retransmission.

The MAC layer also has a specification for an optional Virtual Collision Detection (VCD) mode that includes Request-to-send (RTS) and Clear-to-send (CTS) frames. With VCD active, collisions over the wireless media would be kept to a minimum. Before sending any data, VCD would perform the following steps, as illustrated in Figure 1.15:

1. A clear channel is assessed by the wireless node.
2. A clear channel is identified by the wireless node.
3. A Request to Send (RTS) is sent over the media by the wireless node.
4. A Clear to Send (CTS) acknowledgment is sent by the AP. A zone of silence is created around the AP.
5. The wireless node sends the queued data.
6. The AP replies with Send Acknowledgement (ACK).

The 802.11 general MAC layer also provides power saving features using Traffic Indicator Map (TIM) and Delivery Traffic Indicator Map (DTIM) "beacons." Use of TIMs and DTIMs can greatly increase the effectiveness of wireless LAN deployments using laptops. Power management can save laptop battery life and therefore extend duration of network functionality when operating without a connection to an A.C. power outlet.

As illustrated in Figure 1.16, TIMs are sent periodically by a wireless AP, and provide a listing of the identity of other wireless nodes that have traffic pending. Wireless NIC cards within the wireless node are set at a minimum, and are configured to wake upon receiving a TIM.

DTIMs are similar to TIMs but have broad/multicast traffic indications. They are sent at a lower frequency than TIMs—for instance, one DTIM may be sent for every five TIMs. The recommended power wake setting for NIC cards is at every DTIM. Other user-defined or adaptive wake settings can also be used.

Figure 1.15 802.11 Channel Assessment

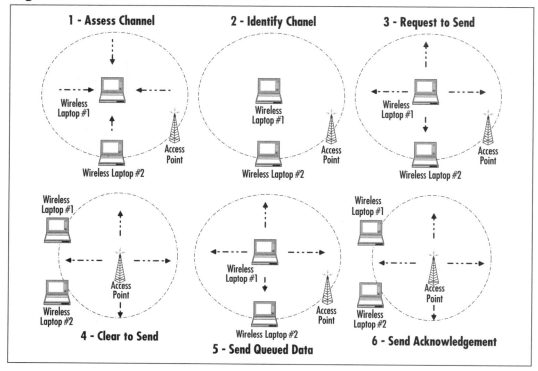

Figure 1.16 Use TIM and DTIM in Power Save Mode

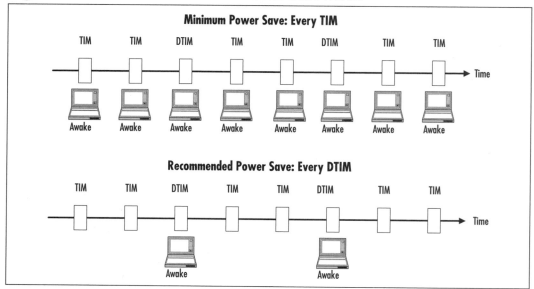

802.11b provides an interference avoidance mechanism through time diversity. This is often referred to as the "wait for the interferer to leave" avoidance mechanism. This, in effect, provides a trivial mass denial of service susceptibility which can be used by attackers to disrupt the operations of the wireless LAN.

The IEEE 802.11a Standard

The IEEE 802.11a standard is the latest IEEE wireless LAN standard to be defined and commercially adopted by equipment manufacturers. Products are planned for 2002 availability.

The 802.11a standard is based on Orthogonal Frequency Division Multiplexing (OFDM) which provides a mechanism for automatically selecting the most optimum waveform within a specified fixed channelization. It offers resistance to multipath signals, fading, impulse noise, and interference.

In the 802.11a wireless LAN specification, OFDM is used to modulate the data and provides a scheme that enables the use of wide band signals in an environment where reflected signals would otherwise disable the receiver from decoding the data transmission contained in the received signal.

802.11b operates over the 5GHz band with a 20MHz spacing allocated between adjacent channels. The 802.11a specification supports data throughput rates ranging from 6 Mbps to 54 Mbps. Range will be limited at the higher rates.

Vendors implementing 802.11a-based equipment are required to support at a minimum the 6 Mbps, 12 Mbps, and 24 Mbps data rates. Vendors can voluntarily support the optional 9 Mbps, 18 Mbps, 36 Mbps, 48 Mbps, and 54 Mbps. A multirate identification mechanism is used to identify and synchronize devices using the best rate.

One of the main impacts resulting from commercial availability of 802.11a wireless LANs is that they will all but make existing 802.11a installations obsolete. Organizations who will already have deployed 802.11b wireless LANs will not be able to also use 802.11a wireless LANs to support the same users base. From a networking perspective, they operate on different radio transmission principles and should be considered completely different networks.

General IEEE 802.11 Wireless LAN Remarks

IEEE 802.11 wireless LANs can operate in either the client/host or peer-to-peer configuration but not both modes simultaneously. Client/host mode is provided using Point Coordination Function (PCF), while peer-to-peer mode is provided using Distributed Coordination Function (DCF). The main issues to supporting peer-to-peer functionality within PCF has to do with how roaming is managed within 802.11.

With the commercial availability of enhancements to the WEP security functionality still years away, users will continue to rely on third-party Virtual Private Network (VPN) software solutions to secure their 802.11 wireless LAN traffic. This will add to the deployment costs and administrative overhead associated with wireless LANs.

While the IEEE 802.11 specification provides a solid framework for robust enterprise grade solutions, provisions are still being made to address the latest developments in LAN applications such as streaming media. While these proposed enhancements are being developed, vendors and implementers are forced to devise their own specifications for supporting voice and video services, quality of service, guidelines for supporting user roaming, defining equipment vendor interoperability and distributed systems administration.

HomeRF

Home data networks are springing up in many of today's multi-PC households. They are being created primarily for sharing data, printers, hard drives and Internet connections among several users. Complex multiline telephone systems are also becoming the norm in the home with the addition of second or third telephone lines, fax lines, and Internet access lines. Home audio and video systems are also being stretched to support a new application: whole house audio.

While wire-line networking is often used to connect the various components in home data, voice, and audio/video networks, it is generally best suited for installations in new homes. In existing homes, network cabling needs to be retrofitted and adapted to each specific environment.

Rarely are all the computers, shared resources, and Internet connections conveniently located in a single room. When telephone, audio speaker, or television extensions need to be added, it is often where existing in-house cabling is not present. In these environments, new cabling is either retrofitted into the walls or run across floors to adjacent rooms. In some cases, cables cannot be run to the desired location. This can result in compromised home environments or nonoptimum placement of equipment.

HomeRF Specification

HomeRF is a wireless networking technology aimed specifically at the networks being created in home environments. The main premise of HomeRF is that home users have different needs than the corporate user, and as such, require solutions tailored to them. HomeRF attempts to address this niche by providing components that are relatively simple to install, easy to use, and are generally more affordable than existing corporate environment grade wireless solutions.

HomeRF is based on several existing voice and data standards and incorporates these into a single solution. It operates over a 2.4GHz ISM wireless band using Frequency Hopping Spread Spectrum (FHSS). Frequency hops occur at a rate of 50 to 100 times per second. Interference resolution is addressed using frequency and time diversity as hopset adaptation with static interferers.

HomeRF uses simple low-power radio transmitters that are akin to those used within the 802.15 Wireless Personal Network in Bluetooth implementations. Transmitters have a range of roughly 150 feet from the base and can be incorporated within the Compact Flash card form factor.

HomeRF provides for 128-bit session encryption based on a 32-bit initialization vector. There are no "open" access modes available as in WEP, and specification-compliant devices cannot pass promiscuous packets above the MAC.

HomeRF MAC layer (see Figure 1.17) provides for three types of communication:

- Asynchronous, connectionless packet data service

- Isochronous, full-duplex symmetric two-way voice service

- Prioritized, repetitive connection-oriented data service

Figure 1.17 The HomeRF Protocol Stack

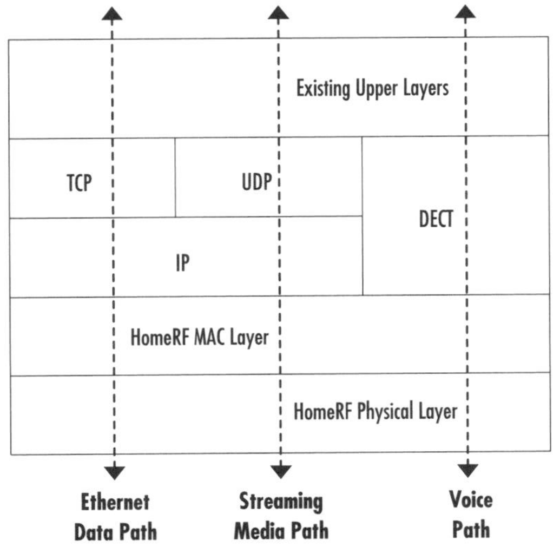

Data Applications

The Data Networking portion of HomeRF is Ethernet-based and relies on the IEEE 802.3 CSMA/CA protocols defined in the 802.11 and OpenAir standards and supports TCP/IP, UDP/IP, IPX, and NETBEUI, among others. The HomeRF specification supports data communications between PCs, peripherals, and data appliances such as portable Web browsing tablets, MP3 players and data-ready phones.

HomeRF Version 1 supports data access rates of 1.6 Mbps and 10 Mbps in the Version 2 standard. Support for 20 Mbps and 40 Mbps implementations of HomeRF are planned for Version 3 and beyond.

HomeRF also supports concurrent host/client and peer-to-peer communication. Host/client communications tend to be favored for voice communications and Internet-centric applications such as Webcasting. Peer-to-peer is better suited to sharing network resources like a DVD drive or a printer.

Telephony Applications

HomeRF telephony is based on TDMA adapted from the Digital Enhanced Cordless Telephony (DECT) standard, which offers a rich set of features that were specifically designed to address the telephony needs of business and home users. Some of the features supported include the intelligent forwarding of incoming calls to cordless extensions, FAX machines, and voice mailboxes, as well as multi-party conferencing. DECT is only applicable in Europe due to the fact that it specifies the use of the 1.9GHz frequency which has been assigned for other purposes in other parts of the world.

The HomeRF base connects to the telephone line instead of the individual cordless telephone handsets. Cordless telephone handsets communicate directly to the HomeRF base and only need a local cradle for battery charging. The use of a cabled base station and unconnected cradles increase the flexibility of phone placement.

Up to eight handsets can be connected to the network. HomeRF provides a facility for supporting handset-to-handset calls in conjunction with external calls to create multiparty calling scenarios.

Audio/Video Applications

HomeRF provides a specification for streaming media sessions with quality-of-service prioritizations. These include audio and video media distribution to remote set-top boxes and wireless speakers in both multi-cast, two-way, and receive-only mode.

Examples of streaming media include MP3 music from a home PC, home theater sound distribution, multiplayer gaming, and MPEG4 video distribution. Provisions have been made to support two-way videoconferencing.

The HomeRF specification supports up to eight prioritized streaming media sessions at any given time. Streaming media is assigned prioritization that is greater than other services such as data networking but below two-way voice calls.

Other Applications

HomeRF is planning to support additional capabilities including Voice over IP (VoIP), home automation, speech-enabled applications, and telemedicine.

802.15 WPAN

Wireless personal area networks (WPANs) are short-range low-power wireless networking technologies providing both voice and data services. WPAN provides a means to create ad-hoc point-to-point networks between other WPAN devices using two-way short-wave radio communications. It operates in a host/client mode where the host is only defined during session establishment.

The basic application of WPAN is for the wireless replacement of cables interconnecting computer peripherals, data terminals, and telephone systems. It can also act as the local delivery mechanism for higher-level wireless networking technologies such as IEEE 802.11 wireless LANs, HomeRF, 2.5G, and 3G, as well as a means for synchronizing devices.

The Bluetooth wireless networking specification developed by Ericsson has now been repatriated within the auspices of the Bluetooth Special Interest group and the IEEE under the IEEE 802.15 WPAN specification. Bluetooth has widespread support among telecommunication equipment vendors, in addition to computer and chip manufacturers.

802.15 WPAN networks operate over the 2.4GHz ISM band using time division multiple access (TDMA). Specifications define short radio link capabilities of up to 10 m (30 feet) and medium range radio link capability up to 100 m (300 feet) and supports voice or data transmission to a maximum capacity of 720 Kbps per channel.

Spread Spectrum is used in frequency hopping to create a full-duplex signal. Hops occur at up to 1600 hops/sec among 79 frequencies spaced at 1MHz intervals to give a high degree of interference immunity

The 802.15 WPAN specification defines both synchronous and asynchronous communications. Synchronous channels are connection-oriented and symmetric, providing up to 64 Kbps in a bi-directional connection between the *master* and a specific *slave*. Synchronous mode is targeted for voice traffic but does not impede the simultaneous transmission of both voice and low-speed data. Up to three synchronous voice channels can be supported simultaneously with each voice channel having access to a 64 Kbps synchronous (voice) channel in each direction.

Asynchronous packets are connectionless and are sent on the over bandwidth. The slaves send information only after they receive information targeted to them from the Master. There are several types of asynchronous channels with different payload size and error correction.

Asynchronous data channels can support maximal 723.2 Kbps asymmetric with up to 57.6 Kbps in the return direction. Asynchronous channels can also be configured for 433.9 Kbps access both ways. A Master can share an asynchronous channel with up to seven simultaneously active slaves forming a *piconet*.

By swapping active and parked slaves out respectively in the piconet, up to 255 slaves can be virtually connected. There is no limitation to the number of slaves that can be parked. Slaves can also participate in different piconets, and a master of one piconet can be a slave in another, thus creating a *scatternet*. Up to ten piconets within range can form a scatternet, with a minimum of collisions. Units can dynamically be added or disconnected to the network. Each piconet is established using a different frequency-hopping channel. All users participating on the same piconet are synchronized to this channel.

The 802.15 WPAN supports a challenge-response routine for authentication. Security functions are supported using the public 48-bit WPAN device address, the private 128-bit user key and a 128-bit pseudorandom number that is generated by the device. A stream cipher is used to encrypt communications.

IEEE 802.15 Task Groups

The IEEE 802.15 WPAN initiative is very active and now comprises four task groups responsible for addressing specific issues relating to physical layer optimizations, MAC layer enhancements, security definitions, and vendor interoperability. The tasks groups are as follows:

- **IEEE 802.15 Task Group 1** The scope of this task group is to define the physical and media access layer specifications for wireless connectivity. These specifications address the needs of fixed, portable, and moving devices within or entering a Personal Operating Space (POS). A POS is a fixed-size area that is centered around a WPAN-enabled device. The POS extends up to 10 meters in all directions, essentially creating a sphere of service for the WPAN-enabled device.

WPAN-enabled devices will typically consist of devices that are carried, worn, or located near or on the body of users. These devices include computers, personal digital assistants, printers, microphones, speakers, headsets, bar code readers, sensors, displays, pagers, and cellular phones.

Task Group 1 intends to establish a basic level interoperability and coexistence between 802.15 WPAN and 802.11 WLAN networks so that data transfers are possible. It also intends to develop QoS specifications to support several classes of service including data and voice.

Lastly, Task Group 1 plans to define a standard for low complexity and low power consumption wireless connectivity.

- **IEEE 802.15 Task Group 2 – The Coexistence Task Group** The scope of this task group is to specifically develop recommended practices which could be used to facilitate coexistence of IEEE 802.15 Wireless Personal Area Networks and IEEE 802.11 Wireless Local Area Networks.

  Task Group 2 is developing a Coexistence Model to quantify the mutual interference of a WLAN and a WPAN. Task Group 2 is also developing a set of Coexistence Mechanisms to facilitate coexistence of WLAN and WPAN devices.

- **IEEE 802.15 Task Group 3 – High Rate** The scope of this task group is to draft and publish a new standard for high-rate WPANs supporting 20 Mbps throughputs or greater. Additional considerations will include providing for low-power, low-cost solutions that address the needs of portable consumer digital imaging and multimedia applications.

  To date, the task group has developed specifications supporting data rates of 11 Mbps, 22 Mbps, 33 Mbps, 44 Mbps, and 55 Mbps. It has also defined protocols to be used in the definition of Quality of Service, physical schemes to minimize power consumption and manufacturing costs.

- **IEEE 802.15 Task Group 4** The purpose of this task group is to investigate a low data rate solution with multimonth to multiyear battery life implemented using a simple design over the ISM band. The application of the working group specifications would include sensors, interactive toys, smart badges, remote controls, and home automation.

  Data rates would be limited to between 20 Kbps and 250 Kbps and would have the ability to operate in either master-slave or peer-to-peer mode. Other considerations include support for critical latency devices, such as joysticks, automatic network establishment by the coordinator, and dynamic device addressing.

A fully resilient protocol with acknowledgment and provisions for retransmissions is expected. Power management to ensure low power consumption over the 16 channels in the 2.4GHz ISM band, ten channels in the 915MHz ISM band, and one channel in the European 868MHz band will also be implemented.

802.15 WPAN Products

Most IEEE 802.15 WPAN implementations will consist of imbedded devices. These will include specialized adapters for mobile phones, PCMCIA cards for notebooks and PCs, high-end mobile phones, headsets, and event monitors.

802.16 WMAN

The 802.16 Wireless Metropolitan Area Network initiative was established in 1998 to create a standard for fixed point-to-multipoint connection-oriented broadband wireless network support over a large area of coverage. The target applications for 802.16 WMAN include broadband wireless access to the Internet and Internet telephony using Voice over IP (VoIP) solutions for enterprise, small business, and home use. These services can be accessed simultaneously and are assigned QoS priorities.

The 802.16 WMAN standard specifies the use of wireless base stations that are connected to public networks, and subscriber stations which provide local building access for an enterprise, small business, or home. Base stations serve subscriber stations.

To facilitate the Wireless Broadband initiative, the 802.16 WMAN committees have chosen to work on several fronts establishing standards for both licensed and unlicensed bands. Licensed band solutions are targeted at the enterprise, whereas unlicensed band solutions target small business and home use. The use of unlicensed bands for small business and home use helps resolve the issues over the shortage of licensed bands and will provide cost savings to solution providers that can be passed on to the price-sensitive home and small business target users.

802.16 WMAN working groups are developing new MAC layer specifications that meet the requirements of both enterprise grade solutions and small business/home solutions. The 802.16.1 MAC is based on the IEEE 802.11 MAC. It was devised to support higher data rates and higher frequency operations and is targeted at large business enterprises. It supports TCP/IP and ATM services among others but not ad-hoc network creation (typically available in 802.11 such as peer-to-peer data transfer) that does not necessarily go through the infrastructure. A scaled down version which does note include services such as ATM is being developed to meet the requirements of small business and home installations. This version supports subscriber-to-subscriber communications.

Security and privacy issues are addressed within the 802.16 WMAN specification using existing standards. Authentication and authorization is based on X.509 certificates with RSA. PKCS support is defined to prevent theft of service and device cloning. The subscriber station manufacturer's X.509 certificate binds a subscriber station's public key to its other identifying information. A trust relation assumed between manufacturer and network operator but a possibility exists to accommodate root authority if required.

Subscriber stations are responsible for maintaining valid authorization keys. Two valid authorization overlapping lifetimes are present within the subscriber station at all times. A reauthorization process is performed periodically where Authorization Key lifetimes are set at seven days with a grace timer of one hour. Key exchanges are likewise performed using a two-level key exchange protocol. 3-DES encryption, meanwhile, is used to secure the payload during key exchange.

General channel encryption is currently defined using 56-bit DES in cipher-block-chaining (CBC) mode but other algorithms can be substituted. The session encryption key initialization vector (IV) is derived from the frame number.

To date, the IEEE 802.16 Wireless Metropolitan Area Network initiative has developed three WMAN specifications:

- **P802.16**
  - This specification defined a physical layer access mechanism supporting the 10GHz to 66GHz frequencies.
  - It defined a MAC layer standard for broad use in 10GHz to 66GHz-based WMAN systems.

- **P802.16a**
  - This amendment to the 802.16 specification defines the physical layer access mechanism supporting implementations using the licensed frequencies in the 2GHz to 11GHz range.

- **P802.16b**
  - This amendment to the 802.16 specification defines the physical layer access mechanism supporting implementations using the unlicensed frequencies in the 2GHz to 11GHz range.

- This standard is referred to as the Wireless High-Speed Unlicensed Metropolitan Area Network or WirelessHUMAN.

IEEE 802.16 Task Groups

The IEEE 802.16 initiative is very active and now comprises four task groups responsible for addressing specific issues relating to physical layer optimizations, MAC layer enhancements, security definitions, and vendor interoperability. The tasks groups are as follows:

- **IEEE 802.16 Task Group 1** The purpose of this task group is to develop physical interfaces for the transmission and reception of wireless data using the 10GHz to 66GHz frequencies.

  To date, the IEEE 802.16 Task Group 1 has developed an air interface for fixed broadband wireless access systems using the 10GHz to 66GHz frequencies.

- **IEEE 802.16 Task Group 2** The aim of this task group is to develop a Coexistence Model to quantify the mutual interference of radio-based data and communication systems and WMAN technologies; and to facilitate coexistence with WLAN and WPAN devices.

  As of September 2001, the task group has completed a coexistence model for fixed broadband wireless access devices operating in the 10GHz to 66GHz frequencies.

- **IEEE 802.16 Task Group 3** The purpose of this task group is to develop physical interfaces for the transmission and reception of wireless data using the licensed 2GHz to 11GHz frequencies.

- **IEEE 802.16 Task Group 4** The function of this task group is to develop physical interfaces for the transmission and reception of wireless data using license-exempt 5GHz frequencies.

Understanding Public Key Infrastructures and Wireless Networking

Traditional wired network security has used Public Key Infrastructures (PKIs) to provide privacy, integrity authentication, and nonrepudiation. Wireless networks need to support the same basic security functionalities in order to meet the minimum accepted standards for security that are expected by users.

Public Key Infrastructures are the components used to distribute and manage encryption and digital signature keys through a centralized service. The centralized service establishes a means of creating third-party trusts between users who may have never met each other before.

PKIs are made up of a Certificate Authority, directory service, and certificate verification service. The Certificate Authority is the application that issues and manages keys in the form of certificates. Directory or look-up services are used to post public information about users or certificates in use. The certificate verification service is an agent of the CA that either directly answers user queries about the validity or applicability of an issued certificate, or supports a directory, look-up, or other third-party agent used to verify certificates.

PKI certificates are akin to end user identities or electronic passports. They are a means of binding encryption or digital signature keys to a user.

Overview of Cryptography

Cryptography has been in use since the days of Julius Caesar. It is the science of changing information into a form that is unintelligible to all but the intended recipient. Cryptography is made up of two parts: encryption and decryption. Encryption is the process of turning clear plaintext or data into ciphertext or encrypted data, while decryption is the process of returning encrypted data or ciphertext back to its original clear plaintext form.

The security behind cryptography relies on the premise that only the sender and receiver have an understanding of how the data was altered to create the obfuscated message. This understanding is provided in the form of keys.

There are generally two types of cryptographic methods, referred to as ciphers, used for securing information: symmetric or private key, and asymmetric public key systems.

Symmetric Ciphers

In symmetric ciphers, the same key is used to encrypt and decrypt a message. Here's how it can be done: Shift the starting point of the alphabet by three positions—the encryption key is now $K=3$.

Standard Alphabet: ABCDEFGHIJKLMNOPQRSTUVWXYZ

Cryptographic Alphabet: DEFGHIJKLMNOPQRSTUVWXYZABC

For example:

Plaintext: WIRELESS SECURITY

Ciphertext: ZLUHOHVV VHFXULWB

The weakness of the system lies in the fact that statistical analysis is based on greater use of some letters in the language than others. Julius Caesar was the first to use a symmetric cipher to secure his communications to his commanders. The key he used consisted of shifting the starting point of the alphabet a certain number of positions and substituting the letters making up a message with the corresponding letter in the cipher alphabet.

The main weakness of this type of encryption is that it is open to statistical analysis. Some languages (like the English language) use some letters more often than others, and as a result cryptanalysts have a starting point from which they can attempt to decrypt a message.

This standard form of symmetric encryption remained relatively unchanged until the 16th century. At this time, Blaise de Vigenere was tasked by Henry the III to extend the Caesar cipher and provide enhanced security. What he proposed was the simultaneous use of several different cryptographic alphabets to encrypt a message. The selection of which alphabet to use for which letter would be determined though the use of a key word. Each letter of the keyword represented one of the cryptographic substitution alphabets. For example:

Standard Alphabet	ABCDEFGHIJKLMNOPQRSTUVWXYZ
Substitution set "A"	ABCDEFGHIJKLMNOPQRSTUVWXYZ
Substitution set "B"	BCDEFGHIJKLMNOPQRSTUVWXYZA
Substitution set "C"	CDEFGHIJKLMNOPQRSTUVWXYZAB

...

Substitution set "Z"	ZABCDEFGHIJKLMNOPQRSTUVWXY

If the keyword were *airwave*, you would develop the cipher text as follows:

Plaintext:	wire	less	secu	rity
Key Word:	airw	avea	irwa	veai
Ciphertext:	wqia	lzws	avyu	mmtg

The main benefit of the Vigenere cipher is that instead of having a one-to-one relationship between each letter of the original message and its substitute, there is a one-to-many relationship, which makes statistical analysis all but impossible. While other ciphers were devised, the Vigenere-based letter substitution scheme variants remained at the heart of most encryption systems up until the mid-twentieth century.

The main difference with modern cryptography and classical cryptography is that it leverages the computing power available within devices to build ciphers that perform binary operations on blocks of data at a time, instead of individual letters. The advances in computing power also provide a means of supporting larger key spaces required to successfully secure data using public key ciphers.

When using binary cryptography, a key is represented as a string of bits or numbers with 2^n keys. That is, for every bit that is added to a key size, the key space is doubled. The binary key space equivalents illustrated in Table 1.1 show how large the key space can be for modern algorithms and how difficult it can be to "break" a key.

Table 1.1 Binary Key Space

Binary Key Length	Key Space
1 bit	2^1 = 2 keys
2 bit	2^2 = 4 keys
3 bit	2^3 = 8 keys
16 bit	2^{16} = 65,536 keys
56 bit	2^{56} = 72,057,594,037,927,936 keys

The task of discovering the one key used, based on a 56-bit key space is akin to finding one red golf ball in a channel filled with white golf balls that is 30 miles wide, 500 feet tall and which runs the distance between L.A. to San Francisco. A 57-bit key would involve finding the one red golf ball in two of these channels sitting side-by-side. A 58-bit key would be four of these channels side-by-side, and so on!

Another advantage of using binary operations is that the encryption and decryption operations can be simplified to use bit-based operations such as XOR, shifts and substitutions, and binary arithmetic operations such as additions, subtractions, multiplications, divisions, and raising to a power.

In addition, several blocks of data, each say 64 bits in length, can be operated on all at once, where portions of the data is combined and substituted with other portions. This can be repeated many times, using a different combination or substitution key. Each repetition is referred to as a round. The resultant ciphertext is now a function of several plaintext bits and several subkeys. Examples of modern symmetric encryption ciphers include 56-bit DES, Triple DES using keys of roughly 120 bits, RC2 using 40-bit and 1280-bit keys, CAST using 40-, 64-, 80-, 128- and 256-bit keys, and IDEA using 128-bit keys among others.

Some of the main drawbacks to symmetric algorithms are that they only provide a means to encrypt data. Furthermore, they are only as secure as the transmission method used to exchange the secret keys between the party encrypting the data, and the party that is decrypting it. As the number of users increases, so does the number of individual keys required to ensure the privacy of the data. As Figure 1.18 illustrates, the number of symmetric keys required becomes exponential.

Figure 1.18 Symmetric Keys Required to Support Private Communications

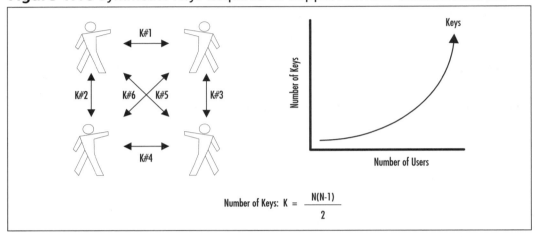

The more a symmetric key is used, the greater the statistical data that is generated which can be used to launch brute force and other encryption attacks. The best way to minimize these risks is to perform frequent symmetric key changeovers. Manual key exchanges have always been bulky and expensive to perform.

Asymmetric Ciphers

Until the advent of asymmetric or public key cryptography in the late 1970s, the main application of cryptography was secrecy. Today, cryptography is used for many things, including:

- Preventing unauthorized disclosure of information
- Preventing unauthorized access to data, networks, and applications
- Detecting tampering such as the injection of false data or the deletion of data
- Prevent repudiation

The basis of asymmetric cryptography is that the sender and the recipient do not share a single key, but rather two separate keys that are mathematically related to one another. Knowledge of one key does not imply any information on what the reverse matching key is. A real world example would be that of a locker with a combination lock. Knowing the location of a locker does not provide any details regarding the combination of the lock that is used to secure the door. The magic behind asymmetric algorithms is that the opposite is also true. In other words, either one of the keys can be used to encrypt data while the other will decrypt it. This relationship makes possible the free distribution of one of the keys in a key pair to other users (referred to as the public key) while the other can remain secret (referred to as the private key), thereby eliminating the need for a bulky and expensive key distribution process.

This relationship allows asymmetric cryptography to be used as a mechanism that supports both encryption and signatures. The main limitations of asymmetric cryptography are that of a slow encryption process and limited size of the encryption payload when compared to symmetric cryptography.

Examples of public key cryptography include RSA, DSA, and Diffie-Hellman.

Elliptic Curve Ciphers

Elliptic curve ciphers are being used more and more within imbedded hardware for their flexibility, security, strength, and limited computational requirements when compared to other encryption technologies.

In essence, elliptic curves are simple functions that can be drawn as looping lines in the (x, y) plane. Their advantage comes from using a different kind of mathematical group for public key computation. They are based on the discrete log problem of elliptic curves.

The easiest way to understand elliptic curves is to imagine an infinitely large sheet of graph paper where the intersections of lines are whole (x, y) coordinates. If a special type of elliptic curve is drawn, it will stretch out into infinity and along the way will intersect a finite number of (x, y) coordinates, rather than a closed ellipse.

At each (x, y) intersection, a dot is drawn. When identified, an addition operation can be established between two points that will yield a third. The addition operation used to define these points forms a finite group and represents the key.

Use of Cryptographic Ciphers in Wireless Networks

Wireless networks use combinations of different cryptographic ciphers to support the required security and functionality within a system. Combinations of symmetric, asymmetric, and elliptic curve cryptography find their way within wireless security protocols including WAP, WEP, and SSL.

Summary

This chapter provided practical knowledge on the various technologies, standards and generalized product offerings used in the deployment of both cellular-based wireless networks and wireless LAN networks. It outlined wireless solutions that can be used to interact with devices contained within a personal space such as in 802.15 Personal Area Networks, within a local area such as in 802.11 Local Area Networks and HomeRF, within a large city using 802.16 Metropolitan Area Networks, and beyond into the world at large using 2G, 2.5G, and 3G cellular networks.

We discussed the many IEEE working groups responsible for developing the 802.11, 802.15, and 802.16 wireless network standards, along with the technologies that make up the 2G, 2.5G, and 3G variants of cellular-based packet data networks.

We provided insight on the main security concerns that exist within each of these wireless environments and the mechanisms offered by standards bodies and equipment vendors such as WAP and WEP to address these issues.

We discussed some of the biggest concerns currently plaguing wireless deployments, namely the flip side of convenience and security. With most wireless devices being small, convenient, and growing in supported features, function and capability sets make them susceptible to both traditional wireless and the new breed of existing LAN and PC attacks. Some of these include device theft, identity theft, code attacks such as viruses, Trojans and worms, and hacker attacks such as man-in-the-middle and denial of service using cheap advanced radio transceiver technology.

With wireless technology deployments being so new to most users and even network administrators, configuration errors and the misapplication of wireless resources to address a particular network architecture requirement will continue to be risks.

By taking a moment to revisit our intrepid wireless PDA user traveling in 2005, we can begin to understand how the convergence of multiple wireless data networking standards and security technologies will make this a real possibility. By merging cellular, LAN, and PAN wireless networking technologies, our intelligent PDAs will open up a world of voice and data communications never before seen. Automatic interactions between devices and networks will become the norm. The convenience of access to people and data resources anytime and anywhere will lead us into a new age of collaboration and work. Multimedia downloads from any office, home, car, or PDA will create new services as well as new uses for remote data. Context- and location-based information will provide insight into localized services, resources, and other availabilities, thereby opening up new forms of niche marketing and industries specializing in the development of wireless applications.

Many risks remain unmanaged and will need to be addressed before this vision of the fully integrated wireless future environment becomes a usable and acceptable reality. Issues over privacy need to be addressed and clearly defined. Trust relationships will need to be established between networks, vendors, and users using PKIs and other technologies. Strong two-factor user authentication needs to be implemented along with end-to-end encryption of user communications. The mobility user credentials such as user IDs, modules, and PINs will need to be addressed using a standard that is compatible with more than one type of device.

Lastly, as with all other security mechanisms, wireless network security will need to balance complexity, user friendliness, effectiveness, reliability, and timeliness with performance requirements and costs. Security and mobility of personal data and communications will be the lynch pins that will uphold the integrity of our wireless future. Clear, usable, and scaleable solutions will need to be defined before we can fully entrust our personal identities and the moments that make up our daily lives to our wireless companions.

Solutions Fast Track

Wireless Technology Overview

☑ Wireless technologies today come in several forms and offer a multitude of solutions applicable to generally one of two wireless networking camps: cellular-based and wireless LANs.

☑ Cellular-based wireless data solutions are solutions that use the existing cell phone and pager communications networks to transmit data.

☑ Wireless LAN solutions are solutions that provide wireless connectivity over a coverage area between 10 and 100 meters. These provide the capabilities necessary to support the two-way data communications of typical corporate or home desktop computers

☑ Open source code does not necessarily have to be free. For example, companies such as Red Hat and Caldera sell their products, which are based on the open source Linux kernel.

☑ Convergence within devices will be the norm over the next two years.

☑ While the majority of cellular-based wireless traffic today mainly consists of voice, it is estimated that by the end of 2003 nearly 35 to −40 percent of cellular-based wireless traffic will be data.

☑ Information appliances will have a big impact on wireless network deployments

☑ Information appliances are single purpose devices that are portable, easy to use, and provide a specific set of capabilities relevant to their function.

☑ Information appliance shipments will outnumber PC shipments this year.

Understanding the Promise of Wireless

☑ Corporate applications of wireless will consist of: Corporate Communications, Customer Service, Telemetry, and Field Service

☑ New wireless services will allow for a single point of contact that roams with the user.

☑ New context (time and location) sensitive applications will revolutionize the way we interact with data.

Understanding the Benefits of Wireless

☑ New end user applications and services are being developed to provide businesses and consumers alike with advanced data access and manipulation

☑ The main benefits of wireless integration will fall primarily into five major categories: convenience, affordability, speed, aesthetics, and productivity.

Facing the Reality of Wireless Today

☑ Fraud remains a big issue.

☑ New more powerful and intelligent devices will provide additional options for attackers.

☑ The WAP standard is a moving target and still has many issues to overcome.

☑ WEP is limited and has many known security flaws.

☑ General wireless security posture: the majority of devices employ weak user authentication and poor encryption. Two-factor authentication, enhanced cryptography, and biometrics are necessary

Examining the Wireless Standards

☑ Cellular-based wireless networking technologies and solutions are categorized into three main groups: 2G Circuit Switched Cellular Wireless Networks, 2.5G Packed Data Overlay Cellular Wireless Networks, and 3G Packet Switched Cellular Wireless Networks.

☑ 3G will provide three generalized data networking throughputs to meet the specific needs of mobile users: High Mobility, Full Mobility, and Limited Mobility.

☑ High Mobility: High Mobility use is intended for generalized roaming outside urban areas in which the users are traveling at speeds in excess of 120 kilometers per hour. This category of use will provide the end user with up to 144 Kbps of data throughput.

☑ Full Mobility: Full Mobility use is intended for generalized roaming within urban areas in which the user is traveling at speeds below 120 kilometers per hour. This category of use will provide the end user with up to 384 Kbps of data throughput.

☑ Limited Mobility: Limited Mobility use is intended for limited roaming or near stationary users traveling at 10 kilometers per hour or less. This category of use will provide the end user with up to 2 Mbps of data throughput when indoors and stationary.

☑ There are four largely competing commercial wireless LAN solutions available: 802.11 WLAN (Wireless Local Area Network), HomeRF, 802.15 WPAN (Wireless Personal Area Network) based on Bluetooth, and 802.16 WMAN (Wireless Metropolitan Area Network).

☑ The 802.11 standard provides a common standardized Media Access Control layer (MAC) that is similar to 802.3 Ethernet (CMSA/CA). It supports TCP/IP, UDP/IP, IPX, NETBEUI and so on, and has a Virtual Collision Detection VCD option. It also supports encrypted communications using WEP encryption. There are still many issues being worked on by the standards bodies, including support for voice and multimedia, QoS specifications, intervendor interoperability, distributed systems, and roaming.

☑ HomeRF is based on existing standards like TCP/IP and DECT. It is a solution aimed at the home wireless LAN market, and supports data, voice, and streaming multimedia.

☑ The 802.15 WPAN standard is based on Bluetooth, and provides a network interface for devices located within a personal area. It supports both voice and data traffic. 802.15 WPAN Task Groups are investigating issues including interoperability with other technologies.

☑ The 802.16 WMAN standard addresses support of broadband wireless solutions to enterprises, small businesses, and homes. Several working group streams are investigating solutions for licensed and unlicensed frequencies.

Frequently Asked Questions

The following Frequently Asked Questions, answered by the authors of this book, are designed to both measure your understanding of the concepts presented in this chapter and to assist you with real-life implementation of these concepts. To have your questions about this chapter answered by the author, browse to **www.syngress.com/solutions** and click on the **"Ask the Author"** form.

Q: I have heard the i-Mode data service for data-ready cell phones in Japan is a huge success with well over 20 million subscribers. What made it so successful?

A: In Japan, as with most countries outside of North America, telephone usage charges are incurred for every minute used. As a result, few people have had access to or have used the Internet on a day-to-day basis and a large pent-up demand existed. i-Mode provided basic text Internet access via data-ready cell phones. Charges were based on total bytes transferred instead of time online. This provided a cost-effective means for users to access even the basic services offered via the Internet.

Q: Will i-Mode be available in North America or Europe?

A: Although i-Mode parent NTT DoCoMo has ownership stakes in several North American and European cellular operators, it is not expected that i-Mode, as it currently exists, will be offered in these markets. This is primarily due to the limited 9.6 Kbps access rates.

Q: Why have WAP deployments in North America had limited success?

A: While security and technology concerns have had an impact on the deployment of WAP-enabled services, the main reason for the slow adoption of WAP has been due to the limited access speeds available to the data-ready cellular handsets. North Americans are used to accessing the content- and graphics-rich Internet. With the data-ready handsets providing a limited viewing screen and access speeds being limited to 9.6 Kbps, users have been forced to rethink how they use the Internet in order to accommodate the limitations of WAP.

Q: Wireless LAN Access Points provide yet another location where users or systems need to present credentials for authentication. Can this be tied to existing login mechanisms so users are not forced to remember another set of user IDs/passwords?

A: While every vendor solution is unique, the majority of solutions currently only offer a standalone approach to user authentication—that is, users are required to use login credentials specific to wireless APs and not the overall network.

Q: The clear benefit of wireless LANs will be the ability to roam physically around an area, as well as logically from one Access Point to another. Is there a specified standard for how this is done, and does it integrate with existing login mechanisms?

A: The IEEE standards working groups are developing a roaming model which will provide the means to support the roaming of users from one wireless AP. At present, most solutions require reauthentication when moving from one wireless AP to another. Vendors who provide a managed roaming capability have developed their own roaming management which may or may not interface with other wireless LAN vendor solutions.

Chapter 2

A Security Primer

Solutions in this chapter:

- **Understanding Security Fundamentals and Principles of Protection**

- **Reviewing the Role of Policy**

- **Recognizing Accepted Security and Privacy Standards**

- **Addressing Common Risks and Threats**

- ☑ **Summary**
- ☑ **Solutions Fast Track**
- ☑ **Frequently Asked Questions**

Introduction

There is not much indication of anything slowing down the creation and deployment of new technology to the world any time in the near future. With the constant pressure to deploy the latest generation of technology today, there is often little time allowed for a full and proper security review of the technology and components that make it up.

This rush to deploy, along with inadequate security reviews, not only allows for the inclusion of security vulnerabilities in products, but also creates new and unknown challenges as well. Wireless networking is not exempt from this, and like many other technologies, security flaws have been identified and new methods of exploiting these flaws are published regularly.

Utilizing security fundamentals developed over the last few decades it's possible to review and protect your wireless networks from known and unknown threats. In this chapter, we will recall security fundamentals and principles that are the foundation of any good security strategy, addressing a range of issues from authentication and authorization, to controls and audit.

No primer on security would be complete without an examination of the common security standards, which will be addressed in this chapter alongside the emerging privacy standards and their implications for the wireless exchange of information.

You'll also lean about the existing and anticipated threats to wireless networks, and the principles of protection that are fundamental to a wireless security strategy.

Understanding Security Fundamentals and Principles of Protection

Security protection starts with the preservation of the *confidentiality*, *integrity*, and *availability* (CIA) of data and computing resources. These three tenets of information security, often referred to as "The Big Three," are sometimes represented by the following figure (Figure 2.1).

As we get into a full description of each of these tenets, it will become clear that to provide for a reliable and secure wireless environment you will need to assure that each tenet is properly protected. To ensure the preservation of "The Big Three," and protect the privacy of those whose data is stored and flows through these data and computing resources, "The Big Three" security tenets are implemented through tried-and-true security practices. These other practices enforce "The Big Three" by ensuring proper authentication for authorized access while allowing for non-repudiation in identification and resource usage methods, and by permitting complete accountability for all activity through audit trails and logs. Some security practitioners refer to Authentication, Authorization, and Audit (accountability) as "AAA." Each of these practices provides the security implementer with tools which they can use to properly identify and mitigate any possible risks to "The Big Three."

Figure 2.1 The CIA Triad

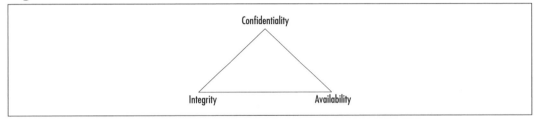

Ensuring Confidentiality

Confidentiality attempts to prevent the intentional or unintentional unauthorized disclosure of communications between a sender and recipient. In the physical world, ensuring confidentiality can be accomplished by simply securing the physical area. However, as evidenced by bank robberies and military invasions, threats exist to the security of the physical realm that can compromise security and confidentiality.

The moment electronic means of communication were introduced, many new possible avenues of disclosing the information within these communications were created. The confidentiality of early analog communication systems, such as the telegraph and telephone, were easily compromised by simply having someone connect to the wires used between sender and recipient.

When digital communications became available, like with many technologies, it was only a matter of time until knowledgeable people were able to build devices and methods that could interpret the digital signals and convert them to whatever form needed to disclose what was communicated. And as technology grew and became less expensive, the equipment needed to monitor and disclose digital communications became available to anyone wishing to put the effort into monitoring communication.

With the advent of wireless communications, the need for physically connecting to a communication channel to listen in or capture confidential communications was eliminated. While you can achieve some security by using extremely tight beam directional antennas, someone still only has to sit somewhere in between the antennas to be able to monitor and possibly connect to the communications channel without having to actually tie into any physical device.

Having knowledge that communications channels are possibly compromised allows us to properly implement our policies and procedures to mitigate the wireless risk. The solution used to ensure "The Big Three" and other security tenets (as we will see in this and other chapters) is encryption.

The current implementation of encryption in today's wireless networks use the RC4 stream cipher to encrypt the transmitted network packets, and the Wired Equivalent Privacy (WEP) protocol to protect authentication into wireless networks by network devices connecting to them (that is, the network adaptor authentication, not the user utilizing the network resources). Both of which, due mainly to improper implementations, have introduced sufficient problems that have made it possible to determine keys used and then either falsely authenticate to the network or decrypt the traffic traveling across through the wireless network.

With these apparent problems, it is strongly recommended that people utilize other proven and properly implemented encryption solutions such as Secure Shell (SSH), Secure Sockets Layer (SSL), or IPSec.

Ensuring Integrity

Integrity ensures the accuracy and completeness of information throughout its process methods. The first communication methods available to computers did not have much in place to ensure the integrity of the data transferred from one to another. As such, it was found that occasionally something as simple as static on a telephone line could cause the transfer of data to be corrupted.

To solve this problem, the idea of a checksum was introduced. A checksum is nothing more than taking the message you are sending and running it through a function that returns a simple value which is then appended to the message being sent. When the receiver gets the complete message, they would then run the message through the same function and compare the value they generate with the value that was included at the end of the message.

The functions that are generally used to generate basic checksums are usually based upon simple addition or modulus functions. These functions can sometimes have their own issues such as the function not being detailed enough to allow for distinctly separate data that could possibly have identical checksums. It is even possible to have two errors within the data itself cause the checksum to provide a valid check because the two errors effectively cancel each other out. These problems are usually addressed through a more complex algorithm used to create the digital checksum.

Cyclic redundancy checks (CRCs) were developed as one of the more advanced methods of ensuring data integrity. CRC algorithms basically treat a message as an enormous binary number, whereupon another large fixed binary number then divides this binary number. The remainder from this division is the checksum. Using the remainder of a long division as the checksum, as opposed to the original data summation, adds a significant chaos to the checksum created, increasing the likelihood that the checksum will not be repeatable with any other separate data stream.

These more advanced checksum methods, however, have their own set of problems. As Ross Williams wrote in his 1993 paper, A Painless Guide to CRC Error Detection Algorithms (www.ross.net/crc/crcpaper.html), the goal of error detection is to protect against corruption introduced by noise in a data transfer. This is good if we are only concerned with protecting against possible transmission errors. However, the algorithm provides no means of ensuring the integrity of an intentionally corrupted data stream. If someone has knowledge of a particular data stream, it is possible to alter the contents of the data and complete the transaction with a valid checksum. The receiver would not have knowledge of the changes in the data because their checksum would match and it would appear as if the data was transferred with no errors.

This form of intentional integrity violation is called a "Data Injection." In such cases, the best way to protect data is to (once again) use a more advanced form of integrity protection utilizing cryptography. Today, these higher levels of protection are generally provided through a series of stronger cryptographic algorithm such as the MD5 or RC4 ciphers.

Wireless networks today use the RC4 stream cipher to protect the data transmitted as well as provide for data integrity. It has been proven (and will be explained in more detail later in this book) that the 802.11 implementation of the RC4 cipher with its key scheduling algorithm introduces enough information to provide a hacker with enough to be able to predict your network's secret encryption key. Once the hacker has your key, they are not only able to gain access to your wireless network, but also view it as if there was no encryption at all.

Ensuring Availability

Availability, as defined in an information security context, assures that access data or computing resources needed by appropriate personnel is both reliable and available in a timely manner. The origins of the Internet itself come from the need to ensure the availability of network resources. In 1957, the United States Department of Defense (DOD) created the Advanced Research Projects Agency (ARPA) following the Soviet launch of Sputnik. Fearing loss of command and control over U.S. nuclear missiles and bombers due to communication channel disruption caused by nuclear or conventional attacks, the U.S. Air Force commissioned a study on how to create a network that could function with the loss of access or routing points. Out of this, packet switched networking was created, and the first four nodes of ARPANET were deployed in 1968 running at the then incredibly high speed of 50 kilobits per second.

The initial design of packet switched networks did not take into consideration the possibility of an actual attack on the network from one of its own nodes, and as the ARPANET grew into what we now know as the Internet, there have been many modifications to the protocols and applications that make up the network, ensuring the availability of all resources provided.

Wireless networks are experiencing many similar design issues, and due to the proliferation of new wireless high-tech devices, many are finding themselves in conflict with other wireless resources. Like their wired equivalents, there was little expectation that there would be a conflict within the wireless spectrum available for use. Because of this, very few wireless equipment providers planned their implementations with features to ensure the availability of the wireless resource in case a conflict occurred.

One method uses tools for building complex overlapping wireless networks came from WIMAN (Wireless Metropolitan Area Networks, at www.wiman.net). In their wireless equipment, they utilized the concept of *pseudo random frequency hopping* over the spread spectrum frequencies available to them.

Frequency hopping is where the wireless equipment changes the frequency used to transmit and receive at scheduled intervals, allowing for wider utilization of the wireless spectrum by multiple devices. WIMAN would generate (or you the user could generate and program) the definition of what channels would be used, and in what order they would jump through those frequencies. WIMAN has configured its equipment to be scheduled to change frequency every 8 milliseconds.

Then by synchronizing base stations through a loop-through heartbeat cable, multiple base stations and their end clients could all run within the same frequency range but hop through the channels used in different sequences, thereby allowing more devices to transmit and receive at the same time while not conflicting or overwriting each others' traffic. Frequency hopping not only allows for the tighter utilization of wireless resources, but also assists in the continuity of your network availability. Unless someone has the ability to broadcast on every frequency you are utilizing, by randomly hopping around those frequencies you reduce the likelihood that the transmission can be overwritten, compromised, or interrupted. As you will see later in this book, the intentional denial of a service or network resource has come to be known as a denial of service (DOS) attack. By having the frequency change automatically through multiple frequencies, products such as the WIMAN Access Points help assure the availability of your wireless network from intentional or unintentional DOS attacks.

Another added benefit of frequency hopping is that anyone wishing to sniff or connect to your network would need to know the frequencies you are using and in what order. 802.11b networks utilized a fixed communications channel, that requires a manual reconfiguration and reset of the wireless device to change the channel used.

Ensuring Privacy

Privacy is the assurance that the information a customer provides to some party will remain private and protected. This information generally contains customer personal non-public information that is protected by both regulation and civil liability law. Your wireless policy and procedures should contain definitions on how to ensure the privacy of customer information that might be accessed or transmitted by your wireless networks. The principles and methods here provide ways of ensuring the protection of the data that travels across your networks and computers.

Ensuring Authentication

Authentication provides for a sender and receiver of information to validate each other as the appropriate entity they are wishing to work with. If entities wishing to communicate cannot properly authenticate each other, then there can be no trust of the activities or information provided by either party. It is only through a trusted and secure method of authentication that we are able to provide for a trusted and secure communication or activity.

The simplest form of authentication is the transmission of a shared password between the entities wishing to authenticate with each other. This could be as simple as a secret handshake or a key. As with all simple forms of protection, once knowledge of the secret key or handshake was disclosed to non-trusted parties, there could be no trust in who was using the secrets anymore.

Many methods can be used to acquire a secret key, from something as simple as tricking someone into disclosing it, to high-tech monitoring of communications between parties to intercept the key as it is passed from one party to the other. However the code is acquired, once it is in a non-trusted party's hands, that party may be able to utilize it to connect to a secure network. That party can then, using additional techniques, falsely authenticate and identify themselves as a valid party, forging false communications, or utilizing the user's access to gain permissions to the available resources.

The original digital authentication systems simply shared a secret key across the network with the entity they wished to authenticate with. Applications such as Telnet, FTP, and POP-mail are examples of programs that simply transmit the password, in clear-text, to the party they are authenticating with. The problem with this method of authentication is that anyone who is able to monitor the network could possibly capture the secret key and then use it to authenticate themselves as you in order to access these same services. They could then access your information directly, or corrupt any information you send to other parties. It might even be possible for them to attempt to gain higher privileged access with your stolen authentication information.

Tools & Traps…

Clear-text Authentication

Clear-text (non-encrypted) authentication is still widely used by many people today, who receive their e-mail through the Post Office Protocol (POP) which, by default, sends the password unprotected in clear-text from the mail client to the server. There are several ways of protecting your e-mail account password, including connection encryption as well as not transmitting the password in clear-text through the network by hashing with MD5 or some similar algorithm.

Encrypting the connection between the mail client and server is the only way of truly protecting your mail authentication password. This will prevent anyone from capturing your password or any of the mail you

Continued

might transfer to your client. Secure Sockets Layer (SSL) is a common the method used to encrypt the connection stream from the mail client to the server and is supported by most mail clients today.

If you only protect the password through MD5 or a similar crypto-cipher, then it would be possible for anyone who happens to intercept your "protected" password to identify it through a brute force attack. A brute force attack is where someone generates every possible combination of characters running each version through the same algorithm used to encrypt the original password until a match is made and your password is found.

Authenticated POP (APOP) is a method used to provide password-only encryption for mail authentication. It employs a challenge/response method defined in RFC1725 that uses a shared timestamp provided by the server being authenticated to. The timestamp is hashed with the username and the shared secret key through the MD5 algorithm.

There are still a few problems with this. The first of which is that all values are known in advance except the shared secret key. Because of this, there is nothing to provide protection against a brute-force attack on the shared key. Another problem is that this security method attempts to protect your password. Nothing is done to prevent anyone who might be listening to your network from then viewing your e-mail as it is downloaded to your mail client.

An example of a brute-force password dictionary generator that can produce a brute-force dictionary from specific character sets can be found at www.dmzs.com/tools/files. Other brute force crackers, including POP, Telnet, FTP, Web and others, can be found at http://packetstormsecurity.com/crackers.

To solve the problem of authentication through sharing common secret keys across an untrusted network, the concept of Zero Knowledge Passwords was created. The idea of Zero Knowledge Passwords is that the parties who wish to authenticate each other want to prove to one another that they know the shared secret, and yet not share the secret with each other in case the other party truly doesn't have knowledge of the password, while at the same time preventing anyone who may intercept the communications between the parties from gaining knowledge as to the secret that is being used.

Public-key cryptography has been shown to be the strongest method of doing Zero Knowledge Passwords. It was originally developed by Whitfield Diffie and Martin Hellman and presented to the world at the 1976 National Computer

Conference. Their concept was published a few months later in their paper, *New Directions in Cryptography*. Another crypto-researcher named Ralph Merkle working independently from Diffie and Hellman also invented a similar method for providing public-key cryptography, but his research was not published until 1978.

Public-key cryptography introduced the concept of having keys work in pairs, an encryption key and a decryption key, and having them created in such a way that it is infeasible to generate one key from the other. The encryption key is then made public to anyone wishing to encrypt a message to the holder of the secret decryption key. Because it is not feasible to extrapolate the decryption key from the encryption key and encrypted message, only the perosn who has the decryption key will be ready to decrypt it.

Public-key encryption generally stores the keys or uses a certificate hierarchy. The certificates are rarely changed and often used just for encrypting data, not authentication. Zero Knowledge Password protocols, on the other hand, tend to use Ephemeral keys. Ephemeral keys are temporary keys that are randomly created for a single authentication, and then discarded once the authentication is completed.

It is worth noting that the public-key encryption is still susceptible to a chosen-cyphertext attack. This attack is where someone already knows what the decrypted message is and has knowledge of the key used to generate the encrypted message. Knowing the decrypted form of the message lets the attacker possibly deduce what the secret decryption key could be. This attack is unlikely to occur with authentication systems because the attacker will not have knowledge of the decrypted message: your password. If they had that, then they would already have the ability to authenticate as you and not need to determine your secret decryption key.

Currently 802.11 network authentication is centered on the authentication of the wireless device, not on authenticating the user or station utilizing the wireless network. There is no public-key encryption used in the wireless encryption process. While a few wireless vendors have dynamic keys that are changed with every connection, most wireless 802.11 vendors utilize shared-key authentication with static keys.

Shared key authentication is utilized by WEP functions with the following steps:

1. When a station requests service, it sends an authentication frame to the Access Point it wishes to communicate with.

2. The receiving Access Point replies to the authentication frame with its own which contains 128 octets of challenge text.

3. The station requesting access encrypts the challenge text with the shared encryption key and returns to the Access Point.

4. The access decrypts the encrypted challenge using the shared key and compares it with the original challenge text. If they match, an authentication acknowledgement is sent to the station requesting access, otherwise a negative authentication notice is sent.

As you can see, this authentication method does not authenticate the user or any resource the user might need to access. It is only a verification that the wireless device has knowledge of the shared secret key that the wireless Access Point has. Once a user has passed the Access Point authentication challenge, that user will then have full access to whatever devices and networks the Access Point is connected to. You should still use secure authentication methods to access any of these devices and prevent unauthorized access and use by people who might be able to attach to your wireless network.

To solve this lack of external authentication, the IEEE 802.11 committee is working on 802.1X, a standard that will provide a framework for 802-based networks authenticating from centralized servers. Back in November 2000, Cisco introduced LEAP authentication to their wireless products, which adds several enhancements to the 802.11 authentication system, including:

- Mutual authentication utilizing RADIUS

- Securing the secret key with one-way hashes that make password reply attacks impossible

- Policies to force the user to reauthenticate more often, getting a new session key with each new session. This will help to prevent attacks where traffic is injected into the datastream.

- Changes to the initialization vector used in the WEP encryption that make the current exploits of WEP ineffective

Not all vendors support these solutions, so your best bet is to protect your network and servers with your own strong authentication and authorization rules.

Ensuring Authorization

Authorization is the rights and permissions granted to a user or application that enables access to a network or computing resource. Once a user has been properly identified and authenticated, authorization levels determine the extent of system rights that the user has access to.

Many of the early operating systems and applications deployed had very small authorization groups. Generally, there were only user groups and operator groups available for defining a user's access level. Once more formal methods for approaching various authorization levels were defined, applications and servers started offering more discrete authorization levels. This can be observed by simply looking at any standard back-office application deployed today.

Many of them provide varying levels of access for users and administrators. For example, they could have several levels of user accounts allowing some users access to only view the information, while giving others the ability to update or query that information and have administrative accounts based on the authorization levels needed (such as only being able to look up specific types of customers, or run particular reports while other accounts have the ability to edit and create new accounts).

As we saw in the previous authentication example, Cisco and others have implemented RADIUS authentication for their wireless devices. Now, utilizing stronger authentication methods, it is possible for you to implement your authorization policies into your wireless deployments.

However, there are many wireless devices that do not currently support external authorization validation. Plus, most deployments only ensure authorized access to the device. They do not control access to or from specific network segments. To fully restrict authorized users to the network devices they are authorized to utilize, you will still need to deploy an adaptive firewall between the Access Point and your network.

This is what was done earlier this year by two researchers at NASA (for more information, see www.nas.nasa.gov/Groups/Networks/Projects/Wireless). To protect their infrastructure, but still provide access through wireless, they deployed a firewall segmenting their wireless and department network. They most likely hardened their wireless interfaces to the extent of the equipments' possibilities by utilizing the strongest encryption available to them, disabling SID broadcast, and only allowing authorized MAC addresses on the wireless network.

They then utilized the Dynamic Host Configuration Protocol (DHCP) on the firewall, and disabled it on their Access Point. This allowed them to expressly define which MAC addresses could receive an IP address, and what the lease lifetime of the IP address would be.

The researchers then went on to turn off all routing and forwarding between the wireless interface and the internal network. If anyone happened to be able to connect to the wireless network, they would still have no access to the rest of the computing resources of the department. Anyone wishing to gain further access would have to go to an SSL protected Web site on the firewall server and authenticate as a valid user. The Web server would authenticate the user against a local RADIUS server, but they could have easily used any other form of user authentication (NT, SecurID, and so on).

Once the user was properly authenticated, the firewall would change the firewall rules for the IP address that user was supposed to be assigned to, allowing full access to only the network resources they are authorized to access.

Finally, once the lease expired or was released for any reason from the DHCP assigned IP address, the firewall rules would be removed and that user and their IP would have to reauthenticate through the Web interface to allow access to the network resources again.

They have yet to release the actual implementation procedure they used, so again it is up to us, the users of wireless networks, to provide proper controls around our wired and wireless resources.

Ensuring Non-repudiation

Repudiation is defined by West's *Encyclopedia of American Law* as "the rejection or refusal of a duty, relation, right or privilege." A repudiation of a transaction or contract means that one of the parties refuses to honor their obligation to the other as specified by the contract. Non-repudiation could then be defined as the ability to deny, with irrefutable evidence, a false rejection or refusal of an obligation.

In their paper "Non-Repudiation in the Digital Environment," Adrian McCullagh and William Caelli put forth an excellent review of the traditional model of non-repudiation and the current trends for crypto-technical non-repudiation. The paper was published online by First Monday, and can be found at www.firstmonday.dk/issues/issue5_8/mccullagh/index.html.

The basis for a repudiation of a traditional contract is sometimes associated with the belief that the signature binding a contract is a forgery, or that the signature is not a forgery but was obtained via unconscionable conduct by a party to the transaction, by fraud instigated by a third party, or undue influence exerted by a third party. In typical cases of fraud or repudiated contracts, the general rule of evidence is that if a person denies a particular signature, the burden of proving that the signature is valid falls upon the receiving party.

Common law trust mechanisms establish that in order to overcome false claims of non-repudiation, a trusted third party needs to act as a witness to the signature being affixed. Having a witness to the signature of a document, who is independent of the transactions taking place, reduces the likelihood that a signer is able to successfully allege that the signature is a forgery. However, there is always the possibility that the signatory will be able to deny the signature on the basis of the situations listed in the preceding paragraph.

A perfect example of a non-repudiation of submissions can be viewed by examining the process around sending and receiving registered mail. When you send a registered letter, you are given a receipt containing an identification number for the piece of mail sent. If the recipient claims that the mail was not sent, the receipt is proof that provides the non-repudiation of the submission. If a receipt is available with the recipient's signature, this provides the proof for the non-repudiation of the delivery service. The postal service provides the non-repudiation of transport service by acting as a Trusted Third Party (TTP).

Non-repudiation, in technical terms, has come to mean:

- In authentication, a service that provides proof of the integrity and origin of data both in an unforgeable relationship, which can be verified by any third party at any time; or

- In authentication, an authentication that with high assurance can be asserted to be genuine, and that cannot subsequently be refuted.

The Australian Federal Government's Electronic Commerce Expert group further adopted this technical meaning in their 1998 report to the Australian Federal Attorney General as:

> *Non-repudiation is a property achieved through cryptographic methods which prevents an individual or entity from denying having performed a particular action related to data (such as mechanisms for non-rejection or authority (origin); for proof of obligation, intent, or commitment; or for proof of ownership.*

In the digital realm, there is a movement to shift the responsibility of proving that a digital signature is invalid to the owner of the signature, not the receiver of the signature, as is typically used in traditional common law methods.

There are only a few examples where the burden of proof falls upon the alleged signer. One such example is usually found in taxation cases where the taxpayer has made specific claims and as such is in a better position to disprove the revenue collecting body's case. Another example would be in an instance of negligence. In a negligence action, if a plaintiff is able to prove that a defendant failed to meet their commitment, then the burden of proof is in effect shifted to the defendant to establish that they have met their obligations.

The problem found in the new digital repudiation definitions that have been created, is that they only take into consideration the validity of the signature itself. They do not allow for the possibility that the signer was tricked or forced into signing, or that their private key may be compromised, allowing the forgery of digital signatures.

With all the recent cases of Internet worms and viruses, it is not hard to imagine there being one that might be specifically built to steal private keys. A virus could be something as simple as a visual basic macro attached to a Word document, or an e-mail message that would search the targets hard drive looking for commonly named and located private key rings which could then be e-mailed or uploaded to some rogue location.

With this and other possible attacks to the private keys, it becomes difficult, under the common law position, for someone attempting to prove the identity of an alleged signatory. This common law position was established and founded in a paper-based environment where witnessing became the trusted mechanism utilized to prevent the non-repudiation of a signature. For a digital signature to be proven valid, however, it will need to be established through a fully trusted mechanism.

Thus for a digitally signed contract to be trusted and not susceptible to repudiation, the entire document handling and signature process must take place within a secured and trusted computing environment. As we will see in some of the documentation to follow, the security policies and definitions created over the years have established a set of requirements necessary to create a secure and trusted computer system.

If we follow the definitions established in the Information Technology Security Evaluation Certification (ITSEC) to create a trusted computing environment of at least E3 to enforce functions and design of the signing process and thus prevent unauthorized access to the private key, then the common law position for digitally signed documents can be maintained. E3 also ensures that the signing function is the only function able to be performed by the signing mechanism by having the source code evaluated to ensure that this is the only process available through the code. If these security features are implemented, then it can be adequately assessed that under this mechanism the private key has not been stolen and as such that any digital signature created under this model has the trust established to ensure the TTP witness and validation of any signature created, preventing any possible repudiation from the signor.

One such example of a secure infrastructure designed and deployed to attempt to provide a digitally secure TTP are the Public Key Infrastructure (PKI) systems available for users of unsecure public networks such as the Internet. PKI consists of a secure computing system that acts as a certificate authority (CA) to issue and verify digital certificates. Digital certificates contain the public key and other identification information needed to verify the validity of the certificate. As long as the trust in the CA is maintained (and with it, the trust in the security of the private key), the digital certificates issued by the CA and the documents signed by them remain trusted. As long as the trust is ensured, then the CA acts as a TTP and provides for the non-repudiation of signatures created by entities with digital certificates issued through the CA.

Accounting and Audit Trails

Auditing provides methods for tracking and logging activities on networks and systems, and links these activities to specific user accounts or sources of activity. In case of simple mistakes or software failures, audit trails can be extremely useful in restoring data integrity. They are also a requirement for trusted systems to ensure that the activity of authorized individuals on the trusted system can be traced to their specific actions, and that those actions comply with defined policy. They also allow for a method of collecting evidence to support any investigation into improper or illegal activities.

Most modern database applications support some level of transaction log detailing the activities that occurred within the database. This log could then be used to either rebuild the database if it had any errors or create a duplicate database at another location. To provide this detailed level of transactional logging, database logging tends to consume a great deal of drive space for its enormous logfile. This intense logging is not needed for most applications, so you will generally only have basic informative messages utilized in system resource logging.

The logging features provided on most networks and systems involve the logging of known or partially known resource event activities. While these logs are sometimes used for analyzing system problems, they are also useful for those whose duty it is to process the logfiles and check for both valid and invalid system activities.

To assist in catching mistakes and reducing the likelihood of fraudulent activities, the activities of a process should be split among several people. This segmentation of duties allows the next person in line to possibly correct problems simply because they are being viewed with fresh eyes.

From a security point of view, segmentation of duties requires the collusion of at least two people to perform any unauthorized activities. The following guidelines assist in assuring that the duties are split so as to offer no way other than collusion to perform invalid activities.

- **No access to sensitive combinations of capabilities** A classic example of this is control of inventory data and physical inventory. By separating the physical inventory control from the inventory data control, you remove the unnecessary temptation for an employee to steal from inventory and then alter the data so that the theft is left hidden.

- **Prohibit conversion and concealment** Another violation that can be prevented by segregation is ensuring that there is supervision for people who have access to assets. An example of an activity that could be prevented if properly segmented follows a lone operator of a night shift. This operator, without supervision, could copy (or "convert") customer lists and then sell them off to interested parties. There have been instances reported of operators actually using the employer's computer to run a service bureau at night.

- **The same person cannot both originate and approve transactions** When someone is able to enter and authorize their own expenses, it introduces the possibility that they might fraudulently enter invalid expenses for their own gain.

These principles, whether manual or electronic, form the basis for why audit logs are retained. They also identify why people other than those performing the activities reported in the log should be the ones who analyze the data in the logfile.

In keeping with the idea of segmentation, as you deploy your audit trails, be sure to have your logs sent to a secure, trusted, location that is separate and non-accessible from the devices you are monitoring. This will help ensure that if any inappropriate activity occurs, the person can't falsify the log to state the actions did not take place.

Most wireless Access Points do not offer any method of logging activity, but if your equipment provides the feature, it should be enabled and then monitored for inappropriate activity using tools such as logcheck. Wireless Access Point logging should, if it's available, log any new wireless device with its MAC address upon valid WEP authentication. It should also log any attempts to access or modify the Access Point itself.

Using Encryption

Encryption has always played a key role in information security, and has been the center of controversy in the design of the WEP wireless standard. But despite the drawbacks, encryption will continue to play a major role in wireless security, especially with the adoption of new and better encryption algorithms and key management systems.

As we have seen in reviewing the basic concepts of security, many of the principles used to assure the confidentiality, integrity, and availability of servers and services are through the use of some form of trusted and tested encryption. We also have seen that even with encryption, if we get tied up too much in the acceptance of the hard mathematics as evidence of validity, it is possible to be tricked into accepting invalid authorization or authentication attempts by someone who has been able to corrupt the encryption system itself by either acquiring the private key through cryptanalysis or stealing the private key from the end user directly.

Cryptography offers the obvious advantage that the material it protects cannot be used without the keys needed to unlock it. As long as those keys are protected, then the material remains protected. There are a few potential disadvantages to encryption as well. For instance, if the key is lost, the data becomes unavailable, and if the key is stolen, the data becomes accessible to the thief.

The process of encryption also introduces possible performance degradation. When a message is to be sent encrypted, time must be spent to first encrypt the information, then store and transmit the encrypted data, and then later decode it. In theory, this can slow a system by as much as a factor of three.

Until recently, distribution and use of strong encryption was limited and controlled by most governments. The United States government had encryption listed as munitions, right next to cruise missiles! As such, it was very difficult to legally acquire and use strong encryption through the entire Internet. With the new changes in trade laws, however, it is now possible to use stronger encryption for internal use as well as with communications with customers and other third parties.

Encrypting Voice Data

Voice communications have traditionally been a very simple medium to intercept and monitor. When digital cell and wireless phones arrived, there was a momentary window in which it was difficult to monitor voice communications across these digital connections. Today, the only equipment needed to monitor cell phones or digital wireless telephones can be acquired at your local Radio Shack for generally less than $100.00.

Most voice communication systems are not designed to ensure the privacy of the conversations on them, so a new industry was created to facilitate those needs. Originally designed for government and military usage, telephone encryption devices give people the option of encrypting their daily calls. A few of these devices are starting to make their way into the commercial market. While a few are being slowed down by organizations such as the National Security Agency (NSA) and the Federal Bureau of Investigation (FBI), who argue that it will prevent their "legal" monitoring of criminal activities, consumer market needs should eventually push these devices into the mainstream.

The Internet, being a communications network, offers people the ability to communicate with anyone, anywhere. Because of this, it didn't take long for the appearance of applications enabling voice communications across the Internet. Many of the early versions, like all budding technologies, did not offer any protection methods for their users. As a result, it's possible that people utilizing Internet voice communications programs could have their communications monitored by someone with access to the data stream between parties. Fortunately, encryption is making its way into some of these programs, and if you're careful, you should be able to find one that uses modern tested and secure encryption algorithms such as Twofish, a popular and publicly-available encryption algorithm created by Bruce Schneier.

Encrypting Data Systems

Data networks have traditionally been susceptible to threats from a trusted insider. However, as soon as someone connects their network to another entity, it introduces possible security compromises from outside sources. Remember, all forms of data communications, from simple modem lines to frame-relay and fiber-optic connections, can be monitored.

There are many network devices available to help protect data confidentiality. RedCreek Communications offers one such hardware device: an IPSec Virtual Private Network. Using VPN hardware, it's possible to segment and protect specific network traffic over wide area network connections.

Reviewing the Role of Policy

Good policy is your first line of defense. A properly designed policy, examines every threat (or tries to) and ensures that confidentiality, integrity, and availability are maintained (or at least cites the known and accepted risks). As we shall see, policy definition begins with a clear identification and labeling of resources being utilized that will build into specific standards that define acceptable use in what's considered an authorized and secure manner. Once a basic standard is defined, you start building specific guidelines and procedures for individual applications and services.

Many wireless manufacturers have responded to security threats hampering their initial product versions by releasing upgrades to their software and drivers. Your security policy should always require that all technology, either existing or newly deployed, have the latest security patches and upgrades installed in a timely manner. However, since the development and release of patches take time, policy and its proper implementation tend to be the first layer of defense when confronting known and unknown threats.

A well-written policy should be more than just a list of recommended procedures. It should be an essential and fundamental element of your organization's security practices. A good policy can provide protection from liability due to an employee's actions, or can form a basis for the control of trade secrets. A policy or standard should also continue to grow and expand as new threats and technologies become available. They should be constructed with the input of an entire organization and audited both internally and externally to assure that the assets they are protecting have the controls in place as specified in the standards, policies, and guidelines.

Damage & Defense...

The Management Commitment

Management must be aware of their needed commitment to the security of corporate assets, which includes protection of information. Measures must be taken to protect it from unauthorized modification, destruction, or disclosure (whether accidental or intentional), and assure its authenticity, integrity, availability and confidentiality.

Fundamental to the success of any security program is senior management's commitment to the information security process and their understanding of how important security controls and protections are to the enterprise's continuity.

The senior management statement usually contains the following elements:

Continued

1. An acknowledgment of the importance of computing resources to the business model.
2. A statement of support for information security throughout the enterprise.
3. A commitment to authorize and manage the definition of the lower level standards, procedures, and guidelines.

Part of any policy definition includes what is required to ensure that the policy is adhered to. The prime object of policy controls is to reduce the effect of security threats and vulnerabilities to the resources being protected. The policy definition process generally entails the identification of what impact a threat would have on an organization, and what the likelihood of that threat occurring would be. Risk analysis (RA) is the process of analyzing a threat and producing a representative value of that threat.

Figure 2.2 displays a matrix created using a small x–y graph representing the threat, and the corresponding likelihood of that threat. The goal of RA is to reduce the level of impact and the likelihood that it will occur. A properly implemented control should move the plotted point from the upper right to the lower left of the graph.

Figure 2.2 Threat versus Likelihood Matrix

An improperly designed and implemented control will show little to no movement in the plotted point before and after the control's implementation.

Identifying Resources

To assess and protect resources, they must first be identified, classified, and labeled so that in the process of performing your risk analysis you are able to document all possible risks to each identified item and provide possible solutions to mitigate those risks.

Security classification provides the following benefits:

- Demonstrates an organization's commitment to security procedures
- Helps identify which information is the most sensitive or vital to an organization
- Supports the tenets of confidentiality, integrity, and availability as it pertains to data
- Helps identify which protections apply to which information
- May be required for regulatory, compliance, or legal reasons

In the public sector, the common categories utilized in the classification of resources are:

- **Public** These are no-risk items which can be disclosed to anyone, as long as they do not violate any individual's right to privacy, and knowledge of this information does not expose an organization to financial loss or embarrassment, or jeopardize security assets. Examples of public information include: marketing brochures, published annual reports, business cards, and press releases.

- **Internal Use** These are low-risk items that due to their technical or business sensitivity are limited to an organization's employees and those contractors covered by a non-disclosure agreement. Should there be unauthorized disclosure, compromise, or destruction of the documents, there would only be minimal impact on the organization, its customers, or employees. Examples of Internal Use information include: employee handbooks, telephone directories, organizational charts, and policies.

- **Confidential** These are moderate-risk items whose unauthorized disclosure, compromise or destruction would directly or indirectly impact an organization, its customers, or employees, possibly causing financial damage to organization reputation, a loss of business, and potential legal action. They are intended solely for use within an organization and are limited to those individuals who have a "need-to-know" security clearance. Examples of confidential items include: system requirements or configurations, proprietary software, personnel records, customer records, business plans, budget information, and security plans and standards.

- **Restricted** These are high-risk critical items whose unauthorized disclosure, compromise, or destruction would result in severe damage to a company, providing significant advantages to a competitor, or causing penalties to the organization, its customers, or employees. It is intended solely for restricted use within the organization and is limited to those with an explicit, predetermined, and stringent "business-need-to-know." Examples of restricted data include: strategic plans, encryption keys, authentication information (passwords, pins, and so on), and IP addresses for security-related servers.

All information, whether in paper, spoken, or electronic form should be classified, labeled, and distributed in accordance to your information classification and handling procedures. This will assist in the determination of what items have the largest threat, and as such, should determine how you set about providing controls for those threats.

Your wireless network contains a few internal items that should be identified and classified, however the overall classification of any network device comes down the level of information that flows through its channels. While using e-mail systems or accessing external sites through your wireless network, you will likely find that your entire network contains restricted information. However, if you are able to encrypt the password, the classification of your network data will then be rated based upon the non-authentication information traveling across your wireless network.

Understanding Classification Criteria

To assist in your risk analysis, there are a few additional criteria that can be used to determine the classification of information resources.

- **Value** Value is the most commonly used criteria for classifying data in the private sector. If someone is valuable to an individual or organization, that will prompt the data to be properly identified and classified.

- **Age** Information is occasionally reclassified to a lower level as time passes. In many government organizations, some classified documents are automatically declassified after a predetermined time period has passed.

- **Useful Life**   If information has become obsolete due to new information or resources, it is usually reclassified.

- **Personal Association**   If information is associated with specific individuals or is covered under privacy law, there might be a need to reclassify it at some point.

Implementing Policy

Information classification procedures offer several steps in establishing a classification system, which provides the first step in the creation of your security standards and policies. The following are primary procedural steps used in establishing a classification system:

1. Identify the administrator or custodian.

2. Specify the criteria of how the information will be classified and labeled.

3. Classify the data by its owner, who is subject to review by a supervisor.

4. Specify and document any exceptions to the classification policy.

5. Specify the controls that will be applied to each classification level.

6. Specify the termination procedures for declassifying the information or for transferring custody of the information to another entity.

7. Create an enterprise awareness program about the classification controls.

Once your information and resources are properly identified and classified, you will be able to define the controls necessary to assure the privacy and security of information regarding your employees and customers. Many industries are required, either by regulation or civil law, to assure that proper policy is in place to protect the security and privacy of non-public personal information. This relationship of policy, guidelines, and legal standards is shown in Figure 2.3.

Figure 2.3 The Hierarchy of Rules

Guidelines refer to the methodologies of securing systems. Guidelines are more flexible than standards or policies and take the varying nature of information systems into consideration as they are developed and deployed, usually offering specific processes for the secure use of information resources. Many organizations have general security guidelines regarding a variety of platforms available within them: NT, SCO-Unix, Debian Linux, Red Hat Linux, Oracle, and so on.

Standards specify the use of specific technologies in a uniform way. While they are often not as flexible as guidelines, they do offer wider views to the technology specified. There are usually standards for general computer use, encryption use, information classification, and others.

Policies are generally statements created for strategic or legal reasons, from which the standards and guidelines are defined. Some policies are based on legal requirements placed on industries such as health insurance, or they can be based upon common law requirements for organizations retaining personal non-public information of their customers.

Policies, standards, and guidelines must be explicit and focused, and must effectively communicate the following subjects:

- Responsibility and authority
- Access control
- The extent to which formal verification is required
- Discretionary/mandatory control (generally only relevant in government or formal policy situations)
- Marking/labeling
- Control of media
- Import and export of data
- Security and classification levels
- Treatment of system output

It is the intent of policy to delineate what an organization expects in the information security realm. Reasonable policy should also reflect any relevant laws and regulations that impact the use of information within an organization.

Damage & Defense...

Sample Wireless Communication Policy

1.0 Purpose

This policy prohibits access to <Company Name> networks via unsecured wireless communication mechanisms. Only wireless systems that meet the criteria of this policy or have been granted an exclusive waiver by InfoSec are approved for connectivity to <Company Name>'s networks.

2.0 Scope

This policy covers all wireless data communication devices (for example, personal computers, cellular phones, PDAs, and so on) connected to any of <Company Name>'s internal networks. This includes any form of wireless communication device capable of transmitting packet data. Wireless devices and/or networks without any connectivity to <Company Name>'s networks do not fall under the purview of this policy.

3.0 Policy

To comply with this policy, wireless implementations must: maintain point-to-point hardware encryption of at least 56 bits; maintain a hardware address that can be registered and tracked (for instance, a MAC address); support strong user authentication which checks against an external database such as TACACS+, RADIUS, or something similar.

Exception: a limited-duration waiver to this policy for Aironet products has been approved if specific implementation instructions are followed for corporate and home installations.

4.0 Enforcement

Any employee found to have violated this policy may be subject to disciplinary action, up to and including termination of employment.

5.0 Definitions

Terms	Definitions
User Authentication	A method by which the user of a wireless system can be verified as a legitimate user independent of the computer or operating system being used.

6.0 Revision History

The System Administration, Networking, and Security Institute (SANS) offers excellent resources for implementing security standards, policies, and guidelines. You can find more information on policy implementation at the SANS Web site at www.sans.org/newlook/resources/policies/policies.htm. There you'll find example policies regarding encryption use, acceptable use, analog/ISDN lines, anti-virus software, application service providers, audits, and many others.

In this section's sidebar, "Sample Wireless Communication Policy," you will find the example wireless policy that defines the standards used for wireless communications.

Recognizing Accepted Security and Privacy Standards

Until recently, there have not been any internationally agreed upon standard principles and procedures for performing security reviews and reporting on the review of the many "targets" that make up our complex technological world. In fact, the targets needing evaluation are ever-expanding and have evolved from physical spaces and wire-connected objects, data applications, and infrastructures to current wireless systems that can be contacted over great distances. Evaluating the security risks of every possible layer of networks and components and applications that make up the various infrastructures is a long and complex undertaking in today's information-rich world.

Reviewing Security Standards

The security standards available today are the result of decades of research and dialog between individuals, corporate entities, and government agencies around the world and have created many new industries—one of which is the laboratories that review and report security risks according to the definitions laid out in these standards. Defining and reviewing security risks, however, is useless if the providers of current and future technologies do not act upon the identified risks.

While we end users of technology wait on the providers of today's tools to implement solid security planning, implementation, and review of their products, there is much we can do to ensure our own infrastructure and applications are secure by following the same principles and procedures defined in today's security standards.

Early Security Standards

One of the first standards to take on the idea of security evaluation criteria is the Trusted Computer Systems Evaluation Criteria (TCSEC), commonly referred to as the Orange Book, which was published by the National Security Agency (NSA) in 1985. The Orange Book is best known for its classification of levels of system security into discrete divisions. The four levels of classification are Division D, Division C, Division B, and Division A, with Division D being the least or minimally protected, and Division A signifying a fully trusted and verified design. In 1991, France, the United Kingdom, Germany, and the Netherlands produced the first attempt at a joint effort international standard Information Technology Security Evaluation Certification (ITSEC). The U.S. Federal Criteria, which replaced the Orange Book, and the Canadian Trusted Computer Product Evaluation Criteria (CTCPEC) were both published in 1993 and added to the growing list of individual standards.

ITSEC went further than TCSEC by separating reliability and assessment from their security functions. A "trust hierarchy" in the reliable operation of the security functions were sectioned into seven evaluation levels. Security functions were associated with measurements or tags resulting from evaluations on the security functions by human "evaluators." Details on ITSEC and the assurance levels it defines can be found at their Web site: www.cesg.gov.uk/assurance/iacs/itsec/index.htm. A quick summary of the assurance levels can be found in Table 2.1.

Table 2.1 Assurance Levels

Assurance Level	Security Functions
E0	Inadequate assurance
E1	A security target and informal architectural design must be produced.
	User/admin documentation gives guidance on Target of Evaluation (TOE) security.
	Security enforcing functions are tested by evaluators or developers.
	TOE is to be uniquely identified and have delivery, configuration, startup, and operational documentation.
	Secure distribution methods to be utilized.

Continued

Table 2.1 Continued

Assurance Level	Security Functions
E2 (or E1 plus)	An informal detailed design, as well as test documentation, must be produced.
	Architecture shows the separation of the TOE into security enforcing and other components.
	Penetration testing searches for errors.
	Configuration control and developer's security is assessed.
	Audit trail output is required during startup and operation.
E3	Source code or hardware drawings to be produced.
	Correspondence must be shown between source code and detailed design.
	Acceptance procedures must be used.
	Implementation languages should be to recognized standards.
	Retesting must occur after the correction of errors.
E4	Formal model of security and semi-formal specification of security enforcing functions, architecture, and detailed design to be produced.
	Testing must be shown to be sufficient.
	TOE and tools are under configuration control with changes audited and compiler options documented.
	TOE to retain security on restart after failure.
E5	Architectural design explains the inter-relationship between security enforcing components.
	Information on integration process and runtime libraries to be produced.
	Configuration control independent of developer.
	Identification of configured items as security enforcing or security relevant, with support for variable relationships between them.
E6	Formal description of architecture and security enforcing functions to be produced.
	Correspondence shown from formal specification of security enforcing functions through to source code and tests.
	Different TOE configurations defined in terms of the formal architectural design.
	All tools subject to configuration control.

Understanding the Common Criteria Model

As none of the standards described in the previous section were globally accepted, the International Organization for Standardization (ISO) began an attempt to create a global standard for security evaluations. This led to the development of the Common Criteria for Information Technology Security Evaluation (CCITSE), known simply as the Common Criteria (CC), which was published in 1999. The Common Criteria defines a general model for selecting and defining Information Technology (IT) security requirements and establishes a standard way of expressing security functional requirements for Targets of Evaluation (TOE).

ISO 17799/BS 7799

The Common Criteria provides an excellent method for identifying, evaluating, and reporting on individual or groups of targets for evaluation. Unfortunately, the Common Criteria does not offer Information Security Management any method or basis for developing organizational security standards and effective security management practices. The British Standards Institute (BSI) provided the beginnings of a solution to this problem when it published BS7799 in February, 1998. BSI sponsored BS7799 to become an international standard and it was incorporated into ISO 17799 and published by the ISO and the International Electrotechnical Commission (IEC) in December 2000.

ISO 7498-2

ISO 7498-2 defines the purpose and objectives of security policies.

Essentially, a security policy states, in general terms, what is and is not permitted in the field of security during the general operation of the system in question. Policy is usually not specific. It suggests what is of paramount importance without saying precisely how the desired results are to be obtained, along the way establishing the topmost level of a security specification.

ISO 10164-8

This section of the ISO Information Technology Open System Interconnection (OSI) System Management document on security audit trail function defines a framework for providing audit trails for system and network activities to ensure secure logging.

ISO 13888

In the Open Distributed Processing Reference Model, the ISO provides the main standards for electronic non-repudiation. ISO/IEC 13888-1 states, "Non-repudiation can only be provided within the context of a clearly defined security policy for a particular application and its legal environment."

The ISO also provides for non-repudiation services for conformance with ISO/IEC 13888-1, -2 and -3 as being:

- **Approval** Non-repudiation of approval service provides proof of who is responsible for approval of the content of a message.

- **Sending** Non-repudiation of sending service provides proof of who sent a message.

- **Origin** Non-repudiation of origin service is a combination of approval and sending services.

- **Submission** Non-repudiation of submission service provides proof that a delivery authority has accepted a message for transmission.

- **Transport** Non-repudiation of transport service provides proof for the message originator that a delivery authority has given the message to the intended recipient.

- **Receipt** Non-repudiation of receipt service provides proof that the recipient received a message.

- **Knowledge** Non-repudiation of knowledge service provides proof that the recipient recognized the content of a received message.

- **Delivery** Non-repudiation of delivery service is a combination of receipt and knowledge services as it provides proof that the recipient received and recognized the content of a message.

The ISO also makes clear that in order for full non-repudiation of both parties to occur, the following steps must be taken:

- All parties must be identified and authenticated.

- All parties must be authorized to perform the function required.

- The integrity of the transaction content must be intact throughout the entire process.

- Certain transaction information needs to be confidential for authorized users only.

- All transactions must be fully audited.

Reviewing Privacy Standards and Regulations

There have been many regulations passed in the U.S. that provide protection for personal non-public privacy and assure standardization within specific industries. Some of this may affect any policy or procedure you deploy.

NAIC Model Act

The National Association of Insurance Commissioners (NAIC) model act of 1980 was adopted to address the issue of confidentiality of personal information obtained by insurance companies.

The Act defines "personal information" as:

> *...any individually identifiable information gathered in connection with an insurance transaction from which judgments can be made about an individual's character, habits, avocations, finances, occupation, general reputation, credit, health or any other personal characteristics including name, address, and medical record information.*

Privileged information generally includes individually identifiable information that: (1) relates to a claim for benefits or a civil or criminal proceeding involving an individual; and (2) is collected in connection with or in reasonable anticipation of a claim for insurance benefits or civil or criminal proceeding involving an individual.

Gramm–Leach–Bliley Act

The Gramm-Leach-Bliley Act (GLBA) allowed financial institutions to consolidate banks, insurance companies, and brokerage firms into financial holdings companies (FHCs). As these institutions were established, a need grew to ensure the protection of customer information that these entities controlled.

This act provides mechanisms to protect the privacy of customer information through:

- **Privacy Policies** Your financial institution must tell you the kinds of information it collects about you and how it uses that information.

- **Right to Opt-Out** Your financial institution must explain how you can prevent the sale of your customer data to third parties.
- **Safeguards** Financial institutions are required to develop policies to prevent fraudulent access to confidential financial information, which must then be disclosed to you.

The relevant sections of the act that pertain to privacy policy disclosure have been extracted from Title V and listed here for your review. A full copy of the act is available at www.house.gov/financialservices/s900lang.htm.

SEC. 503. DISCLOSURE OF INSTITUTION PRIVACY POLICY.

a) DISCLOSURE REQUIRED. — At the time of establishing a customer relationship with a consumer and not less than annually during the continuation of such relationship, a financial institution shall provide a clear and conspicuous disclosure to such consumer, in writing or in electronic form or other form permitted by the regulations prescribed under section 504, of such financial institution's policies and practices with respect to—

1) disclosing non-public personal information to affiliates and non-affiliated third parties, consistent with section 502, including the categories of information that may be disclosed;

2) disclosing non-public personal information of persons who have ceased to be customers of the financial institution; and

3) protecting the non-public personal information of customers.

Such disclosures shall be made in accordance with the regulations prescribed under section 504.

b) Information to be included—the disclosure required by subsection (a) shall include—

1) the policies and practices of the institution with respect to disclosing non-public personal information to non-affiliated third parties, other than agents of the institution, consistent with section 502 of this subtitle, and including—

a) the categories of persons to whom the information is or may be disclosed, other than the persons to whom the information may be provided pursuant to section 502(e); and

b) the policies and practices of the institution with respect to disclosing of non-public personal information of persons who have ceased to be customers of the financial institution;

2) the categories of non-public personal information that are collected by the financial institution;

3) the policies that the institution maintains to protect the confidentiality and security of non-public personal information in accordance with section 501; and

4) the disclosures required, if any, under section 603(d)(2)(A)(iii) of the Fair Credit Reporting Act.

Notes from the Underground…

Policies: A Double-edged Sword

Security policies, while they do not explain exceptions or actual implementation procedures, contain a wealth of information for those who are looking to exploit your resources. If you are required by the Gramm-Leach-Bliley Act or any other such federal, state, or local ruling to disclose to your customers the security policies that have been put in place to protect their information, there is nothing to stop the potential hacker from using this to gather vital data regarding your information system's architecture and security control requirements.

HIPAA

The Health Information Portability and Accountability Act (HIPAA) defined the standards and procedures for gathering, retaining, and sharing customer information in the healthcare sector. Like the GLBA, this places controls on insurance providers to ensure the privacy and confidentiality of customer information. The act also provided for methods of electronic filing while ensuring the protection of any information that might be transmitted.

The act, like many government documents, is long and full of legalese, so I have taken only the sections relevant to information security and displayed them here. A full copy of the act is available at www.hcfa.gov/medicaid/hipaa/content/hipaasta.pdf

STANDARDS FOR INFORMATION TRANSACTIONS AND DATA ELEMENTS

SEC. 1173.

(a) STANDARDS TO ENABLE ELECTRONIC EXCHANGE-

    (1) IN GENERAL—The Secretary shall adopt standards for transactions, and data elements for such transactions, to enable health information to be exchanged electronically, that are appropriate for—

        (A) the financial and administrative transactions described in paragraph (2); and

        (B) other financial and administrative transactions determined appropriate by the Secretary, consistent with the goals of improving the operation of the health care system and reducing administrative costs.

    (2) TRANSACTIONS—The transactions referred to in paragraph (1)(A) are transactions with respect to the following:

        (A) Health claims or equivalent encounter information.

        (B) Health claims attachments.

        (C) Enrollment and disenrollment in a health plan.

        (D) Eligibility for a health plan.

        (E) Health care payment and remittance advice.

        (F) Health plan premium payments.

        (G) First report of injury.

        (H) Health claim status.

        (I) Referral certification and authorization.

    (3) ACCOMMODATION OF SPECIFIC PROVIDERS—The standards adopted by the Secretary under paragraph (1) shall accommodate the needs of different types of health care providers.

(b) UNIQUE HEALTH IDENTIFIERS—

    (1) IN GENERAL—The Secretary shall adopt standards providing for a standard unique health identifier for each individual, employer, health plan, and health care provider for use in the health care system. In carrying out the preceding sentence for each health plan

and health care provider, the Secretary shall take into account multiple uses for identifiers and multiple locations and specialty classifications for health care providers.

(2) USE OF IDENTIFIERS—The standards adopted under paragraph (1) shall specify the purposes for which a unique health identifier may be used.

(c) CODE SETS—

(1) IN GENERAL—The Secretary shall adopt standards that—

(A) select code sets for appropriate data elements for the transactions referred to in subsection (a)(1) from among the code sets that have been developed by private and public entities; or

(B) establish code sets for such data elements if no code sets for the data elements have been developed.

(2) DISTRIBUTION—The Secretary shall establish efficient and low-cost procedures for distribution (including electronic distribution) of code sets and modifications made to such code sets under section 1174(b).

(d) SECURITY STANDARDS FOR HEALTH INFORMATION—

(1) SECURITY STANDARDS- The Secretary shall adopt security standards that—

(A) take into account—

(i) the technical capabilities of record systems used to maintain health information;

(ii) the costs of security measures;

(iii) the need for training persons who have access to health information;

(iv) the value of audit trails in computerized record systems; and

(v) the needs and capabilities of small health care providers and rural health care providers (as such providers are defined by the Secretary); and

(B) ensure that a health care clearinghouse, if it is part of a larger organization, has policies and security procedures which isolate the activities of the health care clearinghouse with respect to processing information in a manner that prevents unauthorized access to such information by such larger organization.

(2) SAFEGUARDS—Each person described in section 1172(a) who maintains or transmits health information shall maintain reasonable and appropriate administrative, technical, and physical safeguards—

(A) to ensure the integrity and confidentiality of the information;

(B) to protect against any reasonably anticipated—

   (i) threats or hazards to the security or integrity of the information; and

   (ii) unauthorized uses or disclosures of the information; and

(C) otherwise to ensure compliance with this part by the officers and employees of such person.

(e) ELECTRONIC SIGNATURE—

(1) STANDARDS—The Secretary, in coordination with the Secretary of Commerce, shall adopt standards specifying procedures for the electronic transmission and authentication of signatures with respect to the transactions referred to in subsection (a)(1).

(2) EFFECT OF COMPLIANCE—Compliance with the standards adopted under paragraph (1) shall be deemed to satisfy Federal and State statutory requirements for written signatures with respect to the transactions referred to in subsection (a)(1).

(f) TRANSFER OF INFORMATION AMONG HEALTH PLANS— The Secretary shall adopt standards for transferring among health plans appropriate standard data elements needed for the coordination of benefits, the sequential processing of claims, and other data elements for individuals who have more than one health plan.

Electronic Signatures in the Global and National Commerce Act

The eSign Act provides for binding implications regarding online contracts. A copy of the act is available at http://frWebgate.access.gpo.gov/cgi-bin/ getdoc.cgi?dbname=106_cong_bills&docid=f:s761enr.txt.pdf, while a Federal

Trade Commission executive report can be found at http://www.ftc.gov/os/2001/06/esign7.htm.

COPPA

The Children's Online Privacy Protection Act of 1998 puts parents in control of information collected from their children online, and is flexible enough to accommodate the many business practices and technological changes occurring on the Internet.

Civil Liability Law

Outside of specific regulation, many individuals and organizations are also bound under civil liability law to assure the privacy and protection of the data they control. Individuals or organizations seeking to recover damages from possible losses incurred fall under U.S. laws regarding tort. A *tort* is some damage, injury, or wrongful act done willfully or negligently for which a civil suit can be brought.

To successfully win a tort case, four basic elements must be established:

1. **Duty** The defendant must have legal duty of care toward the plaintiff.

2. **Breach of Duty** The defendant must have violated a legal duty of care toward the defendant. Usually this violation is the result of "negligence" on the part of the defendant.

3. **Damage** The plaintiff must have suffered harm.

4. **Proximity Cause** The defendant's breach of legal duty must be related to the plaintiff's injury closely enough to be considered the cause or at least one of the primary causes of the harm.

Merriam-Webster's Dictionary of Law defines *duty* as "an obligation assumed (as by contract) or imposed by law to conduct oneself in conformance with a certain standard or to act in a particular way." If your company gathers a customer's information, that information is covered under your security policy. Your company's policy can be more stringent than the law, and create a "duty" between your company and the customer. Even with no contract, your company has an implied duty to the customer to take reasonable steps to ensure the privacy of their information.

If a hacker breaks into your system, the hacker would be liable for trespassing against the company. However, under tort law, your company could be held liable, under negligence, for any injuries the hacker caused to any third party (your customer). For example, if the hacker was able to delete or modify customer orders, then the customer could hold the supplier liable for any damages it sustained by not receiving its order. A court would determine if the company complied with its own policy and whether the company took the necessary actions to protect the information.

Addressing Common Risks and Threats

The advent of wireless networks has not created new legions of attackers. Many attackers will utilize the same attacks for the same objectives they used in wired networks. If you do not protect your wireless infrastructure with proven tools and techniques, and do not have established standards and policies that identify proper deployment and security methodology, then you will find that the integrity of your wireless networks may be threatened.

Experiencing Loss of Data

If you are unable to receive complete and proper information though your network and server services, then those services are effectively useless to your organization. Without having to go through the complex task of altering network traffic, if someone is able to damage sections, then the entire subset of information used will have to be retransmitted. One such method used to cause data loss involves the use of spoofing. Spoofing is where someone attempts to identify themselves as an existing network entity or resource. Having succeeded in this ruse, they can then communicate as that resource causing disruptions that affect legitimate users of those same resources.

This type of threat attacks each of the tenets of security we have covered so far. If someone is able to spoof as someone else, then we can no longer trust the confidentiality of communications with that source, and the integrity of that source will no longer be valid, and, as they have taken over the source, they have the ability to remove or replace the service thereby affecting its availability.

Loss of Data Scenario

If an attacker is able to identify a network resource, they could then either send invalid traffic as that resource, or act as a man-in-the-middle for access to the real resource. A *man-in-the-middle* is created when someone assumes the ID of the legitimate resource, and then responds to client queries for those resources, sometimes offering invalid data in response, or actually acquiring the valid results from the resource being spoofed and returning that result (modified as to how the attacker would like) to the client.

The most common use for spoofing in wireless networks is in the configuration of the network MAC address. If a wireless Access Point has been set up and only allows access from specified MAC addresses, all that an attacker need do is monitor the wireless traffic to learn what valid MAC addresses are allowed and then assign that MAC to their interface. This would then allow the attacker to properly communicate with the network resources being that it now has a valid MAC for communicating on the network.

Experiencing Denial and Disruption of Service

One of the most common attacks used to reduce availability of resources is called a denial of service (DOS). The early ping flood attacks exploited misconfigured network devices and allowed for mass amounts of packets to be sent at specified targets, effectively using the entire targets network or computing resources. This prevented anyone from accessing the targets' resources. Ping floods as well as new and interesting distributed denial of service (DDOS) attacks are still being developed and have been able to disrupt the service of some of the largest Internet service providers around (as was done in the cyberassaults in early 2000 against Buy.com, eBay, CNN, and Amazon.com).

Creating a denial of service (DOS) for a wireless network can be accomplished in a similar fashion to wired network DOS attacks. By only being a node on a wireless network or the network it is connected to, and knowing that there is only a certain amount of bandwidth available on the network or to individual machines connected to the network, it would not be too difficult to create a situation by which the wireless resources might become unavailable to those attempting to utilize the network.

Our own mass deployment of wireless devices is also having an impact on the security and availability of those attempting to utilize them. Many new wireless telephones, baby monitors, and Bluetooth-based devices, share the same 2.4GHz frequency channels as 802.11b networks. That, plus the saturation of so many wireless networks in some areas, provides many opportunities for conflicting signals to be transmitted, causing degradation and possible disruption of service due to the jamming caused by the multiple wireless devices.

As we saw when we reviewed "The Big Three," a DOS attack strikes at the heart of the most fundamental network principle—availability—causing much confusion and loss of productivity.

Disruption of Service Scenario

I was having a discussion with an associate online when he suddenly lost his network connection. When he came back, we were unsure of what had happened, so I decided to call him directly to help debug the situation. As soon as he picked up his telephone, his network connection went offline. He remembered getting a previous call the last time he'd been knocked offline. Upon further investigation, we noticed he'd moved his new wireless telephone next to his wireless network adaptor. As he changed the channel his telephone was currently set for (which are randomly chosen on some telephones when the receiver is picked up), he noticed it was conflicting with the channel he had chosen for his wireless network. In the end, he manually reconfigured his wireless gateway until it was on a channel unaffected by the wireless telephone he was using.

Eavesdropping

Even before wireless networks were introduced, several ways were discovered that allowed analysis of traffic on computer monitors and network cables, without needing to connect to either. One such method developed by the National Security Agency (NSA) is named TEMPEST. There are several theories about the origin of the TEMPEST acronym. One is that it was simply a code word used in the 1960s by the U.S. government. Others believe it to be an acronym for Telecommunications Electronics Material Protected from Emanating Spurius Transmissions, or Transient Electromagnetic Pulse Emanation Standard. Either way, TEMPEST is a technology used to monitor (and protect) devices that emit electromagnetic radiation (EMR) in such a way that it can be used to reconstruct the originally transmitted communications. With such a tool, it is possible to reconstruct the images, and words, displayed on a computer screen from a remote location by receiving the EMR transmitted from the monitor and reconstructing it onto another display.

Wireless networks are even more vulnerable to electronic eavesdropping and do not require complex Van Eck devices. By their very nature, wireless networks are designed to allow people to connect and communicate remotely.

Those who wish to exploit wireless networks have a variety of tools available to them. Many of their tools are simply the same tools used to scan, monitor, and attack wired networks. Make a quick visit to Packet Storm (http://packetstormsecurity.com) and you'll find a plethora of scanning, sniffing, and attack tools, along with detailed documentation and security discussions. To use most of these tools, however, you must first be on a network.

Notes from the Underground…

Is TEMPEST Truly Possible?

In 1985 a Dutch Scientist, Wim van Eck, demonstrated how he could easily pick the emissions of a nearby monitor and display them on another monitor. In his paper, *Electromagnetic Radiation from Video Display Units: An Eavesdropping Risk?* (available at http://jya.com/emr.pdf), Wim describes the problem with the electromagnetic fields produced by electronic devices. Due to his publication and the examples provided, TEMPEST is also sometimes known as "Van Eck Phreaking."

Technology has advanced since the mid 80s and while this risk is still possible, new Liquid Crystal Displays (LCD) and higher shielding in current monitors limit the produced emissions and help protect against TEMPEST attacks.

More information on TEMPEST can be found in Cassi Goodman's *An Introduction to TEMPEST*, available through SANS (System Administration, Networking, and Security) at www.sans.org/infosecFAQ/encryption/TEMPEST.htm, or at *The Complete, Unofficial TEMPEST Information Page*, created by Joel McNamara, which can be found at www.capnasty.org/taf/issue5/tempest.htm.

A large percentage of people who deploy wireless networks set them up with the default insecure settings, and even if they turn on encryption, the default key used is rarely changed. On some gateways, the default key is a shortened version of the network ID that can be identified through either physical examination of the gateway or through clever social engineering.

There is little anyone can do to connect to your network until they know it exists. When modems were the primary communication method used by computers, people looking for other computers to call would sometimes run programs such as Tone Loc to dial mass amounts of numbers in search of other modems that would answer. This form of scanning for modems became known as *war dialing*.

The first generation of tools that could scan for wireless networks were released throughout 2001. Due to their similar scanning functionalities, and the fact that a lot of wireless scanning occurs either in a parking lot or when driving by places utilizing wireless networks, scanning for wireless networks has come to be known as *war driving*. These tools were started with the release of NetStumbler (www.netstumbler.com) for Microsoft Windows platforms, and were soon followed by several Linux war driving tools. To supplement these network detection applications, tools such as AirSnort (http://airsnort.sourceforge.net) were created that would recover WEP encryption keys by passively monitoring transmissions, and once enough packets were gathered, AirSnort could compute the key by analyzing the data in relation to the published WEP exploits.

All of these tools attack the basic concept of confidentiality we reviewed earlier. While WEP and the RC4 stream cipher attempt to protect the confidentiality of the data going through your wireless network, once your secret key is known, unless you are utilizing another encryption layer (SSH, SSL, and so on), your confidentiality will be compromised. Your policy and standards should take this, the other scenarios we outline here, and any other possible threat to the fundamentals of security into account and provide an understanding of the risk as well as possible solutions.

Eavesdropping Scenario

The tools of the wireless network hacker can fit into the palm of your hand, or your backpack, or be mounted directly into your vehicle. Therefore, unless you actually triangulate a hacker's signal or actually observe someone's monitor and see them hacking your network, there is little you can do to determine who is exploiting your wireless resources.

The only tools the modern wireless hacker needs is their computer, a wireless network interface (or several depending on the type of hacking they are doing), and possibly an antenna. Using the free tools available today, all a hacker needs do is travel a short distance to find a wireless network that will allow complete Internet and intranet access. We will get into the utilization of these tools and how they can exploit your resources later in this book.

Preempting the Consequences of an Organization's Loss

There are many obvious consequences to organizations or individuals who deploy technology without a solid understanding of the fundamentals of security. These can involve security breaches, loss of data or trade secrets, loss of market opportunity, loss of reputation or direct financial loss. If any losses occur, an organization can expect to see a direct impact to their reputation and customer confidence, which might result in civil and criminal consequences.

Security Breach Scenario

You need only look at the distributed denial of service attacks leveled at the largest Internet companies in recent years to see how they impact a company's bottom line and its customer confidence. By having your resources offline, especially if you are like eBay or Amazon.com where online channels are your only channels, your company is reduced to nothing more than a corner store with nothing on the shelf.

Having clear and well-defined security standards, policies, and guidelines help prepare for possible attacks and provide solutions should they actually occur. They also add extra legal protection in case a customer, business partner, or shareholder feels proper steps haven't been taken to assure the protection and privacy of the information stored and transmitted through your resources.

Summary

It is only through a solid understanding of security fundamentals, principles, and procedures that you are able to fully identify today's security risks. From this understanding, which is built upon "The Big Three" tenets of security (confidentiality, integrity, and availability) come the basis for all other security practices. The essential practices usually associated with security build upon the concepts of "The Big Three," which provide tools for actually implementing security into systems. The ability to properly authenticate a user or process, before allowing that user or process access to specific resources, protect the CIA directly. If we are able to clearly identify the authenticated user through electronic non-repudiation techniques usually found in encryption tools such as public-key encryption, we can assure that the entities attempting to gain access are who they say they are. Finally, if we log the activities performed, then a third party can monitor the logs and ensure all activity happening on a system complies with the policy and standards defined, and that all inappropriate activity is identified, allowing for possible prosecution or investigation into the invalid activity.

Following these practices, through the use of tested and proven identification and evaluation standards, security risks associated with any object can be fully understood. Once the risks are known, solutions can be provided to diminish these risks as much as possible.

The standard solution is to create a formal security policy along with detailed guidelines and procedures. These guidelines describe the actual implementation steps necessary for any platform to comply with the established security procedure.

By using these standard methods to protect your wireless network, you should be able to develop a clear and concise wireless security plan that incorporates the needs of your organization's highest levels. This plan will allow for the deployment of a wireless network that's as secure as possible, and provide clear exception listings for areas where the risks to your infrastructure cannot be fully controlled.

Solutions Fast Track

Understanding Security Fundamentals and Principles of Protection

☑ "The Big Three" tenets of security are: *confidentiality*, *integrity*, and *availability*.

☑ Requirements needed to implement the principles of protection include proper authentication of authorized users through a system that provides for a clear identification of the users via tested non-repudiation techniques.

☑ Logging or system accounting can be used by internal or external auditors to assure that the system is functioning and being utilized in accordance to defined standards and policies.

☑ Logging can also be the first place to look for evidence should an attack occur. Ensure that logging is going to a trusted third-party site that cannot be accessed by personnel and resources being logged.

☑ These tools are essential to protecting the privacy of customer, partner, or trade secret information.

☑ Encryption has provided many tools for the implementation of these security fundamentals.

☑ Encryption is not the definitive solution to security problems. There is still a possibility that a known secret key could be stolen, or that one of the parties utilizing encryption could be tricked or forced into performing the activity, which would be seen as a valid cryptographic operation as the system has no knowledge of any collusion involved in the generation of the request.

Reviewing the Role of Policy

☑ Once basic fundamentals and principles are understood, then through the creation of policies and standards an organization or entity is able to clearly define how to design, implement, and monitor their infrastructure securely.

☑ Policies must have direct support and sign-in by the executive management of any organization.

☑ A properly mitigated risk should reduce the impact of the threat as well as the likelihood that that threat will occur.

☑ A clear and well-defined classification and labeling system is key to the identification of resources being protected.

☑ Information classification techniques also provide a method by which the items being classified can then have the proper policy or standards placed around them depending on the level or importance, as well as the risk associated with each identified item.

☑ Some organizations are required by their own regulations to have clear and well defined standards and policies.

Recognizing Accepted Security and Privacy Standards

☑ Basic policies are based on years of research by the security community whose members have generated many security standards and legal documents that attempt to protect a company's information.

☑ Some standards provide methods of evaluating and reporting on targets being reviewed for security risks, as well as classifying the systems or resources of an entity.

☑ There are many government policies and regulations that have been enacted to protect the citizens' personal non-public information.

☑ Many businesses that utilize electronic record keeping fall under federal regulation when it comes to providing proper policy and protection of their information. Some of these industries include health care companies, financial services, insurance services, and video stores.

☑ Governments have accepted that Internet communications are going to occur within their own borders as well as internationally. Acts such as the E-Sign act were created to authorize electronic communications, and have activities that occur online have the same legal representation as if they had taken place first-hand.

☑ Many businesses that may not be regulated can also be required under civil liability law to have proper security policies and controls that protect their information.

Addressing Common Risks and Threats

☑ By examining the common threats to both wired and wireless networks, we are able to see how a solid understanding in the basics of security principles allows us to fully assess the risks associated with using wireless and other technologies.

☑ Threats can come from simple design issues, where multiple devices utilize the same setup, or intentional denial of service attacks which can result in the corruption or loss of data.

☑ Not all threats are caused by malicious users. They can also be caused by a conflict of similar resources, such as with 802.11b networks and cordless telephones.

☑ With wireless networks going beyond the border of your office or home, chances are greater that your actions might be monitored by a third party.

☑ Unless your organization has clear and well-defined policies and guidelines you might find yourself in legal or business situations where your data is either compromised, lost, or disrupted. Without a clear plan of action that identifies what is important in certain scenarios, you will not be able to address situations as they occur.

Frequently Asked Questions

The following Frequently Asked Questions, answered by the authors of this book, are designed to both measure your understanding of the concepts presented in this chapter and to assist you with real-life implementation of these concepts. To have your questions about this chapter answered by the author, browse to **www.syngress.com/solutions** and click on the **"Ask the Author"** form.

Q: Do I really need to understand the fundamentals of security in order to protect my network?

A: While you are able to utilize the configuration options available to you from your equipment provider, without a solid background in how security is accomplished you will never be able to protect your assets from the unknown threats that will come against your network through either misconfiguration, backdoors provided by the vendor, or new exploits that have not been patched by your vendor.

Q: Am I required by law to have a security policy?

A: If your organization is a video store, deals with children's records, is associated with the health care or financial industries (and you are located in the United States), then you are most likely required by federal regulation to have a defined security policy, and in some cases you are required to have complete third-party audits of your configuration and policies. If you are not required by legislation, you might still find yourself liable under civil law to provide proper protection for customer or partner information contained within your system.

Q: Some of these standards and policies are old. Do they still apply to me?

A: Some of today's laws are based upon communication laws passed near the beginning of the last century. Until those laws are repealed, you are required to comply with them or face possible litigation. The age of the standards is only sometimes relevant. The concepts defined in them have been used in the creation of many other standards and policies, and will probably be similarly used for many years to come.

Q: Can my customers really sue me or my company for being hacked and having their information leaked or misused?

A: In any situation, if you have an established trust with a customer to maintain their information securely and someone breaks into the building or into their corporate servers, there is a possibility that a customer can pursue litigation against you if it's found you did not have any policies or procedures in place to address the risk associated with this and other threats to the customer's information.

Q: If someone can be forced into performing an activity, why should I bother setting up complex security applications?

A: Without those applications in place, you would find that it does not take direct force to attack you or your information. There has always been the possibility that threats could force individuals in key positions to reveal damaging information and secrets, but there is a greater chance that someone will trick a user into disclosing their password or some other security key. Proper training and education are the best defenses in these situations.

Q: I added a firewall to my design. Why should I also need both a policy and external auditing?

A: Again, a firewall may protect you initially, but what do you do as technology changes, or your staff is replaced? Policies and standards ensure that current and future implementations are built in accordance to the definitions laid out by the organization. Adding logging, as well as internal and third-party auditing of the implemented resources helps assure that the implementations are built in accordance to policy, and that all activity occurring within the environment is in compliance with your standards, guidelines, and policies.

Chapter 3

Wireless Network Architecture and Design

Solutions in this chapter:

- **Fixed Wireless Technologies**

- **Developing WLANs through the 802.11 Architecture**

- **Developing WPANs through the 802.15 Architecture**

- **Mobile Wireless Technologies**

- **Optical Wireless Technologies**

- **Exploring the Design Process**

- **Creating the Design Methodology**

- **Understanding Wireless Network Attributes from a Design Perspective**

- ☑ **Summary**

- ☑ **Solutions Fast Track**

- ☑ **Frequently Asked Questions**

Introduction

No study of the challenge of wireless security would be effective without an understanding of the architecture of wireless networks themselves. In this chapter, you'll learn about the topology of wireless networks, and the logic behind the design. You'll learn about the essential components, including Access Points and wireless Network Interface Cards. You'll also learn the language of wireless LANs, including Media Access Control Layer (MACs), Service Set Identifiers (SSIDs), and MAC protocol data units (MPDU).

Understanding the broadcast nature of wireless is essential to understanding the risk, and in this chapter you'll learn about the most commonly used radio transmission protocols, including Frequency-Hopping Spread spectrum (FHSS), Direct-Sequence Spread Spectrum (DRSS), and Infrared (IR).

The wireless industry, like many other sectors of Information Technology, is advancing at a rapid pace. Driving forces of this advancement are the protocols and standards that provide more and more bandwidth, as well as the convergence of data, voice, and video within a network. This chapter will present the various forms of emerging wireless communication from a service provider perspective, all the way down to the home networking environment. In covering wireless technology from the perspective of the service provider, we'll be discussing Multichannel Multipoint Distribution Service (MMDS), Local Multipoint Distribution Service (LMDS), and Wireless Local Loop (WLL); in covering wireless technologies for the home and enterprise network, we will discuss wireless local area networks (WLANs) and the 802.11 protocol suite. The three primary areas of discussion are *fixed wireless*, *mobile wireless*, and *optical wireless* technology.

We have provided generic architectures under each of these wireless technologies to help you understand their evolution. We also provide a brief overview of why these technologies were developed (that is, the market that they serve), and what new capabilities they will provide. The intention is to provide an overview of the direction of wireless technology. When designing a network, you need to know what functionality is available currently and in the future to make longer term plans.

We will also evaluate the design process with a high-level overview, which will discuss the preliminary investigation and design, followed by implementation considerations and documentation. The goal is to provide the big picture first, and then delve into the details of each step in the process. There are numerous steps—diligently planning the design according to these steps will result in fewer complications during the implementation process. This planning is invaluable because often, a network infrastructure already exists, and changing or enhancing the existing network usually impacts the functionality during the migration period. As you may know, there is nothing worse than the stress of bringing a network to a halt to integrate new services—and especially in the case of introducing wireless capabilities, you may encounter unforeseen complications due to a lack of information, incomplete planning, or faulty hardware or software.

The final portion of this chapter will discuss some design considerations and applications specific to a wireless network. These include signal budgeting, importance of operating system efficiency, signal-to-noise ratios, and security.

Fixed Wireless Technologies

The basic definition of a fixed wireless technology is any wireless technology where the transmitter and the receiver are at a fixed location such as a home or office, as opposed to mobile devices such as cellular phones. Fixed wireless devices normally use utility main power supplies (AC power), which will be discussed later in more detail. The technologies under fixed wireless can be MMDS connectivity models, LMDS, encompassing WLL, Point-to-Point Microwave, or WLAN.

Fixed wireless technologies provide advantages to service providers in several areas. First, just by nature of the wireless technology, fixed wireless systems provide the ability to connect to remote users without having to install costly copper cable or optical fiber over long distances. The service provider can deploy a fixed wireless offering much quicker and at a much lower cost than traditional wireline services. Also, the service provider can provide services via fixed wireless access without having to use the local service provider's last mile infrastructure. The disadvantages to fixed wireless vary, depending on which technology is being used, but some of the issues include line-of-sight and weather issues as well as interference from various sources, and licensing issues. After we discuss service provider implementations of fixed wireless, we will discuss how fixed wireless benefits the home and enterprise users.

Multichannel Multipoint Distribution Service

Allocated by the Federal Communications Commission (FCC) in 1983 and enhanced with two-way capabilities in 1998, Multichannel Multipoint Distribution Service is a licensed spectrum technology operating in the 2.5 to 2.7 GHz range, giving it 200 MHz of spectrum to construct cell clusters. Service providers consider MMDS a complimentary technology to their existing digital subscriber line (DSL) and cable modem offerings by providing access to customers not reachable via these wireline technologies (see Figure 3.1 for an example of a service provider MMDS architecture).

Figure 3.1 MMDS Architecture

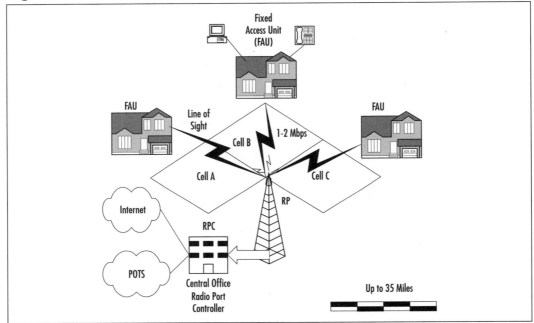

MMDS provides from 1 to 2 Mbps of throughput and has a relative range of 35 miles from the radio port controller (RPC) based on signal power levels. It generally requires a clear line of sight between the radio port (RP) antenna and the customer premise antenna, although several vendors are working on MMDS offerings that don't require a clear line of sight. The *fresnel* zone of the signal (the zone around the signal path that must be clear of reflective surfaces) must be clear from obstruction as to avoid absorption and reduction of the signal energy. MMDS is also susceptible to a condition known as *multipath reflection*. Multipath reflection or interference happens when radio signals reflect off surfaces such as water or buildings in the fresnel zone, creating a condition where the same signal arrives at different times. Figure 3.2 depicts the fresnel zone and the concept of absorption and multipath interference.

Figure 3.2 Fresnel Zone: Absorption and Multipath Issues

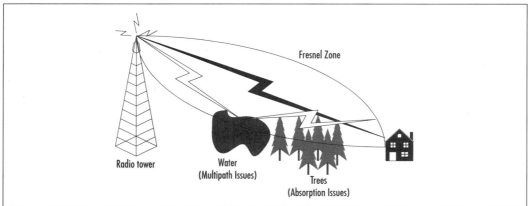

Local Multipoint Distribution Services

Local Multipoint Distribution Service (LMDS) is a broadband wireless point-to-multipoint microwave communication system operating above 20 GHz (28–31 GHz in the US). It is similar in its architecture to MMDS with a couple of exceptions. LMDS provides very high-speed bandwidth (upwards of 500 Mbps) but is currently limited to a relative maximum range of 3 to 5 miles of coverage. It has the same line-of-sight issues that MMDS experiences, and can be affected by weather conditions, as is common among line-of-sight technologies.

LMDS is ideal for short-range campus environments requiring large amounts of bandwidth, or highly concentrated urban centers with large data/voice/video bandwidth requirements in a relatively small area. LMDS provides a complementary wireless architecture for the wireless service providers to use for markets that are not suited for MMDS deployments. Figure 3.3 illustrates a generic LMDS architecture.

Wireless Local Loop

Wireless Local Loop (WLL) refers to a fixed wireless class of technology aimed at providing last-mile services normally provided by the local service provider over a wireless medium. This includes Plain Old Telephone Service (POTS) as well as broadband offerings such as DSL service. As stated earlier, this technology provides service without the laying of cable or use of the Incumbent Local Exchange Carrier (ILEC), which in layman's terms is the Southwestern Bells of the world.

Figure 3.3 Local Multipoint Distribution Services (LMDS) Architecture

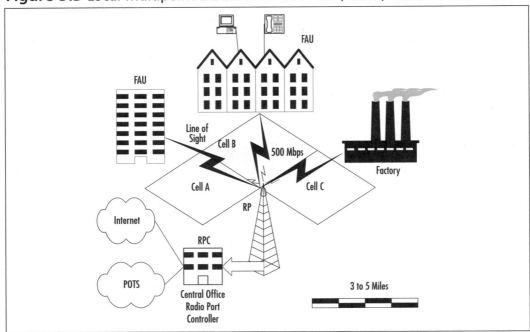

The generic layout involves a point–to–multipoint architecture with a central radio or radio port controller located at the local exchange (LE). The RPC connects to a series of base stations called radio ports (RPs) via fixed access back to the LE. The RPs are mounted on antennas and arranged to create coverage areas or sectored cells. The radios located at the customer premise, or fixed access unit (FAU), connects to an external antenna optimized to transmit and receive voice/data from the RPs. The coverage areas and bandwidth provided vary depending on the technology used, and coverage areas can be extended through the use of repeaters between the FAU and the RPs. Figure 3.4 provides a generic depiction of a wireless local loop architecture.

Point-to-Point Microwave

Point-to-Point (PTP) Microwave is a line–of–sight technology, which is affected by multipath and absorption much like MMDS and LMDS. PTP Microwave falls into two categories: licensed and unlicensed, or spread spectrum. The FCC issues licenses for individuals to use specific frequencies for the licensed version. The advantage with the licensed PTP Microwave is that the chance of interference or noise sources in the frequency range is remote. This is critical if the integrity of the traffic on that link needs to be maintained. Also, if the link is going to span a long distance or is in a heavily populated area, the licensed version is a much safer bet since the probability of interference is greater in those cases. The drawback to licensed PTP Microwave is that it may take a considerable amount of time for the FCC to issue the licenses, and there are fees associated with those licenses. Unlicensed PTP Microwave links can be used when a licensed PTP Microwave is not necessary and expediency is an issue.

Figure 3.4 Wireless Local Loop Architecture

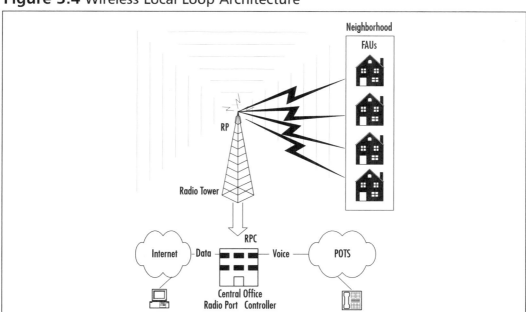

Since PTP can span long distances, determined mostly by the power of the transmitter and the sensitivity of the receiver, as well as by traditional weather conditions, many different aspects need to be considered in designing a PTP Microwave link. First, a site survey and path analysis need to be conducted. Obstructions and curvature of the earth (for links over six miles) determine the height of the towers or the building required to build the link in a line-of-sight environment. As stated earlier, the fresnel zone must be clear of obstructions and reflective surfaces to avoid absorption and multipath issues. Predominant weather conditions can limit the distance of the PTP Microwave link since the signal is susceptible to a condition called *rain fade*. The designers must take the predicted amount of signal degradation in a projected area and factor that into the design based on reliability requirements for the PTP Microwave link. Figure 3.5 gives a basic depiction of a PTP Microwave link.

Figure 3.5 Point-to-Point Microwave

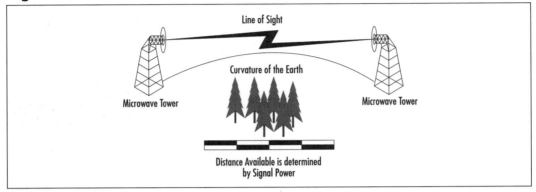

Wireless Local Area Networks

Benefits of fixed wireless can also provide value to the enterprise and home networks. This is where wireless capabilities get exciting for the end user. The benefits are literally at your fingertips. Imagine sitting at your desk when your boss calls announcing an emergency meeting immediately—there is a document on its way to you via e-mail that will be the focus of the meeting. Before wireless, you would first have to wait for your computer to receive the e-mail, then perhaps print the document before traveling to the meeting; with a laptop, you would have to consider cords, batteries, and connections. After the meeting, you would go back to your desk for any document changes or further correspondence by e-mail. In a wireless environment, you can receive the e-mail and read the document while you are on your way to the meeting, and make changes to the document and correspond with other attendees real-time during the meeting.

Why the Need for a Wireless LAN Standard?

Prior to the adoption of the 802.11 standard, wireless data-networking vendors made equipment that was based on proprietary technology. Wary of being locked into a relationship with a specific vendor, potential wireless customers instead turned to more standards-based wired technologies. As a result, deployment of wireless networks did not happen on a large scale, and remained a luxury item for large companies with large budgets.

The only way wireless local area networks (WLANs) would be generally accepted would be if the wireless hardware involved had a low cost and had become commodity items like routers and switches. Recognizing that the only way for this to happen would be if there were a wireless data-networking standard, the Institute of Electrical and Electronics Engineers' (IEEE's) 802 Group took on their eleventh challenge. Since many of the members of the 802.11 Working Group were employees of vendors making wireless technologies, there were many pushes to include certain functions in the final specification. Although this slowed down the progress of finalizing 802.11, it also provided momentum for delivery of a feature-rich standard left open for future expansion.

On June 26, 1997, the IEEE announced the ratification of the 802.11 standard for wireless local area networks. Since that time, costs associated with deploying an 802.11–based network have dropped, and WLANs rapidly are being deployed in schools, businesses, and homes.

In this section, we will discuss the evolution of the standard in terms of bandwidth and services. Also, we will discuss the WLAN standards that are offshoots of the 802.11 standard.

NOTE

The IEEE (www.ieee.org) is an association that develops standards for almost anything electronic and /or electric. Far from being limited to computer-related topics, IEEE societies cover just about any technical practice, from automobiles to maritime, from neural networks to super-conductors. With 36 Technical Societies covering broad interest areas, more specific topics are handled by special committees. These other committees form Working Groups (WGs) and Technical Advisory Groups (TAGs) to create operational models that enable different vendors to develop and sell products that will be compatible. The membership of these committees and groups are professionals who work for companies that develop, create, or manufacture with their technical practice. These groups meet several times a year to discuss new trends within their industry, or to continue the process of refining a current standard.

What Exactly Does the 802.11 Standard Define?

As in all 802.x standards, the 802.11 specification covers the operation of the media access control (MAC) and physical layers. As you can see in Figure 3.6, 802.11 defines a MAC sublayer, MAC services and protocols, and three physical (PHY) layers.

Figure 3.6 802.11 Frame Format

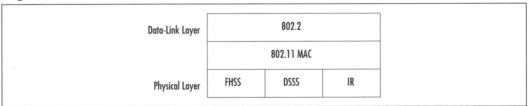

The three physical layer options for 802.11 are infrared (IR) baseband PHY and two radio frequency (RF) PHYs. Due to line-of-sight limitations, very little development has occurred with the Infrared PHY. The RF physical layer is composed of Frequency Hopping Spread Spectrum (FHSS) and Direct Sequence Spread Spectrum (DSSS) in the 2.4 GHz band. All three physical layers operate at either 1 or 2 Mbps. The majority of 802.11 implementations utilize the DSSS method.

FHSS works by sending bursts of data over numerous frequencies. As the name implies, it hops between frequencies. Typically, the devices use up to four frequencies simultaneously to send information and only for a short period of time before hopping to new frequencies. The devices using FHSS agree upon the frequencies being used. In fact, due to the short time period of frequency use and device agreement of these frequencies, many autonomous networks can coexist in the same physical space.

DSSS functions by dividing the data into several pieces and simultaneously sending the pieces on as many different frequencies as possible, unlike FHSS, which sends on a limited number of frequencies. This process allows for greater transmission rates than FHSS, but is vulnerable to greater occurrences of interference. This is because the data is spanning a larger portion of the spectrum at any given time than FHSS. In essence, DHSS floods the spectrum all at one time, whereas FHSS selectively transmits over certain frequencies.

Designing & Planning…

Additional Initiatives of the 802 Standards Committee

802.1 LAN/MAN Bridging and Management 802.1 is the base standard for LAN/MAN Bridging, LAN architecture, LAN management, and protocol layers above the MAC and LLC layers. Some examples would include 802.1q, the standard for virtual LANs, and 802.1d, the Spanning Tree Protocol.

802.2 Logical Link Control Since Logical Link Control is now a part of all 802 standards, this Working Group is currently in hibernation (inactive) with no ongoing projects.

802.3 CSMA/CD Access Method (Ethernet) 802.3 defines that an Ethernet network can operate at 10 Mbps, 100 Mbps, 1 Gbps, or even 10 Gbps. It also defines that category 5 twisted pair cabling and fiber optic cabling are valid cable types. This group identifies how to make vendors' equipment interoperate despite the various speeds and cable types.

802.4 Token-Passing Bus This Working Group is also in hibernation with no ongoing projects.

802.5 Token Ring Token Ring networks operate at 4 mps or 16 Mbps. Currently, there are Working Groups proposing 100 mb Token Ring (802.5t) and Gigabit Token Ring (802.5v). Examples of other 802.5 specs would be 802.5c, Dual Ring Wrapping, and 802.5j, fiber optic station attachment.

802.6 Metropolitan Area Network (MAN) Since Metropolitan Area Networks are created and managed with current internetworking standards, the 802.6 Working Group is in hibernation.

802.7 Broadband LAN In 1989, this Working Group recommended practices for Broadband LANs, which were reaffirmed in 1997. This group is inactive with no ongoing projects. The maintenance effort for 802.7 is now supported by 802.14.

802.8 Fiber Optics Many of this Working Group's recommended practices for fiber optics get wrapped into other Standards at the Physical Layer.

Continued

802.9 Isochronous Services LAN (ISLAN) Isochronous Services refer to processes where data must be delivered within certain time constraints. Streaming media and voice calls are examples of traffic that requires an isochronous transport system.

802.10 Standard for Interoperable LAN Security (SILS) This Working Group provided some standards for Data Security in the form of 802.10a, Security Architecture Framework, and 802.10c, Key Management. This Working Group is currently in hibernation with no ongoing projects.

802.11 Wireless LAN (WLAN) This Working Group is developing standards for Wireless data delivery in the 2.4 GHz and 5.1 GHz radio spectrum.

802.12 Demand Priority Access Method This Working Group provided two Physical Layer and Repeater specifications for the development of 100 Mbps Demand Priority MACs. Although they were accepted as ISO standards and patents were received for their operation, widespread acceptance was overshadowed by Ethernet. 802.12 is currently in the process of being withdrawn.

802.13 This standard was intentionally left blank.

802.14 Cable-TV Based Broadband Comm Network

This Working Group developed specifications for the Physical and Media Access Control Layers for Cable Televisions and Cable Modems. Believing their work to be done, this Working Group has no ongoing projects.

802.15 Wireless Personal Area Network (WPAN) The vision of Personal Area Networks is to create a wireless interconnection between portable and mobile computing devices such as PCs, peripherals, cell phones, Personal Digital Assistants (PDAs), pagers, and consumer electronics, allowing these devices to communicate and interoperate with one another without interfering with other wireless communications.

802.16 Broadband Wireless Access The goal of the 802.16 Working Group is to develop standards for fixed broadband wireless access systems. These standards are key to solving "last-mile" local-loop issues. 802.16 is similar to 802.11a in that it uses unlicensed frequencies in the unlicensed national

Continued

information infrastructure (U-NII) spectrum. 802.16 is different from 802.11a in that Quality of Service for voice/video/data issues are being addressed from the start in order to present a standard that will support true wireless network backhauling.

Does the 802.11 Standard Guarantee Compatibility across Different Vendors?

As mentioned earlier, the primary reason WLANs were not widely accepted was the lack of standardization. It is logical to question whether vendors would accept a nonproprietary operating standard, since vendors compete to make unique and distinguishing products. Although 802.11 standardized the PHY, MAC, the frequencies to send/receive on, transmission rates and more, it did not absolutely guarantee that differing vendors' products would be 100 percent compatible. In fact, some vendors built in backward-compatibility features into their 802.11 products in order to support their legacy customers. Other vendors have introduced proprietary extensions (for example, bit-rate adaptation and stronger encryption) to their 802.11 offerings.

To ensure that consumers can build interoperating 802.11 wireless networks, an organization called the Wireless Ethernet Compatibility Alliance (WECA) tests and certifies 802.11 devices. Their symbol of approval means that the consumer can be assured that the particular device has passed a thorough test of interoperations with devices from other vendors. This is important when considering devices to be implemented into your existing network, because if the devices cannot communicate, it complicates the management of the network—in fact, essentially you will have to deal with two autonomous networks. It is also important when building a new network because you may be limited to a single vendor.

Since the first 802.11 standard was approved in 1997, there have been several initiatives to make improvements. As you will see in the following sections, there is an evolution unfolding with the 802.11 standard. The introduction of the standard came with 802.11b. Then along came 802.11a, which provides up to five times the bandwidth capacity of 802.11b. Now, accompanying the ever-growing demand for multimedia services, is the development of 802.11e. Each task group, outlined next, is endeavoring to speed up the 802.11 standard, making it globally accessible, while not having to reinvent the MAC layer of 802.11:

- **The 802.11d Working Group** is concentrating on the development of 802.11 WLAN equipment to operate in markets not served by the current standard (the current 802.11 standard defines WLAN operation in only a few countries).

- **The 802.11f Working Group** is developing an *Inter-Access Point Protocol*, due to the current limitation prohibiting roaming between Access Points made by different vendors. This protocol would allow wireless devices to roam across Access Points made by competing vendors.

- **The 802.11g Working Group** is working on furthering higher data rates in the 2.4 GHz radio band.

- **The 802.11h Working Group** is busy developing Spectrum and Power Management Extensions for the IEEE 802.11a standard for use in Europe.

802.11b

Ignoring the FHSS and IR physical mediums, the 802.11b PHY uses DSSS to broadcast in any one of 14 center-frequency channels in the 2.4 GHz Industrial, Scientific, and Medical (ISM) radio band. As Table 3.1 shows, North America allows 11 channels; Europe allows 13, the most channels allowed. Japan has only one channel reserved for 802.11, at 2.483 GHz.

Table 3.1 802.11b Channels and Participating Countries

Channel Number	Frequency GHz	North America	Europe	Spain	France	Japan
1	2.412	X	X			
2	2.417	X	X			
3	2.422	X	X			
4	2.427	X	X			
5	2.432	X	X			
6	2.437	X	X			
7	2.442	X	X			
8	2.447	X	X			
9	2.452	X	X			
10	2.457	X	X	X	X	

Continued

Table 3.1 Continued

Channel Number	Frequency GHz	North America	Europe	Spain	France	Japan
11	2.462	X	X	X	X	
12	2.467		X		X	
13	2.472		X		X	
14	2.483					X

There are many different devices competing for airspace in the 2.4 GHz radio spectrum. Unfortunately, most of the devices that cause interference are especially common in the home environment, such as microwaves and cordless phones. As you can imagine, the viability of an 802.11b network depends on how many of these products are near the network devices.

One of the more recent entrants to the 802.11b airspace comes in the form of the emerging Bluetooth wireless standard. Though designed for short-range transmissions, Bluetooth devices utilize FHSS to communicate with each other. Cycling through thousands of frequencies a second, this looks as if it poses the greatest chance of creating interference for 802.11. Further research will determine exactly what—if any—interference Bluetooth will cause to 802.11b networks. Many companies are concerned with oversaturating the 2.4 GHz spectrum, and are taking steps to ensure that their devices "play nicely" with others in this arena.

These forms of interference will directly impact the home user who wishes to set up a wireless LAN, especially if neighbors operate interfering devices. Only time will tell if 802.11b will be able to stand up against these adversaries and hold on to the marketplace.

802.11a

Due to the overwhelming demand for more bandwidth and the growing number of technologies operating in the 2.4 GHz band, the 802.11a standard was created for WLAN use in North America as an upgrade from the 802.11b standard. 802.11a provides 25 to 54 Mbps bandwidth in the 5 GHz spectrum (the unlicensed national information infrastructure [U-NII] spectrum). Since the 5 GHz band is currently mostly clear, chance of interference is reduced. However, that could change since it is still an unlicensed portion of the spectrum. 802.11a still is designed mainly for the enterprise, providing Ethernet capability.

802.11a is one of the physical layer extensions to the 802.11 standard. Abandoning spread spectrum completely, 802.11a uses an encoding technique called Orthogonal Frequency Division Multiplexing (OFDM). Although this encoding technique is similar to the European 5-GHz HiperLAN physical layer specification, which will be explained in greater detail later in the chapter, 802.11a currently is specific to the United States.

As shown in Table 3.2, three 5-GHz spectrums have been defined for use with 802.11a. Each of these three center-frequency bands covers 100 MHz.

Table 3.2 802.11a Channels Usable in the 5-GHz U-NII Radio Spectrum

Regulatory Area	Frequency Band	Channel Number	Center Frequencies
USA	U-NII Lower Band 5.15 - 5.25 GHz	36	5.180 GHz
		40	5.200 GHz
		44	5.220 GHz
		48	5.240 GHz
USA	U-NII Middle Band 5.25 - 5.35 GHz	52	5.260 GHz
		56	5.280 GHz
		60	5.300 GHz
		64	5.320 GHz
USA	U-NII Upper Band 5.725 - 5.825 GHz	149	5.745 GHz
		153	5.765 GHz
		157	5.785 GHz
		161	5.805 GHz

802.11e

The IEEE 802.11e is providing enhancements to the 802.11 standard while retaining compatibility with 802.11b and 802.11a. The enhancements include multimedia capability made possible with the adoption of quality of service (QoS) functionality as well as security improvements. What does this mean for a service provider? It means the ability to offer video on demand, audio on demand, high-speed Internet access and Voice over IP (VoIP) services. What does this mean for the home or business user? It allows high-fidelity multimedia in the form of MPEG2 video and CD quality sound, and redefinition of the traditional phone use with VoIP.

QoS is the key to the added functionality with 802.11e. It provides the functionality required to accommodate time-sensitive applications such as video and audio. QoS includes queuing, traffic shaping tools, and scheduling. These characteristics allow priority of traffic. For example, data traffic is not time sensitive and therefore has a lower priority than applications like streaming video. With these enhancements, wireless networking has evolved to meet the demands of today's users.

Developing WLANs through the 802.11 Architecture

The 802.11 architecture can best be described as a series of interconnected cells, and consists of the following: the wireless device or station, the Access Point (AP), the wireless medium, the distribution system (DS), the Basic Service Set (BSS), the Extended Service Set (ESS), and station and distribution services. All of these working together providing a seamless mesh gives wireless devices the ability to roam around the WLAN looking for all intents and purposes like a wired device.

The Basic Service Set

The core of the IEEE 802.11 standard is the Basic Service Set (BSS). As you can see in Figure 3.7, this model is made up of one or more wireless devices communicating with a single Access Point in a single radio cell. If there are no connections back to a wired network, this is called an *independent Basic Service Set.*

Figure 3.7 Basic Service Set

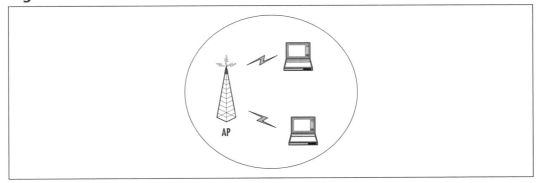

If there is no Access Point in the wireless network, it is referred to as an *ad-hoc network.* This means that all wireless communications is transmitted directly between the members of the ad-hoc network. Figure 3.8 describes a basic ad-hoc network.

Figure 3.8 Ad-Hoc Network

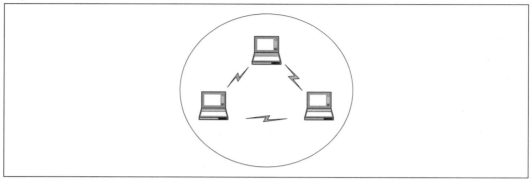

When the BSS has a connection to the wired network via an AP, it is called an *infrastructure BSS*. As you can see in the model shown in Figure 3.9, the AP bridges the gap between the wireless device and the wired network.

Figure 3.9 802.11 Infrastructure Architecture

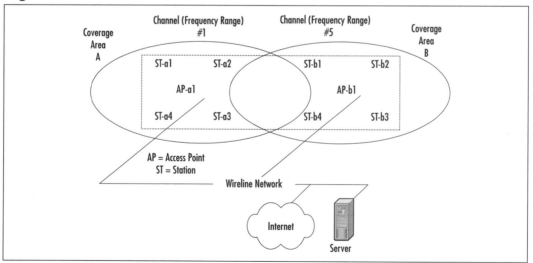

Since multiple Access Points exist in this model, the wireless devices no longer communicate in a peer-to-peer fashion. Instead, all traffic from one device destined for another device is relayed through the AP. Even though it would look like this would double the amount of traffic on the WLAN, this also provides for traffic buffering on the AP when a device is operating in a low-power mode.

The Extended Service Set

The compelling force behind WLAN deployment is the fact that with 802.11, users are free to move about without having to worry about switching network connections manually. If we were operating with a single infrastructure BSS, this moving about would be limited to the signal range of our one AP. Through the Extended Service Set (ESS), the IEEE 802.11 architecture allows users to move between multiple infrastructure BSSs. In an ESS, the APs talk amongst themselves forwarding traffic from one BSS to another, as well as switch the roaming devices from one BSS to another. They do this using a medium called the distribution system (DS). The distribution system forms the spine of the WLAN, making the decisions whether to forward traffic from one BSS to the wired network or back out to another AP or BSS.

What makes the WLAN so unique, though, are the invisible interactions between the various parts of the Extended Service Set. Pieces of equipment on the wired network have no idea they are communicating with a mobile WLAN device, nor do they see the switching that occurs when the wireless device changes from one AP to another. To the wired network, all it sees is a consistent MAC address to talk to, just as if the MAC was another node on the wire.

Services to the 802.11 Architecture

There are nine different services that provide behind-the-scenes support to the 802.11 architecture. Of these nine, four belong to the *station services* group and the remaining five to the *distribution services* group.

Station Services

The four station services (*authentication*, *de-authentication*, *data delivery*, and *privacy*) provide functionality equal to what standard 802.3 wired networks would have.

The authentication service defines the identity of the wireless device. Without this distinct identity, the device is not allowed access to the WLAN. Authentication can also be made against a list of MACs allowed to use the network. This list of allowable MAC addresses may be on the AP or on a database somewhere on the wired network. A wireless device can authenticate itself to more than one AP at a time. This sort of "pre-authentication" allows the device to prepare other APs for its entry into their airspace.

The de–authentication service is used to destroy a previously known station identity. Once the de–authentication service has been started, the wireless device can no longer access the WLAN. This service is invoked when a wireless device shuts down, or when it is roaming out of the range of the Access Point. This frees up resources on the AP for other devices.

Just like its wired counterparts, the 802.11 standard specifies a data delivery service to ensure that data frames are transferred reliably from one MAC to another. This data delivery will be discussed in greater detail in following sections.

The privacy service is used to protect the data as it crosses the WLAN. Even though the service utilizes an RC4–based encryption scheme, it is not intended for end–to–end encryption or as a sole method of securing data. Its design was to provide a level of protection equivalent to that provided on a wired network— hence its moniker Wireless Equivalency Protection (WEP).

Distribution Services

Between the Logical Link Control (LLC) sublayer and the MAC, five distribution services make the decisions as to where the 802.11 data frames should be sent. As we will see, these distribution services make the roaming handoffs when the wireless device is in motion. The five services are *association*, *reassociation*, *disassociation*, *integration*, and *distribution*.

The wireless device uses the association service as soon as it connects to an AP. This service establishes a logical connection between the devices, and determines the path the distribution system needs to take in order to reach the wireless device. If the wireless device does not have an association made with an Access Point, the DS will not know where that device is or how to get data frames to it. As you can see in Figure 3.10, the wireless device can be authenticated to more than one AP at a time, but it will never be associated with more than one AP.

As we will see in later sections dealing with roaming and low-power situations, sometimes the wireless device will not be linked continuously to the same AP. To keep from losing whatever network session information the wireless device has, the reassociation service is used. This service is similar to the association service, but includes current information about the wireless device. In the case of roaming, this information tells the current AP who the last AP was. This allows the current AP to contact the previous AP to pick up any data frames waiting for the wireless device and forward them to their destination.

Figure 3.10 Wireless Authentication through the Association Service

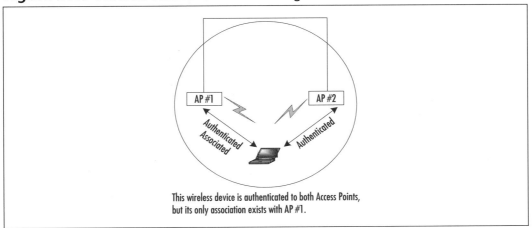

The disassociation service is used to tear down the association between the AP and the wireless device. This could be because the device is roaming out of the AP's area, the AP is shutting down, or any one of a number of other reasons. To keep communicating to the network, the wireless device will have to use the association service to find a new AP.

The distribution service is used by APs when determining whether to send the data frame to another AP and possibly another wireless device, or if the frame is destined to head out of the WLAN into the wired network.

The integration service resides on the APs as well. This service does the data translation from the 802.11 frame format into the framing format of the wired network. It also does the reverse, taking data destined for the WLAN, and framing it within the 802.11 frame format.

The CSMA-CA Mechanism

The basic access mechanism for 802.11 is carrier sense multiple access collision avoidance (CSMA–CA) with binary exponential backoff. This is very similar to the carrier sense multiple access collision detect (CSMA–CD) that we are familiar with when dealing with standard 802.3 (Ethernet), but with a couple of major differences.

Unlike Ethernet, which sends out a signal until a collision is detected, CSMA–CA takes great care to not transmit unless it has the attention of the receiving unit, and no other unit is talking. This is called *listening before talking* (LBT).

Before a packet is transmitted, the wireless device will listen to hear if any other device is transmitting. If a transmission is occurring, the device will wait for a randomly determined period of time, and then listen again. If no one else is using the medium, the device will begin transmitting. Otherwise, it will wait again for a random time before listening once more.

The RTS/CTS Mechanism

To minimize the risk of the wireless device transmitting at the same time as another wireless device (and thus causing a collision), the designers of 802.11 employed a mechanism called Request To Send/Clear To Send (RTS/CTS).

For example, if data arrived at the AP destined for a wireless node, the AP would send a RTS frame to the wireless node requesting a certain amount of time to deliver data to it. The wireless node would respond with a CTS frame saying that it would hold off any other communications until the AP was done sending the data. Other wireless nodes would hear the transaction taking place, and delay their transmissions for that period of time as well. In this manner, data is passed between nodes with a minimal possibility of a device causing a collision on the medium.

This also gets rid of a well-documented WLAN issue called *the hidden node*. In a network with multiple devices, the possibility exists that one wireless node might not know all the other nodes that are out on the WLAN. Thanks to RST/CTS, each node hears the requests to transmit data to the other nodes, and thus learns what other devices are operating in that BSS.

Acknowledging the Data

When sending data across a radio signal with the inherent risk of interference, the odds of a packet getting lost between the transmitting radio and the destination unit are much greater than in a wired network model. To make sure that data transmissions would not get lost in the ether, *acknowledgment* (ACK) was introduced. The acknowledgement portion of CSMA-CA means that when a destination host receives a packet, it sends back a notification to the sending unit. If the sender does not receive an ACK, it will know that this packet was not received and will transmit it again.

All this takes place at the MAC layer. Noticing that an ACK has not been received, the sending unit is able to grab the radio medium before any other unit can and it resends the packet. This allows recovery from interference without the end user being aware that a communications error has occurred.

Configuring Fragmentation

In an environment prone to interference, the possibility exists that one or more bits in a packet will get corrupted during transmission. No matter the number of corrupted bits, the packet will need to be re-sent.

When operating in an area where interference is not a possibility, but a reality, it makes sense to transmit smaller packets than those traditionally found in wired networks. This allows for a faster retransmission of the packet to be accomplished.

The disadvantage to doing this is that in the case of no corrupted packets, the cost of sending many short packets is greater than the cost of sending the same information in a couple of large packets. Thankfully, the 802.11 standard has made this a configurable feature. This way, a network administrator can specify short packets in some areas and longer packets in more open, noninterfering areas.

Using Power Management Options

Because the whole premise of wireless LANs is mobility, having sufficient battery power to power the communications channel is of prime concern. The IEEE recognized this and included a power management service that allows the mobile client to go into a sleep mode to save power without losing connectivity to the wireless infrastructure.

Utilizing a 20-byte Power Save Poll (PS-Poll) frame, the wireless device sends a message to its AP letting it know that is going into power-save mode, and the AP needs to buffer all packets destined for the device until it comes back online. Periodically, the wireless device will wake up and see if there are any packets waiting for it on the AP. If there aren't, another PS-Poll frame is sent, and the unit goes into a sleep mode again. The real benefit here is that the mobile user is able to use the WLAN for longer periods of time without severely impacting the battery life.

Multicell Roaming

Another benefit to wireless LANs is being able to move from wireless cell to cell as you go around the office, campus, or home without the need to modify your network services. Roaming between Access Points in your ESS is a very important portion of the 802.11 standard. Roaming is based on the ability of the wireless device to determine the quality of the wireless signal to any AP within reach, and decide to switch communications to a different AP if it has a stronger or cleaner signal. This is based primarily upon an entity called the signal-to-noise (S/N) ratio. In order for wireless devices to determine the S/N ratio for each AP in the network, Access Points send out *beacon* messages that contain information about the AP as well as link measurement data. The wireless device listens to these beacons and determines which AP has the clearest and cleanest signal. After making this determination, the wireless device sends authentication information and attempts to reassociate with the new AP. The reassociation process tells the new AP which AP the device just came from. The new AP picks up whatever data frames that might be left at the old AP, and notifies the old AP that it no longer needs to accept messages for that wireless device. This frees up resources on the old AP for its other clients.

Even though the 802.11 standard covers the concepts behind the communications between the AP and the DS, it doesn't define exactly how this communication should take place. This is because there are many different ways this communication can be implemented. Although this gives a vendor a good deal of flexibility in AP/DS design, there could be situations where APs from different vendors might not be able to interoperate across a distribution system due to the differences in how those vendors implemented the AP/DS interaction. Currently, there is an 802.11 Working Group (802.11f) developing an Inter-Access Point Protocol. This protocol will be of great help in the future as companies who have invested in one vendor's products can integrate APs and devices from other vendors into their ESSs.

Security in the WLAN

One of the biggest concerns facing network administrators when implementing a WLAN is data security. In a wired environment, the lack of access to the physical wire can prevent someone from wandering into your building and connecting to your internal network. In a WLAN scenario, it is impossible for the AP to know if the person operating the wireless device is sitting inside your building, passing time in your lobby, or if they are seated in a parked car just outside your office. Acknowledging that passing data across an unreliable radio link could lead to possible snooping, the IEEE 802.11 standard provides three ways to provide a greater amount of security for the data that travels over the WLAN. Adopting any (or all three) of these mechanisms will decrease the likelihood of an accidental security exposure.

The first method makes use of the 802.11 Service Set Identifier (SSID). This SSID can be associated with one or more APs to create multiple WLAN segments within the infrastructure BSS. These segments can be related to floors of a building, business units, or other data-definition sets. Since the SSID is presented during the authentication process, it acts as a crude password. Since most end-users set up their wireless devices, these SSIDs could be shared among users, thus limiting their effectiveness. Another downside to using SSIDs as a sole form of authentication is that if the SSID were to be changed (due to an employee termination or other event), all wireless devices and APs would have to reflect this change. On a medium-sized WLAN, rotating SSIDs on even a biannual basis could prove to be a daunting and time-consuming task.

As mentioned earlier in the station services section, the AP also can authenticate a wireless device against a list of MAC addresses. This list could reside locally on the AP, or the authentication could be checked against a database of allowed MACs located on the wired network. This typically provides a good level of security, and is best used with small WLAN networks. With larger WLAN networks, administering the list of allowable MAC addresses will require some back-end services to reduce the amount of time needed to make an addition or subtraction from the list.

The third mechanism 802.11 offers to protect data traversing the WLAN was also mentioned earlier in the section on station services. The *privacy* service uses a RC-4 based encryption scheme to encapsulate the payload of the 802.11 data frames, called Wired Equivalent Privacy (WEP). WEP specifies a 40-bit encryption key, although some vendors have implemented a 104-bit key. As mentioned previously, WEP is not meant to be an end-to-end encryption solution. WEP keys on the APs and wireless devices can be rotated, but since the 802.11 standard does not specify a key-management protocol, all key rotation must be done manually. Like the SSID, rotating the WEP key would affect all APs and wireless users and take significant effort from the network administrator.

Some network designers consider WLANs to be in the same crowd as Remote Access Service (RAS) devices, and claim the best protection is to place the WLAN architecture behind a firewall or Virtual Private Network (VPN) device. This would make the wireless client authenticate to the VPN or firewall using third-party software (on top of WEP). The benefit here is that the bulk of the authenticating would be up to a non-WLAN device, and would not require additional AP maintenance.

The uses of 802.11 networks can range from homes to public areas like schools and libraries, to businesses and corporate campuses. The ability to deploy a low-cost network without the need to have wires everywhere is allowing wireless networks to spring up in areas where wired networks would be cost prohibitive. The 802.11 services allow the wireless device the same kind of functionality as a wired network, yet giving the user the ability to roam throughout the WLAN.

Next, we will discuss another wireless technology breakthrough, appealing to the truly free-spirited. This emerging technology is capable of providing a personal network that moves along with you wherever you go. Let's say you receive a text message on your cellular and personal communications services (PCS) phone and would like to transfer the contents into your PDA. No problem—with the 802.15 standard, this is possible no matter where you are. And if you happen to be in a public place and someone near you is using the same technology, there is no need to worry, because your information is encrypted.

Developing WPANs through the 802.15 Architecture

Wireless personal area networks (WPANs) are networks that occupy the space surrounding an individual or device, typically involving a 10m radius. This is referred to as a personal operating space (POS). This type of network adheres to an ad-hoc system requiring little configuration. The devices in a WPAN find each other and communicate with little effort by the end user.

WPANs generally fall under the watchful eyes of the IEEE 802.15 working group (technically, 802.15 networks are defined as *short-distance wireless networks*). The growing trend toward more "smart" devices in the home and the increasing number of telecommuters and small office/home office (SOHO) users is driving the demand for this section of the wireless industry. Another driving requirement for this segment is the need for simplistic configuration of such a network. As this segment grows, the end users involved are not the technically elite, early technology adopters, but the average consumer. The success of this segment is rooted in its ability to simplify its use while maintaining lower costs. In addition, various efforts are under way to converge the 802.11 and 802.15 standards for interoperability and the reduction of interference in the 2.4 GHz space. Since this is the same unlicensed range shared by numerous wireless devices such as garage door openers, baby monitors, and cordless phones, 802.15 devices must be able to coexist. They fall under two categories. The first is the collaborative model where both standards not only will coexist with interference mitigated, but also will interoperate. The second is the noncollaborative model, where the interference is mitigated but the two standards do not interoperate.

Bluetooth

Bluetooth technology was named after Harold Blaatand (Bluetoothe) II, who was the King of Denmark from 940–981 and was generally considered a "unifying figurehead" in Europe during that period. The unification of Europe and the unification of PDAs and computing devices is the parallelism that the founders of this technology sought to create when they chose the name *Bluetooth*. Bluetooth began in 1994 when Ericsson was looking for inexpensive radio interfaces between cell phones and accessories such as PDAs. In 1998, Ericsson, IBM, Intel, Nokia, and Toshiba formed the Bluetooth Special Interest Group (SIG) and expanded to over 1000 members by 1999, including Microsoft. However, the Bluetooth technology is currently behind schedule and the projected cost of $5 per transceiver is not being realized. This combined with the expansion and success of the 802.11 standard may threaten the survivability of this technology.

Bluetooth is primarily a cable replacement WPAN technology that operates in the 2.4 GHz range using FHSS. One of the main drivers for the success of the Bluetooth technology is the proposition of low-cost implementation and size of the wireless radios. Bluetooth networks are made up of *piconets*, which are loosely fashioned or *ad-hoc* networks. Piconets are made up of one master node and seven simultaneously active slaves or an almost limitless number of virtually attached but not active (standby) nodes. Master nodes communicate with slaves in a hopping pattern determined by a 3-bit Active Member Address (AMA). Parked nodes are addressed with an 8-bit Parked Member Address, (PMA). Up to ten piconets can be colocated and linked into what is called *scatternets*. A node can be both a master in one piconet and a slave in another piconet at the same time, or a slave in both piconets at the same time. The range of a Bluetooth standard piconet is 10 meters, relative to the location of the master. Bluetooth signals pass through walls, people, and furniture, so it is not a line-of-sight technology. The maximum capacity of Bluetooth is 740 Kbps per piconet (actual bit rate) with a raw bit rate of 1 Mbps. Figure 3.11 provides a logical depiction of several piconets linked together as a scatternet.

Since Bluetooth shares the 2.4 GHz frequency range with 802.11b, there is a possibility for interference between the two technologies if a Bluetooth network is within ten meters of an 802.11b network. Bluetooth was designed to be a complementary technology to the 802.11 standard and the IEEE Task Group f (TGf) is chartered with proposing interoperability standards between the two technologies. Bluetooth has also been working with the FCC and FAA to provide safe operation on aircraft and ships. Figure 3.12 gives a broad view of the envisioned uses of Bluetooth as a technology (more information on Bluetooth can be obtained at www.bluetooth.com).

Figure 3.11 Bluetooth Piconet and Scatternet Configuration

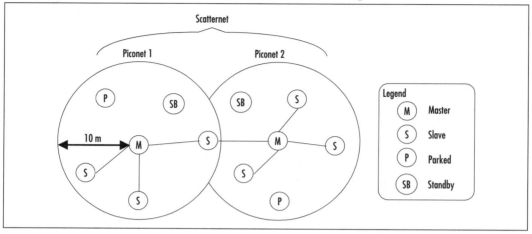

Figure 3.12 Bluetooth Uses

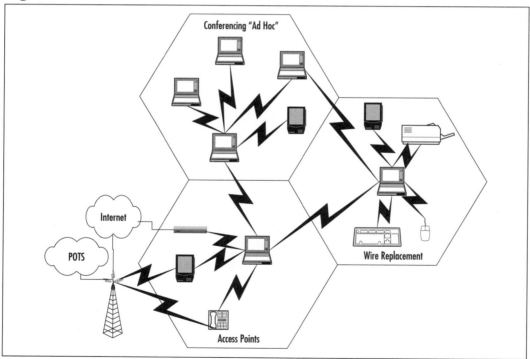

HomeRF

HomeRF is similar to Bluetooth since it operates in the 2.4 GHz spectrum range and provides up to 1.6 Mbps bandwidth with user throughput of about 650 Kb/s. HomeRF has a relative range of about 150 feet as well. Home RF uses FHSS as its physical layer transmission capability. It also can be assembled in an ad hoc architecture or be controlled by a central connection point like Bluetooth. Differences between the two are that HomeRF is targeted solely towards the residential market—the inclusion of the Standard Wireless Access Protocol (SWAP) within HomeRF gives it a capability to handle multimedia applications much more efficiently.

SWAP combines the data beneficial characteristics of 802.11's CSMA-CA with the QoS characteristics of the Digital Enhanced Cordless Telecommunications (DECT) protocol to provide a converged network technology for the home. SWAP 1.0 provides support for four DECT toll quality handsets within a single ad-hoc network. SWAP 1.0 also provides 40-bit encryption at the MAC layer for security purposes.

SWAP 2.0 will extend the bandwidth capabilities to 10 Mbps and provide roaming capabilities for public access. It also provides upward scalability for support of up to eight toll quality voice handsets based on the DECT protocol within the same ad-hoc network. The QOS features are enhanced by the addition of up to eight prioritized streams supporting multimedia applications such as video. SWAP 2.0 extends the security features of SWAP 1.0 to 128 bits encryption. For more information on HomeRF, go to www.homerf.com.

High Performance Radio LAN

High Performance Radio LAN (HiperLAN) is the European equivalent of the 802.11 standard. HiperLAN Type 1 supports 20 Mbps of bandwidth in the 5 GHz range. HiperLAN Type 2 (HiperLAN2) also operates in the 5 GHz range but offers up to 54 Mbps bandwidth. It also offers many more QoS features and thus currently supports many more multimedia applications than its 802.11a counterpart. HiPerLAN2 is also a connection-oriented technology, which, combined with its QoS and bandwidth, gives it applications outside the normal enterprise networks.

Mobile Wireless Technologies

The best way to describe *mobile wireless* is to call it your basic cellular phone service. The cell phone communications industry has migrated along two paths; the United States has generally progressed along the Code Division Multiple Access (CDMA) path, with Europe following the Global System for Mobile Communications (GSM) path. However, both areas' cellular growth has progressed from analog communications to digital technologies, and both continents had an early focus on the voice communication technology known as 1G and 2G (the G stands for *generations*). Emerging technologies are focused on bringing both voice and data as well as video over the handheld phones/devices. The newer technologies are referred to as 2.5G and 3G categorically. A linear description of the evolution of these two technologies is presented in the following sections.

Figure 3.13 illustrates a generic cellular architecture. A geographic area is divided into cells; the adjacent cells always operate on different frequencies to avoid interference—this is referred to as *frequency reuse*. The exact shape of the cells actually vary quite a bit due to several factors, including the topography of the land, the anticipated number of calls in a particular area, the number of man-made objects (such as the buildings in a downtown area), and the traffic patterns of the mobile users. This maximizes the number of mobile users.

Figure 3.13 Basic Cell Architecture

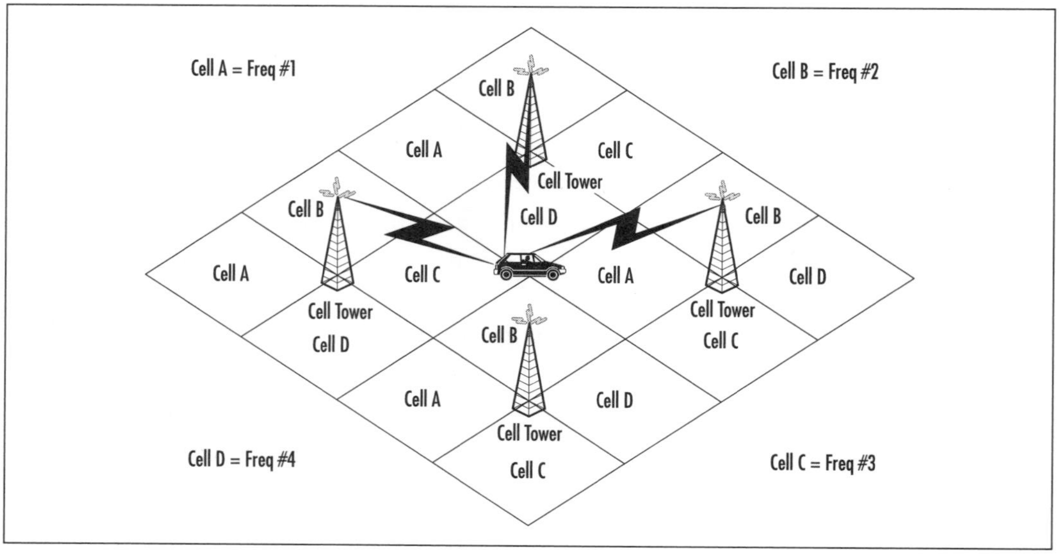

A lower powered antenna is placed at a strategic place, but it is not in the center of the cell, as you might think. Instead, the transmitter is located at a common point between adjacent cells. For example, in Figure 3.13, a base station is built at the intersection of cells A, B, C, and D. The tower then uses directional antennas that point inward to each of the adjacent cells. Other transmitters subsequently are placed at other locations through the area. By using the appropriately sized transmitter, frequencies in one particular cell are also used in nearby cells. The key to success is making sure cells using the same frequency cannot be situated right next to each other, which would result in adverse effects. The benefit is that a service provider is able to reuse the frequencies allotted to them continually so long as the system is carefully engineered. By doing so, more simultaneous callers are supported, in turn increasing revenue.

As a cell phone moves through the cells, in a car for example, the cell switching equipment keeps track of the relative strength of signal and performs a handoff when the signal becomes more powerful to an adjacent cell site. If a particular cell becomes too congested, operators have the ability to subdivide cells even further. For example, in a very busy network, the operator may have to subdivide each of the cells shown in Figure 3.12 into an even smaller cluster of cells. Due to the lower powered transmitters, the signals do not radiate as far, and as we mentioned, the frequencies are reused as much as we desire as long as the cells are spaced apart appropriately.

Mobile technology has developed with various protocols associated with each generation. These protocols will be explained in greater detail in the following sections, after we introduce the migration scheme.

First Generation Technologies

The introduction of semiconductor technology and the smaller microprocessors made more sophisticated mobile cellular technology a reality in the late 1970s and early 1980s. The *First Generation* (1G) technologies started the rapid growth of the mobile cellular industry. The most predominant systems are the Advanced Mobile Phone System (AMPS), Total Access Communication System (TACS), and the Nordic Mobile Telephone (NMT) system. However, analog systems didn't provide the signal quality desired for a voice system. These systems provided the foundation for the growth of the industry into the digital systems characterized by 2G.

Second Generation Technologies

The need for better transmission quality and capacity drove the development of the *Second Generation* (2G) systems and brought about the deployment of digital systems in the mobile industry. The U.S. companies like Sprint PCS predominantly gravitated towards the CDMA systems; most of the rest of the world embraced the GSM systems. Dual band mobile phones were created to allow roaming between digital 2G coverage areas through analog 1G areas. The CDMA and GSM 2G technologies are currently incompatible. The globalization of the world economy and the market for mobile data capabilities fueled the development of the 2.5G and 3G technologies. Both provide a migration path towards convergence of the two standards (GSM and CDMA) toward a globally interoperable mobile system. Both 2.5G and 3G also provide a migration path for a fully converged mobile voice/data/video system.

2.5G Technology

With the beginning of convergence came the development of new protocols created to optimize the limited bandwidth of mobile systems. The Wireless Access Protocol (WAP) was one of the first specifications for protocols created to meet these challenges by creating more efficient applications for the mobile wireless environment. The General Packet Radio Service (GPRS) was created to provide a packet-switched element (classical data) to the existing GSM voice circuit-switched architecture. In addition, GPRS seeks to increase the relative throughput of the GSM system fourfold, using a permanent IP connection from the handset to the Internet. Enhanced Data Rates for GSM Evolution (EDGE) was created as a further extension to the GSM data rates but is not limited to the time division multiple access (TDMA)-based GSM systems. EDGE's acceptance in the market to date is limited, and as with any technology, may be affected by the low acceptance rate. Many mobile service providers may migrate directly from existing GSM/GPRS systems directly to 3G systems.

Third Generation Technologies

The promise of the *Third Generation* (3G) mobile wireless technologies is the ability to support applications such as full motion video that require much larger amounts of bandwidth. This capability is known as Broadband and generally refers to bandwidths in excess of 1 Mbps. Wideband CDMA and cdma2000 are two versions of systems designed to meet this demand; however, they still are not globally compatible. A global group of standards boards called the Third-Generation Partnership Project (3GPP) has been created to develop a globally compatible 3G standard so the global interoperability of mobile systems can be a reality. The standard this group has developed is named the Universal Mobile Telecommunications System (UMTS). For more information on 3G and UMTS, go to www.umts.com.

Figure 3.14 illustrates the progression of the mobile wireless industry.

Figure 3.14 Mobile Wireless Progression

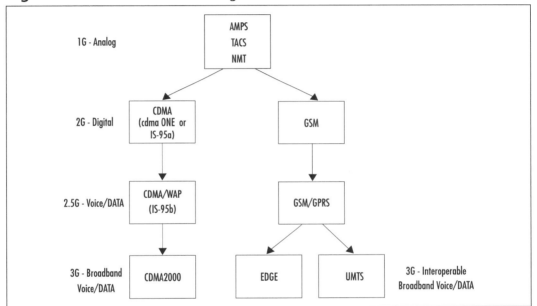

Wireless Application Protocol

The *Wireless Application Protocol* (WAP) has been implemented by many of the carriers today as the specification for wireless content delivery. WAP is an open specification that offers a standard method to access Internet-based content and services from wireless devices such as mobile phones and PDAs. Just like the OSI reference model, WAP is nonproprietary. This means anyone with a WAP-capable device can utilize this specification to access Internet content and services. WAP is also not dependent on the network, meaning that WAP works with current network architectures as well as future ones.

WAP as it is known today is based on the work of several companies that got together in 1997 to research wireless content delivery: Nokia, Ericsson, Phone.com, and Motorola. It was their belief at that time that the success of the wireless Web relied upon such a standard. Today, the WAP Forum consists of a vast number of members including handset manufacturers and software developers.

WAP uses a model of accessing the Internet very similar in nature to the standard desktop PC using Internet Explorer. In WAP, a browser is embedded in the software of the mobile unit. When the mobile device wants to access the Internet, it first needs to access a WAP gateway. This gateway, which is actually a piece of software and not a physical device, optimizes the content for wireless applications. In the desktop model, the browser makes requests from Web servers; it is the same in wireless. The Web servers respond to URLs, just like the desktop model, but the difference is in the formatting of the content. Because Internet-enabled phones have limited bandwidth and processing power, it makes sense to scale down the resource-hungry applications to more manageable ones. This is achieved using the Wireless Markup Language (WML). A WML script is used for client-side intelligence.

Global System for Mobile Communications

The *Global System for Mobile Communications* (GSM) is an international standard for voice and data transmission over a wireless phone. Utilizing three separate components of the GSM network, this type of communication is truly portable. A user can place an identification card called a Subscriber Identity Module (SIM) in the wireless device, and the device will take on the personal configurations and information of that user. This includes telephone number, home system, and billing information. Although the United States has migrated toward the PCS mode of wireless communication, in large part the rest of the world uses GSM.

The architecture used by GSM consists of three main components: a *mobile station*, a *base station subsystem*, and a *network subsystem*. These components work in tandem to allow a user to travel seamlessly without interruption of service, while offering the flexibility of having any device used permanently or temporarily by any user.

The mobile station has two components: mobile equipment and a SIM. The SIM, as mentioned, is a small removable card that contains identification and con-nection information, and the mobile equipment is the GSM wireless device. The SIM is the component within the mobile station that provides the ultimate in mobility. This is achieved because you can insert it into any GSM compatible device and, using the identification information it contains, you can make and receive calls and use other subscribed services. This means that if you travel from one country to another with a SIM, and take the SIM and place it into a rented mobile equipment device, the SIM will provide the subscriber intelligence back to the network via the mobile GSM compatible device. All services to which you have subscribed will continue through this new device, based on the information contained on the SIM. For security and billing purposes, SIM and the terminal each have internationally unique identification numbers for independence and identification on the network. The SIM's identifier is called the International Mobile Subscriber Identity (IMSI). The mobile unit has what is called an International Mobile Equipment Identifier (IMEI). In this way a user's identity is matched with the SIM via the IMSI, and the position of the mobile unit is matched with the IMEI. This offers some security, in that a suspected stolen SIM card can be identified and flagged within a database for services to be stopped and to prevent charges by unauthorized individuals.

The base station subsystem, like the mobile station, also has two components: the base transceiver station and the base station controller. The base transceiver station contains the necessary components that define a cell and the protocols associated with the communication to the mobile units. The base station controller is the part of the base station subsystem that manages resources for the transceiver units, as well as the communication with the mobile switching center (MSC). These two components integrate to provide service from the mobile station to the MSC.

The network subsystem is, in effect, the networking component of the mobile communications portion of the GSM network. It acts as a typical class 5 switching central office. It combines the switching services of the core network with added functionality and services as requested by the customer. The main component of this subsystem is the MSC. The MSC coordinates the access to the POTS network, and acts similarly to any other switching node on a POTS network. It has the added ability to support authentication and user registration. It coordinates call hand-off with the Base Station Controller, call routing, as well as coordination with other subscribed services. It utilizes Signaling System 7 (SS7) network architecture to take advantage of the efficient switching methods. There are other components to the network subsystem called *registers*: visitor location register (VLR) and home location register (HLR). Each of these registers handles call routing and services for mobility when a mobile customer is in their local or roaming calling state. The VLR is a database consisting of visitor devices in a given system's area of operation. The HLR is the database of registered users to the home network system.

General Packet Radio Service

General Packet Radio Service (GPRS), also called GSM-IP, sits on top of the GSM networking architecture offering speeds between 56 and 170 Kbps. GPRS describes the bursty packet-type transmissions that will allow users to connect to the Internet from their mobile devices. GPRS is nonvoice. It offers the transport of information across the mobile telephone network. Although the users are always on like many broadband communications methodologies in use today, users pay only for usage. This provides a great deal of flexibility and efficiency. This type of connection, coupled with the nature of packet-switched delivery methods, truly offers efficient uses of network resources along with the speeds consumers are looking for. The data rates offered by GPRS will make it possible for users to partake in streaming video applications and interact with Web sites that offer multimedia, using compatible mobile handheld devices. GPRS is based on Global System for Mobile (GSM) communication and as such will augment existing services such as circuit-switched wireless phone connections and the Short Message Service (SMS).

Short Message Service

Short Message Service (SMS) is a wireless service that allows users to send and receive short (usually 160 characters or less) messages to SMS-compatible phones. SMS, as noted earlier, is integrated with the GSM standard. SMS is used either from a computer by browsing to an SMS site, entering the message and the recipient's number, and clicking **Send**, or directly from a wireless phone.

Optical Wireless Technologies

The third wireless technology we'll cover in this chapter is *optical*, which marries optical spectrum technology with wireless transmissions.

An optical wireless system basically is defined as any system that uses modulated light to transmit information in open space or air using a high-powered beam in the optical spectrum. It is also referred to as *free space optics* (FSO), *open air photonics*, or *infrared broadband*. FSO systems use low-powered infrared lasers and a series of lenses and mirrors (known as a telescope) to direct and focus different wavelengths of light towards an optical receiver/telescope. FSO is a line-of-sight technology and the only condition affecting its performance besides obstruction is fog, and to a lesser degree, rain. This is due to the visibility requirements of the technology. Fog presents a larger problem than rain because the small dense water particles deflect the light waves much more than rain does. The technology communicates bi-directionally (that is, it is full duplex) and does not require spectrum licensing. Figure 3.15 represents a common FSO implementation between buildings within a close proximity, which is generally within 1000 feet, depending on visibility conditions and reliability requirements. Some FSO vendors claim data rates in the 10Mbps to 155Mbps range with a maximum distance of 3.75 kilometers, as well as systems in the 1.25 Gbps data rate range with a maximum distance of 350 meters. The optical sector is growing in capability at a rapid rate, so expect these data rates and distance limits to continue to increase.

Figure 3.15 Free Space Optical Implementation

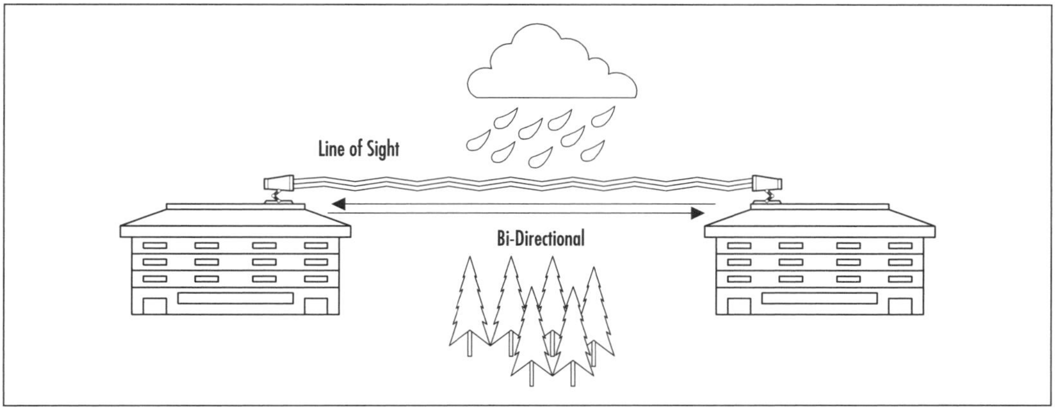

Exploring the Design Process

For years, countless network design and consulting engineers have struggled to streamline the design and implementation process. Millions of dollars are spent defining and developing the steps in the design process in order to make more effective and efficient use of time. Many companies, such as Accenture (www.accenture.com), for example, are hired specifically for the purpose of providing processes.

For the network recipient or end user, the cost of designing the end product or the network can sometimes outweigh the benefit of its use. As a result, it is vital that wireless network designers and implementers pay close attention to the details associated with designing a wireless network in order to avoid costly mistakes and forego undue processes. This section will introduce you to the six phases that a sound design methodology will encompass—conducting a preliminary investigation regarding the changes necessary, performing an analysis of the existing network environment, creating a design, finalizing it, implementing that design, and creating the necessary documentation that will act as a crucial tool as you troubleshoot.

Conducting the Preliminary Investigation

Like a surgeon preparing to perform a major operation, so must the network design engineer take all available precautionary measures to ensure the lifeline of the network. Going into the design process, we must not overlook the network that is already in place. In many cases, the design process will require working with an existing legacy network with preexisting idiosyncrasies or conditions. Moreover, the network most likely will be a traditional 10/100BaseT wired network. For these reasons, the first step, conducting a preliminary investigation of the existing system as well as future needs, is vital to the health and longevity of your network.

In this phase of the design process, the primary objective is to learn as much about the network as necessary in order to understand and uncover the problem or opportunity that exists. What is the impetus for change? Almost inevitably this will require walking through the existing site and asking questions of those within the given environment. Interviewees may range from network support personnel to top-level business executives. However, information gathering may also take the form of confidential questionnaires submitted to the users of the network themselves.

It is in this phase of the process that you'll want to gather floor-plan blueprints, understand anticipated personnel moves, and note scheduled structural remodeling efforts. In essence, you are investigating anything that will help you to identify the *who*, *what*, *when*, *where*, and *why* that has compelled the network recipient to seek a change from the current network and associated application processes.

In this phase, keep in mind that with a wireless network, you're dealing with three-dimensional network design impacts, not just two-dimensional impacts that commonly are associated with wireline networks. So you'll want to pay close attention to the *environment* that you're dealing with.

Performing Analysis of the Existing Environment

Although you've performed the preliminary investigation, oftentimes it is impossible to understand the intricacies of the network in the initial site visit.

Analyzing the existing requirement, the second phase of the process, is a critical phase to understanding the inner workings of the network environment.

The major tasks in this phase are to understand and document all network and system dependencies that exist within the given environment in order to formulate your approach to the problem or opportunity. It's in this phase of the process that you'll begin to outline your planned strategy to counter the problem or exploit the opportunity and assess the feasibility of your approach. Are there critical interdependencies between network elements, security and management systems, or billing and accounting systems? Where are they located physically and how are they interconnected logically?

Although wireless systems primarily deal with the physical and data-link layers (Layers 1 and 2 of the OSI model), remember that, unlike a traditional wired network, access to your wireless network takes place "over the air" between the client PC and the wireless Access Point. The point of entry for a wireless network segment is critical in order to maintain the integrity of the overall network. As a result, you'll want to ensure that users gain access at the appropriate place in your network.

Creating a Preliminary Design

Once you've investigated the network and identified the problem or opportunity that exists, and then established the general approach in the previous phase, it now becomes necessary to create a preliminary design of your network and network processes. All of the information gathering that you have done so far will prove vital to your design.

In this phase of the process, you are actually transferring your approach to paper. Your preliminary design document should restate the problem or opportunity, report any new findings uncovered in the analysis phase, and define your approach to the situation. Beyond this, it is useful to create a network topology map, which identifies the location of the proposed or existing equipment, as well as the user groups to be supported from the network. A good network topology will give the reader a thorough understanding of all physical element locations and their connection types and line speeds, along with physical room or landscape references. A data flow diagram (DFD) can also help explain new process flows and amendments made to the existing network or system processes.

It is not uncommon to disclose associated costs of your proposal at this stage. However, it would be wise to communicate that these are estimated costs only and are subject to change. When you've completed your design, count on explaining your approach before the appropriate decision-makers, for it is at this point that a deeper level of commitment to the design is required from both you and your client.

It is important to note that, with a wireless network environment, terminal or PC mobility should be factored into your design as well as your network costs. Unlike a wired network, users may require network access from multiple locations, or continuous presence on the network between locations. Therefore, additional hardware or software, including PC docking stations, peripherals, or applications software may be required.

Finalizing the Detailed Design

Having completed the preliminary design and received customer feedback and acceptance to proceed, your solution is close to being implemented. However, one last phase in the design process, the detailed design phase, must be performed prior to implementing your design.

In the detailed design phase, all changes referenced in the preliminary design review are taken into account and incorporated into the detailed design accordingly. The objective in this phase is to finalize your approach and capture all supporting software and requisite equipment on the final Bill Of Materials (BOM). It is in this phase that you'll want to ensure that any functional changes made in the preliminary design review do not affect the overall approach to your design. Do the requested number of additional network users overload my planned network capacity? Do the supporting network elements need to be upgraded to support the additional number of users? Is the requested feature or functionality supported through the existing design?

Although wireless networking technology is rapidly being embraced in many different user environments, commercial off-the-shelf (COTS) software is on the heels of wireless deployment and is still in development for broad applications. As a result, you may find limitations, particularly in the consumer environment, as to what can readily be supported from an applications perspective.

Executing the Implementation

Up to this point, it may have felt like an uphill battle; however, once that you've received sign-off approval on your detailed design and associated costs, you are now ready to begin the next phase of the design process—implementing your design. This is where the vitality of your design quickly becomes evident and the value of all your preplanning is realized.

As you might have already suspected, this phase involves installing, configuring, and testing all supporting hardware and software that you have called for in your network design. Although this may be an exhilarating time, where concept enters the realm of reality, it is vital that you manage this transition in an effective and efficient manner. Do not assume that the implementation is always handled by the network design engineer. In fact, in many large-scale implementations, this is rarely the case.

The key in this phase of the process is minimizing impact on the existing network and its users, while maximizing effective installation efforts required by the new network design. However, if your design calls for large-scale implementation efforts or integration with an existing real-time network or critical system process, I would highly recommend that you utilize skilled professionals trained in executing this phase of the project. In doing so, you'll ensure network survivability and reduce the potential for loss in the event of network or systems failure.

There are many good books written specifically on the subject of project management and implementation processes that outline several different approaches to this key phase and may prove useful to you at this point. At a minimum, from a wireless network perspective, you'll want to build and test your wireless infrastructure as an independent and isolated network, whenever possible, prior to integrating this segment with your existing network. This will aid you in isolating problems inherent to your design and will correct the outstanding issue(s) so that you may complete this phase of the process. Similarly, all nodes within the wireless network should be tested independently and added to the wireless network in building-block fashion, so that service characteristics of the wireless network can be monitored and maintained.

Capturing the Documentation

Although the last phase of this process, capturing the documentation, has been reserved for last mention, it is by no means a process to be conducted solely in the final stages of the overall design process. Rather, it is an iterative process that actually is initiated at the onset of the design process. From the preliminary investigation phase to the implementation phase, the network design engineer has captured important details of the existing network and its behavior, along with a hardened view of a new network design and the anomalies that were associated with its deployment.

In this process phase, capturing the documentation, the primary focus is to preserve the vitality and functionality of the network by assembling all relevant network and system information for future reference. Much of the information you've gathered along the way will find its way into either a user's manual, an instructional and training guide, or troubleshooting reference material. Although previous documentation and deliverables may require some modification, much can be gleaned from the history of the network design and implementation process. Moreover, revisiting previous documentation or painstakingly attempting to replicate the problem itself may result in many significant findings.

For these reasons, it is crucial to your success to ensure that the documentation procedures are rigorously adhered to throughout the design and implementation process. Beyond network topology maps and process flow diagrams, strongly consider using wire logs and channel plans wherever possible. Wire logs provide a simple description of the network elements, along with the associated cable types, and entry and exit ports on either a patch panel or junction box. Channel plans outline radio frequency (RF) channel occupancy between wireless Access Points. Trouble logs are also invaluable tools for addressing network issues during troubleshooting exercises. In all cases, the information that you have captured along the way will serve to strengthen your operational support and system administration teams, as well as serve as an accurate reference guide for future network enhancements.

Creating the Design Methodology

There are many ways to create a network design, and each method must be modified for the type of network being created. Earlier, we outlined the necessary phases for a sound design methodology (preliminary investigation, analysis, preliminary design, detailed design, implementation, and documentation). Nevertheless, network types can vary from service provider to enterprise, to security, and so on. As wireless networking becomes more commonplace, new design methodologies tuned specifically for the wireless environment will be created.

Creating the Network Plan

Every good network design begins with a well thought out plan. The *network plan* is the first step in creating a network design. It is where information regarding desired services, number of users, types of applications, and so forth is gathered. This phase is the brainstorming phase during which the initial ideas are put together. The planning stage can be one of the longest segments of a network design, because it is dependent on several factors that can be very time consuming.

However, if each planning step is thoroughly completed, the architecture and design stages move along much more quickly.

Gathering the Requirements

The first and most important step in creating a network plan is to gather the requirements. The requirements will be the basis for formulating the architecture and design. If a requirement is not identified at the beginning of the project, the entire design can miss the intended goal of the network. The requirements include:

- **Business Requirements** A few examples of possible business requirements are budget, time frame for completion, the impact of a network outage, and the desired maintenance window to minimize the negative effects of an outage.

- **Regulatory Issues** Certain types of wireless networks (such as MMDS) require licenses from the FCC. If the wireless network is going to operate outside of the public RF bands, the regulatory issues need to be identified.

- **Service Offerings** This is the primary justification for the design of a new network or migration of an existing network. Simply, these are services or functionality the network will provide to the end users.

- **Service Levels** Committed information rate (CIR) is an example of a service level agreement (SLA). This involves the customer's expectation of what the service provider guarantees to provide.

- **Customer Base** This establishes who the anticipated end users are, and what their anticipated applications and traffic patterns are.

- **Operations, Management, Provisioning, and Administration Requirements** This identifies how the new network will impact the individuals performing these job functions, and whether there will be a need to train these individuals.

- **Technical Requirements** This can vary from a preferred equipment vendor to management system requirements.

- **Additional Information** Any additional information that can affect the outcome of the design.

Once all of the requirements have been collected, it is recommended that a meeting be set up with the client to ensure that no key information is missing. This is important because it not only keeps the client involved, but also allows both the client and network architect to establish and understand the expectations of the other. Once you get client buy-off on the goals and requirements of the network, you can proceed with baselining the existing network.

Baselining the Existing Network

The reason you need to baseline the existing network is to provide an accurate picture of the current network environment. This information will be used later on to identify how the new design will incorporate/interface with the existing network. When conducting the baseline, be sure to include the following considerations:

- Business processes
- Network architecture
- IP addressing
- Network equipment
- Utilization
- Bandwidth
- Growth
- Performance
- Traffic patterns
- Applications
- Site identification/Surveys
- Cost analysis

With proper identification of these items, you will gain a good understanding of both the existing network and get an idea of any potential issues or design constraints. In the case of utilization—that is, *overutilization*—unless kept under a watchful eye, it can contribute to a less-than-optimized network. Therefore, by evaluating the health of the existing network, you can either eliminate or compensate for potential risks of the new network. In addition to monitoring network conditions, it is also a good idea to perform site surveys in this step, to identify any possible problems that are not identified in either the requirements collection or the baseline monitoring.

Analyzing the Competitive Practices

When you compare the client's business and technology plan to the competitors' in the same industry, you can learn what has and hasn't worked and why. Once you have evaluated and understand the industry practices, you can identify what not to do as well. This is a potential opportunity for a network architect to influence the functionality, in terms of services and choice of technology, that will facilitate the desired network. The primary reason the architect is involved is because of his or her knowledge of the technology—not only how it works, but also how it is evolving.

Beginning the Operations Planning

The operations systems support daily activities of telecommunications infrastructures. The purpose of this step is to identify all of the elements required for the operations system. Depending on the needs of the client, any or all of the following processes need to be identified:

- Pre-order
- Order management
- Provisioning
- Billing
- Maintenance
- Repair
- Customer care

If your client is not planning on offering any services with the new design, then this step can be skipped. Once the operations planning step is complete, you can move on to the *gap analysis*.

Performing a Gap Analysis

The *gap analysis* will be a comparison of the existing network to the future requirements. The information obtained through the gathering of requirements and baselining of the current network provide the data needed to develop a gap analysis. The gap analysis is a method of developing a plan to improve the existing network, and integrate the new requirements. The documented result should include the following items:

- Baseline
- Future requirements
- Gap analysis
- Alternative technology options
- Plan of action

Once the client reviews and accepts the requirements' definition document and gap analysis, the time frame required to complete the project becomes more evident. At this point, the client should have a good understanding of what the current network entails and what it will take to evolve into their future network. Once this step is complete, the next task is to create a *technology plan*.

Creating a Technology Plan

This step involves identifying the technology that will enable the business goals to be accomplished. There can be several different technology plans—a primary plan and any number of alternatives. The alternative plans can be in anticipation of constraints not uncovered yet, such as budget. Being able to provide alternatives allows the client some options; it provides them with a choice regarding the direction of their network and the particular features that are of top priority. Oftentimes, until a plan is devised and on paper, the "big picture" (the process from ideas to a functioning network) can be somewhat difficult to realize fully.

The *technology plan* should identify what types of equipment, transport, protocols, and so on will be used in the network. Make sure that the plan has both a short-term focus (usually up to a year), and a long-term outlook (typically a 3 to 5 year plan). Creating a good technology plan requires that you understand the existing technology, migration paths, and future technology plans. There are several steps you can take when creating a technology plan. Some of the more important steps include:

- Business assessment
- Future requirements analysis
- Current network assessment
- Identifying technology trends and options
- Mapping technology to client needs

The technology plan will not contain specific details about how the new network will operate—it will identify the technologies that will enable the network.

Creating an Integration Plan

Whenever a new service, application, network component, or network is added to an existing network, an integration plan needs to be created. The *integration plan* will specify what systems will be integrated, where, and how. The plan should also include details as to what level of testing will be done prior to the integration. Most importantly, the integration plan must include the steps required to complete the integration. This is where the information from the gap analysis is utilized. As you may recall, the gap analysis provides information on what the network is lacking, and the integration plan provides the information on how the gaps will be resolved.

Beginning the Collocation Planning

If the network needs to locate some of its equipment off the premises of the client, collocation agreements will need to be made. Specifically with wireless networks, if you plan on connecting buildings together and you lease the buildings, you will need to collocate the equipment on the rooftops. Depending on the amount of collocation required, this step can be skipped or it can be a significantly large portion of the plan phase.

Performing a Risk Analysis

It is important to identify any risks that the client could be facing or offering its perspective customers. Once the risks have been identified, you will need to document and present them to the client. The way to identify risks is by relating them to the return they will provide (such as cost savings, increased customer satisfaction, increased revenue, and so on). An easy way to present the various risks is in a matrix form, where you place risk on the horizontal axis and return on the vertical axis. Assign the zero value of the matrix (lower left corner) a low setting for both risk and return, and assign the max value (upper right corner) a high setting. This provides a visual representation of the potential risks. Once the matrix is created, each service can be put in the matrix based on where they fit. An example of this would be providing e-mail service, which would be put in the lower left corner of the matrix (low risk, low return).

This is important because you are empowering the client to make certain decisions based on industry and technological information. For example, if the client is planning on offering a service and is unaware that the service is high risk with low return, the client will need to offset or eliminate the risk. Perhaps the client could offer a service package pairing the high risk, low return with a low risk, high return service. After all, the goal is to help make your client successful. Once the client accepts the risk analysis, the *action plan* can be created.

Creating an Action Plan

Once all of the previous planning steps have been completed, an action plan needs to be created. The *action plan* identifies the recommended "next steps." The recommended next steps can either identify what needs to be done to prepare for the architecture phase (such as a project plan), or what action needs to be taken to clarify/correct any problems encountered during the planning phase. For example, with a situation as indicated in the risk analysis section previously, the action plan may need to provide a solution to a particular risk. Basically, the action plan functions to address any open issues from the information gathering stages. This step is to ensure all of the required information has been obtained in order to provide the best solution for the client. As soon as the action plan is created and approved, the planning deliverables can be prepared.

Preparing the Planning Deliverables

The last step in the plan phase is to gather all information and documentation created throughout the plan and put them into a deliverable document. This is somewhat of a sanity checkpoint, in terms of making the client fully aware of the plans you have devised and what to expect for the remainder of the project. Some of the items to include in the document are:

- Requirements document

- Current environment analysis

- Industry practices analysis

- Operations plan

- Gap analysis

- Technology plan

- Collocation plan

- Risk analysis

- Action plan

Once the planning deliverable document is complete and has been presented to the client, the next phase of the network design can begin.

Developing the Network Architecture

The *network architecture* is also referred to as a *high-level* design. It is a phase where all of the planning information is used to begin a conceptual design of the new network. It does not include specific details to the design, nor does it provide enough information to begin implementation. (This will be explained in greater detail in the following sections.) The architecture phase is responsible for marrying the results of the planning phase with the client's expectations and requirements for the network.

Reviewing and Validating the Planning Phase

The first step in developing a network architecture is to review and validate the results of the planning phase. Once you have thoroughly gone through the results of the planning phase, and you understand and agree to them, you are finished with this step and can move on to creating a high level topology. The reason that this step is included here is that many times teams on large projects will be assembled but the architecture team can consist of people that were *not* in the plan team. This step is to get everyone familiar with what was completed prior to his or her participation.

Creating a High-Level Topology

A *high-level topology* describes the logical architecture of a network. The logical architecture should describe the functions required to implement a network and the relationship between the functions. The logical architecture can be used to describe how different components of the network will interoperate, such as how a network verifies the authentication of users. The high-level topology will not include such granularity as specific hardware, for example; rather, it illustrates the desired functionality of the network. Some of the components to include in the high-level topology are:

- Logical network diagrams
- Functional network diagrams
- Radio frequency topology
- Call/Data flows

- Functional connectivity to resources
- Wireless network topology

Creating a Collocation Architecture

Once the *collocation plan* has been complete, a more detailed architecture needs to be created. The architecture should include information that will be used as part of the requirements package that you give to vendors for bids on locations. Information to include in the requirements includes:

- Power requirements in Watts
- Amperage requirements
- Voltage (both AC and DC) values
- BTU dissipated by the equipment
- Equipment and cabinet quantity and dimensions
- Equipment weight
- Equipment drawings (front, side, top, and back views)
- Environmental requirements

The intention of this type of architecture is to provide information to assist in issuing either a request for information (RFI) or a request for proposal (RFP) to a vendor(s). It is in the best interest of the client to include enough information about the network requirements to evoke an adequate response from the vendor, but not give away information that potentially could be used for competitive intelligence.

Defining the High-Level Services

The services that the client plans on offering their customers will usually help determine what the necessary equipment requirements will be. These services should match up with the services identified in the risk portion of the plan phase. Once the services have been identified, they need to be documented and compared against the risk matrix to determine what services will be offered. The client typically will already have identified the types of services they are interested in providing, but this is an opportunity to double-check the client's intentions. Any services that will not be offered need to be removed from the architecture. Once you have presented the documented services and get the client's service offering list, you can move on to creating a high-level physical design.

Creating a High-Level Physical Design

The *high-level physical design* is the most important step in the architecture phase and is usually the most complicated and time consuming. A lot of work, thought, and intelligence go into this step. It defines the physical location and types of equipment needed throughout the network to accomplish its intended operation. It does not identify specific brands or models of equipment, but rather functional components such as routers, switches, Access Points, etc. The high-level physical design takes the RF topology, for example, completed in the high-level topology step, and converts that to physical equipment locations. Due to the many unknowns with RF engineering, several modifications and redesigns may be necessary before this step is complete. Upon acceptance of the high-level physical design, the operations services needs to be defined.

Defining the Operations Services

The purpose of defining the *operations services* is to identify the functionality required within each operations discipline. Some of the more common operations disciplines include:

- order
- Order management
- Provisioning
- Billing
- Maintenance
- Repair
- Customer care

Once the functionality for each discipline has been defined, documented, and accepted, you are ready to create a high-level operations model.

Creating a High-Level Operating Model

If a network can't be properly maintained once built, then its success and even its life can be in jeopardy. The purpose of creating a *high-level operating model* is to describe how the network will be managed. Certainly a consideration here is how the new network management system will interoperate with the existing management system. Some of the steps that need to be considered when creating a high-level operating model include:

- Leveraging technical abilities to optimize delivery of management information

- Providing an easily managed network that is high quality and easy to troubleshoot

- Identifying all expectations and responsibilities

The high-level operating model will be used later to create a detailed operating model. Once the high-level operating model has been developed and accepted by the client, you can proceed with evaluating the products for the network.

Evaluating the Products

In some cases, the step of evaluating the products can be a very lengthy process. Depending on the functionality required, level of technology maturity, and vendor availability/competition, this can take several months to complete. When evaluating products, it is important to identify the needs of the client and make sure that the products meet all technical requirements. This is where the responses from the RFI/RFP will be evaluated. However, if the project is not of a large scale, it may be the responsibility of the design engineer to research the products available on the market. Once the list of products has been identified, an evaluation needs to be performed to determine which vendor will best fit the client. There are several factors that affect the decision process including:

- Requirement satisfaction

- Cost

- Vendor relationship

- Vendor stability

- Support options

- Interoperability with other devices

- Product availability

- Manufacturing lag time

The result of this step should leave you with each product identified to the model level for the entire network. Once the products have been identified, an action plan can be created.

Creating an Action Plan

The *action plan* will identify what is necessary to move on to the design phase. The action plan's function is to bridge any gaps between the architectural phase and the actual design of the network. Some of the items for which an action plan can be given are:

- Create a project plan for the design phase
- Rectify any problems or issues identified during the architecture phase
- Establish equipment and/or circuit delivery dates

This is another checkpoint in which the network architect/design engineer will verify the progression and development direction of the network with the client. Once the action plan is complete and approved by the client, the network architecture deliverables can be created.

Creating the Network Architecture Deliverable

During this step, all of the documents and information created and collected during the architecture phase will be gathered and put into a single location. There are several different options for the location of the deliverable, such as:

- Master document
- CD-ROM
- Web page

Any and all of the methods listed can be used for creating the architecture deliverable. One thing to include in this step is the deliverables from the plan phase as well. This lets the client reference any of the material up this point. Also, as new documents and deliverables are developed, they should be added. Once the architecture deliverable has been completed and it has been presented to the client, the detailed design phase can begin.

Formalizing the Detailed Design Phase

The *detailed design phase* of the NEM is the last step before implementation begins on the network. This phase builds on the architecture phase and fills in the details of each of the high-level documents. This is the shortest and easiest phase of the design (assuming the plan and architecture phase was completed thoroughly and with accurate information). Basically, the detail design is a compilation of the entire planning process. This is absolutely where the rewards of the prior arduous tasks are fully realized.

Reviewing and Validating the Network Architecture

The first step of a detailed design phase is to review and validate the network architecture. The network architecture is the basis for the design, and there must be a sanity check to ensure that the architecture is on track. This involves making sure all of the functionality is included. As you did at the beginning of the architecture phase, you may be validating work done by other people. Once the network architecture has been validated, you begin the detailed design by creating a detailed topology.

Creating the Detailed Topology

The *detailed topology* builds on the high-level topology, adding information specific to the network topology, such as:

- Devices and device connectivity
- Data/Voice traffic flows and service levels
- Traffic volume
- Traffic engineering
- Number of subscribers
- IP addressing
- Routing topology
- Types of technology
- Location of devices
- Data-link types
- Bandwidth requirements
- Protocols
- Wireless topology

The detailed topology is a functional design, not a physical design. The detailed topology is where client dreams become a reality. By this point the client should be fully aware of what they would like the network to offer, and your job is to make it happen. In addition to the documented results, you should have detailed drawings of the various topologies listed earlier. Once the detailed topology is complete, a detailed collocation design can be created.

Creating a Detailed Service Collocation Design

As with the detailed topology, the detailed service collocation design builds on the collocation architecture. This step will provide the details necessary to install equipment in collocation facilities. Include the following information with the design:

- Network Equipment Building Standards (NEBS) compliance
- Facilities
- Cabling

Once the detailed service collocation design is complete and accepted by the client, it can be presented to the collocation vendor for approval. Once the vendor approves the design, the implementation phase for collocation services can begin.

Creating the Detailed Services

This step will define and document the specific services that the client will offer to its customers. The services offered are a continuation of the services list identified in the high-level services design step. When creating the design, be sure to include information such as timeline for offering. This information will most likely be of interest to the client's marketing department. You can easily understand that in a service provider environment, the customers and the resulting revenue justify the network. Some of the information to provide with each service includes:

- Service definition
  - Service name
  - Description
  - Features and benefits
  - SLAs
- Service management
- Functionality

- Configuration parameters
- Access options
- Third-party equipment requirements
- Service provisioning
- Network engineering
- Customer engineering
- Service options

Not only do you need to provide information regarding when these services will be available, but you should include how they will be offered and how they will interface with the network. Once the detailed services have been created, they can be put to the implementation process.

Creating a Detailed Physical Design

The detailed physical design builds on the high-level physical design. It specifies most of the physical details for the network including:

- Equipment model
- Cabling details
- Rack details
- Environment requirements
- Physical location of devices
- Detailed RF design

The detailed physical design builds on information identified in the following documents:

- High-level physical design
- Detailed topology
- Detailed service collocation
- Product evaluation
- Site survey details

The detailed physical design is a compilation of these items as well as finalized equipment configuration details including IP addressing, naming, RF details, and physical configuration. When you finish this step you should have a detailed physical drawing of the network as well as descriptions of each of the devices.

Creating a Detailed Operations Design

The *detailed operations design* builds on the high-level operations design. The purpose of this step is to specify the detailed design of the support systems that will be implemented to support the network. Some of the results of this step include determining vendor products, identifying technical and support requirements, and determining costs. Major steps in this phase include:

- Develop systems management design
- Develop services design
- Develop functional architecture
- Develop operations physical architecture analysis and design
- Develop data architecture
- Develop OSS network architecture
- Develop computer platform and physical facilities design

The detailed operations design is complete when it is documented and reviewed. After it is complete, the detailed operating model can be designed. Due to the fact that the operations network can be very small (or nonexistent), or that it could be an entirely separate network with its own dedicated staff, the specific details for this step in the design process has been summarized. In large network projects, the operations design can be a completely separate project, consisting of the full NLM process.

Creating a Detailed Operating Model Design

This step is intended to describe the operating model that will optimize the management of the network. The detailed design builds on the high-level operating model. When creating the detailed design you should answer as many of the following questions as possible:

- Which organizations will support what products and services, and how?
- Who is responsible for specific tasks?
- How will the organization be staffed?

- How do the different organizations interact?

- How long will a support person work with an issue before escalating it?

- How will an escalation take place?

- Which procedures will be automated?

- What tools are available to which organization?

- What security changes are required?

Depending on the size of the network, the management network may be integrated in the main network, or it could be its own network. Additionally, the management network might run on the single network administrator's PC (for a very small network), or it could be run in a large Network Operations Center (NOC) staffed 24 hours a day, or anywhere in between. Because of the variations in size and requirements to network management, only a brief description is provided on what needs to be done. On larger networks, often the management design is an entirely separate design project deserving its own NLM attention.

Creating a Training Plan

Depending on the size of the new network and the existing skill set of the staff, the *training plan* can vary greatly. Interviewing existing staff, creating a skills matrix, and comparing the skills matrix to the skills needed to operate the network can help determine training needs. If the client wants to perform the implementation on his or her own, that needs to be considered when reviewing the matrix. Once the training needs have been determined, create a roadmap for each individual, keeping future technologies in mind. Once the roadmaps have been created and the client accepts them, this step is finished.

Developing a Maintenance Plan

This step in the design phase is intended to plan and identify how maintenance and operations will take place once the network is operational. The *maintenance plan* should cover all pieces of the network including operations and management. Also, the plan needs to take the skill set and training needs into consideration. Once a maintenance plan is developed and the client agrees to it, the implementation plan can be developed.

Developing an Implementation Plan

The *high-level implementation plan* should be an overview of the major steps required to implement the design. It should be comprehensive and it should highlight all steps from the design. Things to include in this step should be time-lines, impact on existing network, and cost. The implementation plan and the detailed design documents will be the basis for the next phase: implementing the network design.

Creating the Detailed Design Documents

The *detailed design documents* should be a summarized section of all of the documents from the entire design phase, as well as the architecture and plan deliverables. As with the architecture deliverable, we recommend that you present this information in several forms, including (but not limited to) CD-ROM, a single design document, or a dedicated Web site. Once this step is complete, the design phase of the project is finished. The next step is to move on to the implementation phase and install the new network. The details for the implementation phase are specific to each design.

Now that you have been through a detailed examination of the how and why of network design, let's look at some design principles specific to wireless networking.

Understanding Wireless Network Attributes from a Design Perspective

In traditional short-haul microwave transmission (that is, line-of-sight microwave transmissions operating in the 18 GHz and 23 GHz radio bands), RF design engineers typically are concerned with signal aspects such as fade margins, signal reflections, multipath signals, and so forth. Like an accountant seeking to balance a financial spreadsheet, an RF design engineer normally creates an RF budget table, expressed in decibels (dB), in order to establish a wireless design. Aspects like transmit power and antenna gain are registered in the assets (or plus) column, and free space attenuation, antenna alignment, and atmospheric losses are noted in the liabilities (or minus) column. The goal is to achieve a positive net signal strength adequate to support the wireless path(s) called for in the design.

As we continue to build a holistic view of the design process, it is important to take into account those signal characteristics unique to wireless technologies from several design perspectives. We will explore both sides of the spectrum, so to speak, examining characteristics that are unique and beneficial to implementation—as well as those that make this medium cumbersome and awkward to manage. Equally important is the ability to leverage these attributes and apply them to meet your specific needs. Ultimately, it is from this combined viewpoint of understanding RF signal characteristics as well as exploiting those wireless qualities that we approach this next section.

For the sake of clarity, however, it is worth reiterating that the wireless characteristics described in the following sections are not focused on traditional short-haul licensed microwave technologies. Furthermore, it is not our intent to delve deeply into radio frequency theory or the historical applications of line-of-sight Point-to-Point Microwave. Rather, the purpose at this juncture is to entice you into exploring the possibilities of unlicensed wireless technologies by examining their characteristics from several design perspectives.

Application Support

Interest in wireless LAN technologies has skyrocketed dramatically over the last few years. Whether the increase in popularity stems from the promise of mobility or the inherent ability to enable a network with minimal intrusion, interest in wireless LAN technologies remains high. However, these aspects by themselves do not validate the need to embrace a wireless network—or any other network for that matter. To understand the real cause for adopting a network, wireless or otherwise, we must look to the intrinsic value of the network itself. What is the purpose of the network? How will the network enhance my current processes? Does the overall benefit of the network outweigh all operational, administrative, and maintenance (OAM) costs associated with deploying it?

In our search to find that intersection between cost and benefit, we ultimately come to the realization that it is the applications and services that are supported over the network that bring value to most end users. Except for those truly interested in learning how to install, configure, or support wireless or wireline networks, most users find the value of a given network to be in the applications or services derived from what is on the network. So then, how do unlicensed wireless technologies enhance user applications, and what are some of the associated dependencies that should be considered to support these applications or services?

It is undisputed that one of the key aspects of wireless technology is the inherent capability to enable mobility. Although wireless applications are still largely under development, services that accommodate demands for remote access are emerging rapidly. From *web clipping*, where distilled information requested on behalf of a common user base is posted for individual consumption upon request, to e-mail access and retrieval from remote locations within the network footprint, wireless personal information services are finding their place in our mobile society.

At this point, it should be realized that one wireless application dependency is found in the supporting form factor or device. Speculation is rampant as to what the ultimate "gadget" will look like. Some believe that the ultimate form factor will incorporate data and voice capabilities, all within a single handheld device. There is movement in the marketplace that suggests corporations and service providers are embracing a single device solution. We only need to look at their own cellular phones or newly released products like the Kyocera QCP 6035 that integrate PDA functionality with cellular voice to see this trend taking hold.

On the other hand, technologies like Bluetooth point to, perhaps, a model whereby applications and services are more easily supported by a two-form factor approach. Although still in the early development stage, with a Bluetooth enabled wireless headset communicating to a supporting handheld device or wristwatch, both voice and data communications may be supported without compromising session privacy or ergonomic function. As a result, from an applications perspective, knowing what physical platform will be used to derive or deliver your application or service is an important design consideration.

Power consumption and operating system efficiency are two more attributes that should be considered when planning applications and services over wireless LAN technologies. Many of us are aware of the importance of battery life, whether that battery is housed in a cellular telephone, laptop, or even the TV remote control. However, it should not go without mention that these two factors play a significant role in designing applications and services for wireless networking.

Unlike normal desktop operations, whereby the PC and supporting peripherals have ready access to nearby wall outlets to supply their power budget, developers that seek to exploit the mobile characteristics of wireless LAN are not afforded the same luxury. As a result, power consumption, heat dissipation, and operating system efficiencies are precious commodities within the mobile device that require preservation whenever the opportunity exists. Companies like Transmeta Corporation understand these relationships and their value to the mobile industry, and have been working diligently to exploit the operating system efficiencies of Linux in order to work beyond these constraints. Nevertheless, applications and service developers should take into account these characteristics in order to maintain or preserve service sessions.

Beyond these immediate considerations, the design developer may be limited in terms of what types of services, including supporting operating systems and plug-ins, are readily available. Synchronous- or isochronous-dependent services may prove difficult to support, based on the wireless transport selected. Therefore, take caution as you design your wireless service or application.

Subscriber Relationships

Unlike wired LAN topologies, where physical attachment to the network is evidenced merely by tracing cables to each respective client, physical connectivity in a wireless network is often expressed in decibels (dB) or decibel milliwatts (dBm). Simply put, these are units of measure that indicate signal strength expressed in terms of the signal levels and noise levels of a given radio channel, relative to 1 watt or 1 milliwatt, respectively. This ratio is known as a signal-to-noise (S/N) ratio, or SNR. As a point of reference, for the Orinoco RG1000 gateway, the SNR level expressed as a subjective measure is shown in Figure 3.16.

Figure 3.16 SNR Levels for the Orinoco RG1000

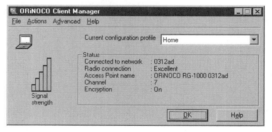

From a wireless design perspective, subscriber relationships are formed, not only on the basis of user authentication and IP addressing, as is common within a wired network, but also on the signal strength of a client and its location, a secure network ID, and corresponding wireless channel characteristics.

Like traditional short-haul microwave technologies, 802.11 direct sequence spread spectrum (DSSS) wireless technology requires frequency diversity between different radios. Simply stated, user groups on separate Access Points within a wireless LAN must be supported on separate and distinct channels within that wireless topology. Similarly, adjacent channel spacing and active channel separation play an important role when planning and deploying a wireless network. These aspects refer to the amount of space between contiguous or active channels used in the wireless network. From a design perspective, the integrity and reliability of the network is best preserved when the channels assigned to Access

Points in the same wireless network are selected from opposite ends of the wireless spectrum whenever possible. Failure to plan in accordance with these attributes most likely will lead to cochannel interference, an RF condition in which channels within the wireless spectrum interfere with one another. In turn, this may cause your service session to lock up, or it may cause severe network failure or total network collapse. Other attributes that depend on subscriber relationships involve network security.

Physical Landscape

Even if adequate channel spacing, sound channel management, and RF design principles are adhered to, other wireless attributes associated with the given environment must be taken into account. As mentioned at the onset of this section, antennas are constructed with certain gain characteristics in order to transmit and receive information. This attribute of the antenna serves to harness wireless information for transmission or reception; through the use of modulation and demodulation techniques, the transmitted signal ultimately is converted into useable information. However, the propensity of antennas to transmit and receive a signal is regulated largely by the obstructions, or lack thereof, between the transmit antenna and the receive antenna.

Make no mistake, although radio-based spread spectrum technologies do not require line-of-sight between the transmitter and corresponding receiver, signal strength is still determined by the angle in which information is received. The following diagnostic screens in Figures 3.17 and 3.18 show impacts to data when the angle of reception from the emitted signal is changed by less than five degrees.

Figure 3.17 Diagnostic

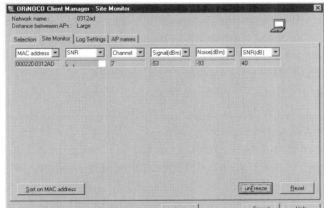

Figure 3.18 Diagnostic

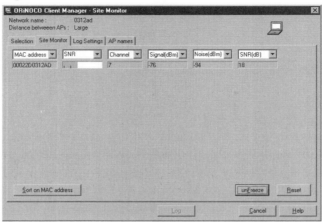

From a physical landscape perspective, we can easily see how physical obstructions may affect signal quality and overall throughput. As such, placement of antennas, angles of reception, antennae gain and distance to the radio should be considered carefully from a design perspective.

Obviously, with each type of antenna, there is an associated cost that is based on the transport characteristics of the wireless network being used. Generally speaking, wireless radios and corresponding antennas that require support for more physical layer interfaces will tend to cost more, due to the additional chipset integration within the system. However, it might also be that the benefit of increased range may outweigh the added expense of integrating more radios to your design.

Beyond the physical environment itself, keep in mind that spectral capacity, or available bits per second (bps), of any given wireless LAN is not unlimited. Couple this thought of the aggregate bandwidth of a wireless transport with the density of the users in a given area, and the attribute of *spatial density* is formed. This particular attribute, spatial density, undoubtedly will be a key wireless attribute to focus on and will grow in importance proportionate to the increase in activity within the wireless industry. The reason for this is very clear. The wireless industry is already experiencing congestion in the 2.4 GHz frequency range. This has resulted in a "flight to quality" in the less congested 5 GHz unlicensed spectrum. Although this frequency range will be able to support more channel capacity and total aggregate bandwidth, designers should be aware that, as demand increases, so too will congestion and bandwidth contention in that spectrum. Because of the spectral and spatial attributes of a wireless LAN, we recommend that no more than 30 users be configured on a supporting radio with a 10BaseT LAN interface. However, up to 50 users may be supported comfortably by a single radio with a 100BaseT LAN connection.

Network Topology

Although *mobility* is one of the key attributes associated with wireless technologies, a second and commonly overlooked attribute of wireless transport is the *ease of access*. Let's take a moment to clarify. Mobility implies the ability of a client on a particular network to maintain a user session while roaming between different environments or different networks. The aspect of roaming obviously lends itself to a multitude of services and applications, many yet to be developed. Is mobility the only valuable attribute of wireless technology?

Consider that market researchers predict that functional use of appliances within the home will change dramatically over the next few years. With the emergence of the World Wide Web, many companies are seizing opportunities to enhance their products and product features using the Internet. Commonly referred to as IP appliances, consumers are already beginning to see glimmers of this movement. From IP-enabled microwave ovens to Internet refrigerators, manufacturers and consumers alike are witnessing this changing paradigm. But how do I connect with my refrigerator? Does the manufacturer expect there to be a phone jack or data outlet behind each appliance? As we delve into the details of the wiring infrastructure of a home network, it becomes apparent that the value of wireless technology enables more than just mobility. It also provides the ease of access to devices without disrupting the physical structure of the home.

Whether these wireless attributes are intended for residential use via HomeRF, or are slated for deployment in a commercial environment using 802.11b, mobility and ease of access are important considerations from a design perspective and have a direct impact on the wireless network topology. From a network aspect, the wireless designer is faced with how the wireless network, in and of itself, should function. As stated earlier in this book, wireless LANs typically operate in either an ad-hoc mode or an infrastructure mode. In an ad-hoc configuration, clients on the network communicate in a peer-to-peer mode without necessarily using an Access Point via the Distributed Coordination Function (DCF) as defined in the 802.11b specification. Alternatively, users may prescribe to the network in a client/server relationship via a supporting Access Point through the Point Coordination Function (PCF) detailed in the 802.11b specification. It should be determined early in the design process how each client should interact with the network. However, beyond a client's immediate environment, additional requirements for roaming or connectivity to a disparate subnetwork in another location may be imposed. It is precisely for these reasons that mobility and wireless access must be factored in from the design perspective early in the design process and mapped against the network topology.

Finally, wireless access should also be viewed more holistically from the physical point of entry where the wireless network integrates with the existing wired infrastructure. As part of your planned network topology, once again, the impacts to the overall network capacity—as well as the physical means of integrating with the existing network—should be considered. The introduction of wireless clients, whether in whole or in part, most likely will impact the existing network infrastructure.

Summary

This chapter provides an overview of differences and purposes of the emerging technologies in the wireless sector. The three primary areas of discussion are *fixed wireless*, *mobile wireless*, and *optical wireless* technology.

We began with a discussion of the fixed wireless technologies that include Multichannel Multipoint Distribution Service (MMDS), Local Multipoint Distribution Service (LMDS), Wireless Local Loop (WLL) technologies, and the Point-to-Point Microwave technology. The primary definition of a fixed wireless technology is that the transmitter and receiver are both in a fixed location. Service providers consider MMDS a complimentary technology to their existing digital subscriber line (DSL) and cable modem offerings; LMDS is similar, but provides very high-speed bandwidth (it is currently limited in range of coverage). Wireless Local Loop refers to a fixed wireless class of technology aimed at providing last mile services normally provided by the local service provider over a wireless medium. Point-to-Point (PTP) Microwave is a line-of-sight technology that can span long distances. Some of the hindrances of these technologies include line of sight, weather, and licensing issues.

In 1997, the Institute of Electrical and Electronics Engineers (IEEE) announced the ratification of the 802.11 standard for wireless local area networks. The 802.11 specification covers the operation of the media access control (MAC) and physical layers; the majority of 802.11 implementations utilize the DSSS method that comprises the physical layer. The introduction of the standard came with 802.11b. Then along came 802.11a, which provides up to five times the bandwidth capacity of 802.11b. Now, accompanying the ever-growing demand for multimedia services is the development of 802.11e.

The 802.11 architecture can be best described as a series of interconnected cells, and consists of the following: the wireless device or station, the Access Point (AP), the wireless medium, the distribution system (DS), the Basic Service Set (BSS), the Extended Service Set (ESS), and station and distribution services. All these working together providing a seamless mesh allows wireless devices the ability to roam around the WLAN looking for all intents and purposes like a wired device.

High Performance Radio LAN (HiperLAN) is the European equivalent of the 802.11 standard. Wireless personal area networks (WPANs) are networks that occupy the space surrounding an individual or device, typically involving a 10m radius. This is referred to as a personal operating space (POS). This type of network adheres to an ad-hoc system requiring little configuration. Various efforts are under way to converge the 802.11 and 802.15 standards for interoperability and the reduction of interference in the 2.4 GHz space.

Bluetooth is primarily a cable replacement WPAN technology that operates in the 2.4 GHz range using FHSS. One of the main drivers for the success of the Bluetooth technology is the proposition of low-cost implementation and size of the wireless radios. HomeRF is similar to Bluetooth but is targeted solely toward the residential market.

The second category of wireless technology covered in the chapter is *mobile wireless*, which is basically your cell phone service. In this section we described the evolution of this technology from the analog voice (1G) to the digital voice (2G) phases. We continued with a discussion of the next generation technologies including the digital voice and limited data phase (2.5G) to the broadband multimedia (3G) phase, which supports high data rate voice, video, and data in a converged environment.

An *optical wireless* system basically is defined as any system that uses modulated light to transmit information in open space or air using a high-powered beam in the optical spectrum. It is also referred to as free space optics (FSO); it has growing capabilities in the infrared arena for bi-directional communication. It does not require licensing.

Designing a wireless network is not an easy task. Many wireless attributes should be considered throughout the design process. In the preliminary stages of your design, it is important to query users in order to accommodate their needs from a design perspective. Keep in mind that with wireless networks, attributes such as mobility and ease of access can impact your network in terms of cost and function.

The architecture phase is responsible for taking the results of the planning phase and marrying them with the business objectives or client goals. The architecture is a high-level conceptual design. At the conclusion of the architecture phase, the client will have documents that provide information such as a high-level topology, a high-level physical design, a high-level operating model, and a collocation architecture.

The design phase takes the architecture and makes it reality. It identifies specific details necessary to implement the new design and is intended to provide all information necessary to create the new network. At the conclusion of the design phase, the design documents provided to the client will include a detailed topology, detailed physical design, detailed operations design, and maintenance plan.

Hopefully this chapter has provided you with enough basic understanding of the emerging wireless technologies to be able to differentiate between them. The information in this chapter affords you the ability to understand which technology is the best solution for your network design. Evaluate the advancements in these technologies and see how they may impact your organization.

Solutions Fast Track

Fixed Wireless Technologies

☑ In a fixed wireless network, both transmitter and receiver are at fixed locations, as opposed to mobile. The network uses utility power (AC). It can be point-to-point or point-to-multipoint, and may use licensed or unlicensed spectrums.

☑ Fixed wireless usually involves line-of-sight technology, which can be a disadvantage.

☑ The *fresnel* zone of a signal is the zone around the signal path that must be clear of reflective surfaces and clear from obstruction, to avoid absorption and reduction of the signal energy. *Multipath reflection* or interference happens when radio signals reflect off surfaces such as water or buildings in the fresnel zone, creating a condition where the same signal arrives at different times.

☑ Fixed wireless includes Wireless Local Loop technologies, Multichannel Multipoint Distribution Service (MMDS) and Local Multipoint Distribution Service (LMDS), and also Point-to-Point Microwave.

Developing WLANs through the 802.11 Architecture

☑ The North American wireless local area network (WLAN) standard is 802.11, set by the Institute of Electrical and Electronics Engineers (IEEE); HiperLAN is the European WLAN standard.

☑ The three physical layer options for 802.11 are infrared (IR) baseband PHY and two radio frequency (RF) PHYs. The RF physical layer is comprised of Frequency Hopping Spread Spectrum (FHSS) and Direct Sequence Spread Spectrum (DSSS) in the 2.4 GHz band.

☑ WLAN technologies are not line-of-sight technologies.

☑ The standard has evolved through various initiatives from 802.11b, to 802.11a, which provides up to five times the bandwidth capacity of 802.11b—now, accompanying the every growing demand for multimedia services is the development of 802.11e.

☑ 802.11b provides 11 Mbps raw data rate in the 2.4 GHz transmission spectrum.

☑ 802.11a provides 25 to 54 Mbps raw data rate in the 5 GHz transmission spectrum.

☑ HiperLAN type 1 provides up to 20 Mbps raw data rate in the 5 GHz transmission spectrum.

☑ HiperLAN type 2 provides up to 54 Mbps raw data rate and QOS in the 5 GHz spectrum.

☑ The IEEE 802.11 standard provides three ways to provide a greater amount of security for the data that travels over the WLAN: use of the 802.11 Service Set Identifier (SSID); authentication by the Access Point (AP) against a list of MAC addresses; use of Wired Equivalent Privacy (WEP) encryption.

Developing WPANs through the 802.15 Architecture

☑ Wireless personal area networks (WPANs) are networks that occupy the space surrounding an individual or device, typically involving a 10m radius. This is referred to as a personal operating space (POS). WPANs relate to the 802.15 standard.

☑ WPANs are characterized by short transmission ranges.

☑ Bluetooth is a WPAN technology that operates in the 2.4 GHz spectrum with a raw bit rate of 1 Mbps at a range of 10 meters. It is not a line-of-sight technology. Bluetooth may interfere with existing 802.11 technologies in that spectrum.

☑ HomeRF is similar to Bluetooth but targeted exclusively at the home market. HomeRF provides up to 10 Mbps raw data rate with SWAP 2.0.

Mobile Wireless Technologies

☑ Mobile wireless technology is basic cell phone technology; it is not a line-of-sight technology. The United States has generally progressed along the Code Division Multiple Access (CDMA) path, with Europe following the Global System for Mobile Communications (GSM) path.

☑ Emerging technologies are known in terms of *generations*: 1G refers to analog transmission of voice; 2G refers to digital transmission of voice; 2.5G refers to digital transmission of voice and limited bandwidth data; 3G refers to digital transmission of multimedia at broadband speeds (voice, video, and data).

☑ The Wireless Application Protocol (WAP) has been implemented by many of the carriers today as the specification for wireless content delivery. WAP is a nonproprietary specification that offers a standard method to access Internet-based content and services from wireless devices such as mobile phones and PDAs.

☑ The Global System for Mobile Communications (GSM) is an international standard for voice and data transmission over a wireless phone. A user can place an identification card called a Subscriber Identity Module (SIM) in the wireless device, and the device will take on the personal configurations and information of that user (telephone number, home system, and billing information).

Optical Wireless Technologies

☑ Optical wireless is a line-of-sight technology in the infrared (optical) portion of the spread spectrum. It is also referred to as free space optics (FSO), open air photonics, or infrared broadband.

☑ Optical wireless data rates and maximum distance capabilities are affected by visibility conditions, and by weather conditions such as fog and rain.

☑ Optical wireless has very high data rates over short distances (1.25 Gbps to 350 meters). Full duplex transmission provides additional bandwidth capabilities. The raw data rate available is up to a 3.75 kilometer distance with 10 Mbps.

☑ There are no interference or licensing issues with optical wireless, and its data rate and distance capabilities are continuously expanding with technology advances.

Exploring the Design Process

☑ The design process consists of six major phases: preliminary investigation, analysis, preliminary design, detailed design, implementation, and documentation.

☑ In the early phases of the design process, the goal is to determine the cause or impetus for change. As a result, you'll want to understand the existing network as well as the applications and processes that the network is supporting.

☑ Because access to your wireless network takes place "over the air" between the client PC and the wireless Access Point, the point of entry for a wireless network segment is critical in order to maintain the integrity of the overall network.

☑ PC mobility should be factored into your design as well as your network costs. Unlike a wired network, users may require network access from multiple locations or continuous presence on the network between locations.

Creating the Design Methodology

☑ The NEM is broken down into several categories and stages; the category presented in this chapter is based on the execution and control category, for a service provider methodology. The execution and control category is broken down into planning, architecture, design, implementation, and operations.

☑ The planning phase contains several steps that are responsible for gathering all information and documenting initial ideas regarding the design. The plan consists mostly of documenting and conducting research about the needs of the client, which produces documents outlining competitive practices, gap analysis, and risk analysis.

☑ The architecture phase is responsible for taking the results of the planning phase and marrying them with the business objectives or client goals. The architecture is a high-level conceptual design. At the conclusion of the architecture phase, a high-level topology, a high-level physical design, a high-level operating model, and a collocation architecture will be documented for the client.

☑ The design phase takes the architecture and makes it reality. It identifies specific details necessary to implement the new design and is intended to provide all information necessary to create the new network, in the form of a detailed topology, detailed physical design, detailed operations design, and maintenance plan.

Understanding Wireless Network Attributes from a Design Perspective

☑ It is important to take into account signal characteristics unique to wireless technologies from several design perspectives. For example, power consumption and operating system efficiency are two attributes that should be considered when planning applications and services over wireless LAN technologies.

☑ Spatial density is a key wireless attribute to focus on when planning your network due to network congestion and bandwidth contention.

Frequently Asked Questions

The following Frequently Asked Questions, answered by the authors of this book, are designed to both measure your understanding of the concepts presented in this chapter and to assist you with real-life implementation of these concepts. To have your questions about this chapter answered by the author, browse to **www.syngress.com/solutions** and click on the **"Ask the Author"** form.

Q: What does the G stand for in 1G, 2G, 2.5G, and 3G mobile wireless technologies?

A: It stands for *generation* and the use of it implies the evolutionary process that mobile wireless is going through.

Q: What are the primary reasons that service providers use a Wireless Local Loop (WLL)?

A: The primary reasons are speed of deployment, deployment where wireline technologies are not practical, and finally, for the avoidance of the local exchange carrier's network and assets.

Q: Why is digital transmission better than analog in mobile wireless technologies?

A: Digital transmissions can be reconstructed and amplified easily, thus making it a cleaner or clearer signal. Analog signals cannot be reconstructed to their original state.

Q: Why does fog and rain affect optical links so much?

A: The tiny water particles act as tiny prisms that fracture the light beam and minimize the power of the signal.

Q: What is the difference between an ad-hoc network and an infrastructure network?

A: Ad-hoc networks are ones where a group of network nodes are brought together dynamically, by an Access Point (AP), for the purpose of communicating with each other. An infrastructure network serves the same purpose but also provides connectivity to infrastructure such as printers and Internet access.

Q: Several customers want me to give them up-front costs for designing and installing a network. When is the most appropriate time to commit to a set price for the job?

A: Try to negotiate service charges based on deliverables associated with each phase of the design process. In doing so, you allow the customer to assess the cost prior to entering into the next phase of the design.

Q: I'm very confused by all the different home network standards. Is there any way that I can track several of the different home networking standards from a single unbiased source?

A: Yes. There are several means of tracking various home network standards and initiatives. For comprehensive reports in the home network industry, I would suggest contacting Parks Associates at www.parksassociates.com. The Continental Automated Buildings Association (CABA) at www.caba.org is another good source for learning about home network technologies from a broad and unbiased perspective.

Q: I am trying to create a design of a wireless campus network and I keep finding out new information, causing me to change all of my work. How can I prevent this?

A: If you have done a thorough job in the planning phase you should already have identified all of the requirements for the project. Once you identify all of the requirements, you need to meet with the client and make sure that nothing was overlooked.

Chapter 4

Common Attacks and Vulnerabilities

Solutions in this chapter:

- The Weaknesses in WEP
- Conducting Reconnaissance
- Sniffing, Interception, and Eavesdropping
- Spoofing and Unauthorized Access
- Network Hijacking and Modification
- Denial of Service and Flooding Attacks
- The Introduction of Malware
- Stealing User Devices

☑ Summary

☑ Solutions Fast Track

☑ Frequently Asked Questions

Introduction

Information Security has often been compared to fighting wildfires—no sooner do you think you have one fire under control than another two pop up behind you. No sooner had vendors implemented standards like 802.11 and Bluetooth than security experts, academics, and hackers exposed a host of vulnerabilities. These vulnerabilities questioned the suitability of the currently available wireless devices as enterprise network solutions, at least without implementing additional security controls (such as firewalls).

And while many of the attacks are similar in nature to attacks on wired networks, it's essential to understand the particular tools and techniques that attackers use to take advantage of the unique way wireless networks are designed, deployed, and maintained.

In this chapter we will explore the attacks that have exposed the vulnerabilities of wireless networks, and in particular the weaknesses inherent in the security standards. Through a detailed examination of these standards we will identify how these weaknesses have lead to the development of new tools and tricks that can be used to exploit your wireless networks. We will look at the emergence and threat of "war driving" technique and how it is usually the first step in an attack on wireless networks.

As we progress through our examination it will become apparent that even with the best protection available, wireless networks can be monitored and accessed with little effort from the attacker. We will even see how simple household devices can render your wireless network useless!

Through the examination of these and other scenarios, we will see just how vulnerable wireless networks are but also offer possible solutions to mitigating this risk.

To properly understand the state of wireless networks, we must start with how 802.11 is defined and deployed. It is only through a solid understanding of the technical specifications that you will be able to clearly see how attackers are able to exploit the weaknesses found within 802.11—specifically, the design and implementation of the Wired Equivalent Privacy (WEP) protocol.

The Weaknesses in WEP

The Institute of Electrical and Electronics Engineers' (IEEE) 802.11 standard was first published in 1999 and describes the Medium Access Control (MAC) and physical layer specifications for wireless local and metropolitan area networks (see www.standards.ieee.org). The IEEE recognized that wireless networks were significantly different from wired networks and due to the nature of the wireless medium there would need to be additional security measures implemented to assure that the basic protections provided by wired networks were available.

The IEEE determined that access and confidentiality control services, along with mechanisms for assuring the integrity of the data transmitted, would be required to provide wireless networks with functionally equivalent security to that which is inherent to wired networks. To protect wireless users from casual eavesdropping and provide the equivalent security just mentioned, the IEEE introduced the *Wired Equivalent Privacy* (WEP) algorithm.

As with many new technologies, there have been significant vulnerabilities identified in the initial design of WEP. Over the last year security experts have utilized the identified vulnerabilities to mount attacks to WEP that have defeated all security objectives WEP set out to achieve: network access control, data confidentiality, and data integrity.

Criticisms of the Overall Design

The IEEE 802.11 standard defines WEP as having the following properties:

- **It is reasonably strong** The security afforded by the algorithm relies on the difficulty of discovering the secret key through a brute force attack. This in turn is related to the length of the secret key and the frequency of changing keys.

- **It is self-synchronizing** WEP is self-synchronizing for each message. This property is critical for a data-link level encryption algorithm, where "best effort" delivery and packet loss rates may be very high.

- **It is efficient** The WEP algorithm is efficient and may be implemented in either hardware or software.

- **It may be exportable** Every effort has been made to design the WEP system operation so as to maximize the chances of approval by the U.S. Department of Commerce for export from the U.S. of products containing a WEP implementation.

- **It is optional** The implementation and use of WEP is an IEEE 802.11 option.

Attempting to support the U.S. export regulations, the IEEE has created a standard that introduces a conflict with the first of these properties, that WEP should be "reasonably strong." In fact the first property even mentions that the security of the algorithm is directly related to the length of the key. Just as was shown in the Netscape Secure Sockets Layer (SSL) Challenge in 1995 (www.cypherspace.org/~adam/ssl), the implementation of a shortened key length such as those defined by U.S. export regulations shortens the time it takes to discover that key though a brute force attack.

Several implementations of WEP provide an extended version that supports larger keys. While many advertise that the extended version provides a 128-bit key, the actual key length available is 104-bit; either one should make a brute force attack on the WEP key virtually impossible for all but the most resourceful of entities. However, as Jesse R. Walker describes in his document "Unsafe at Any Key Size: An Analysis of WEP Encapsulation" from October of 2000 (http://grouper.ieee.org/groups/802/11/Documents/DocumentHolder/0-362.zip), there are several problems with the design of WEP that introduce significant shortcuts, which we will examine below, for determining the secret key used to encrypt the data.

Possibly the most egregious of the principles stated in the standard is the last one, the item that states that WEP itself is *optional* to the implementation. As many people who are users of technology know, when people install new equipment they generally do just enough to make it work and then never touch it again once it is operational. Many of the manufacturers of wireless equipment have, until recently, been shipping their equipment with WEP disabled as the default setting.

The IEEE recognized that allowing WEP and other privacy features to be optional introduced a significant security risk. This was even noted in section 8.2.1 of the WEP introduction, which recommended strongly against utilizing data protection without authentication. If the intent of IEEE was to create a medium that provides similar protections to that found in wired environments, then the utilization of data protection without proper authentication would compromise any wireless network, as anyone could connect to the network just as if they were physically able to connect to a wired network, without having or needing any physical security controls (as if your network had a spare cable run out into the street for anyone driving by to use as they wish). It has been argued by the security community that the option to not use privacy or protected authentication should either not be allowed or should not be the default installation option. These issues, along with other end-user problems we will examine, are causing people and organizations to deploy their wireless networks with these default settings, leaving them wide open for possible misuse by authorized and unauthorized users.

Weaknesses in the Encryption Algorithm

The IEEE 802.11 standard, as well as many manufacturers' implementations, introduces additional vulnerabilities that provide effective shortcuts to the identification of the secret WEP key. The standard identifies in section 8.2.3 that "implementers should consider the contents of higher layer protocol headers and information as it is consistent and introduce the possibility of" collision. The standard then goes on to define the *initialization vector* (IV) as a 24-bit field that, as we will see, will cause significant reuse of the initialization vector leading to the degradation of the RC4 cipher used within WEP to such a point that it is easily attacked.

To understand the ramifications of these issues, we need to examine the way that WEP is utilized to encrypt the data being transmitted. The standard defines the WEP algorithm as "a form of electronic codebook in which a block of plaintext is bit-wise XORed with a pseudorandom key sequence of equal length. The key sequence is generated by the WEP algorithm." The sequence of this algorithm can be found in Figure 4.1.

Figure 4.1 WEP Encipherment Block Diagram

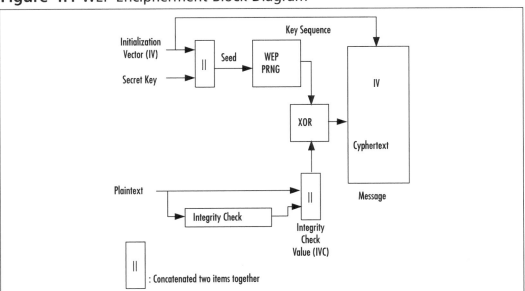

The secret key is concatenated with (linked to) an IV and the resulting seed is input to the pseudorandom number generator (PRNG). The PRNG uses the RC4 stream cipher (created by RSA Inc.) to output a key sequence of pseudo-random octets equal in length to the number of data octets that are to be transmitted. In an attempt to protect against unauthorized data modification, an integrity check algorithm operates on the plaintext message to produce a checksum that is concatenated onto the plain text message to produce the integrity check value (IVC). Encipherment is then accomplished by mathematically combining the IVC and PRNG output through a bit-wise XOR to generate the ciphertext. The IV is concatenated onto the ciphertext and the complete message is transmitted over the radio link.

One well-known problem with stream ciphers is that if any messages are encrypted with the same IV and key, then an attacker is able to use the known and reused IV to reveal information about the plaintext message. One such attack is where two encrypted messages are bit-wise XORed together. If the separate ciphertext messages use the same IV and secret key, the process of XORing the messages effectively cancels out the key stream and results in the XOR of the two original plaintexts. If the plaintext of one of the messages is known then the plaintext of the other message could be easily obtained from the result of this operation.

If the data encrypted with the stream cipher has enough items encrypted with the same IV, the problem of attacking the secret key becomes easier. The reuse of the same keystream introduces what is known as *depth* to the analysis. Frequency analysis, dragging cribs, and other classical techniques provide methods to utilize an increased keystream reuse depth to solve the computation of plaintext from encrypted messages.

In September of 1995, Andrew Roos of Vironix Software Laboratories in Westville, South Africa published a paper on the sci.crypt Usenet newsgroup titled "A Class of Weak Keys in the RC4 Stream Cipher" (www.dmzs.com/~dmz/WeakKeys.txt). Through Roos' work it was shown that the state table used to generate RC4 keys is not properly initialized. This raised the possibility that some of the initial 256 bytes of data produced by RC4 would be less correlated with the key than they should be, which would make it easier to analyze the data encrypted under these keys. David Wegner from the University of California at Berkeley independently came to the same conclusion at about the same time (www.cs.berkeley.edu/~daw/my-posts/my-rc4-weak-keys). In fact, RSA Security has routinely recommended that the implementers of the RC4 cipher either hash or discard the first 256 bytes of data output from the stream.

Stream ciphers are also susceptible to plaintext and chosen ciphertext attacks. An attacker need only send e-mail to an intended target or get the target to visit a known Web site. While this activity may appear innocent, if the attacker is sniffing the target's wireless traffic, they then know both the IV and the plaintext transmitted. A simple calculation of these two items will then produce the secret key that can be used to not only allow the attacker have access to the wireless network, but also allow the attacker to decrypt all future encrypted packets transmitted through the wireless network.

The possibility of these attacks to the IV used in IEEE 802.11 networks were identified early on by the IEEE and independently by Walker. Walker explained that the 24-bit IV appended to the shared key creates a possible keyspace of 2^{24} keys. The basic problem with this available keyspace is that in a standard 802.11 network, a single Access Point running at 11 Mbps can exhaust the entire keyspace within an hour. A larger network with multiple Access Points will exhaust the keyspace at an even faster rate.

To make matters even worse, many implementers of IEEE 802.11 equipment reset their IV every time the device is reset. As most wireless networks are portable devices, it can be concluded that many of these devices will be initialized every day, often first thing in the morning as people begin their day. Having many clients reset their IV to 0 at almost the same time and incremented through the day introduces an increased likelihood that there will be additional IV collisions, allowing for more ciphertext attacks on the data.

At the start of this section, we mentioned that the IEEE standard warned implementers to the possible security problems that could be introduced from the protocols built upon the 802.11 Data-Link layer. Most wireless networks deployed utilize IEEE 802.11 as the Data-Link layer for Transmission Control Protocol /Internet Protocol (TCP/IP) networks. Every packet transmitted now contains an IP datagram that contain large amounts of known plaintext information. The information that can be assumed from each IP datagram allows an attacker to recover a partial key stream for every frame transmitted. Over time an attacker can induce further packet information, and if enough information is gathered then the attacker could possibly calculate the original seed utilized by the RC4 cipher. Utilizing both a TCP datagram inference as well as repeated IV packets significantly decreases the time necessary to determine either future plaintext or the secret key.

The security community has also raised significant questions about the generation of the seed for the PRNG. Having the seed generated by linking the secret key to the IV increases the chances and likelihood of an attacker being able to determine the secret key out of ciphertext attacks. If an attacker is able to attack the encrypted data and infer the IV schedule and details of enough plaintext IP datagrams, then it is possible that they could compute the original secret key value from this data.

In January of 2001, researchers at the University of California at Berkeley independently concluded the same results as Walker and others regarding WEP IV weaknesses (www.isaac.cs.berkeley.edu/isaac/wep-faq.html). They additionally disclosed that the integrity check performed with CRC-32 is not a cryptographically secure authentication code. Cyclic redundancy checks (CRCs) were developed as one of the more advanced methods of ensuring the integrity of data. As we noted in our review of the principle of data integrity from Chapter 2, CRCs were designed to correct for errors within a data stream, not protect against malicious attacks to the data and checksum itself.

The standard defines "the WEP checksum" as "a linear function of the message." The consequence of this property is that it allows for controlled modifications of the ciphertext without disrupting the checksum. Similarly, the RC4 itself is a linear function. As such, the entities that make up the CRC and RC4 terms can be reordered without disrupting the results of the computations. The researchers concluded by noting that an attacker need only know the original ciphertext and desired plaintext difference in order to calculate the desired information, allowing for an attacker to modify a packet with only partial knowledge of its contents.

Researchers from AT&T Laboratories were the first to implement an actual attack on IEEE 802.11 wireless networks using open source software and off-the-shelf equipment. With their implementation it was possible through passive monitoring of a wireless network to recover up to the 128-bit secret key. While they did not release the software they built, it was clearly noted in the document that such software only took them a few hours to create. As a result it was only a short amount of time until the security community was seeing new tools such as AirSnort (http://airsnort.sourceforge.net) and WEPCrack (http://wepcrack.sourceforge.net) released to the world.

Weaknesses in Key Management

The IEEE 802.11 standard specifically outlines that the secret key used by WEP needs to be controlled by an external key management system. At the date of publication the only external management available to users of wireless networks utilizes Remote Authentication Dial-In User Service (RADIUS) authentication, which is generally not in use or available to today's small businesses and home users.

Damage & Defense...

Solutions to Key and User Management Issues

As we saw in our review of authentication principles in Chapter 2, Cisco responded to the lack of solid authentication by creating an authentication scheme based on the Extensible Authentication Protocol (EAP) called EAP-Cisco Wireless or LEAP. This solution provides enterprises that have external RADIUS servers the ability to solve many of the identified attacks to IEEE 802.11.

For those who do not have a RADIUS server, Hewlett-Packard has tested and published a proposed alternative solution to managing WEP secret keys (www.hpl.hp.com/techreports/2001/HPL-2001-227.pdf). Their solution utilizes a modified DHCP server running under Linux. The modified server not only responds to requests for IP numbers, but also uses public-private key encryption to authenticate the user and assign session-based WEP secret keys.

While this is not a commercial package, it appears as if the solutions that will be available to the next generation of wireless networks are being built from a solid understanding of the current weaknesses in both WEP and secret-key management.

The standard additionally defines that there can be up to four secret keys stored in a globally shared array. Each message transmitted contains a key identifier indicating the index of which key was used in the encryption. Changing between these keys on a regular basis would reduce the number of IV collisions, making it more difficult for those wishing to attack your wireless network. However, each time you change your key it is a manual process.

Changing your encryption key with the Lucent ORiNOCO card can be accomplished by bringing up the Client Manager, selecting **Action** and then **Add/Edit Configuration Profile**. Once the Add/Edit Configuration profile dialog box comes up, select the profile you wish to edit and click on **Edit Profile**. The dialog box for Edit Configuration will come up. Click on the **Encryption** tab and you will see the encryption options, as shown in Figure 4.2.

Here you can edit the configuration keys and select the key you wish to utilize to encrypt your packets.

Figure 4.2 Lucent ORiNOCO Encryption Edit Dialog

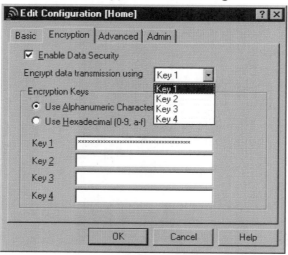

As you can see, this process is quite involved and one might expect many people will rarely change the key they are using—especially home users, once they realize they will have to also define the key for their Access Point (AP) each time as well. In fact, many people who deploy wireless networks for both home and offices tend to just use the default WEP secret key. In many cases this key is standardized in such a way that attackers need only refer to their list of manufactures' defaults once they have identified which equipment you are using (which is provided in the gateway broadcast messages attackers utilize to identify your network).

Within the standard there is another configuration defined that allows for separate keys for each client connection. Utilizing separate keys will significantly reduce the number of IV collisions. This is because the seed used for the PRNG is made up of the concatenation of the secret key and the IV. If the key is unique for each client then the seed is also unique. The attacker would have to attack each client individually, thus making it take significantly longer and requiring additional resources to mount the attack. Not many manufacturers provide this option, and when available it tends to be more expensive and require additional resources (such as RADIUS).

These more advanced solutions, such as LEAP from Cisco, also provide for the external key managed system specified in the standard that provides additional features, such as creating a new session key when the 24-bit IV keyspace is used up. For those who do not have LEAP, they will find that they will generate a significant amount of IV collisions from standard network utilization allowing potential attackers the ability to mount the above-mentioned attacks much easier.

Through our analysis of the WEP algorithm as well as several manufacturers' implementations we have seen that there are significant weaknesses introduced into any implementation of WEP. These weaknesses are due to the way the standard has defined how WEP is to be implemented. No matter what size we expand the secret key to, the problems identified will allow the attacker quick and painless access to any key used.

As there are not many solutions available outside of external additional resources, the only real solution available to people looking to ensure the protection of their wireless resources is to change the deployed secret key on a regular basis and utilize additional security mechanisms such as SSL and strong two-factor authentication.

Weaknesses in User Behavior

Manufacturers today should have learned from more than 30 years of selling high-tech devices that many people do not change default configuration options. One of the largest criticisms of implementations of 802.11 is that the default settings used "out of the box," as well as default encryption settings, are either extremely weak or simple to overcome.

One of the "features" of wireless networks is that they announce themselves to anyone who happens to be listening. This announcement includes their name (secure set identifier [SSID]), equipment type, as well as other significant information that is extremely valuable to the wireless attacker. Many manufacturers ship their devices with this option turned on by default. Some do not have any option to turn it off!

Many users who are fortunate enough to have enabled WEP also tend to either use the default password provided by the equipment, or use simple passwords that in some cases either match the company name or even the SSID or part of the MAC address used in the network! Security professionals have pointed to such weak password practices as one of the most common ways intruders are able to access resources.

While it might seem like a good idea to use the MAC address for your WEP secret key, there are several reasons for not doing so. While the address looks like it is a fairly random and hard-to-guess sequence of numbers and letters, these numbers are actually standardized. In fact, if an attacker knows the manufacturer, he will be able to look up the MAC addresses assigned to that manufacturer (http://standards.ieee.org/regauth/oui/index.shtml). So if you have enabled WEP and utilized your MAC address as the WEP secret key, but not disabled the broadcast or announcement of your network, an attacker should be able to fully identify what you are running and what your possible secret key could be.

Notes from the Underground…

Lucent Gateways Broadcast SSID in Clear on Encrypted Networks

It has been announced (at www.securiteam.com/securitynews/5ZP0I154UG.html) that the Lucent Gateway allows an attacker an easy way to join a closed network.

Lucent has defined an option to configure the wireless network as "closed." This option requires that to associate with the wireless network a client must know and present the SSID of the network. Even if the network is protected by WEP, part of the broadcast messages that the gateway transmits in cleartext includes the SSID. All an attacker need do is sniff the network to acquire the SSID, and they are then able to associate with the network.

If WEP is enabled, they will still need to determine the secret key, but there are several methods of acquiring that information as well.

These easily deduced keys will lead to the development of tools to brute force the secret key—in fact, it is in the development plans for the WEPCrack project. Brute force attacks generally start by examining if the wireless configuration is utilizing one of the manufacturers' default passwords. For example, some 3Com products' default password is "comcomcom," while the Lucent default password is the last five digits of the Network ID (which is broadcast if you have the broadcast feature enabled). In fact the ORiNOCO five-digit key is limited to HEX characters (0-9, a-f), which leaves only 1,118,480 possible combinations that an attacker needs to try in order to find your key (this number is reduced to 1,048,576 possible combinations if only five-character passwords are tested). If the brute force attack uses a little logic, the key should be able to be found in a relatively short amount of time.

Conducting Reconnaissance

In his renowned book *The Art of War*, philosopher and military strategist Sun Tzu counsels on the importance of knowing your enemy. In order to understand the first steps in an attack on a wireless network, it is necessary to understand how an attacker would find, assess, and exploit a target.

Finding a Target

Utilizing new tools created for wireless networks and thousands of existing identification and attack techniques and utilities, attackers of wireless networks have many avenues to your network. The first step to attacking a wireless network involves finding a network to attack. The first popular software to identify wireless networks was NetStumbler (www.netstumbler.org). NetStumbler is a Windows application that listens for information, such as the SSID, being broadcast from APs that have not disabled the broadcast feature. When it finds a network, it notifies the person running the scan and adds it to the list of found networks.

As people began to drive around their towns and cities looking for wireless networks, NetStumbler added features such as pulling coordinates from Global Positioning System (GPS) satellites and plotting that information on mapping software. This method of finding networks is very reminiscent of a way hackers would find computers when they only had modems to communicate. They would run programs designed to search through all possible phone numbers and call each one looking for a modem to answer the call. This type of scan was typically referred to as *war dialing*; driving around looking for wireless networks has come to be known as *war driving*. We'll cover a few sample war drive scenarios in this book.

NetStumbler.org created place that people can upload the output of their war drives for inclusion in a database that can graph the location of wireless networks that have been found (www.netstumbler.org/nation.php). Output of discovered and uploaded wireless networks as of January 2002 can be seen in Figure 4.3.

Similar tools soon became available for Linux and other UNIX-based operating systems which contained many additional utilities hackers use to attack hosts and networks once access is found. A quick search on www.freshmeat.net

or www.packetstormsecurity.com for "802.11" will reveal several network identification tools as well as tools to configure and monitor wireless network connections.

Figure 4.3 Networks Discovered with NetStumbler (as of January 2002)

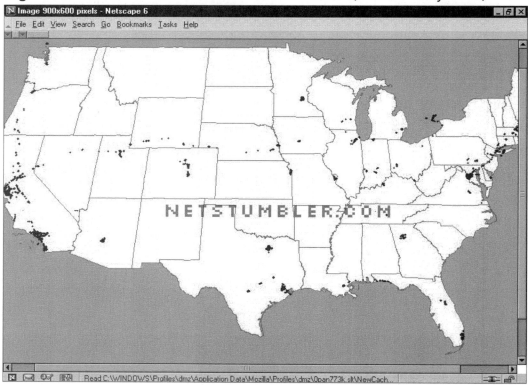

Finding Weaknesses in a Target

If a network is found without encryption enabled, which reports are showing to be more than half of the networks found so far, then the attacker has complete access to any resource the wireless network is connected to. They can scan and attack any machines local to the network, or launch attacks on remote hosts without any fear of reprisal, as the world thinks the attack is coming from the owner of the wireless network.

If the network is found with WEP enabled, then the attacker will need to identify several items to reduce the time it will take to get onto the wireless network. First, utilizing the output of NetStumbler or one of the other network discovery tools, the attacker will identify the SSID, network, MAC address, and any other packets that might be transmitted in cleartext. There is generally vendor information that is received in NetStumbler results, which an attacker can use to determine which default keys to attempt on the wireless network.

If the vendor information has been changed or is unavailable, then there is still the SSID and network name and address that can be used to identify the vendor or owner of the equipment (many people use the same network name as the password, or use the company initials or street address as their password). If the SSID and network name and address has been changed from the default setting, then a final network-based attempt could be to use the MAC address to identify the manufacturer.

If none of these options work, there is still the possibility of a physical review. Many public areas are participating in the wireless revolution. An observant attacker will be able to use physical and wireless identification techniques—physically you will find antennas, APs, and other wireless devices that are easily identified by the manufacturer's casing and logo.

Exploiting Those Weaknesses

A well-configured wireless Access Point will not stop a determined attacker. Even if the network name and SSID are changed and the secret key is manually reconfigured on all workstations on a somewhat regular basis, there are still avenues that the attacker will take to compromise the network.

If there is easy access near to the wireless network such as a parking lot or garage next to the building being attacked, then the only thing an attacker needs is patience and AirSnort or WEPCrack. When these applications have captured enough "weak" packets (IV collisions, for example) they are able to determine the secret key currently in use on the network. Quick tests have shown that an average home network can be cracked in an overnight session. This means that to assure your network protection, you would need to change your WEP key at least two times per day, or keep your eyes open for any vehicles that look suspicious (with an antenna sticking out the window, for instance) parked outside your home or business for hours or days at a time.

If none of these network tools help in determining which default configurations to try, then the next step is to scan the traffic for any cleartext information that might be available. As we saw earlier there are some manufacturers, such as Lucent, that have been known to broadcast the SSID in cleartext even when WEP and closed network options are enabled. Using tools such as Ethereal (www.ethereal.com) and TCPDump (www.tcpdump.org) allow the attacker to sniff traffic and analyze it for any cleartext hints they may find.

As a last option, the attacker will go directly after your equipment or install their own. The number of laptops or accessories stolen from travelers is rising each year. At one time these thefts were perpetrated by criminals simply looking to sell the equipment, but as criminals become more savvy, they are also after the information contained within the machines. Once you have access to the equipment, you are able to determine what valid MAC addresses can access the network, what the network SSID is, and what secret keys are to be used.

An attacker does not need to become a burglar in order to acquire this information. A skilled attacker will utilize new and specially designed malware and network tricks to determine the information needed to access your wireless network. It would only take a well-scripted Visual Basic script that could arrive in e-mail (targeted spam) or through an infected Web site to extract the information from the user's machine and upload it to the attacker.

With the size of computers so small today (note the products at www.mynix.com/espace/index.html and www.citydesk.pt/produto_ezgo.htm) it wouldn't take much for the attacker to simply create a small Access Point of their own that could be attached to your building or office and look just like another telephone box. Such a device, if placed properly, will attract much less attention than someone camping in a car or van in your parking lot.

Sniffing, Interception, and Eavesdropping

Originally conceived as a legitimate network and traffic analysis tool, sniffing remains one of the most effective techniques in attacking a wireless network, whether it's to map the network as part of a target reconnaissance, to grab passwords, or to capture unencrypted data.

Defining Sniffing

Sniffing is the electronic form of eavesdropping on the communications that computers have across networks. In the original networks deployed, the equipment tying machines together allowed every machine on the network to see the traffic of others. These repeaters and hubs, while very successful for getting machines connected, allowed an attacker easy access to all traffic on the network by only needing to connect to one point to see the entire network's traffic.

Wireless networks function very similar to the original repeaters and hubs. Every communication across the wireless network is viewable to anyone who happens to be listening to the network. In fact the person listening does not even need to be associated with the network to sniff!

Sample Sniffing Tools

The hacker has many tools available to attack and monitor your wireless network. A few of these tools are Ethereal and AiroPeek (www.wildpackets.com/products/airopeek) in Windows, and TCPDump or ngrep (http://ngrep.sourceforg.net) within a UNIX or Linux environment. These tools work well for sniffing both wired and wireless networks.

All of the above software packages function by putting your network card in what is called *promiscuous mode*. When in this mode, every packet that goes past the interface is captured and displayed within the application window. If the attacker is able to acquire your WEP password, then they can utilize features within AiroPeek and Ethereal to decrypt either live or post-capture data.

Sniffing Case Scenario

By running NetStumbler, the hacker will be able to find possible targets. As shown in Figure 4.4, we have found several networks that we could attack.

Figure 4.4 Discovering Wireless LANS with NetStumbler

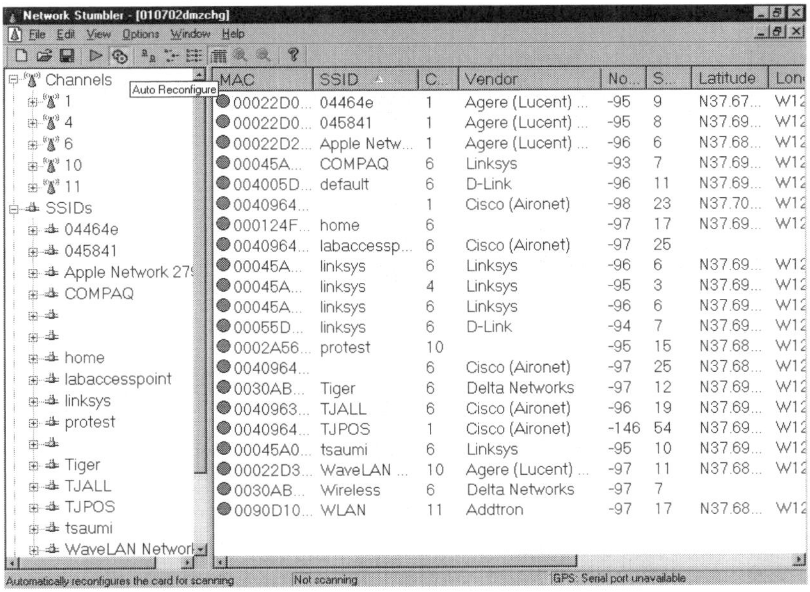

Once the hacker has found possible networks to attack, one of the first tasks is to identify who the target is. Many organizations are "nice" enough to include their name or address in the network name. For those that do not display that information there is a lot we can gather from their traffic that allows us to determine who they could be.

Utilizing any of the mentioned network sniffing tools, the unencrypted network is easily monitored. Figure 4.5 shows our network sniff of the traffic on the wireless network. From this we are able to determine who their Domain Name System (DNS) server is, and what default search domain and default Web home page they are accessing. With this information, it is easy to identify who the target is and determine if they are worth attacking.

Figure 4.5 Sniffing with Ethereal

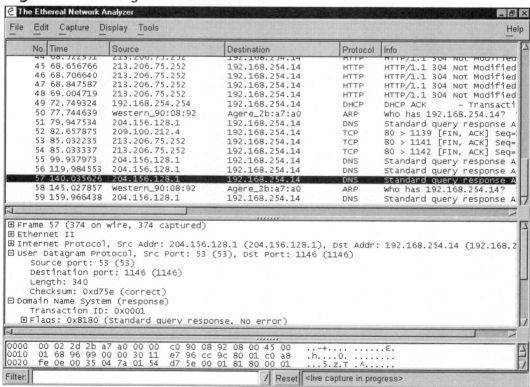

If the network is encrypted, then the first place to start is locating the physical location of the target. NetStumbler has the ability to display the signal strength of the networks you have discovered. This can be seen in Figure 4.6.

Utilizing this information, the attacker need just drive around and look for where the signal strength increases and decreases to determine the home of the wireless network.

Figure 4.6 Using Signal Strength to Find Wireless Networks

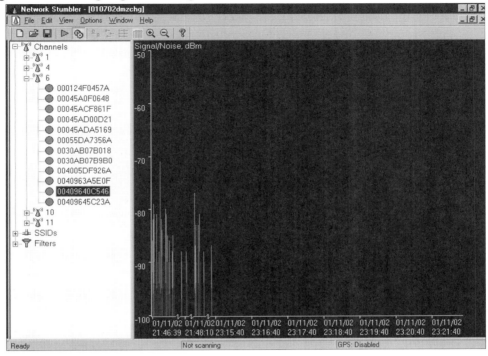

To enhance the ability to triangulate the position of the wireless network, the attacker can utilize directional antennas to focus the wireless interface in a specific direction. An excellent source for wireless information, including information on the design of directional antennas is the Bay Area Wireless Users Group (www.bawug.org).

Protecting Against Sniffing and Eavesdropping

One protection available to wired networks was the upgrade from repeaters and hubs to a switched environment. These switches would send only the traffic intended over each individual port, making it difficult (although not impossible) to sniff the entire network's traffic. This is not an option for wireless due to the nature of wireless itself.

The only way to protect your wireless users from attackers who might be sniffing is to utilize encrypted sessions wherever possible: Use SSL for e-mail connections, Secure Shell (SSH) instead of Telnet, and Secure Copy (SCP) instead of File Transfer Protocol (FTP).

To protect your network from being discovered with NetStumbler, be sure to turn off any network identification broadcasts, and if possible, close down your network to any unauthorized users. This will prevent tools such as NetStumbler from finding your network to begin with. However, the knowledgeable attacker will know that just because you are not broadcasting your information does not mean that your network can't be found.

All the attacker need do is utilize one of the network sniffers to monitor for network activity. While not as efficient as NetStumbler, it is still a functional way to discover and monitor networks. Even encrypted networks will show traffic to the sniffer, even if you are not broadcasting who you are. Once they have identified your traffic, the attacker will then be able to utilize the same identification techniques to begin an attack on your network.

Spoofing and Unauthorized Access

The combination of weaknesses in WEP, and the nature of wireless transmission, has highlighted the art of *spoofing* as a real threat to wireless network security. Some well publicized weaknesses in user authentication using WEP have made authentication spoofing just one of an equally well tested number of exploits by attackers.

Defining Spoofing

One definition of spoofing is where an attacker is able to trick your network equipment into thinking that the connection they are coming from is one of the valid and allowed machines from its network. There are several ways to accomplish this, the easiest of which is to simply redefine the MAC address of your wireless or network card to be a valid MAC address. This can be accomplished in Windows through a simple Registry edit, or in UNIX with a simple command from a root shell. Several wireless providers also have an option to define the MAC address for each wireless connection from within the client manager application that is provided with the interface.

There are several reasons that an attacker would spoof your network. If you have closed out your network to only valid interfaces through MAC or IP address filtering, then if they are able to determine a valid MAC or IP address, they could then reprogram their interface with that information, allowing them to connect to your network impersonating a valid machine.

IEEE 802.11 networks introduce a new form of spoofing, authentication spoofing. As described in their paper "Intercepting Mobile Communications: The Insecurities of 802.11," the authors identified a way to utilize weaknesses within WEP and the authentication process to spoof authentication into a closed network. The process of authentication, as defined by IEEE 802.11, is a very simple process. In a shared-key configuration, the AP sends out a 128-byte random string in a cleartext message to the workstation wishing to authenticate. The workstation then encrypts the message with the shared key and returns the encrypted message to the AP. If the message matches what the AP is expecting, then the workstation is authenticated onto the network and access is allowed.

As described in the paper, if an attacker has knowledge of both the original plaintext and ciphertext messages, then it is possible to created a forged encrypted message. By sniffing the wireless network, an attacker is able to accumulate many authentication requests, each of which include the original plaintext message and the returned ciphertext-encrypted reply. From this it is easy for the attacker to identify the keystream used to encrypt the response message. This could then be used to forge an authentication message that the AP will accept as a proper authentication.

Sample Spoofing Tools

The wireless hacker does not need many complex tools to succeed in spoofing a MAC address. In many cases these changes are either features of the wireless devices, or easily changed through a Windows Registry modification or from a simple command line option. Once a valid MAC is identified the attacker need only reconfigure their device to trick the AP into thinking they are a valid user.

The ability to forge authentication onto a wireless network is a complex process. There are no known "off the shelf" packages available that will provide these services. An attacker will need to either have to create their own tool, or take the time to decrypt the secret key using AirSnort or WEPCrack.

Spoofing Case Scenario

Once the hacker has identified the target they are going to attack, the next step is to become part of the wireless network. If your network is set up to only allow valid MAC addresses, then the first step the attacker will need to take is to determine what MAC addresses are valid.

If your network has not enabled encryption, then the attacker need only sniff the traffic to determine what MAC addresses are valid. As you can see in Figure 4.7, changing the MAC address assigned to your workstation's wireless interface is simply accomplished by editing the configuration of the network connection and changing the MAC address to a specifically defined address.

Figure 4.7 Changing MAC Address in Lucent ORiNOCO

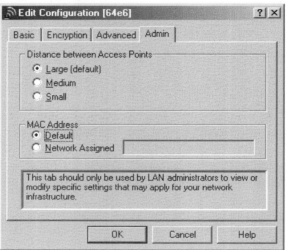

If the attacker is using Windows 2000, and their network card supports reconfiguring the MAC address, then there is another way to reconfigure this information. If your card supports this feature, it can be changed by going to the **Start** menu and selecting **Settings** and then bringing up the Control Panel. Once the Control Panel is up, select **System** option. Once the System Properties dialog box appears, select the **Hardware** tab and choose **Device Manager**. Within the device manager, under the **Network Adaptors**, you should find your interface. If you open the properties to this interface you should have an **Advanced** tab. Many network adaptors allow you to reconfigure the MAC address of the card from this area.

Now that the hacker is utilizing a valid MAC address, they are able to access any resource available from your wireless network. If you have WEP enabled, then the hacker will have to either identify your secret key, or as we will see below, capture the key through malware or stealing the user's notebook.

Protecting Against Spoofing and Unauthorized Attacks

There is little that can be done to prevent these attacks. The best protection involves several additional pieces to the wireless network. Using an external authentication source, such as RADIUS or SecurID, will prevent an unauthorized user from accessing the wireless network and resources it connects with.

If the attacker has reconfigured their machine to use a valid MAC address, then there is little that can be done, except the above-mentioned additional external authentication. The only additional protection that can be provided is if you utilize secure connections for all host services accessed by the network. If SSH and SSL are used, then it is possible to require valid client certificates to access those resources. Even if a hacker were able to access the network, this would keep them from accessing your critical systems.

However, it is worth noting that even with this, and without utilizing either a dynamic firewall or RADIUS WEP authentication, an attacker could be able to get onto your network. Even if you protect your critical systems, they will still have access to all workstations on the network, as well as all networks that are connected to the wireless network. It would then be possible to compromise those resources and from there acquire the valid information they need to access your systems.

Network Hijacking and Modification

There are numerous techniques available for an attacker to "hijack" a wireless network or session. And unlike some attacks, network and security administrators may be unable to tell the difference between the hijacker and a legitimate passenger.

Defining Hijacking

There are many tools available to the network hijacker. These tools are based upon basic implementation issues within almost every network device available today. As TCP/IP packets go through switches, routers, and APs, each device looks at the destination IP address and compares it with the IP addresses it knows to be local to it. If the address is not in the table, then the device hands the packet off to its default gateway.

This table is used to coordinate the IP address with what MAC addresses are local to the device. In many situations this list is a dynamic list that is built up from traffic that is passing through the device and through Address Resolution

Protocol (ARP) notifications from new devices joining the network. There is no authentication or verification that the request that is received by the device is valid. So a malicious user is able to send messages to routing devices and APs stating that their MAC address is associated with a known IP address. From then on, all traffic that goes through that router destined for the hijacked IP address will be handed off to the hacker's machine.

If the attacker spoofs as the default gateway or a specific host on the network, then all machines trying to get to the network or the spoofed machine will connect to the attacker's machine instead of where they had intended. If the attacker is clever, then they will only use this to identify passwords and other necessary information and route the rest of the traffic to the intended recipient. This way the end user has no idea that this "man-in-the-middle" has intercepted their communications and compromised their passwords and information.

Another clever attack that is possible is through the use of rogue APs. If the attacker is able to put together an AP with enough strength, then it is possible that the end users may not be able to tell which AP is the real one to use. In fact most will not even know that another is available. Using this, the attacker is able to receive authentication requests and information from the end workstation regarding the secret key and where they are attempting to connect.

These rogue APs can also be used to attempt to break into more tightly configured wireless APs. Utilizing tools such as AirSnort and WEPCrack requires a large amount of data to be able to decrypt the secret key. A hacker sitting in a car in front of your house or office is easily identified, and will generally not have enough time to finish acquiring enough information to break the key. However, if they install a tiny machine that is able to be easily hidden, then this machine could sit there long enough to break the key and possibly act as an external AP into the wireless network it has hacked.

Sample Hijacking Tools

Attackers who wish to spoof more than their MAC address have several tools available to them. Most of the tools available are for use under a UNIX environment and can be found through a simple search for "ARP Spoof" at http://packetstormsecurity.com. With these tools, the hacker can easily trick all machines on your wireless network into thinking that the hacker's machine is another machine. Through simple sniffing on the network, an attacker can determine which machines are in high use by the workstations on the network. If they then spoof themselves as one of these machines, then they could possibly intercept much of the legitimate traffic on the network.

AirSnort and WEPCrack are freely available. And while it would take additional resources to build a rogue AP, these tools will run from any Linux machine.

Hijacking Case Scenario

Now that we have identified the network to be attacked, and spoofed our MAC address to become a valid member of the network, it is possible to gain further information that is not available through simple sniffing. If the network being attacked is using Secure Shell (SSH) to access their hosts, then it might be easier to just steal a password than attempt to break into the host using any exploit that might be available.

By just ARP spoofing their connection with the AP to be that of the host they are wishing to steal the passwords from, all wireless users who are attempting to SSH into the host will then connect to the rogue machine. When they attempt to sign on with their password, the attacker is then able to, first, receive their password, and second, pass on the connection to the real end destination. If the attacker does not do the second step, then it will increase the likelihood that their attack will be noticed as users will begin to complain that they are unable to connect to the host.

Protection against Network Hijacking and Modification

There are several tools that can be used to protect your network from IP spoofing with invalid ARP requests. These tools, such as ArpWatch, will notify an administrator when ARP requests are seen, allowing the administrator to take appropriate action to determine if there is indeed someone attempting to hack into the network.

Another option is to statically define the MAC/IP address definitions. This will prevent the attacker from being able to redefine this information. However, due to the management overhead in statically defining all network adaptors' MAC address on every router and AP, this solution is rarely implemented. In fact, many APs do not offer any options to define the ARP table and it would depend upon the switch or firewall you are using to separate your wireless network from your wired network.

There is no way to identify or prevent any attackers from using passive attacks, such as from AirSnort or WEPCrack, to determine the secret key used in an encrypted wireless network. The best protection available is to change the secret key on a regular basis and add additional authentication mechanisms such as RADIUS or dynamic firewalls to restrict access to your wired network once a user has connected to the wireless network. However, if you have not properly secured every wireless workstation, then an attacker need only go after one of the other wireless clients to be able to access the resources available to it.

Denial of Service and Flooding Attacks

The nature of wireless transmission, and especially the use of spread spectrum technology, makes a wireless network especially vulnerable to *denial of service* (DoS) attacks. The equipment needed to launch such an attack is freely available and very affordable. In fact many homes and offices contain equipment necessary to deny service to their wireless network.

Defining DoS and Flooding

A denial of service occurs when an attacker has engaged most of the resources a host or network has available, rendering it unavailable to legitimate users. One of the original DoS attacks is known as a *ping flood*. A ping flood utilizes misconfigured equipment along with bad "features" within TCP/IP to cause a large number of hosts or devices to send an ICMP echo (ping) to a specified target. When the attack occurs it tends to use much of the resources of both the network connection and the host being attacked. This will then make it very difficult for any end users to access the host for normal business purposes.

In a wireless network there are several items that can cause a similar disruption of service. Probably the easiest is through a confliction within the wireless spectrum by different devices attempting to use the same frequency. Many new wireless telephones use the same frequency as 802.11 networks. Through either intentional or unintentional uses of this, a simple telephone call could prevent all wireless users from accessing the network.

Another possible attack would be through a massive amount of invalid (or valid) authentication requests. If the AP is tied up with thousands of spoofed authentication attempts, then any users attempting to authenticate themselves would have major difficulties in acquiring a valid session.

As we saw earlier, the attacker has many tools available to hijack network connections. If a hacker is able to spoof the machines of a wireless network into thinking that the attackers machine is their default gateway, then not only will the attacker be able to intercept all traffic destined to the wired network, but they would also be able to prevent any of the wireless network machines from accessing the wired network. To do this the hacker need only spoof the AP and not forward connections on to the end destination, preventing all wireless users from doing valid wireless activities.

Sample DoS Tools

There is not much that is needed to create a wireless DoS. In fact many users create these situations with the equipment found within their home or office. In a small apartment building you could find several APs as well as many wireless telephones. It would not take much for these users to create many DoS attacks on their own networks as well as on those of their neighbors.

A hacker wishing to DoS a network with a flood of authentication strings will also need to be a well skilled programmer. There are not many tools available to create this type of attack, but as we have seen in the attempts to crack WEP, much of the programming required does not take much effort or time. In fact, a skilled hacker should be able to create such a tool within a few hours. When done, this simple application, when used with standard wireless equipment, could possibly render your wireless network unusable for the duration of the attack.

Creating a hijacked AP DoS will require additional tools that can be found on many security sites. See the section above for a possible starting point to acquiring some of the ARP spoofing tools needed. These tools are not very complex and are available for almost every computing platform available.

DoS and Flooding Case Scenario

Many apartments and older office buildings do not come prewired for the high-tech networks that many people are using today. To add to the problem, if there are many individuals setting up their own wireless networks, without coordinating the installs, then there will be many possible problems that will be difficult to detect.

There are only so many frequencies available to 802.11 networks. In fact once the frequency is chosen, it does not change until someone manually reconfigures it. With these problems it is not hard to imaging the following situation from occurring.

A person goes out and purchases a wireless Access Point and several network cards for his home network. When he gets home to his apartment and configures his network he is extremely happy with how well wireless actually works. Then all of a sudden none of the machines on the wireless network are able to communicate. After waiting on hold for 45 minutes to get though to tech support for the device, the network magically starts working again so he hangs up.

Later that week the same problem occurs, only this time he decides to wait on hold. While waiting he goes onto his porch and begins discussing his frustration with his neighbor. During the conversation his neighbor's kids come out and say that their wireless network is not working.

So they begin to do a few tests (still waiting on hold, of course). First the man's neighbor turns off his AP (which is generally off unless the kids are online, to "protect" their network). Once this is done the wireless network starts working again. Then they turn on the neighbor's AP again and the network stops working again.

At this point, tech support finally answers and he describes what has happened. The tech-support representative has seen this situation several times and informs the user that he will need to change the frequency used in the device to another channel. He explains that what has happened is that the neighbor's network is utilizing the same channel, causing the two networks to conflict. Once he changes the frequency, everything starts working properly.

Protecting Against DoS and Flooding Attacks

There is little that can be done to protect against DoS attacks. In a wireless environment the attacker does not need to even be in the same building or neighborhood. With a good enough antenna, the attacker is able to send these attacks from a great distance away. There is no indication that there is any reason for the disruption.

This is one of the valid times to use NetStumbler in a non-hacking context. By using NetStumbler it is possible to identify any other networks that might be conflicting with your network configuration. However, NetStumbler will not identify other DoS attacks or other equipment that is causing conflicts (such as wireless telephones).

The Introduction of Malware

Despite the downplaying of the risk of viruses and other malware to wireless devices like PDAs, there's little argument that a legitimate wireless device connected to a trusting wireless network makes an ideal delivery vehicle for a variety of malicious code attacks.

Many of the recently published exploits against Windows users are through either rogue worms spreading their way through the Internet or through cleverly created Web sites that pull the information directly from a user's computer.

One of the most known of these types of attacks was through a hack on E-Bay. Through the use of JavaScript, anyone who visited the infected E-Bay auction would disclose their E-Bay password to the holder of the auction without any knowledge that it had happened. There was little that E-Bay could do to prevent this without disabling JavaScript (which they chose to not do as it was widely used by their customers). As a result, people were opening up access to their accounts without any knowledge that it was happening.

Tools & Traps…

Acquiring Lucent WEP Keys from Windows Registry or Linux Configuration

Many wireless configurations store the WEP secret key either in cleartext on the local file system or in weakly encrypted configuration entries, so it would not take much for a good hacker to create an application that targets these keys directly.

The Lucent ORiNOCO cards store this information within the Windows Registry. Many Windows users do not even disable remote Registry editing, so an attacker need only pull the information directly from the machine to acquire the WEP keys needed to gain access to the wireless network.

A tool was created by Cquire.net and released in November of 2001 (www.cqure.net/tools03.html) that takes the secret key as stored in the Registry and decrypts it into a key that can be used by the attacker.

Their example has the Win2k Registry at //HKEY_LOCAL_MACHINE\ SYSTEM\CurrentControlSet\Control\Class\{4D36E972-E325-11CE-BFC1-08002BE10318}\0009\.

This same information can be found in the Win98 Registry at HKEY_LOCAL_MACHINE\System\CurrentControlSet\Services\Class\Net\ 0004\Config04, or any \Net\XX\ device that has \ConfigXX\Encryption and DesiredSSID.

Below you will see an example of running the Lucent recovery tool against a key found within my own Windows Registry.

```
D:\>lrc -d "G?TIUEA]dEMAdZV'dec(6*?9:V:,'VF/

    (FR2)6^5*'*8*W6;+GB>,7NA-'ZD-X&G.H2J/

    8>M0(JP0XVS1HbV29.Y3):\3YF_4IRb56"
```

Continued

www.syngress.com

```
Lucent Orinoco Registry Encryption/Decryption

Version 0.2b

Anders Ingeborn, iXsecurity 2001

Decrypted WEP key is: BADPW
```

Windows machines are not the only ones susceptible to this type of attack. Many Linux machines store their secret key in cleartext within a generally world-readable file. On many Linux machines this information can be found in /etc/pcmcia/wireless.opts. The same rogue attack program could easily be modified to attack this file on any Linux machine it finds.

Stealing User Devices

While many security administrators may still consider the theft of a laptop, PDA, or Web phone to be of minimal importance in the war against hackers, hackers consider any Web-enabled device a valuable prize that could reveal vital user identification, authentication, and access information necessary to break into a wireless network.

With these devices now worth more than their replacement value, law enforcement is seeing a rise in the type of device being stolen, as well as a change in who it is stolen from. Recently there was significant press regarding the loss of several notebooks from the Federal Bureau of Investigation (FBI). While it was reported that there was no top-secret information lost, there was doubtless much information contained within the machines that is extremely valuable to the hacker.

If any of these devices contained information on how to access a home network for the individual it was stolen from then it is possible that the perpetrator would be able to access restricted information through the wireless network of the end user. If the notebook contained any PGP keyrings, then it could be possible to utilize the private key of whomever the notebook was stolen from to send forged e-mail, or even decrypt any encrypted messages on the system. This would require that the passphrase of the private key be known, or brute-forced.

Another situation several years ago highlights the risks with stolen equipment. A large manufacturer that provided equipment needed to run extensive network backbones kept a "secured" server in one of its data-centers. This server contained, in encrypted form, the information necessary to log on to all equipment deployed for their customers with service contracts.

This data-center was raided by armed individuals that were able to overpower the guard (most guards in data-centers are there to watch for inappropriate activity, not stop an armed assault on the facility) and gain access to the machines in the center. They then removed the one "secure" server and left the center.

The manufacturer later informed their users that this situation had occurred, but to comfort them also noted that the information necessary to access the maintained equipment was protected by encryption. It is my belief that as these attackers knew the specific target they were after, they also had additional "insider information" and were not stopped by the encryption protecting the remote access information.

While this is an extreme case, it clearly highlights the possible threats to any machine that might play an essential part in gaining access to restricted places. Technical criminals know what and whom they are attacking and will stop at nothing to acquire all that is needed to gain access—especially in a wireless environment, where armed assault is not necessary, since a clever IT pickpocket should be able to gather the equipment from the intended target with minimal troubles.

Summary

Through a careful examination of the design of WEP we have identified signifi-cant weaknesses in the algorithm. These weaknesses, along with implementation flaws, have lead to the creation of many new tools that can be used to attack wireless networks. These tools allow for the attacker to identify a wireless net-work through *war driving* and then crack the secret key by passively listening to the encrypted transmissions. Once they have access to the secret key, only those that have deployed additional security measures will have some additional protec-tion for the rest of their infrastructure.

Even if you have a incident response plan and procedure defined in your security standards, if an attack is not known to be happening, then there is little that can be done to mitigate or rectify the intrusion. The entire discovery and WEP-cracking process is passive and undetectable. It is only at the point of attacking other wireless hosts or spoofing their attacking machine as a valid host that the attack becomes noticeable. However, many installations do not imple-ment system logging nor have standards and practices requiring monitoring of those logs for inappropriate activity.

None of these actions will provide protection against one of the oldest attacks known—theft. There is little that can be done to protect your resources if critical information, such as network passwords and access definitions, can be acquired by only gaining access to notebooks or backups. High-tech criminals are creating custom malware that can access this information through spam or disguised Web sites.

While wireless networks are making computing easier and more accessible, understanding the design and implementation weaknesses in 802.11 will help you in preventing attacks. And at times when attacks are unavoidable, by knowing how and where the attackers will come, you may be able to identify when they are attempting to gain access and respond as defined in your standards and inci-dent response practices.

Solutions Fast Track

The Weaknesses in WEP

☑   Wired Equivalent Privacy (WEP) is only optional for implementers of 802.11 equipment.

☑ The design of WEP initialization vector (IV) is weak and allows for identification of secret keys.

☑ Many implementers of WEP reset the IV each time the machine cycles, allowing for easier identification of secret key

☑ IEEE knew early on in the development of 802.11 that there was a weakness in the IV used in WEP.

☑ Cyclic redundancy checks (CRCs) used to "protect" data only ensure that data was transmitted properly. Clever attackers are able to modify packets and still have valid CRCs.

☑ RC4, used as the stream cipher in WEP, has weak keys in the first 256 bytes of data. No implementations correct for this flaw.

☑ The seed used for WEP is simply the combination of the secret key and IV, and the IV is broadcast in cleartext, making it easier for attackers to deduce the secret key used in encryption.

☑ WEP either supports no keys or a shared key management system. Any stronger key management system need to be deployed by the consumer and very few products support external key management systems.

Conducting Reconnaissance

☑ The first popular software to identify wireless networks was NetStumbler.

☑ NetStumbler discovered wireless Access Points (APs) set up to broadcast network information to anyone listening.

☑ The APs broadcast information includes much information that can often be used to deduce the WEP key if encryption is activated.

☑ More than 50 percent of these networks have been identified as being non-encrypted.

☑ If the WEP key is not the system default. or is easily deduced from the secure set identifier (SSID) or the network name, several programs exist to exploit the weaknesses within WEP to identify the secret key.

☑ An attacker can send e-mail or other messages to the wireless networks through their wired/Internet connection to introduce additional known plaintext, making it easier to deduce the secret key.

☑ An attacker can either sit outside the wireless network or install remote APs using the small computers available today.

☑ High-tech attackers can use malware to gain access to secret key or other authentication information stored on users' machines.

Sniffing, Interception, and Eavesdropping

☑ Electronic eavesdropping, or *sniffing*, is passive and undetectable to intrusion detection devices.

☑ Tools to sniff networks are available for Windows (such as Ethereal and AiroPeek) and UNIX (such as tcpdump and ngrep).

☑ Sniffing traffic allows attackers to identify additional resources that can be compromised.

☑ Even encrypted networks have been shown to disclose vital information in cleartext, such as the network name, that can be received by attackers sniffing the wireless local area network (LAN).

☑ Any authentication information that is broadcast can often be simply replayed to services requiring authentication (NT Domain, WEP Authentication, and so on) to access resources.

☑ The use of virtual private networks, Secure Sockets Layer (SSL), and Secure Shell (SSH) helps protect against wireless interception.

Spoofing and Unauthorized Access

☑ Due to the design of the Transmission Control Protocol/Internet Protocol (TCP/IP), there is little that can be done to prevent Media Access Control/IP (MAC/IP) address spoofing.

☑ Only through static definition of MAC address tables can this type of attack be prevented, however. due to significant overhead in management. this is rarely implemented.

☑ Only through diligent logging and monitoring of those logs can address spoofing attacks be identified.

☑ Wireless network authentication can be easily spoofed by simply replaying another node's authentication back to the AP when attempting to connect to the network.

☑ Many wireless equipment providers allow for end-users to redefine the MAC address within their cards through the configuration utilities that come with the equipment.

☑ External two-factor authentication such as RADIUS or SecurID should be implemented to additionally restrict access requiring strong authentication to access the wireless resources.

Network Hijacking and Modification

☑ Due to the design of TCP/IP, some spoof attacks allow for attackers to hijack or take over network connections established for other resources on the wireless network.

☑ If an attacker hijacks the AP, then all traffic from the wireless network gets routed through the attacker, so they are then able to identify passwords and other information other users are attempting to use on valid network hosts.

☑ Many users are easily susceptible to these man-in-the-middle attacks, often entering their authentication information even after receiving many notifications that SSL or other keys are not what they should be.

☑ Rogue APs can assist the attacker by allowing remote access from wired or wireless networks.

☑ These attacks are often overlooked as just faults in the user's machine, allowing attackers to continue hijacking connections with little fear of being noticed.

Denial of Service and Flooding Attacks

☑ Many wireless networks within a small space can easily cause network disruptions and even denial of service (DoS) for valid network users.

☑ If an attacker hijacks the AP and does not pass traffic on to the proper destination, then all users of the network will be unable to use the network.

☑ Flooding the wireless network with transmissions can also prevent other devices from utilizing the resources, making the wireless network inaccessible to valid network users.

☑ Wireless attackers can utilize strong and directional antennas to attack the wireless network from a great distance.

☑ An attacker who has access to the wired network can flood the wireless AP with more traffic than it can handle, preventing wireless users from accessing the wired network.

☑ Many new wireless products utilize the same wireless frequencies as 802.11 networks. A simple cordless telephone could create a DoS situation for the network more easily than any of the above mentioned techniques.

The Introduction of Malware

☑ Attackers are taking the search for access information directly to end users.

☑ Using exploits in users' systems, custom crafted applications can access Registry or other storage points to gain the WEP key and send it back to the attacker.

☑ New exploits are available every day for all end-user platforms.

☑ Malware attacks are already happening against Internet users.

☑ Even if the information is encrypted, it is often encrypted weakly, allowing for the attacker to quickly pull the cleartext information out.

☑ Keeping your software up to date and knowing where these exploits might come from (Web browser, e-mail, server services running when they shouldn't, and so on) is the only protection available.

Stealing User Devices

☑ Criminals have learned the value of the information contained in electronic devices.

☑ Notebook computers are smaller to run with than a bank vault!

☑ By obtaining just your wireless network card, an attacker would now have access to a valid MAC address used in your wireless network.

☑ When equipment is stolen, end users often do not think that the thief was after the data on the machine; instead they tend to believe that the thief was only after the machine itself.

☑ Your security policy should contain plans for dealing with authentication information stolen along with the theft of a machine.

Frequently Asked Questions

The following Frequently Asked Questions, answered by the authors of this book, are designed to both measure your understanding of the concepts presented in this chapter and to assist you with real-life implementation of these concepts. To have your questions about this chapter answered by the author, browse to **www.syngress.com/solutions** and click on the **"Ask the Author"** form.

Q: How do I prevent an attacker from discovering my wireless network?

A: If your equipment supports disabling network broadcasts, then by doing so your network will not be discovered by NetStumbler. However, if the attacker is simply sniffing on the same frequency as your network, then they will still detect traffic from your network and identify your wireless LAN.

Q: If I have enabled WEP, am I now protected?

A: No. There are tools that can break all WEP keys by simply monitoring the network traffic for generally less than 24 hours.

Q: If an attacker breaks my WEP key, will they be able to access my network?

A: Yes, once your WEP key is broken, then unless you have additional network protection such as RADIUS or VPN restricted access, then the attacker will be able to access anything your wireless network is connected to.

Q: Is there any solution available besides RADIUS to do external user and key management?

A: No, there are plans from manufacturers to identify other ways of doing the user/key management, but to date there is nothing available.

Q: Does an attacker need expensive custom equipment to detect and attack my network?

A: No, the attacker needs only the equipment they will normally use for everyday work: a notebook computer and a wireless network card.

Q: Does an attacker need to have in-depth programming skills to find and attack my network?

A: No, there are several "off-the-shelf" tools available to anyone wishing to detect and compromise wireless networks. Many of these tools are open source and are being expanded to provide additional features by the security and hacker communities.

Q: Can my new wireless telephone really break my wireless network?

A: Yes, many of these devices utilize the same frequency range, and if the base station and APs are near each other they can cause network conflicts.

Q: I've set up my AP to only allow "authorized" MAC addresses. Does this prevent an attacker from connecting to my network?

A: No, the attacker can simply redefine their MAC address to that of a valid one, or steal a valid network card from one of your users and then access the wireless network. If this is a concern, then you should investigate additional authentication methods such as RADIUS.

Chapter 5

Wireless Security Countermeasures

Solutions in this chapter:

Introduction

Securing your wireless networking activities from the hordes of hackers requires a balanced blend of security intelligence, policy adjustments, standards, tactics, technologies, and, yes, user participation. Over-reliance on any one of these ingredients to the exclusion of others increases the risk of creating a vulnerability—which an attacker would be delighted to bring to your attention!

In this chapter, we will look at how you can maximize the features of existing security standards like Wired Equivalent Privacy (WEP). We will also examine the effectiveness of Media Access Control (MAC) and protocol filtering as a way of minimizing opportunity. Lastly, we will look at the security advantages of using virtual private networks (VPNs) on a wireless network, as well as discuss the importance of convincing users of the role they can play as key users of the network.

The original 802.11 standards are woefully inadequate for securing wireless local area networks (WLANs), which are gaining popularity in the home, small office/home offices (SOHOs), enterprises, and public access areas. Although the standards provide a methodology of accessing or extending the LAN wirelessly, and that offers comfort to users in the form of mobility, it leaves devices vulnerable to rudimentary attacks from hackers. This chapter will arm you with the ability to thwart such attacks.

We will show you how to completely protect all areas of the wireless network in sufficient manner so as to minimize the risk, by utilizing some proven methods of protection (like VPN solutions, firewalls, authentication, subnetting, and encryption) along with some new twists. Bear in mind that security—like any other discipline in the IT world—is not static. As technology advances, new gaps will invariably arise and need to be secured. Further, as sophistication of the hackers increases, so too will the need for appropriate placement of countermeasures to mitigate the threats involved. We will explore this information as well.

Although this chapter promises to be quite extensive on content, it is intentionally light in a few areas: You will not find white papers for IP Security (IPSec), Point-to-Point Tunneling Protocol (PPTP), Layer 2 Tunneling Protocol (L2TP), or other VPN technologies. You will not find a description of the cryptographic algorithms, Kerberos authentication, or great detail on the IP stack for IPv4 or IPv6. Each of these plays a part in securing your WLAN, but we are concerned primarily with making sure you take the appropriate steps required to secure it.

There will be a section at the end that covers where to go next. For starters, an Internet search using an engine such as Google.com for "wireless security" (or "wireless insecurity," as it is sometimes called!) will produce a number of links to valuable resources for information. Keep in mind, however, that much of the information and tools necessary for *breaking into* your WLAN is also found on the World Wide Web. In this way, the search will assist you in getting hacking information straight from the horse's mouth, so to speak.

Now that the formalities are out of the way, let's get started with protecting your network! If you are going to install a WLAN, but haven't already selected an AP, remember that security starts with the equipment you purchase. Do your research. Find an AP that has features such as WEP support, Dynamic Host Configuration Protocol (DHCP) support, built-in firewalls, support for Remote Authentication Dial-In User Service (RADIUS) authentication, the ability to "close" the network, VPN client or server support, routing, Network Address Translation (NAT), and most of all, technical support! After all, no matter how many of the previous features the hardware platform supports, if you have difficulty configuring them, let alone implementing them, the features won't matter. If you aren't familiar with these concepts, you will be by the end of this chapter. Once you have made your purchase, read the rest of the chapter to learn what these features can do to secure your WLAN.

If you already have an AP, this chapter is for you. You may have some limitations based on the AP you have purchased, but all APs can benefit from various security measures contained in this chapter. You must consider the feature set you have chosen. Does it support WEP? What levels? 40 bit? 128 bit? Does it support VPNs? In this chapter, we will be looking at a couple of APs that are in wide deployment, and their security feature set. We will be using these APs as examples throughout the chapter to reflect the types of configurations that will ultimately provide you with the threat mitigation you are looking for.

Revisiting Policy

No security policy should be set in stone, yet many security administrators still forget to adjust corporate security policy to accommodate wireless networks and the users who depend on them. Wireless users have unique needs that policy must address. Roaming capabilities, ease of capture of Radio Frequency (RF) traffic, dedicated segments and more stringent rule sets are all areas of policy that must be reflected upon cautiously in order to begin the securing process from a policy perspective. It is critical that the administrator take diligent care in creating effective policy to protect the users, their data, and other corporate assets.

Any wireless security plan must include a review of policy to make sure wireless systems and users are included, that there is an effective mechanism to distribute updated policies to all users, and that these policies can be monitored, tested, and enforced. Let's briefly review policy to bring to mind some common sense elements when creating an effective policy for the wireless users.

Essentially policy is the set of rules that governs the management, use, implementation, and interaction of corporate assets. These assets include human resources, intellectual capital, hardware, software, networks and infrastructure, and data. In order for these resources to be used securely, they must be easily accessible for trusted users, while barriers are maintained for untrusted users. Accessibility also requires the integrity of the data to be protected and verified, such that the user is not adversely affected. Integration of checksums, parity, and authentication headers in IPSec are good support mechanisms for integrity checks. Also, protection such as anti-virus programs and a good disaster recovery plan are all part of the security policy as it pertains to reliability.

Resources should be sufficiently advertised to authenticated users. At first this may seem odd when speaking about security, but part of security encompasses the availability of resources to parties who need them. In this case, you do not want to advertise to unauthorized intruders, but you do want to advertise to your authorized users. Filtering MAC addresses and protocols fit here in your security posture.

Bear in mind that not all users require access to the same data. For example, payroll department information advertised to the entire company would cause severe problems. Therefore, even within the boundaries of authorized and authenticated users, there are delineations of groups that require a different set of rules governing access. We are dealing with wireless users, so the policy must reflect authorized wireless access. In this light, services should be advertised only after a sufficient authorization transaction has been successfully completed. This is where RADIUS, TACACS, or other authentication servers, and the use of user-authenticated VPN equipment falls into place.

Further, policy must reflect changes in corporate structure. If policy fails to comply with reorganization, it will be as effective as last year's virus definitions against this year's variety. In the case of wireless users, when securing the WLAN, you must take care not to alter the policy without the proper user notification. Altering this policy without the proper distribution of information may lead to limiting access to the intended users. Insert the education and securing of users here in your policy.

Under some circumstances, changes won't have the same severe impact on the end users, because many policies are handled at the application level and can be applied to the users via login scripts and group policy in Windows environments. However, in the case of the WLAN settings, such as the WEP Key, alterations without end user notification will lead to no access whatsoever!

Addressing the Issues with Policy

Wireless users have unique needs that policy must address. It is critical that the administrator takes diligent care in creating effective policy to protect the users, their data, and corporate assets. But just what is an effective policy for wireless users? Let's look at some common sense examples of good wireless policy.

First, wireless LANs are an "edge" technology. As such, policy should reflect a standard consistent with end users attempting to gain access to network resources from "the edge." In the case of wired LANs, typically you would set some standard physical access restrictions. This type of restriction would protect the LAN from certain types of attacks. You might also create group policies on the PC for authentication and access restrictions to corporate domains, and so long as there is no inside threat, the LAN is secured. (This scenario is unlikely in that disgruntled employees are representative of a solid portion of network hacking/misuse.) If you can't physically access the media, you cannot break in. If you do not furnish a valid username and password despite physical access, in most cases you cannot break in. Certainly there are some other methods of attack so long as you have physical access, but for all intents and purposes in this discussion the typical, aspiring hacker is locked out. This assists in implementing the more stringent rule set as required by edge and remote access. We will get more into that later.

In a wireless environment, the rules change. How do you stop access to RF? RF travels through, around, and is reflected off objects, walls, and other physical barriers. RF doesn't have the feature-rich security support that the typical wired network has. Despite that once you are connected to the LAN you can use the features of the wired Ethernet/IP security model, what about the signal from the AP to the client and visa versa? Because of this access methodology, wireless poses some interesting policy challenges.

One of these challenges—ease of capture of RF traffic—can be overcome by preventing the broadcast of the Secure Set Identifier (SSID) to the world from the AP. Much like the Network Basic Input/Output System (NETBIOS) in the Windows world that broadcasts shares, the AP typically broadcasts the SSID to allow clients to associate. This is an advertisement for access to what we would like to be a restricted WLAN. Therefore, a good policy in the WLAN space is to prevent the AP from broadcasting this information. Instead, set up the AP to only respond to clients that already have the required details surrounding the Basic Service Set (BSS). This means that when the client attempts to associate, the AP challenges the client for the SSID and WEP encryption key information before allowing access. Of course, there are still ways to capture the traffic, but with this minor policy rule, the level of difficulty has been exponentially increased from the default implementation.

This security policy works well in the WLAN space until a technically savvy, but security ignorant, user installs a rogue AP because they wish to have their own personal AP connected to the WLAN. Although we will cover rogue APs in further detail later, the fact is, this poses a strong threat to the overall network security posture, and must be prohibited.

What's in a name? It's imperative that a standard naming convention and WEP policy be set in place to prevent the standard defaults from being utilized. You wouldn't want your password published to the world in a set of instructions on how to access your PC, but that is exactly the case when speaking of WLAN defaults. They are published, documented, and presented as the default settings of the wireless space built from that specific hardware, and this is a *good* thing. Without this information, we would not be able to implement the hardware. However, to prevent unauthorized access, it's critical that the default settings are not left in place. A further consideration would be not using easily guessed names such as the company name. This should be part of your security policy for new hardware/software integration and goes toward assisting in the mitigation of capturing RF traffic.

With respect to roaming needs, these policies should not change from room to room or AP to AP. A consistent rule set (more stringent than normally internally trusted users) should be put in place across all APs where users are likely to roam while connected wirelessly. When choosing your AP, you can also add to ease of use for your wireless users by getting hardware that supports true roaming as opposed to having to lose connectivity momentarily while reassociating with another AP. The temporary loss of connectivity could lead to account lock out and the need to reauthenticate in upper layers.

Finally, strong authentication and encryption methods make it even more difficult to attack the access mechanisms, which is why the organization must include the appropriate use of authentication and encryption in its policy. Use of RADIUS or VPN solutions for authentication and tunneling sits nicely in the gap for the added protection. These authentication tools even serve as a standalone security feature for open networks where disabling the SSID is not an option.

All in all, policy should reflect these general guidelines if you intend to secure the WLAN access to corporate assets. We will be exploring each in detail throughout this chapter to give you the information you need to secure your WLAN. Don't make the mistake of using just one of these options. Instead, look at your security policy as a tightly bound rope consisting of multiple threads. Each thread is another layer of security. In this case, your security policy will remain strong despite the failure of one or two threads. At no time do you want one solution to be the only boundary between maintaining your valuables and losing them.

Analyzing the Threat

Threat analysis boils down to the science of assigning a dollar value to an arbitrary or statistical potential of harm by taking the cost of the reactionary activities in the restoration process and comparing that cost with the investment of security countermeasures to prohibit the harm. This is a difficult and arduous process, but invaluable and absolutely necessary if you are actually going to maintain business during the information age.

You might not have conducted such an exercise for a while, but with the lack of boundaries typical of a wired network, it's essential that you understand and account for the complexity and challenges wireless introduces with respect to targets. Obviously you can't protect every asset one hundred percent of the time, but this exercise can help you to define the wireless border, prioritize assets, and protect those most vulnerable to attack through the wireless network.

When trying to look at threats there are two types of extremes: paranoia, which means that you consider everything to be a potential threat, and what I call the Ostrich method of burying your head in the sand and figuring there's no need for security.

The truth lies somewhere between these two extremes. Because of inherent limitations on types of access or because of hardware or software implementations, there will undoubtedly be some degree of acceptable risk with respect to that threat. Risk is knowing what the threat is, but leaving no or weak security measures because the costs of higher degrees of security are prohibitive. So, how do we find the happy medium? Are there mechanisms or checklists that serve as a guide for threat analysis?

The good news is there are some legitimate guides to recommendations for analyzing threat or risk. The bad news is applying those templates to the many types of networks, corporations, policies, and culture that exists is like trying to look good in a pair of "one size fits all" pants. This is why your own custom analysis is so vital to the security process.

Logically the first thing to do when analyzing threat is to define who poses a threat and ascertain what they are interested in. Then, by viewing current policy, corporate structure, and network infrastructure to see how these guidelines can be leveraged to fit your network needs, you can begin to mentally formulate an action plan. Perhaps it may even be an inaction plan based on your needs. But first you need to quantify the threat in relation to risk. In order to perform this task, ask yourself two questions:

- What are my vulnerabilities?
- What could the potential cost be of recovering from a situation where one of these vulerabilities has been exploited?

These two questions will ultimately determine your final course of action for securing your WLAN (further detail about vulnerabilities can be found in Chapter 6).

Threat Equals Risk Plus Vulnerability

Let's define some terms to allow you to get an understanding of threat, risk, and vulnerability. *Threat* implies a force with a direction. An example of threat would be a charging bull headed straight for you. A bull fenced in and chained to a post without strength to break either barrier is no threat no matter how menacing it appears. *Risk* is defined over time. In other words, if this same bull has weakened the chain so that in time it will break, if you stand inside the fence long enough you will place yourself at risk. Even further defined, if the bull has finally broken the chain, and you are inside the fence, although he may not be charging now, you are still at risk. The bull is not yet a threat, but you are at risk. Now, let's look at *vulnerability*. In this instance, you are vulnerable in several ways: you cannot outrun the bull (placing ineffective policy in your organization); and you are not able to withstand the impact if he manages contact (pretending there is no threat and not addressing policy).

First, let's try to look at the difference between risk and vulnerability. Vulnerability identifies a weakness in implementation or software or hardware that allows access to various resources unauthorized. This is definitely an item to consider when securing your network. Think of it as a house with an open window. Once an intruder has circled the house enough times, and sufficiently searched for weaknesses, he might find this open window. But just because the window is open doesn't mean that he is guaranteed access. This window might be out of reach, or it might be too small to gain entrance, or it might be secured with another mechanism not yet visible. Just because vulnerability exists doesn't mean it is automatically exploitable. There are other circumstances that may mitigate the threat.

Let's suppose the window is open sufficiently to allow entrance, and no other security mechanisms prevent intrusion. Now that the intruder is in the house, we have identified the exploitable vulnerability. An exploitable vulnerability constitutes potential risk. Let's use our example to identify risk. Risk describes the potential loss measured against the vulnerabilities. In our case, the risk so far is that if there is vulnerability (that is, the window is open), the intruder can gain entrance. This may or may not equate to potential loss. If the house is abandoned, is there the potential for loss of valuables? What if the intruder gains entrance to an occupied home that stores all valuables in a safe? What if this safe is offsite? All of these are mitigating factors for analyzing threat, and quantifying how legitimate the risk is for a given vulnerability.

Another factor in analyzing threat is determining where the threat is likely to come from. The Trojan horse is an oft-used security euphemism for identity spoofing, but it is just as accurate in representing any misplaced trust as it is in regards to internal security. Perimeter security measures can be nearly impenetrable, but if the threat is already within the gate, then high walls and huge locks won't secure your valuables! For this reason, you must pause to ask yourself, "Who would want to hack my network?" This question cannot be answered without reviewing what it is they may be after.

Disgruntled employees always make the short list for potential hackers. Typically, we tend to secure from the outside, but those operating in the trusted environment are even more of a threat than their anonymous external counterparts. An angry employee may just be after a little revenge. Or the hacker may simply be some curious techno-geek who recently acquired some new software or hardware and wants to try it out. IT departments are replete with technical gurus capable of bypassing security policy for the pleasure of Internet perusal and downloading. Of course, there is the potential for corporate espionage and other malfeasance, but that is the rarity.

What makes your network worth attacking? Most home users have nothing to really fear except their neighbor borrowing their Internet connection. Quite honestly, a shrewd entrepreneur could pay for an Internet service provider (ISP) account by sharing his RF with paying neighbors. On the other hand, if one is a bank, a government agency, or another entity that houses potentially valuable information, the list of justifications for attack grows exponentially. Analyzing threat is tied to who you are and what you do. At this point, we will assume you have some valuable information, or privacy concerns that make analyzing threat important. So, you must apply some general guidelines for analyzing threat and then drill down into specific need. Here is a list of some guidelines for analyzing the threat:

- Identify assets
- Identify the method of accessing these valuables from an authorized perspective
- Identify the likelihood that someone other than an authorized user can access the valuables identified
- Identify potential damages
  - Defacement
  - Modification
  - Theft
- Destruction of data
- Identify the cost to replace, fix, or track the loss
- Identify security countermeasures
- Identify the cost in implementation of the countermeasures
  - Hardware
  - Software
  - Personnel
  - Procedures
  - Limitations on access across the corporate structure
- Compare costs of securing the resource versus the cost of damage control

In the case of valuables, this will differ for each organization. Some companies value the client information, because there are regulations tied to their security. Other companies are tied to the financial market value data that significantly impacts bottom line performance. Still other companies value trade secrets.

In all cases, some universal rules apply, such as not allowing the average worker to obtain financial records for peers. Great care must be taken to identify each and every valuable. It is highly beneficial to sit down in a meeting with the heads of various departments to determine what is of value to each of them, since they are the ones closest to the pain if their resources are compromised. In this way, you will gain their trust, confidence, and most importantly their "buy in." Making them part of the process will go a long way toward getting complete information and cooperation.

Ask these group members how the resources are accessed and handled in order to determine dependencies and traffic requirements. If the payroll department needs access to records you have "secured" from them, it makes their job impossible. Nothing could be more detrimental than the poor implementation of good policy, or worse, poor policy because of lack of communication.

Look at the likelihood that someone would attempt to gain access to the various group members' valuables. In certain circumstances, although the information is valuable to the department, it would be of little value to a hacker—if this is the case, you need that department to *admit* this. If you make decisions on their behalf, based on your outsider viewpoint, you could be headed for interoffice squabbles galore. Invariably you will lose the political power of teamwork. If you determine someone malicious would be interested in gaining a department's information, review the method of authorized access. Are there weaknesses, such as a universal account for all people in the department? This would allow an intruder to use this account anonymously. Or are there multiple accounts, but highly standardized usernames and passwords making password guessing easy? Each of these cases has some significant security flaws. These and other factors need to be considered before your final security policy is set in stone when analyzing threat.

Once you have identified the valuables, determined who accesses them, and who may want to get unauthorized access to them, the next step is to evaluate the types of threats and the potential harm caused by an exploited vulnerability. This information needs to then be weighed against the cost of securing the vulnerabilities. The cost can be as minute as the time spent restoring a defaced Web site with a backup held on a disk or as great as replacing destroyed data (if possible) because of a self-replicating virus, along with the customer relationships lost because of it. Although replacing a defaced Web site is annoying, the threat and cost is pretty minimal as compared to the virus that damages data in every one of the servers on site.

Notes from the Underground…

Weak Authentication

A security organization conducted an unpublished study that shows many people choose the same weak passwords, usually related to local culture and events. As an example, in Denver, use of the password "Broncos" (referring to the local football team) might be widely used. If there are insufficient characters making up the password, then adding a "1" at the end is the typical response. (Broncos1 for an eight-character requirement standard.) Born out, this means that if a hacker gains access to one account, odds are he'll find another account with the same password. Combining this with a highly standardized user account naming convention implies severe weaknesses.

Using the virus example, let's look at some of the thought processes involved for analyzing that threat. Viruses pose interesting challenges themselves. The question is: how long has it been resident before becoming active? In order to attempt to restore from backup, you would need to go far enough back to get a good copy of data. In addition, all the information that has been corrupted since the time of the last good copy could be lost. At the very least, it may take a long time to reestablish the system. This scenario poses greater challenges than the defaced Web site—likewise, the cost of recovery is greater. In this case, it is necessary to calculate the cost of potentially angry customers, management, and specialized engineers in a disaster recovery effort against the cost of securing the data with a firewall, anti–virus software, and a good authentication mechanism. So you see how costs can vary depending on the type of threat.

Also, keep in mind that costs are not always uniform or monetary. Costs could also be the loss of valuable employees who feel alienated by the policy you have set in place. If your security countermeasures fail to take into account the need for political buy-in, as well as data availability to those that need it, ultimately you will be fighting an uphill battle against your peers.

This information is good for all networks, but what about wireless networks specifically? How are they special? What are the contributing factors that would lead an administrator to generate a policy specific to the wireless security model? Here is a list of WLAN security guidelines that nearly everyone can benefit from:

- Alter the defaults!

- Treat the AP like a Remote Access Server (RAS).

- Specify IP ranges that are earmarked for the WLAN only.

- Use the highest-rated, supported security feature available on your AP.

- Apply consistent authorization rules across the edge of the network for all users.

Once these rules are set in place, they will act as a starting point for securing your wireless network. Let's look at each rule and determine why this is a sound practice for your network.

Alter the defaults! First off, you need to alter the default passwords and SSIDs on your APs. It may seem trite to discuss it in this forum, but quite honestly, this is the number one cause for WLAN insecurity. Many administrators place the AP on the network and walk away, having never altered any default information. This default information is widely published on the Internet, and therefore is public knowledge. Once you set that AP up with the defaults in place, you might as well ask someone to browse your network.

Treat the AP like a Remote Access Server. Why treat APs like RAS servers? This is a no-brainer. RF is not held under the same restrictions as wired media. In a wired network, companies have full control of all wires within their building up to the point where the ISP connection is set. And under their control, to the extent that they patrol, is who is allowed access to server farms, wiring closets, and patch panels. In other words, they have limited their vulnerability for a complete stranger to gain wired access to the network from within. RF, on the other hand, has properties that allow hackers to sit in a neighboring building and attack your network resources without restraint, or sit out in the parking lot and attack other corporate networks over the Internet from your network! You wonder who is hogging all the bandwidth on your WLAN? It might be a disgruntled employee parked out front downloading MP3s or objectionable content from the Web. For this reason, you must treat WLANs like access from locations outside your jurisdiction. In this way, you need strong authentication and protocol filters. More information on that subject will be provided later.

Specify IP ranges that are earmarked for the WLAN only. By specifying IP address ranges specific to the WLAN, you isolate the WLAN for logging and access purposes. Most APs will bridge wireless traffic to the LAN they are connected to. Bridging takes place at the Data Link layer of the Open Systems Interconnect (OSI) reference model. Even if hackers can get access to the Data Link layer, but cannot get access to the Network layer, they are limited to the WLAN for traffic perusal. Specifying an IP range that is outside the scope of the defaults adds a layer of protection to your WLAN.

Use the highest-rated, supported security feature available on your AP. It is definitely recommended to implement the highest-rated security feature supported by the AP. In many cases, the AP will support VPN traffic destined for a server that will authenticate the user, and then provide access to resources set in the permissions for that user. Some APs only support WEP. If that is the case, if it supports WEP 40 and 128, use 128! The harder you make it, the better your chances for protection. Again, as we get further into the chapter, we will speak more about securing by WEP.

Apply consistent authorization rules across the edge of the network for all users. Applying consistent authorization rules across the network prevents a special account from getting privileged access that could potentially harm the network. If the traffic is captured via a wireless sniffer such as Airopeek, this special account can be just as vulnerable as any other, and could lead to extra mischief based on the extended permissions.

What is Airopeek? Covered in the previous chapter, Airopeek is a program designed to work with wireless cards that are set to promiscuous mode to gather traffic over the wireless network. It is costly, but as with all hacker tools, once there is a copy in circulation, there are knockoffs and bootleg copies available on hacker sites. Using this program, a hacker can sit outside the confines of the office, perhaps in a neighboring office or building and capture traffic. This traffic can be analyzed and used to gain entry.

Other shareware programs available include NetStumbler and AiroSnort. NetStumbler can be used to identify open networks reporting Extended SSID (ESSID), whether or not WEP is enabled, and the manufacturer of the AP. If the defaults are used, hackers find an easy target using published information for gaining entry to your network. Airosnort is a UNIX-based command line utility used much the same way as Airopeek. (Of course, if the hacker knows UNIX you'll probably be faced with a real techno-geek! But that's no reason to give up. Read on. We'll stop him, too!)

Now you are armed with some of the peripheral and some general guideline information regarding WLANs and what the possibilities are for analyzing threat and mitigating it. You have discovered some of the threats and learned methods for sorting the information. You have also been given some best practices for implementing policy on your WLAN, as well as general information on the hows and whys of it. Given this, you are ready to actually get into the design and deployment phase of your secure WLAN.

Designing and Deploying a Secure Network

As mentioned previously, your choice of product and vendor, combined with your network design and deployment, will significantly contribute in determining your degree of vulnerability. It is therefore critical to choose your wireless vendors carefully: "think" security into the design of your network, and deploy the network with all security options at their most appropriate settings. The questions then are:

- What should I be looking for in an Access Point?
- Who offers these Access Points?

First things first: the AP you are looking for should fit into the threat analysis structure we just created. It should also meet some minimum requirements such as disabling the broadcast of the SSID, 128-bit WEP encryption, Wi-Fi compatibility, and the ability to pass VPN traffic.

Another recommendation is to check into their path to migrate to 802.11a. Will there be a firmware revision to cover it, or a forklift upgrade? What about 802.11g? No one wants to pay for hardware that is obsolete in a year.

These standards are not the highest in the world by any stretch, but when building security, there is no silver bullet that fixes all gaps. Instead, you build *layers of security* that mitigate the threat. The layering approach, in addition to offering multiple points of security, also provides flexibility in the hardware you choose, understanding that not every budget includes the availability of funds for the latest and greatest.

Who offers APs? The list is extensive. Pretty much every major player in networking offers some form of 802.11b device support. In addition to that there is a long list of SOHO companies like Linksys and SMC, and newcomers like Colubris Networks making waves in the industry.

Because we are looking at the enterprise and need to limit space, we will focus on two of the leading vendors' models: Cisco's Aironet and Agere's ORiNOCO AP-1000. Don't think that these are the only models to consider. The fact is Colubris' AP product offering is complete and has all the security feature support needed. The Colubris 1054 is a terrific enterprise level AP with a built-in VPN server and client. It also rates high with respect to throughput under VPN load.

Both the ORiNOCO Access Point from Agere and the popular Cisco Aironet Series support the disabling of broadcast of the SSID; a critical component of the secure WLAN model. Both support 128-bit WEP encryption, and can be configured to pass VPN traffic; but even more importantly they are Wi-Fi compliant, which means they interoperate with other Wi-Fi-compliant devices.

These standards alone make these two APs a success on the beginnings of a secure WLAN. You will find some failings, too, but as always there are ways to improve everything. An AP fairly new to the scene that has an interesting security feature is the Colubris CN1050. This AP supports all the general features of the ORiNOCO and the Aironet, but also has an integrated VPN client and server. This will allow inter AP traffic to be encrypted for added security in an infrastructure environment. Note that individual users will not be affected by this increased security unless they install and make use of VPN software on their mobile devices.

Tools & Traps...

Access Point Matrix

You can find a good access point matrix on the Web at www.bawug.org/ap_table.html. This matrix compares many of the products available in a number of categories, such as VPN support and number of supported users, as well as throughput.

There are other good products on the market, with lots of documentation; decide for yourself which AP fits your financial constraints and business goals.

Once you have decided which vendor to use and verified their support capabilities, the next step is identifying the architecture of the WLAN. Questions that should be asked in this stage are:

- Who needs the access?

- In each location, how many users require access?

- Are there other wireless devices in the vicinity that could cause interference with your WLAN?

These questions relate to the physical layout of the network. Unlike their wired counterparts, where physical location of hardware is relatively unimportant, WLANs depend greatly on the physical layout for security. For example, you would not place a directional antenna in the window of the building facing into the wild blue yonder. This would allow anyone within a given distance limitation (up to 25 km) the ability to receive signal from the WLAN. Likewise, part of security policy requires making data available to those who need it. Not providing sufficient coverage can become a support headache and could easily change into reengineering the design altogether.

Most APs have a distance limitation of approximately 100 meters in a straight line, and 30 meters around objects that cause reflection of the signal. This distance provides up to 11 Mbps. At greater distances, you can get 5.5 Mbps, 2 Mbps, and then 1 Mbps. This is auto-adjusted for the best bandwidth for a given distance. (Although APs claim 11 Mbps, actual per user throughput is closer to 5 to 7 Mbps. This isn't too much of an issue for home and remote access users, because they are used to 1 and 2 Mbps at most with DSL or a cable modem.)

One significant thought in terms of bandwidth relates to the number of users on the AP. If there are up to 50 users in a space with only 1 AP, then logically you have to divide 11 Mbps between the 50 users. It works out to be (with no VPN or WEP overhead) 220 Kbps. Once you add the overhead generated by these security protocols, that number is going to drop significantly.

NOTE

When placing APs in the same broadcast vicinity, different broadcast channels need to be configured on each AP. Not doing so will result in a drop in bandwidth. This condition is based on collisions and interference issues with the frequency spectrum utilized. The 802.11b standard uses a limited ISM band in the 2.4GHz range. In order to access the wireless media, Collision Sense Medium Access with Collision Avoidance (CSMA/CA) with Clear to Send (CTS) and Request to Send (RTS) packets and back-off algorithms for preventing collisions and retransmissions are employed. In effect, there will be an increased number of collisions, and therefore much of the time will be spent either in retransmission, or waiting on the back-off algorithm.

In this scenario, you would want to place a few APs together to provide some load balancing. This will allow you the extra bandwidth to support VPN tunnels or WEP encryption.

Sometimes, the opposite is true—you may have just a few users scattered across a vast expanse. In this case, a good antenna can allow users to access the AP from a greater distance away. Make sure to consider that as you allow authorized users access to the WLAN via antenna, you are extending the invitation to would-be intruders as well.

When placing the AP, keep in mind the physical aspect of security. The AP should not be in a location that allows easy access to the hardware. While it should be placed in a strategic location that allows for maximum RF coverage, it should also be out of the reach of potential attackers. If placed in a physically unprotected environment, the AP can be reset physically and will return to defaults. When that happens, that AP could be vulnerable long enough for a vandal to compromise it and cause some significant damages, if not allow a hacker to gain access to the wired portion of the network and discover information that could lead to the eventual compromise of the WLAN. Consider thievery, too—make sure your $500 to $1000 investments don't end up walking out the door with someone.

Once you have placed the hardware with coverage in mind, you may have elected to use an antenna to extend the range.

If you do use an antenna, here are a few rules of thumb:

- Use the appropriate antenna for the task based on lobe and gain considerations.

- Place the antenna in a location that allows functionality while reducing security risk.

Consider the fact that using an antenna is a benefit for both the authorized individual and the intruder. Sure it can extend coverage, but can you see where the new RF footprint ends? You may be opening up your WLAN to the company upstairs, or those in the building next door. Because the quality of antennas varies, and the exact signal direction and strength can be somewhat unpredictable, it is wise to avoid them whenever possible, but when the need arises, perform an exhaustive RF site survey and place them appropriately.

If you do need an antenna, use one that suits your needs. If you need a wide footprint of coverage, use a standard omni; if you need focused access, use a directional. You might use several directional antennas to create strong coverage in a small area. Or you might use an omni directional to expand the radius of a single coverage area. In either case, be sure to understand the limitations and benefits of both. A good design with security in mind will prevent unnecessary follow up on neighboring office suites that might be browsing and hacking your internal resources.

In summary, consider the coverage area, and whether or not you will need to use antennas. Understand the benefits and limitations of the design you are employing. Make sure you aren't allowing excessive RF into unsecured areas, but apply coverage to all who need access. Good design sets the stage for a secure WLAN.

Implementing WEP

Despite its critics, WEP still offers a reasonable level of security, providing all its features are used properly. This means greater care in key management, avoiding default options, and making sure adequate encryption is enabled at every opportunity.

Proposed improvements in the standard should overcome many of the limitations of the original security options, and should make WEP more appealing as a security solution. Additionally, as WLAN technology gains popularity, and users clamor for functionality, both the standards committees as well as the hardware vendors will offer improvements. This means you should make sure to keep abreast of vendor-related software fixes and changes that improve the overall security posture of your WLAN.

Most APs advertise that they support WEP in at least 40-bit encryption, but often the 128-bit option is also supported. For corporate networks, 128-bit encryption-capable devices should be considered as a minimum. With data security enabled in a closed network, the settings on the client for the SSID and the encryption keys have to match the AP when attempting to associate with the network, or it will fail. In the next few paragraphs, we will discuss WEP as it relates to the functionality of the standard, including a standard definition of WEP, the privacy created, and the authentication.

Defining WEP

802.11 as a standard covers the communication between WLAN components. RF poses challenges to privacy in that it travels through and around physical objects. As part of the goals of the communication, a mechanism needed to be implemented to protect the privacy of the individual transmissions that in some way mirrored the privacy found on the wired LAN. Wireless Equivalency Privacy is the mechanism created in the standard as a solution that addresses this goal. Because WEP utilizes a cryptographic security countermeasure for the fulfillment of its stated goal of privacy, it has the added benefit of becoming an authentication mechanism. This benefit is realized through a shared key authentication that allows the encryption and decryption of the wireless transmissions. There can be many keys defined on an AP or a client, and they can be rotated to add complexity for a higher security standard for your WLAN policy. This is a must!

WEP was never intended to be the absolute authority in security. Instead, the driving force was privacy. In cases that require high degrees of security, other mechanisms such as authentication, access control, password protection, and virtual private networks should be utilized.

Creating Privacy with WEP

Let's look at how WEP creates a degree of privacy on the WLAN. WEP comes in several implementations: no encryption, and 40-bit and 128-bit encryption. Obviously, no encryption means no privacy. Transmissions are sent in the clear, and can be viewed by any wireless sniffing application that has access to the RF propagated in the WLAN. In the case of the 40- and 128-bit varieties (just as with password length), the greater the number of characters (bits) the stronger the encryption. The initial configuration of the AP will include the set up of the shared key. This shared key can be in the form of either alphanumeric, or hexadecimal strings, and is matched on the client.

WEP uses the RC4 encryption algorithm, a stream cipher developed by noted cryptographer Ron Rivest (the "r" in RSA). Both the sender and receiver use the stream cipher to create identical pseudorandom strings from a known shared key. The process entails the sender to logically XOR the plaintext transmission with the stream cipher to produce the ciphertext. The receiver takes the shared key and identical stream and reverses the process to gain the plaintext transmission.

A 24-bit Initialization Vector (IV) is used to create the identical cipher streams. The IV is produced by the sender, and is included in the transmission of each frame. A new IV is used for each frame to prevent the reuse of the key weakening the encryption. This means that for each string generated, a different value for the RC4 key will be used. Although a secure policy, consideration of the components of WEP bear out one of the flaws in WEP. Because the 24-bit space is so small with respect to the potential set of initialization vectors, in a short period of time, all keys are eventually reused. Unfortunately, this weakness is the same for both the 40- and 128-bit encryption levels.

To protect against some rudimentary attacks that insert known text into the stream to attempt to reveal the key stream, WEP incorporates a checksum in each frame. Any frame not found to be valid through the checksum is discarded. All in all this sounds secure, but WEP has well-documented flaws which we will cover more extensively in Chapter 6. Let's review the process in a little more detail to gain a better understanding of the behind the scenes activities that are largely the first line of defense in WLAN security.

The WEP Authentication Process

Shared key authentication is a four-step process that begins when the access point receives the validated request for association. After the AP receives the request, a series of management frames are transmitted between the stations to produce the authentication. This includes the use of the cryptographic mechanisms employed by WEP as a validation.

Strictly with respect to WEP, in the authorization phase, the four steps break down in the following manner:

1. The requestor (the client) sends a request for association.

2. The authenticator (the AP) receives the request, and responds by producing a random challenge text and transmitting it back to the requestor.

3. The requestor receives the transmission, ciphers the challenge with the shared key stream and returns it.

4. The authenticator decrypts the challenge text and compares the values against the original. If they match, the requestor is authenticated. On the other hand, if the requestor doesn't have the shared key, the cipher stream cannot be reproduced, therefore the plaintext cannot be discovered, and theoretically, the transmission is secured.

WEP Benefits and Advantages

WEP provides some security and privacy in transmissions to prevent curious or casual browsers from viewing the contents of the transmissions held between the AP and the clients. In order to gain access, the degree of sophistication of the intruder has to improve, and specific intent to gain access is required. Let's view some of the other benefits of implementing WEP:

- All messages are encrypted using a checksum to provide some degree of tamper resistance.

- Privacy is maintained via the encryption. If you do not have the key, you can't decrypt the message.

- WEP is extremely easy to implement. Set the encryption key on the AP, repeat the process on each client, and voilà! You're done!

- WEP provides a very basic level of security for WLAN applications.

- WEP keys are user definable and unlimited. You do not have to use pre-defined keys, and you can and should change them often.

WEP Disadvantages

As with any standard or protocol, there are some inherent disadvantages. The focus of security is to allow a balance of access and control while juggling the advantages and disadvantages of each implemented countermeasure for security gaps. The following are some of the disadvantages of WEP:

- The RC4 encryption algorithm is a known stream cipher. This means it takes a finite key and attempts to make an infinite pseudorandom key stream in order to generate the encryption.

- Once you alter the key—which should be done often—you have to tell everyone so they can adjust their settings. The more people you tell, the more public the information becomes. Some of the newer software and devices on the market (notably Cisco products) support automatically regenerating new keys at specified time periods. This is a great security feature that can alleviate this concern.

- Used on its own, WEP does not provide adequate WLAN security.

- WEP has to be implemented on every client as well as every AP to be effective.

The Security Implications of Using WEP

From a security perspective, you have mitigated the curious hacker who lacks the means or desire to really hack your network. If you have enabled WEP as instructed in the previous pages, someone has to be actively attempting to break into your network in order to be successful. If that is the case, then using the strongest form of WEP available is important. Because WEP relies on a known stream cipher, it is vulnerable to certain attacks. By no means is it the final authority and should not be the only security countermeasure in place to protect your network—and ultimately your job!

Implementing WEP on the Aironet

As you can see in the following, the Cisco AP340 supports 128-bit encryption. It is configured with either a HTTP connection pictured here, or a serial connection. The serial interface is cryptic and in no way intuitive. If you plan on administering many Aironet devices, it may be better to use the Web interface. In Figure 5.1, you see the Web interface for an AP340. By using the drop-down menu, you can select "**Full Encryption**" and then "**128 bit**" for the Key size. Finally, select the **WEP Key** radio button for the transmission key and type the string.

Figure 5.1 WEP Configuration on the Aironet

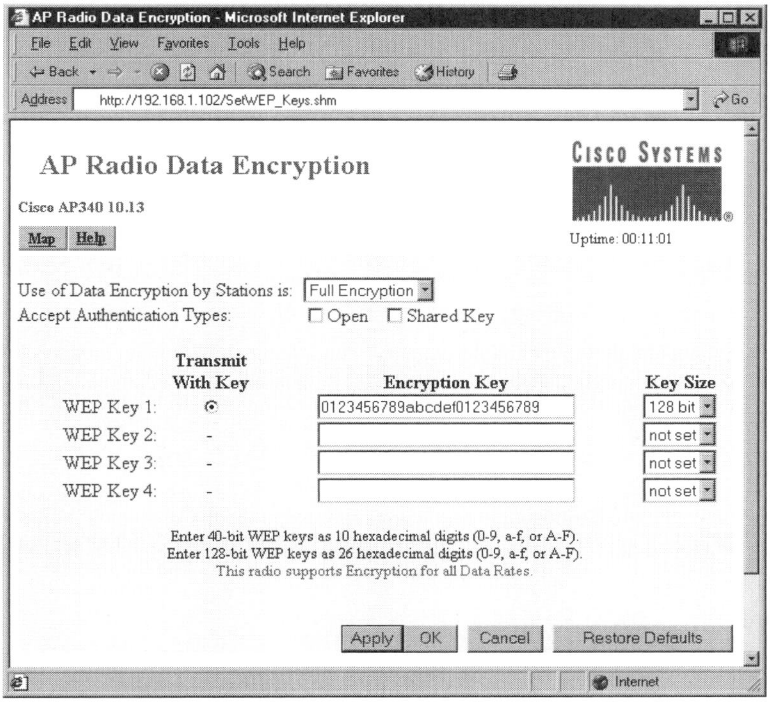

Implementing WEP on the ORiNOCO AP-1000

The following is the dialogue box for configuring the SSID. By selecting the **Security** button, the dialogue box shown in Figure 5.2 allows the configuration of the security model.

Figure 5.2 AP Configuration—Wireless Interfaces on the ORiNOCO

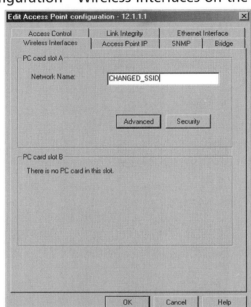

Figure 5.3 shows the dialogue box for configuring the WEP encryption key. Select the **Enable Encryption** dialogue box, and type the alphanumeric string. The ability to close the network is also configured here by selecting the **Closed Wireless System** dialogue box.

Securing a WLAN with WEP: A Case Scenario

Imagine a fictional company, R&R Enterprises, that needs to secure its WLAN. R&R has recently purchased several ORiNOCO AP 1000s. This company has determined that in order to provide mobility for their lab workers, they will implement wireless LAN technologies. Security is of great concern because the lab workers are perfecting the new and improved formula for a proprietary medicine code-named "Anti-Chimera." The lab facility is approximately 500 square feet, shaped in a rectangle, and there are roughly 30 users. About 100 feet down the corridor off the main lab entrance is a conference room where when not working, the lab workers participate in brainstorming activities. This room also needs to have wireless access. Figure 5.4 illustrates the layout. The AP is indicated by the location of the access points as placed by the administrator. The inner circle represents the area of 11 Mbps coverage, while the outer circle represents the 5.5 Mbps coverage. Placement was determined as a result of the need for an area of coverage, as well as redundancy because of the number of users within the room at any given time.

Figure 5.3 Wireless Security Setup Dialogue Box

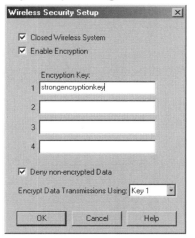

Figure 5.4 Case Scenario Office Layout

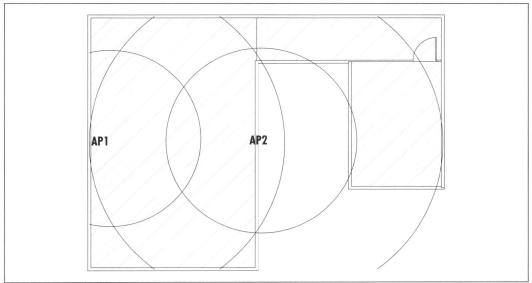

After settling on two APs in the lab set strategically for optimum coverage—each at approximately one half the distance of the overall length of the room on opposite walls—the first order of business was to set up the BSS. This will not be an ad-hoc network. Instead, we will set it up as an infrastructure configuration. Because of the proximity of the devices, different channels will be used for each AP.

After all of the appropriate wiring is completed, the administrator will open up the administration utility for the ORiNOCO access point installed on a management station from the software provided with the AP. As a priority, he will set a password on the management utility to prevent unauthorized administrative access.

Once the admin is logged in and has the password altered appropriately, he will then select the dialogue box for the ESSID, and type a network name according to a unique predetermined naming convention. This same SSID will be applied to all the APs; even the AP covering the conference room. After this is completed, he will select the radio button that closes the network (essentially disabling responses to probes from clients set to "any," and also preventing the AP from broadcasting the SSID.)

Next, the administrator will select the radio button enabling data security. This will bring up a WEP dialogue box. The admin will select hex or alphanumeric depending on preference, and type a string of characters to create the WEP key. The administrator will then reboot the AP, and the settings will take effect. In order for anyone to gain access at this point, they must each have their Wi-Fi-compatible card with the correct SSID and with the appropriate level of encryption enabled, with the matching string value.

R&R Enterprises now has a reasonable degree of security. Based on what you have learned so far, can you think of any risks associated with this setup? Make sure to consider availability of data, and location and strength of the APs. We will speak more on R&R's network in upcoming sections.

Filtering MACs

MAC filtering is one of the simplest ways to minimize the threat of a number of attacks, and although it's more practical on smaller networks, it's still a viable option for larger wireless networks. In both cases, it is extremely simple to implement and is by far the best true network security mechanism to avoid basic attacks. It can be performed at the ingress switch attached to the AP or on the AP itself, if a mechanism to do so exists. Both the Cisco Aironet and the ORiNOCO APs offer such a security mechanism.

Defining MAC Filtering

What does it mean to filter MACs? Just what is a MAC? Without getting into the OSI reference model details, a MAC address is a 48-bit hexadecimal hardware address. It is also called the *burned-in* address, because it does not change. While it's true that some hardware devices are configurable, the burned-in MAC address given at the time the card was manufactured does not change. The first 24 bits relate to the hardware manufacturer, and are common to all network hardware manufactured by that entity. The remaining 24 bits make up a unique identifier for each piece of hardware. Usually each network adapter is numbered in sequence for this unique number.

This unique number identifies the client to the rest of the local network and because it is unique, you can trace by hardware address exactly which node is attempting access to your network. More importantly you can set up filters to prevent intruders from your trusted network. This can be useful especially on the very edge of the network where the majority of potential attackers are likely to be. How would you go about doing that?

If you look at the size of the Internet and all the nodes it contains, it would make no sense to attempt to write a rule to block every MAC address out there; nor could you. Instead, administrators deny all addresses except those trusted. As part of the overall policy for the network, it makes sense to be aware of all trusted hardware devices in use. As we just saw, each of these devices has a MAC address of some kind to allow it to communicate on the network. Keeping track of the MAC addresses along with hardware models and serial numbers will assist in good record keeping as well as network security. Instead of a long list of deny rules, there should be an implicit deny and several permits. Each MAC address to be used on the WLAN should be recorded and configured on the AP for permission to access the network. Set this up at the switch or the AP, whichever has the capability and is furthest from your trusted network.

The reason for the point at which the filtering should take place is simple. Preventing it at the switch allows the AP to provide wireless access. If there is an intruder who was savvy enough to get by your encryption and SSID combination, they are probably able to figure out how to access wireless devices on the LAN. The filter will prevent corporate attacks for a time, but the WLAN is still wide open.

If instead the filter is on the AP, there is a much slimmer chance of getting by the encryption and SSID combination, as well as the MAC filter. In this scenario, the filter will work to prevent access by any hardware except trusted hardware.

Upon attempting to associate with the AP, the MAC filter will recognize the untrusted MAC, and prevent traffic from traversing the AP to the trusted network. The client may still be able to associate to the AP, but traffic is stopped.

At this point, it becomes vital to note that MAC filtering alone is not sufficient. MAC filtering should be implemented in conjunction with logging, as well as a policy that dictates times when a given MAC address is allowed to access resources. This can pose some challenges, but it will prevent a hacker from snooping a trusted MAC address, reconfiguring his own card with it, and then gaining access while the trusted user is home watching television. Logging will alert the admin to suspicious activities leading up to the attack, and possibly provide evidence if the policy of your establishment is to prosecute hackers.

Do you see how we are building layers of security? We are not just applying a single remedy or quick fix; instead, we are applying incremental, and reasonable layers of defense that avoid excessive administrative overhead. Granted, the larger your network, the longer your list of allowed devices, but it's well worth the hassle, especially from an inventory or records standpoint.

MAC Benefits and Advantages

The benefits of filtering MAC addresses boil down to access control. If you remember in the beginning of the chapter, we talked about treating the WLAN as a remote access technology. It makes sense to apply your access control to the WLAN. In this way, you prevent intrusion as close to the edge as possible. The following is a list of advantages:

- Predefined users are accepted.

- Filtered MACs do not get access.

- It provides a good first level of defense.

MAC Disadvantages

The main disadvantage of using MAC filters is the administrative overhead. This, of course, depends on the actual number of wireless nodes accessing the network. The problem becomes even more of an issue when employees are reassigned or let go. The hardware should be removed from the permit list to prevent malicious attempts at reciprocity. The same can be said when temporary help is assigned, when someone gets hired, or if new hardware is purchased. The new hardware addresses have to be added to the permit list, further expanding the administrative overhead. Even more grind on the overhead is the fact that MAC filters should be logged and monitored for maximum effectiveness. A log is useless if it is not examined regularly. At the very least there should be alerts set up. Here is where you really have to balance the cost of implementation against the cost of cleaning up an intrusion.

Another downside is one we have already covered: on some wireless devices, the MAC addresses can be programmed. If someone sniffs the traffic, they can learn the MAC address from the well-known location in a frame. By monitoring usage, the intruder can attempt to gain access using an authorized user's MAC address once the user is no longer present.

Security Implications of MAC Filtering

From a security perspective, MAC filtering occurs at Layer 2 of the OSI reference model—meaning traffic bound for any address is ultimately attempting to breach Layer 3 in order to gain wider access to network resources. If they are filtered at Layer 2, none of the processing of the extraneous bits is required.

If you log the access attempts—and you should be logging them—this can alert the administrator to potential attempts to hack the network and help stop the intruder before they really get started. In order for this to be effective, someone has to be looking at the logs—which leads us back to administrative overhead.

Implementing MAC Filters on the AP-1000

Creating a MAC filter on the AP-1000 is easy. In the **Access Control** tab of the **Edit Access Point** configuration screen, select the **AP Authentication** button, as shown in Figure 5.5.

The **Setup Access Control** dialogue box appears. Select **Add**, as shown in Figure 5.6.

In the **Add MAC Address** dialogue box (see Figure 5.7), type the MAC address that should be permitted (all others will then be automatically denied). The AP-1000 will reboot and apply the new configuration settings. This process will take about 20 seconds.

Figure 5.5 AP Configuration—Access Control on the ORiNOCO

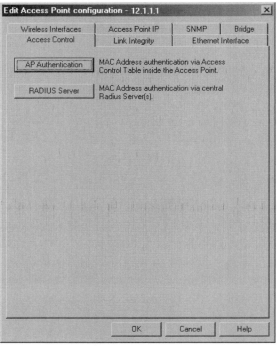

Figure 5.6 AP Setup Access Control

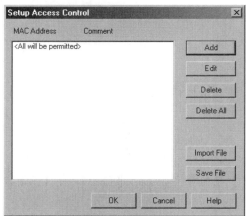

Figure 5.7 The Add MAC Address Dialogue Box

Implementing MAC Filters on the Aironet 340

Figure 5.8 shows the interface for the Cisco Aironet 340 AP. As you can see, Cisco employs a fairly user-friendly interface with an intuitive configuration method. Type the MAC address in the **Dest MAC Address** dialogue box and select the appropriate **Allowed** or **Disallowed** radio button to determine which MAC to perform the action upon, and which action should be taken. Finally, select **Add**, then **Apply** to make the configuration complete.

Figure 5.8 Managing MACs on the Aironet

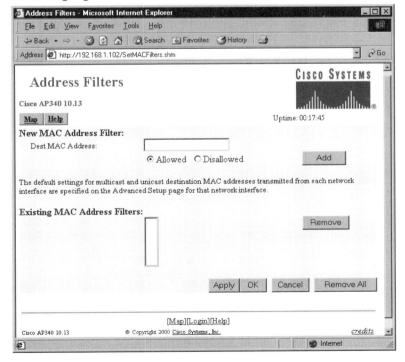

Figure 5.9 illustrates what the Cisco Aironet 340 AP interface looks like when MAC addresses have been entered into the configuration. As you can see, MAC address 00:02:2D:09:7E:C3 has been disallowed, while 00:02:2D:09:7E:C3 has been allowed. Note that the 00:02:2D points out the hardware manufacturer of the wireless card, while the remainder of the address is the globally unique identification number within that manufacturer's license.

Figure 5.9 Managing MACs on the Aironet

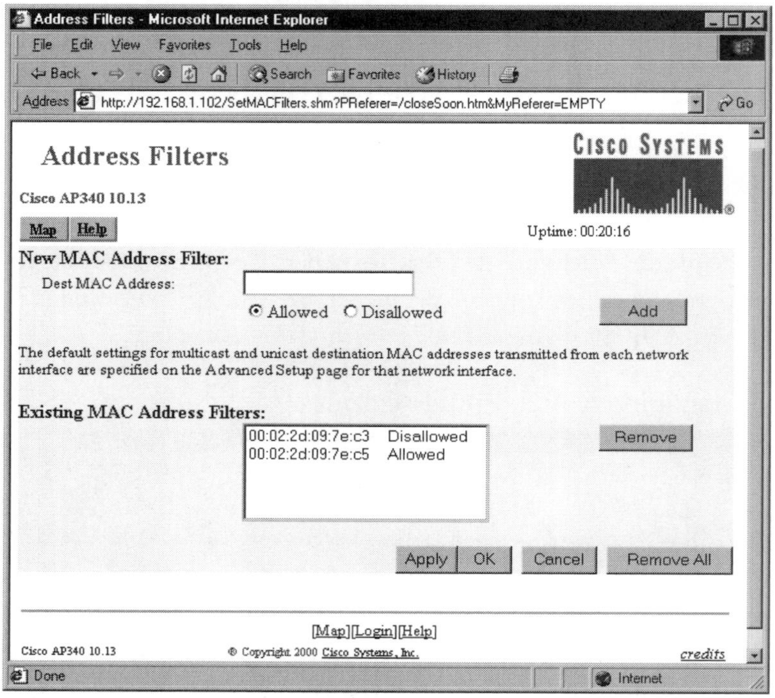

Filtering MAC Addresses: A Case Scenario

Our fictional company, R&R Enterprises, in their zeal to block access to their Anti-Chimera formula, has already established a closed network with 128-bit WEP encryption. The next logical step is to filter entry by recording all MAC addresses of the trusted lab workers, and then entering them in the AP as Allowed (as shown in the preceding). Thereafter, all other MAC addresses attempting access will be denied.

Because the administrators were diligent in reading this chapter, they implemented logging and applied a policy to disable all access after normal business hours. The administrator checks the logs each morning, and notes any dubious activity. Without a doubt, if someone gets past these initial steps, they are sure to be noticed.

Filtering Protocols

Like MAC filtering, protocol filtering is another way of minimizing risk. But care must be taken in setting up the filtering rules, enforcing them properly, and testing their effectiveness. Poorly implemented protocol filters can result in intermittent access, no access, and/or no security.

When considering the need to filter protocols, the underlying premise is that there is going to be some degree of access to the edge devices, but you should want to prevent certain known threats, and unnecessary processing of packets across the network.

Defining Protocol Filters

Protocol filters are set in place on routers and access devices that correspond to the edge of the network as far from the destination as possible. The rationale for their placement is to prevent unnecessary bandwidth usage and packet processing. They are implemented in the form of a firewall rules set that follows the pattern of denying or permitting types of traffic based on port ID (like port 25) or well-known protocol names such as the Simple Mail Transfer Protocol (SMTP).

Filtering protocols is a relatively effective method of restricting WLAN users from attempting SNMP access to the wireless devices to alter configurations. In this way, the administrator can allow the administrative group access solely from the wired side of the LAN, or via console access. Certainly, the case could be made that access is already restricted by password authentication, but remember, we build layers of security to protect areas of weakness.

Another good policy with respect to protocol filtering on the WLAN is preventing the use of large Internet Control Message Protocol (ICMP) packets and other such protocols from being used as DoS agents. You should also filter FTP from the WLAN if not otherwise required. After all, if there is only 11 Mbps of bandwidth to divide between multiple users, a user attempting to dawdle while downloading MP3s significantly impacts the remainder of the network users. Because of the CSMA/CA architecture, each node is given access for a particular duration until that message has been completed.

Earlier, we discussed MAC filtering. MAC filtering sits at Layer 2 of the OSI reference model and prevents users from gaining access to the Data Link layer. Protocol filtering rests on Layers 3 and 4, depending on which protocols you intend to filter. If you filter IP layer traffic such as certain IP addresses, those addresses will not be able to access the network. In the case of filtering FTP, the client can access the network, but cannot utilize FTP services.

As mentioned earlier, it is imperative to test these filters once enabled, because if implemented improperly they can cause users whom you do not wish to filter to be affected. Anyone who has worked in the networking industry knows that the first thing to ask when users are complaining of lack of access is who changed what on the network devices! By the same token, if you want to restrict access to an FTP server, it is wise to place the access list on the ingress of the network, as opposed to the egress. That way the traffic doesn't have to traverse the network, being processed by multiple devices only to be dropped at the end.

Many of the higher end APs support protocol filtering. Although specific in nature with respect to usage, protocol filters offer another layer of security to the overall security posture of the corporate environment.

Protocol Filter Benefits and Advantages

Protocol filters provide some benefits that would be difficult to implement otherwise. Some of these benefits include restricting traffic types not conducive to productivity, protecting networks from denial of service attacks, and restricting brute force attacks for administrative access. You can even restrict chatty protocols and unwanted advertising of services from gaining access to the network.

Protocol Filter Disadvantages

Some of the disadvantages of protocol filtering include the unwitting restriction of valid users. As the administration of the network becomes harder, and the processing of devices intensifies, the potential to overtax the system with large rule sets arises. These rules, if implemented improperly, can conflict with one another and lead to unexpected results. All in all, in order to use protocol filtering, a good understanding of the network layout, resource location, and user need is required.

Security Implications of Using Protocol Filters

One implication seen far too often is the common gathering at the water cooler to discuss the angst over the latest administrative restriction that was implemented and the network-wide outage it caused. This results in a negative view of security and may lead to internal circumvention of policy.

On the other hand, there is no better mechanism for preventing unwanted traffic, aside from powering down the offending nodes or unplugging the switch the various subnets are attached to.

Using Closed Systems and Networks

Using closed access systems is a valuable step towards controlling access to the AP. It is critical, however, that security administrators establish a closed system at the first installation to ensure that the network has identified only the access points with which it is allowed to connect, that proper passwords have been assigned to identify these stations, and that the closed network is assigned a name not easily guessed or discovered by attackers. Much like weak passwords, an easily guessed SSID can allow access that is more devastating because it offers a false sense of security. For this reason, avoid the usage of dictionary words for SSID and passwords.

Defining a Closed System

A *closed system* is one which does not respond to clients with the "Any" SSID assigned, nor does it broadcast the SSID to the clients at large. Instead, as the client scans for APs in range with which to associate, it expects the correct management frame containing the SSID that matches its own configuration. This is a simple definition, but carries the overall meaning. To get more specific though, let's look at what happens in an open network to determine exactly what *closing* it means.

An unassociated client device is in constant state of scanning until it associates with an AP. This state of scanning is where the client on each channel announces itself and requests permission to associate with any AP within range. There may be no RF close enough to receive the desperate cries for help from the adapter. If this is the case, the adapter continues to announce its identification in the form of its hardware address and requests a group to join—in the form of an AP and network. Eventually, the client comes in contact with an AP willing to listen to it. When this happens, the client remembers which channel the response came from and sticks to it. The AP announces its network name or SSID and whether or not data security is required. This is where the authentication begins with respect to the section on WEP. The client, all too willing to join, replies with an

"Any" for SSID (or the proper one, if configured) and the ciphertext challenge response for matching on the AP for correct WEP identification. The AP responds with an "OK, let's rock," or a "Sorry, you must be from out of town. Try the next window." If this transfer concludes successfully, the client is considered associated with the AP. The AP will then let all the other APs on the WLAN know that this client is associated with it, and to forward all stored messages destined for this client.

Association is more interrogative in a closed system. The same overall process is followed, but the AP does not announce the SSID. Instead, it challenges the client for the information. If the client says "Any," the AP will not respond. Only if the proper SSID and encryption key are supplied, will the AP associate the client device.

It is *not* recommended that you accept client associations with the SSID set to "Any," and further that you disable the broadcast of the SSID from the AP. This effectively closes the network. If the SSID is set to a name that is difficult to guess, then this process becomes a rudimentary method of access control, as communication cannot take place without this parameter being verified. This means that the SSID on the client has to match the settings on the AP. If they match, it means your client has passed the access control in that the device settings are correct.

Now that you know what a closed system is and what it implies, why would you use a closed system? The answer is more along the lines of "Why *wouldn't* you use a closed system?" The benefits of preventing random snooping and unauthorized access far outweighs this passive mechanism of preventing hackers from obtaining information about your WLAN.

Closed System Benefits and Advantages

The benefits of running closed networks boil down to the difference between a bar and a private club. It is the closing of the door on the unwashed masses that creates the privacy desired. In the same way, "closing the network" helps keep out those who would like to snoop your network ID, or find out whether or not you have WEP enabled. That information alone could give an intruder all the information they need to begin dissecting your WLAN. If the defaults are not altered, then with a couple of changes, anyone can surf your network or the World Wide Web right from their car in your parking lot. The following is a list of advantages:

- AP does not accept unrecognized network requests.
- It is an excellent security feature for preventing NetStumbler snooping software.

- It is easy to implement.
- Closing your network is passive and requires no other efforts.

Closed System Disadvantages

There aren't really any disadvantages to implementing a closed system. Once the network information is distributed to all the authorized users, it is a passive lock on your network. If there were any disadvantages to speak of, they would be:

- Administration for new users, new hardware, and other changes.
- New software installations will require the repeated distribution of the network information (SSID, WEP keys), thus weakening the policy.

Security Implications of Using a Closed System

Security is benefited greatly by closing your network. Think of the SSID and WEP as a car, and closing the network as deep tinting the glass. You can see out, but they can't see in. You get all the benefits you want, while the disadvantages are minimal. One item to note however (because this feature works in conjunction with the SSID and encryption), is that if this layer is compromised, wholesale changes will need to be made to correct the issue. All clients and APs will need to be addressed with a new SSID and encryption keys. Please, close the network. If your Access Point does not support this feature, rethink your choice of vendor equipment.

A Closed Environment on a Cisco Aironet Series AP

Figure 5.10 shows the Web interface for the Cisco Aironet AP340. As you can see, this interface sets the SSID and disables the null association for the closed environment. Additionally, there is the granularity of configuration for tweaking the WLAN, including various thresholds. That's not our focus here, but in terms of deploying a WLAN, it demonstrates the robust nature of the Cisco hardware.

A Closed Environment on an ORiNOCO AP-1000

Closing the Wireless LAN from the AP-1000 is as simple as checking the **Closed Wireless System** box in the **Wireless Security Setup** dialogue box (as shown in Figure 5.11), and selecting **OK**. The AP will reboot: a process that takes about

20 seconds, and voilà! The network is closed. Note that the WEP string is configured as earlier discussed.

Figure 5.10 Closing the WLAN on the Aironet

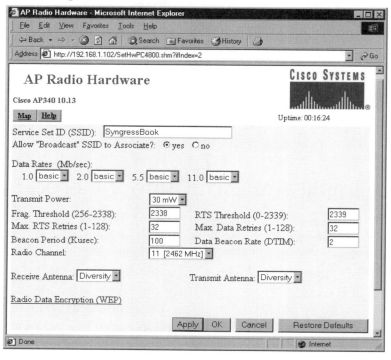

Figure 5.11 The Wireless Security Setup Dialogue Box

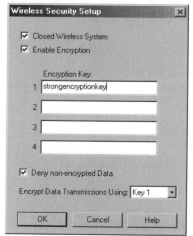

Implementing a Closed System: A Case Scenario

The president of our fictional R&R Enterprises has presented an article on the security issues surrounding WEP for WLANs and demanded countermeasures. The administrator of the WLAN immediately spoke to the lab workers on the Anti-Chimera project, and told them they need to be certain the SSID is set correctly in their client configuration. The administrator told them that by lunch, the network would be closed. After some initial protesting by the lab workers, the administrator explained what closed meant, and that the network would still be accessible to them (the authorized users), but not to anyone who did not have the correct client configuration.

As part of the corporate policy of R&R, the lab workers were compelled to sign an agreement to not divulge the settings for the WLAN client stations. This was an easy sell, because all the workers took great pride in the potential of developing unhindered this miracle medicine.

Enabling WEP on the ORiNOCO Client

Figure 5.12 shows the client software for the ORiNOCO card. Here the client enables WEP in order to communicate with the AP on R&R's wireless network. As you can see, there are methods of configuring multiple WEP keys and selecting which to use for rotating WEP.

Figure 5.12 The ORiNOCO Client Configuration

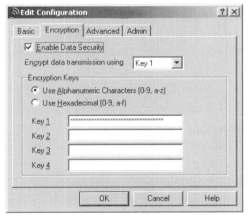

Allotting IPs

Allotting IP address spaces specific to the WLAN space is a good security countermeasure to consider from a couple points of view. Most APs can serve as DHCP servers, or at least allow DHCP traffic to transverse the network out to the WLAN client. Other implementations require static IP addresses for WLAN users. There are good arguments for each, which we'll discuss in the following sections.

Defining IP Allocation on the WLAN

WLANs take advantage of the same TCP/IP stack as Ethernet or Token Ring access methods. Wireless is more or less the Physical and Data Link layer of the access architecture. The TCP/IP stack sits on top of this architecture and allows seamless integration to the wired LAN. This allows the security tactics used in typical IP networks to be just as effective in the WLAN space. So, why would you allot specific IP addresses to the WLAN—as opposed to just allowing the LAN segment they're attached to act as an IP address?

Again, the answer to this question goes back to the fact that WLANs should be treated as remote access. It is not typical that a hacker with his laptop walks into your building, takes an Ethernet cable, and attaches to the nearest data port. This is due to the fact that your Ethernet is limited to your cabled offices, and is segmented according to the various VLANs required by the corporate structure and policy.

Wireless, on the other hand, doesn't politely stop at the wall or data port. In this case, the data port is an invisible barrier called an association with an access point. It is because of this fact that the remote access association should be regarded as priority.

So in this manner, it is necessary to take a certain IP address space or subnet and allot it to the WLAN. In this way, the administrator can look at the logs of potential intrusions and recognize immediately if they originated from the WLAN. If the same IP space were used as the local Ethernet segment, the administrator would have to do some preliminary paring down before the threat could be isolated. This certainly provides ample rationale for setting the IP address space specific to the WLAN, but how do you deliver it to the client? Do you use DHCP? Do you perform NAT? Do you provide static IP addresses? The answer is going to vary depending on the particular implementation your office uses. We'll look at some of the advantages and disadvantages of each in the next two sections.

Deploying IP over the WLAN: Benefits and Advantages

Why would you use DHCP? DHCP in certain cases makes the most sense, because of the nature of the network. If a construction company moves into a space for a few months in order to build a housing track or a set of buildings, an AP and a few wireless clients make great sense. There are no cables to run and the mobility provides the flexibility required to fully gain the benefit of WLAN access. Drop an AP in a central location, configure it for DHCP, and away you go. This provides for minimal configuration and maximum flexibility.

You could use DHCP in the corporate environment as well. Again, you are minimizing configuration on the client and the potential of weakness in access by providing DNS and default gateway information. You are also registering your clients on your network for logging purposes. In addition, the ability of the DHCP server in the SOHO office to provide NAT support protects users from the Internet threat by hiding addresses. In this way, when DHCP users are accessing the corporate network environment remotely, hackers who attempt to scan for devices will find the AP as the DHCP server only, and in that way no other devices are found.

This introduces some challenges though as well. If a hacker breaks your WEP key and in essence has the ability to associate with your AP, he will also receive an IP address from DHCP upon association. In this way, the address space for your WLAN is compromised. For that reason, assigning static IP addresses to your wireless clients can become very attractive.

Although it does introduce more client configuration challenges, the curbing of delivering Layer 3 access to devices not trusted on the network is highly advantageous. For this reason, statically assigning addresses is a viable option. These addresses should still come from a pool of addresses that are assigned to remote access and more specifically from the WLAN remote access portion of the network.

Deploying IP over the WLAN: Disadvantages

From a DHCP perspective, we have already discussed some of the disadvantages of utilizing DHCP for Layer 3 accesses. WEP can be broken. Traffic can be sniffed, and if there are Layer 3 access vulnerabilities, you could be giving a hacker a free pass to the network via DHCP, which is the last thing you want.

From a static perspective, the main disadvantage is the administrative overhead of keeping track of all the IP addresses in use. This issue compounds itself as the use of the WLAN increases. Many companies forecast a high probability of utilizing some version of WLAN technology in the near future even if it is 802.11G or 802.11A. Also, the potential for duplicate IP addresses bears mentioning, as it can cause trouble when static IP is the standard policy.

Security Implications of Deploying IP over the WLAN

DHCP as a means for deploying IP over the WLAN requires additional layers of security by virtue of the fact that hackers will get a free pass in the case of DHCP. Static IP ranges cause hackers to guess what your subnet is for WLAN.

IP requires the issue of duplicate IP addresses to be taken into account, as well as the distribution of the IP address space to users. Self-administration for Layer 3 connectivity results in the potential of the address space being utilized improperly by the trusted users.

Deploying IP over the WLAN: A Case Scenario

Although the administrator for the WLAN at R&R Enterprises initially set the AP to route DHCP requests to the DHCP server for Layer 3 addressing of the WLAN, he determined that because he did not initiate the closed system for a period of weeks, there might be additional threats concerning the WLAN. Perhaps an intruder already gathered a little information about the WLAN, including the subnet? He couldn't altogether prevent that from happening, but he certainly didn't want to publish information about his network. He also thought that if someone had gotten past WEP, they would have been served an IP address!

Immediately, the administrator notified the lab workers of the risks, and that there would be a change effective by lunch that day. He would go around to each client and set each IP address manually. He then determined to record this information, and cross reference it with the MAC addresses already recorded. This way the logs would be an automatic identification of a particular user's device for each event logged. The savvy admin then created an ACL preventing mismatched addresses to traverse the WLAN. He further tightened the straps by creating an ACL that denied all outgoing sender IP addresses except those assigned to the lab workers. This would prevent an intruder from arbitrarily setting up an IP within the subnet.

Satisfied with this next step, the administrator reflected on what security countermeasures he had placed and what they prevented. So far, he thought, an intruder must overcome the following:

- Uncover RF in the 2.4 Gig range to find a WLAN, because it is a closed system

- Break the 128-bit WEP encryption key

- Get past a MAC filter

- Discover what the IP address range is on the WLAN and find an address not in use

- Get past an ACL governing MAC/IP pair

Using VPNs

Use of virtual private networks has soared in recent years, and improvements in security matched by reductions in price will only increase their appeal. Properly configured, VPNs can come to the aid of wireless security, providing valuable authentication benefits, and perhaps eliminating the risk posed by the WEP shared key. It is no secret that as broadband access becomes more readily available, more and more users are able to telecommute. This has given rise to the awareness of VPN architectures and their use. A VPN essentially encrypts transmissions in such a fashion as to cause the nodes to be associated in a point-to-point relationship. This means one sender, one receiver, and no intermediary intelligence devices that can decrypt the transmission's contents.

In the Point-to-Point Tunneling Protocol, the most widely understood VPN mechanism, this process is performed according to the following method:

The traffic is sent down the protocol stack in a normal manner. The IP address of the intended destination is placed as usual in the IP header. Once it is passed to the Data Link layer, it is then transported back up the protocol stack to the IP layer again. Another IP header is added, which is formed with the destination address of the VPN server. It is then passed down the stack again and sent as normal. The VPN server receives the packet, strips off the headers until only the original packet is left. It is then forwarded on to the original destination. This is invisible from the perspective of the destination unless the destination is the VPN server. A similar function is performed on the Layer 2 Tunneling Protocol. IPSec is slightly different and utilizes an authentication and encryption on each packet (you can find out more about it and scan the RFCs listed by visiting www.ietf.org/html.charters/ipsec-charter.html).

Applying those techniques to the wireless space has enhanced the security model of wireless LANs—at one time, it was the sole mechanism utilized to ensure security, without which wireless would have been left on the discussion table and not implemented. VPNs continue to play a role in securing the WLAN. Colubris networks has gone so far as to implement a built-in VPN client on their AP, to allow individual users—regardless of VPN client ability—to use the VPN portion of the network connection back to the corporate network. Many other AP designers have started to implement this concept as well. It is no small feature and is changing the face of security perception regarding wireless in the networking community.

Network operating systems have long included VPN clients in their architecture to enhance their value to the telecommuting world. Now WLAN users can utilize the built-in IPSec, L2TP, and PPTP clients in Windows 2000 and enhanced versions in Windows XP. This prevents the requirement of distributing third-party clients to all your workstations and lowers the total cost of ownership.

There are many scenarios where this can be implemented. We will examine some of them now. In the first scenario, we will look at the most common implementation of security in the WLAN space. It is the VPN server on the corporate network, which provides authentication requirements and then terminates the VPN tunneled packets. This procedure allows secure access to the corporate network.

In this case, you create a VPN client connection on the client. This connection will point to the VPN server on the protected network. Until this connection is authorized, the WLAN traffic is inhibited beyond the BSS. This means that you can send non-VPN traffic to local stations in the same subnet connected to the same BSS. Traffic destined outside that BSS is blocked until authenticated by the VPN server. The client associates with AP, then must authenticate to the VPN server. Once that is completed, the client has protected access to the corporate network.

In another case, the VPN server can provide the necessary VPN services to tunnel data and distribute it to the appropriate destination, while a RADIUS server provides the authentication mechanism. The Remote Access Dial-In User Service has been the de facto standard for remote access authentication, authorization, and accounting, and provides a very granular approach to providing degrees of access. In the case of authentication, it matches credentials to determine identity. In the case of authorization, it matches identification credentials with a set of governing rules to allow access to network resources. Finally, in the case of accounting, it logs various configurable parameters to create a trail of use. In this case, the RADIUS server is established on the corporate network behind the VPN server for an additional layer of security.

In a third scenario, the VPN server is provided locally via the AP. Some APs can be configured as VPN servers and thus the traffic from the client to the AP is protected under the same encryption model as the previous example, but with one major advantage: It is the AP that provides the authentication, and therefore the entire communication is encrypted via VPN authentication mechanisms, instead of allowing a brief time (as in the previous example) where traffic is unprotected. This case provides more protection, with one limitation. The APs must support VPN traffic as a server, which introduces account limitations. The traffic, limited to 11 Mbps in the first place, becomes slightly more choked out with the fact that there is more overhead resulting from the tunneling process. In the design of an environment relying heavily on VPN architectures, it is important to provide the appropriate redundancy within the coverage area, which will result in a greater distribution of bandwidth.

VPN Benefits and Advantages

The benefits of VPN services are concise and can be listed on one hand, but the value associated behind those benefits cannot be expressed without an understanding of the risk associated with the loss of mission-critical data.

First of all, there is the fact that it is a point-to-point emulation that allows each node to appear as though all conversations are limited to a single conversation between only the two participants.

Secondly, the use of VPNs provides transmissions that are encrypted with multiple keys changing every defined time interval. This prevents anyone without those keys from gaining access to the data at all. Of course, this method of communication has its roots in telecommuting, so we would be remiss if we left out the fact that it is heavily relied upon by the work-from-home remote users.

Finally, another benefit is not just individual users connecting to corporate resources, but also branch offices connecting over the Internet. If the branch office has a DSL account, it is much cheaper and of significantly more bandwidth than a legacy ISDN BRI connection. In this case, the VPN provides the security.

VPN Disadvantages

Generally speaking, VPNs can be complex, difficult to set up, and difficult to administer. They should use a strong encryption algorithm such as 3DES.

They also require a re-keying period that sufficiently addresses the known text to ciphertext comparison vulnerabilities of a VPN, much like corporations that require the change of passwords for users at regular intervals.

Advantages of VPN client and server networks can quickly evaporate if the overhead is not calculated and contingency plans are not made for the resulting bottleneck. VPN communication places an additional 15 to 20 percent overhead on the network. Those figures are significant and must be taken into account.

VPNs can also be rendered useless if the security settings on user systems or devices can be compromised. This would allow an attacker to gather all the data from a user's system or device, and make use of it to access resources protected by the VPN.

Further, as with any security policy, it adds responsibilities to the administrator. Depending on the size of the network, and the number and type of security policies implemented in your particular environment, you could be adding staff with every new countermeasure. Administrators would have to make sure the setup is correct for servers and clients, and that the VPN server itself is redundant, and can handle the intense processing required. Clients without the VPN client set up and enabled on their device will not gain access. This can lead to frustrations on the part of technically challenged users.

Finally, there is the matter of making sure the users are set up properly. In this case, it requires some complex set up for the end users and their client connections, as well as the server set up and the connecting devices and underlying architecture.

Security Implications of Using a VPN

VPNs are the most widely used security mechanism for remote access. We discussed earlier the necessity of handling WLAN traffic as remote access—VPNs fall into that role nicely. When considering this countermeasure, keep in mind that although it is highly secure, it requires the appropriate underlying policies that prevent remote access outside the boundaries of VPNs, otherwise the VPN is rendered somewhat irrelevant.

As a closing thought, the VPN structure of the network you are implementing should tie directly into the policy of the network in general. Although the WLAN should be treated as a remote access technology, it is not necessary to implement an entirely separate network space for the WLAN. The same VPN server used prior to WLAN access should be utilized. One of the key advantages of wireless is the relatively inexpensive cost of implementation. To create an entirely new architecture for wireless defeats the purpose of reducing cost of ownership.

Layering Your Protection Using a VPN

Figure 5.13 represents a VPN from both the wired and the wireless perspective. The wireless device equipped with a VPN client can use its wireless connection to VPN through the AP to the VPN cluster in the DMZ. This VPN cluster will terminate the VPN tunnel while the RAS server provides authentication. Finally, the authenticated traffic will be passed through the firewall for a final layer of security prior to hitting the protected LAN. The remote site will also use this VPN only from the wired perspective—the same as you should already be familiar with.

Figure 5.13 VPN Architecture

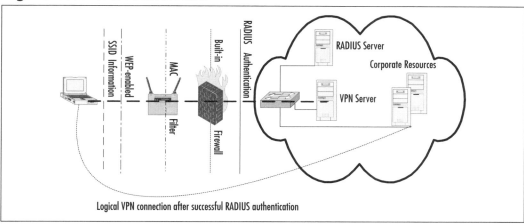

As you look at this diagram, you should be instantly alerted to the number of layers of security in place to protect the corporate environment. These will be WEP-enabled—the RAS server providing one layer of authentication and the VPN server providing an encrypted tunnel for a point-to-point link to the client while providing yet another layer of authentication.

Here you will notice first the need for the client to have the appropriate SSID information. If not, the AP will not accept a connection. Next, you'll see that even with the correct SSID, if the WEP key does not match, the AP will not grant a connection. Even if that information is correct, if the MAC is not recognized, the AP will not grant access. If all that information is correct on the client, but the IP address does not fall into the correct category, or if the protocol in use is not permitted, the built in firewall will block the traffic. Further, when initially supplying information, if the authentication username and password do not match a legitimate account on the RADIUS server, access is not granted. Once authenticated, if the VPN configuration matches the VPN server on the network, not only are you finally granted access, but your traffic is encrypted from start to finish.

Utilizing a VPN: A Case Scenario

R&R Enterprises had a significant setback in their plans for securing the WLAN. Part of the security mechanisms set in place, such as access control lists and logging, were causing significant deterioration in network performance because of the added processing required for each transmission. The lab workers complained that they could not be productive because packets were being dropped, and timeouts were occurring.

After reviewing all of the possibilities, the administrator decided to remove the ACLs and instead utilize a VPN. He theorized that although this would add overhead with respect to frame size and computing on the far ends, transmission on the intermediary devices, which were straining under the previous loads could handle the minor increase in bandwidth requirements.

An IPSec client was agreed upon and loaded on each wireless workstation. The VPN server provided an added layer of authentication, as well as adding an even stronger security posture than the previous model. A password policy was created to ensure minimum password length, and rotation with a four-password memory was instituted to prevent the reuse of previous passwords that might have become compromised.

Again the administrator rested, well-knowing that intruders would have virtually no access whatsoever to the WLAN. Each layer of security builds on the previous, providing stopgaps and additional hurdles that make the attempted hack into this network statistically impossible. Theoretically, even if these countermeasures could be compromised, it would take longer to break in than it would to create the Anti-Chimera medicine and patent it.

Securing Users

No security program will be complete without the willing participation of informed users. This is especially important in a wireless network, because of the limitations in the security model. WEP demands proper key setup and distribution for access. There are also vulnerabilities with respect to theft and misuse of portable devices. A disgruntled employee determined to get revenge could easily circumvent security mechanisms, because they are likely to have the information necessary. It is necessary that in considering securing users we touch on limiting administrative access to authorized personnel.

There are two extremes in securing users: security without regard to the thoughts, ideas, and interests of employees; and group effort security through education of good strong policy. The first states that users are secure despite their best efforts in a non-combative yet adversarial relationship with the administrator. In this scenario, the administrator institutes a policy whereby users follow procedures or get no access. This is certainly a secure model in the sense that users have to comply to get the network resources they need, however it causes users to attempt to find ways around the policy. The issue here is the active imagination of the user who doesn't like the policy, and therefore determines that they will attempt to circumvent it in some way. An example of this would be bringing in a modem from home and connecting it to their own workstation for remote access. Certainly, this extreme will cause them to have their hands full when security audits come to town.

The second extreme requires (and is based on) buy-in to the security model adopted by the administrator. This model demonstrates a collaborative effort where each user feels some obligation to the security model, and compliance is based on desire rather than force. Although this method is harder to implement and is more costly upfront because it requires education of the end users, the payoff is a typically more secure model with fewer headaches. Again, the reason comes down to the education of the end user, and the buy-in factor that allows many people to be self-policed, with some expected agreed upon policies. Let's talk about some strong yet appropriate measures for securing the user.

- Educate the users to the threats and where they are at risk.

- Provide policies that enable them to successfully secure themselves.

- Create accounts and policies that secure users "behind the scenes."

- Evaluate policy against required user activity to prevent adversarial relationships.

Educate the user as to the risk. If the user is made aware that they could be vulnerable, they are not only more cautious as to how they spend their time, but are also willing to listen to recommendations when it comes to protecting themselves.

Passwords and authentication are areas that end users need to be educated on—wireless or not. Administrators need to establish the expectation that the security policy is both useful and helpful, and that the requirements are mandatory. Weak passwords and poor authentication models make up a significant portion of the vulnerabilities found in networks. Users need to be educated on strong passwords of a minimum of eight characters in length using both upper- and lowercase letters, with special characters interspersed within. No dictionary words should be used. They need to understand that these passwords will, out of necessity, be changed at a regular interval to prevent someone from gaining the secret. They need to be educated on the authentication process so they understand that without the strong password and interval change, their work is at risk. The net of it is this: internal marketing for security is every bit as important a tool as policy, architecture, or a super-security-smart security team.

Provide policies that enable them to successfully secure themselves. It is important to force the users to alter their passwords at regular intervals. Of course, you already received buy-in for the process, but you have to follow it up with the action of the requirement. There are many ways to get this to happen. If you just tell users to do it, some will go along, but you won't get 100 percent compliance. If you force it from your Network Operating System (NOS), however, this will get the compliance you are looking for. Bear in mind that even though you have the users behind you in the security policy, if you force password alteration too often, the administrative cost of resets, and the irritation level of the users will grow. Users need access to resources to perform various tasks, and if they feel overbearing security policies are hindering their job, they will rebel. A good interval is dependent on a number of factors, but every 60 days is a good average.

The next part of this is the password length. Making sure the password has at least eight characters is absolutely necessary. Volumes of books could be written as to why, but it boils down to this extreme example. If your password is only 1 alphanumeric character in length, how many guesses do I have to make before I get it right? Thirty-six. Because of the nature of probabilities as the number of characters increases, the number of guesses increases exponentially. Add to that the complexity of upper- and lowercase letters, as well as preventing common strings of letters such as dictionary words, and the passwords become extremely difficult to break. You only need the passwords to be difficult enough to break that it becomes too costly for the hacker to spend the time, money, and energy to attempt it.

Creating policies that work seamlessly and largely go unnoticed so users are secured without administratively having to perform some task goes a long way toward cutting administrative costs. In order to do this, you must set policy restrictions that work in the background. Filtering traffic that users don't know exists can accomplish this goal. This averts the feeling of having lost a right. The more security tasks are left in the hands of the user, the less effective the policy is going to be. Users want to do their jobs, not be security administrators. Make sure they don't have access to resources from an account perspective that they should not have. Filter protocols, as we have already discussed, create security policies for individual resources to prevent the unwitting breach of security policy. An example of this would be preventing a user from being able to share local volumes.

Finally, as mentioned earlier, there is user buy-in. If you do not allow appropriate access to resources, and impose severely restrictive rule sets that ultimately hinder productivity, the end users will rebel and attempt to subvert the security policy. Respecting the end users and their role in the corporate environment is of the highest importance. Without them, your security is unnecessary. It is in this scenario where the disgruntled employee is provided the impetus to wreak havoc on devices within the network. Because of this, it is vital that administrative access to devices, as part of the security policy, be limited to certain trusted users. In some extreme cases (military, for example), there are multiple individuals who each have a portion of a long random password, and who are each required to be present in order to make administrative changes. Certainly, this scenario isn't always practical, but it serves as an example of how to secure from within.

Now that we have examined passwords and how to secure users from an abstract perspective, what are some of the rule sets that should be in place with respect to wireless 802.11b?

No rogue access points. No one should be bringing in their own AP to allow them access to the corporate network environment. Not only can they allow hackers access to corporate resources, but also if they do not understand the 2.4 Gig wireless ISM band, they could be severely limiting other users access to the resources they need by using a channel that is already in production.

Inventory all wireless cards and their corresponding MAC addresses. Standardize on a specific brand of card. Allow only those cards accepted in inventory in your MAC filter.

No antennas without administrative consent. If someone brings in an antenna and connects it to the corporate network, you have created the possibility that your signal can now be accessed from great distances (up to 25 km!). In this way, the potential intruder can work on attacking your network from a distance using Airsnort and NetStumbler.

Strong passwords on wireless network devices. Standard users should not have logical administrative access to the AP. In the case of physical access, the AP should be placed where either all users would readily see loss, or where no one can actually get to the AP. Placing the AP physically in a location that prevents reset, or theft, or physical contact outside of a lock and key is an excellent choice.

End User Security Benefits and Advantages

One advantage of securing users is preventing one of the largest points of failure. It allows all of your security measures to work together while adding one more important layer to the protective model.

Another advantage is found in the policy remaining in unhindered while the users do their jobs without the adversarial relationship. No security policy is effective if the end user is constantly trying to subvert it from within. Ultimately, it will allow for far more vulnerabilities than an administrator can keep up with.

A majority of users policing themselves and peers with respect to the security policy is infinitely more effective than a forced policy. Users may also be willing to offer ideas and suggestions to secure their own areas of responsibility that the administrator might never have imagined a need for. This is due to the fact that end users recognize the idea of personal work and the need for security more than corporate work and need. To many users, corporate security is an amorphous concept without personal effects. But when the policy is brought to the individual, personal pride in accomplishment plays a role in development of the policy. Many individually secured users add up to corporate security.

End User Security Disadvantages

In this scenario, a disadvantage is that there will not be 100 percent cooperation. And in this regard, it can be a limiting factor in that it only takes one breach in the ship to sink it. Users will tend to secure their stations based on the idea that it is a common goal, and that the machines and resources around them are also more or less equally secured. This could lead to unwitting vulnerabilities.

Also, securing individuals is an expensive proposition. It requires training and administrative overhead that otherwise wouldn't be a concern. This also dovetails into a second vulnerability in that the information in the training sessions must be dispersed in order to become valuable. If it is dispersed, there is a greater likelihood it will be spread beyond the ears that need it. Also, if a user is disgruntled and wants to cause mischief, they are aware of the policies and will know of ways to circumvent these policies. These are challenges that can be overcome to some extent, but will ultimately need to be kept in mind.

User Security: A Case Scenario

As we have seen in the previous case scenarios, at each turn the administrator discussed the security policy changes with the relevant parties. He also gained their support by educating them, and including them in the process. He educated them about some of the countermeasures and how to prevent them from losing their valued access. Even more important, the admin responded when the users explained of the issues concerning productivity surrounding a security policy initially thought to be good. From a threat mitigation perspective, it was a good policy; but from an availability standpoint, it was not effective.

As you read these case scenarios and glean information from them, the expectation is that you recognize the need for multiple layers of security, the availability of multiple security countermeasures in general, and the need to incorporate them within a sound policy that accounts for the production, as well as the protection, of corporate assets.

Summary

With respect to securing your WLAN, not to mention the success of your security strategy overall, *policy* is the place to start—policies such as preventing administrative access from unauthorized internal users, treating the WLAN like remote access, altering the defaults, and keeping consistent rule sets across your network.

It's important to start by undertaking a process of threat analysis, conducting an evaluation of resources that are potential targets for intruders. Next, you must identify the potential intruders, and the overall best practices to thwart their activities. Identifying assets and assigning value, threat, vulnerability, and risk is a key component of setting policy. Make certain you know what intruders are likely to find, and what they are most interested in finding. For any given threat, a lack of barriers and a high degree of inescapability ensures your vulnerability.

Even if from a high-level perspective, think security into the design of your WLAN. Review the AP hardware and the security supported by the platform, the placement of the AP for security, and the minimum requirements for the device you decide upon.

The next step is the development and planning of your WLAN. Utilize the highest supported security feature within the existing hardware, and make sure WEP is enabled. WEP has its merits and benefits and although there are some limitations, there is no reason to ignore its use. Periodic WEP key changes should take place in order to prevent certain known plaintext attacks. This chapter focused briefly on MAC filters and utilizing built-in firewalls, as well as closing the network system by disabling the broadcast of the SSID as an added layer of authentication. MAC filtering should be used in conjunction with logging failures to see if there is an attempted breach. Protocol filters are to be used cautiously when necessary to segment traffic.

In addition, when making a new purchase, select hardware that supports a strong migration path for 802.11a and 802.11g. This new hardware should also support all the same security countermeasures as the existing one, as well as any new and improved strategies. Once you have decided on the hardware, place it where theft is unlikely, but where there is optimum coverage for those that need it.

As some added countermeasures, consider allotting the IP address space and weigh the advantages and disadvantages of both static and dynamically assigned addresses. Static addresses prevent a hacker from automatically being dealt an IP, where dynamic addresses ease the use of the WLAN with respect to already daunting administrative tasks. To seal the WLAN from other possible threats that could potentially get far enough to overcome the significantly complex obstacles already in place, you could add a strong VPN with IPSec clients. What you are actually trying to do is create enough mitigating layers to protect the assets so that the value of the target is nil by the time the intruder finally gains access—if he does at all.

Finally, employ a security posture that cooperates with end users in making a holistic security approach. Care should be given to securing from internal threats by placing administrative access in specific hands. It's important to balance administrative powers between enough personnel that mitigation of internal risk is maintained. All your efforts will be thwarted from within if there isn't sufficient buy-in from those you are attempting to secure.

Solutions Fast Track

Revisiting Policy

☑ Policy is the set of rules that governs the management, use, implementation, and interaction of corporate assets. These assets include human resources, intellectual capital, hardware, software, networks and infrastructure, and data.

☑ Resources must be easily accessible for trusted users, while barriers are maintained for untrusted users.

☑ Policy must reflect changes in corporate structure. If policy fails to comply with reorganization, it will be as effective as last year's virus definitions against this year's virus.

☑ Wireless local area networks (WLANs) are an "edge" technology. Policy should reflect a standard consistent with end users attempting to gain access to network resources from the "edge."

Analyzing the Threat

☑ Analyzing the threat is the first step in securing any network.

☑ Recognize what threat, vulnerability, and risk mean as they pertain to securing your network.

☑ Identify assets and assign risk.

☑ Identify potential intruders and begin to formulate a mitigation plan.

Designing and Deploying a Secure Network

- ☑ Alter the defaults!

- ☑ Treat the Access Point (AP) like a Remote Access Server (RAS).

- ☑ Specify Internet Protocol (IP) ranges that are earmarked for the WLAN only.

- ☑ Use the highest-rated, supported security feature available on your AP.

- ☑ Consider the fact that using an antenna in a benefit for both the authorized and the intruder.

- ☑ Apply consistent authorization rules across the edge of the network for all users.

- ☑ Deploy hardware where it is not easily tampered with.

Implementing WEP

- ☑ To protect against some rudimentary attacks that insert known text into the stream to attempt to reveal the key stream, Wired Equivalent Privacy (WEP) incorporates a check sum in each frame. Any frame not found to be valid through the check sum is discarded.

- ☑ Used on its own, WEP does not provide adequate WLAN security.

- ☑ WEP has to be implemented on every client as well as every AP to be effective.

- ☑ WEP keys are user definable and unlimited. You do not have to use predefined keys, and you can and should change them often.

- ☑ Implement the strongest version of WEP available and keep abreast of the latest upgrades to the standards.

Filtering MACs

- ☑ Apply Media Access Control (MAC) filters as a first line of defense. Each MAC address to be used on the WLAN should be recorded and configured on the AP for permission to access the network.

☑ Log failures and review the logs to determine if someone is attempting to breach security.

Filtering Protocols

☑ Filtering protocols is a relatively effective method for restricting WLAN users from attempting Simple Network Management Protocol (SNMP) access to the wireless devices to alter configurations, and for preventing the use of large Internet Control Message Protocol (ICMP) packets and other such protocols that can be used as Denial of Service (DoS) agents.

☑ Filter all the appropriate protocols and addresses to maintain control of the data traversing your network.

Using Closed Systems and Networks

☑ Ease of capture of Radio frequency (RF) traffic can be overcome by preventing the broadcast of the Secure Set Identifier (SSID) to the world from the AP.

☑ Close the network to prevent null association whenever possible.

☑ Distribute the necessary client configuration information to WLAN users securely.

Allotting IPs

☑ Determine which method of allotting IPs best suits your organization: static or dynamically assigned addresses. Static addresses prevent a hacker from automatically being dealt an IP, where dynamic addresses ease the use of the WLAN with respect to already daunting administrative tasks.

☑ Static IP ranges make hackers have to guess what your subnet is for WLAN.

Using VPNs

☑ Use virtual private network (VPN) services where appropriate. They are the single most secure method of remote access available.

☑ Some APs (like Colubris Networks and Nokia) have built in VPNs for ease of implementation.

Securing Users

☑ Educate your users as to the risk associated with the uses of WLANs and the need for agreement in security policy. They are your single largest point of failure in your security model.

☑ Include the users in the process for the best information upon which to base decisions.

☑ Enforce the policies to the extent that it remains productive.

Frequently Asked Questions

The following Frequently Asked Questions, answered by the authors of this book, are designed to both measure your understanding of the concepts presented in this chapter and to assist you with real-life implementation of these concepts. To have your questions about this chapter answered by the author, browse to **www.syngress.com/solutions** and click on the **"Ask the Author"** form.

Q: Where can I find an explanation of the weaknesses of WEP?

A: University of California at Berkeley has members participating in this discussion that add significant value to the conversation. The following is a good link: www.drizzle.com/~aboba/IEEE.

Q: Security seems so vast. What is the starting point for determining security needs?

A: There is no standard starting point. Analyze what it is that you do, and where in the process it can be threatened. Sophisticated hackers (the ones you need to worry about) are interested in the value of the data for an exchange of financial reward. Ask yourself this question, "Where can I be hurt the worst?" Then secure that position!

Q: How can I tell if my WLAN is secure?

A: There are a few products out there that provide common threat analysis for wired LANs such as ISS's Scanner tools, Nessus, whisker, and the like. There are few that are specific to WLANs. Once you have implemented the concepts contained in this chapter, it might be a good idea to hire an outside consulting firm to check it for you. They are versed in security, as well as wireless, and have the tools available to check avenues of vulnerability.

Q: How many users can function adequately on one AP with VPN enabled?

A: This depends on the hardware in use, and the application accessed. The Colubris Series APs advertise a maximum of 30 users using the VPN client, but it's more likely that number is closer to 20. Depending on the amount of bandwidth you require per user, that number is going to fluctuate accordingly.

Q: Where can I find some information on WLAN security improvement initiatives?

A: Search the Web for vendor sites. Vendors typically respond to the needs of customers in order to generate and maintain revenue streams. They will be struggling to be the first to implement the latest security mechanisms developed. Eventually, the best countermeasure will become standardized and be widely deployed.

Q: What features are the minimums for an adequate security posture?

A: At a minimum, you should close the network, enable WEP, and employ a MAC filter. Change your WEP key often. This should be enough in many environments until the level of sophistication of the intruders significantly increases. However, if you do have a more virulent intruder after your network, and you have the budget, deployment of a strong VPN would be your logical next step.

Chapter 6

Circumventing Security Measures

Solutions in this chapter:

- **Planning and Preparations**
- **Exploiting WEP**
- **War Driving**
- **Stealing User Devices**
- **MAC Filtering**
- **Bypassing Advanced Security Mechanisms**
- **Exploiting Insiders**
- **Installing Rogue Access Points**
- **Exploiting VPNs**

- ☑ **Summary**
- ☑ **Solutions Fast Track**
- ☑ **Frequently Asked Questions**

Introduction

No security measure is perfect on its own merit. In some cases, multiple security measures have to be put in place to cover a single vulnerability—yet it seems that no sooner is a security mechanism deemed safe, than an attacker pokes a hole right through it!

Although network administrators may have thought they could secure their wireless network by changing the default settings, knowledgeable attackers can find their way through using several different means.

In this chapter, we'll look at the most worrying methods that attackers have used to bypass security mechanisms. We'll also look at the threat of *war driving*, which is rapidly gaining respect as a legitimate and effective attack strategy.

The use of shared keys and hard-coded Media Access Control (MAC) addresses in order to control access to the wireless local area network (WLAN) makes device theft a very effective technique in defeating wireless security measures.

With a notable increase in crimes and attacks by trusted insiders, it's likely that unauthorized insiders with special knowledge will be able to find effective countermeasures against even the toughest security measures. And while virtual private networks (VPNs) can provide an additional layer of security to a wireless network, they are not a perfect solution. We will discuss some of the problems associated with VPN security, many of them directly connected to user behavior, home computing, and working on the road.

Planning and Preparations

From a broad perspective, attackers fall into two categories: the bored and the determined. The former will only attempt to breach the security of your network if it can be accomplished with a minimum of effort. These types of attackers like to use premade scripts to gauge how difficult it will be to penetrate your defenses and will move on to an easier target if the network has defenses adequate enough to frustrate them.

A determined attacker may spend weeks or even months conducting reconnaissance on a potential target. Their primary objective is to gather the information necessary to prepare an attack that will result in the greatest success with the lowest risk of detection or capture. This attacker will most likely begin with passive and non-intrusive attacks, such as war driving, to first uncover potential targets, and then map the discovered networks to identify specific characteristics and vulnerabilities. Numerous war driving studies have shown how easy it is for an attacker using very basic and affordable equipment to not only identify numerous wireless networks in a relatively small area, but to identify the many organizations who have not even implemented the Wired Equivalent Privacy (WEP) security measures available to them.

Finding a Target

With few exceptions (such as Starbucks and other public wireless Internet service providers[ISPs]), most companies with a corporate-sponsored wireless network will not announce their existence to the outside world. In order to avoid providing an incentive for hacking, most companies will only release information about their WLANS to the employees who will be using them.

In preparation for intrusion, a hacker will have to discover if a wireless network exists, as well as determine the boundaries of the wireless network. We'll discuss some of the methods they use in the following section.

Choosing the Tools and Equipment Required for Attack

The first piece of equipment needed will be a computer. Although a personal computer may suffice for testing purposes, typically a laptop will be used (for mobility reasons).

The second item needed is an 802.11 radio. Typically mounted within a PCMCIA card, these radios will be used to identify and locate the radio signals from the target network. USB radios may also be employed, but are most commonly used to connect to wireless networks, not look for them.

Almost all PCMCIA-based 802.11b radios have a built-in antenna, or the ability to connect to an external antenna. Depending on the signal strength of the target network, an external antenna might be needed to maintain a connection to the network.

Finally, we come to the most important ingredient to this recipe, software. Several wireless network discovery programs can be used, depending on your operating system and your budget. While Windows users can download NetStumbler for free, it only works with certain 802.11 cards and discovers *open networks*. For the discovery of *closed networks*, Windows users can use Ethernet sniffing programs like Network Associates' Sniffer Wireless or WildPacket's AiroPeek. (We will discuss "open" and "closed" networks in more detail in the following section.) Many Unix-based wireless network discovery tools exist, the most notable being Ethereal. Each of these programs has special requirements regarding the wireless cards they work with, as well as the specific version of firmware and drivers necessary for proper operation.

Detecting an Open System

When the Institute of Electrical and Electronic Engineers' (IEEE) 802.11 specification was being developed, various methods were proposed by which wireless stations could attach onto the network. The finished specification declares that in order for a device to attach to the WLAN, it would need to know the network name or Service Set Identifier (SSID) of the wireless network. A network administrator, however, can configure the wireless network to accept incoming connections if the end-device is looking for a wireless network with an "empty value" SSID. These sorts of networks are termed *open systems* or *open networks*.

It is important to make a clear distinction here. Even though a network may be defined as "open," it does not necessarily mean that this network can be easily compromised. The only information passed back to the end-device is that a wireless network exists, and the value of that WLAN's SSID. It is up to the network administrator to know that if he wishes to broadcast his networks' SSID that some additional access controls need to be implemented in order to protect against hacking attempts.

This is how a program like NetStumbler (shown in Figure 6.1) operates. The program sends out a radio beacon with an "empty set" SSID. Access Points (APs) configured to accept these connections will hear this beacon and respond with a radio transmission listing their SSID as well as other related information.

Figure 6.1 Network Stumbler's Main Window

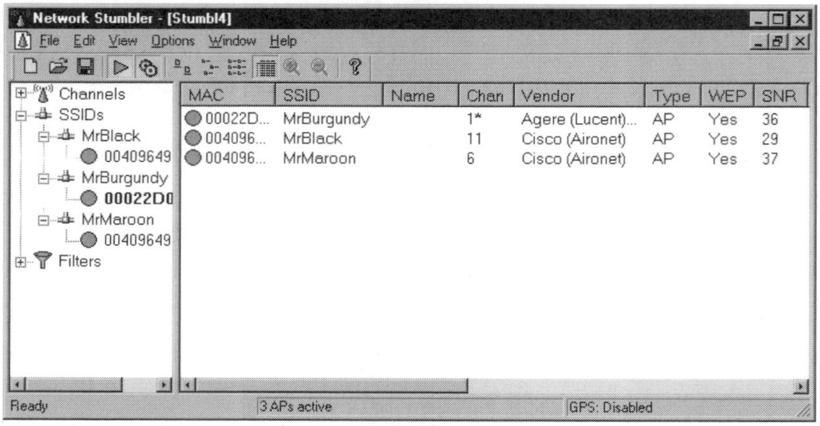

AiroPeek, and other wireless sniffers, will display all traffic being heard on the wireless card, regardless of whether the AP is sending out beacons or not. As long as the AP is within the range of the wireless sniffer, all traffic can be captured, recorded, and saved for future analysis.

Detecting a Closed System

If a network administrator has configured his APs to ignore the "empty set" SSID beacons, programs like NetStumbler will not be able to ascertain the existence of that WLAN. These "closed" networks can be determined through the use of a Wireless Protocol Analysis software like Ethereal, Sniffer Wireless, or AiroPeek. These programs can capture the raw 802.11b frames and decode their contents. It is while looking though the decoded frames that a person can see the SSID of the "closed" network, the 802.11b channel frequency it is operating on, as well as traffic that might be traversing the WLAN at that time.

Additionally, these "closed" networks can also be found through the use of a Radio Frequency (RF) spectrum analyzer, such as the one shown in Figure 6.2. If the analyzer supports the 2.4GHz frequencies, it may be possible to uncover their existence, channel of use, and signal strength. This is handy if you are planning to deploy a WLAN and want to check for potential interference. If you want to find the network's SSID, or see any traffic, you will have to use a protocol analyzer for those details.

Exploiting WEP

There have been a number of well-publicized exploitations and defeats of the security mechanisms at the heart of WEP, from weaknesses in the encryption algorithm to weaknesses in key management. While steps have being taken to overcome these weaknesses, attackers are not suffering from a lack of networks to exploit.

The first warnings regarding WEP's vulnerability to compromise came in the fall of 2000 when Jesse Walker published a document called "Unsafe at any Size: An Analysis of the WEP Encryption." In this document, Walker underscored the main weakness of WEP—the fact that it reinitializes the encrypted data stream every time an Ethernet collision occurs. Even though the 802.11 protocol attempts to avoid them with CDMA/CA, collisions are a reality that will occur. If someone is listening in on the wireless conversation, they capture the Initialization Vector information transmitted with each frame and in a matter of hours have all the data needed to recover the WEP key.

Figure 6.2 Spectrum Analysis Shows What Seems to Be an AP Operating on Channel Seven

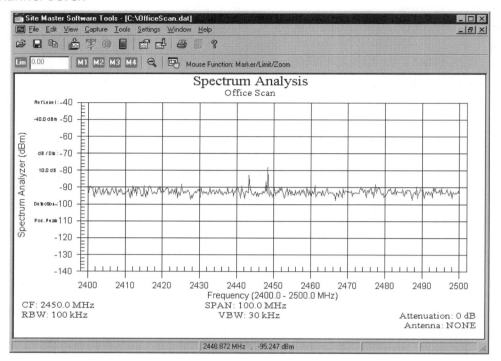

While many experts have made similar discoveries regarding this and other ways to recover WEP keys, these were usually academic and only showed that the potential for vulnerability existed. This all changed with the introduction of AirSnort and WEPcrack. Both of these programs saw an initial release in the summer of 2001, and moved the recovery of WEP keys from being a theoretical to something anyone could do—if they had a wireless card based on the PRISM2 chipset.

Security of 64-bit versus 128-bit Keys

It might seem obvious to a non-technical person that something protected with a 128-bit encryption scheme would be more secure than something protected with a 64-bit encryption scheme. This, however, is not the case with WEP. Since the same vulnerability exists with both encryption levels, they can be equally broken within similar time limits.

With 64-bit WEP, the network administrator specifies a 40-bit key—typically ten hexadecimal digits (0-9, a-f, or A-F). A 24-bit initialization vector (IV) is appended to this 40-bit key, and the RC4 key scheme is built from these 64-bits of data. This same process is followed in the 128-bit scheme. The Administrator specifies a 104-bit key—this time 26 hexadecimal digits (0-9, a-f, or A-F). The 24-bit IV is added to the beginning of the key, and the RC4 key schedule is built.

As you can see, since the vulnerability comes from capturing predictably weak initialization vectors, the size of the original key would not make a significant difference in the security of the encryption. This is due to the relatively small number of total initialization vectors possible under the current WEP specification. Currently, there are a total of 2^{24} possible IV keys. You can see that if the WEP key was not changed within a strictly-defined period of time, all possible IV combinations could be heard off of a 802.11b connection, captured, and made available for cracking within a short period of time. This is a flaw in the design of WEP, and bears no correlation to whether the wireless client is using 64-bit WEP or 128-bit WEP.

Acquiring a WEP Key

As mentioned previously, programs exist that allow an authenticated and/or unassociated device within the listening area of the AP to capture and recover the WEP key. Depending on the speed of the machine listening to the wireless conversations, the number of wireless hosts transmitting on the WLAN, and the number of IV retransmissions due to 802.11 frame collisions, the WEP key could be cracked as quickly as in a couple of hours. Obviously, if an attacker attempts to listen to a WEP-protected network when there was very little network traffic, it would take much longer to be able to get the data necessary to crack WEP.

Armed with a valid WEP key, an intruder can now successfully negotiate association with an AP, and gain entry onto the target network. Unless other mechanisms like MAC filtering are in place, this intruder is now able to roam across the network and potentially break into servers or other machines on the network. If MAC filtering is occurring, another procedure must be attempted to get around this. This will be covered in the "MAC Filtering" section later in the chapter.

Damage & Defense...

WEP Re-keying—Friend or Foe?

Since WEP key retrieval is now possible by casual attackers, it does not make sense to keep the same static WEP key in a production role for an extended period of time. If your WEP key is static, is could be published into the underground by a hacker and still be used in a production WLAN six months to a year later.

One of the easiest ways to mitigate the risk of WEP key compromise is to regularly change the WEP key your APs and clients use.

While this may be an easy task for small WLANs, the task becomes extremely daunting when you have dozens of APs and hundreds of clients to manually re-key.

Both Cisco and Funk Software have released Access Control servers that implement rapid WEP re-keying on both APs as well as the end-user client. Utilizing this form of software, even if a WEP key was to be discovered, you could rest assured that within a specified period of time, that particular key would no longer be valid.

War Driving

War driving has become the common term given for people who drive around with wireless equipment looking for other wireless networks. Another term used synonymously is "Access Point Discovery." But no matter what name the practice goes by, it is commonplace to hear stories of people who drive around their city looking to see if they can find others who have installed a wireless network.

A number of recent demonstrations have highlighted the simplicity and effectiveness of war driving in locating wireless networks. If the Access Points of the discovered networks are located behind the firewall, war driving can be the vital first step in identifying a target that thinks it's secure.

Part of the novelty of war driving is how easy it is to discover wireless networks. All you have to do is toss your laptop in the car and do a little driving. You could be going to get groceries, taking your pet to the vet, or just driving to the mall, and all the while your laptop is discovering and recording wireless networks along the way.

The numbers of "Open" WLANs are proportionate to the size of the city; they can be detected in small towns and large cities alike. Even a mid-sized rural county seat in the Midwest was noted to have over 60 open WLANS. In more metropolitan cities, some "AP Jockeys" have disclosed figures nearer the thousand mark.

Tools & Traps…

Is It Easy to Pinpoint the Location of an AP?

Even with the use of a Global Positioning System (GPS), it can be difficult to determine the exact location of a "beaconing" Access Point. Things like weather conditions and the amount of seasonal foliage can vary an outdoor AP's signal-to-noise ratio, thus creating different seasonal 802.11 footprints. While locating an indoor AP is easier, structural reflections and building materials can cause reflective patterns that make it a little more difficult that one might think.

What Threat Do These "Open Networks" Pose to Network Security?

The easiest answer to this question lies in the fact that APs are not typically treated as an outside access device such as a modem. APs are often located outside a firewall, but instead will sit inside the company's production network. Even if WEP encryption is used on this network (studies have shown that the majority of them will fail to enable even this form of weak protection) it is then a simple matter to change the SSID settings on the 802.11b radio, crack WEP, and gain entry onto the target network.

What Tools Are Necessary to Perform a War Drive?

Although war driving does not require much more than the equipment listed in the section "Open Network Discovery," there are a few things that can enhance the experience like a GPS device and a personal firewall.

If your GPS unit has a serial port, you can plug GPS Latitude/Longitude data into your NetStumbler results. This data will assist you in building a map of where the open systems are in your city as seen in Figure 6.3. (To protect those who have left their APs on the default settings, we have removed identifying markings from the map.)

Figure 6.3 Matching Discovered APs to a Map through Latitude/Longitude Triangulation

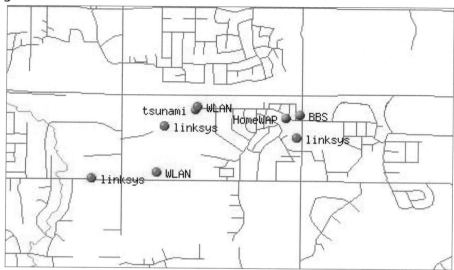

The other handy item to have along is a personal firewall that will block *all* Internet Protocol (IP) traffic. This may seem like an odd item at first, but it is very important. Since 802.11b is a Layer 1/ Layer 2 protocol, it is entirely possible to perform a war drive and not pass any IP traffic while mapping out the Access Points discovered. (The Zone Alarm personal firewall from Zone Labs is perfect for this purpose, as it will block *all* inbound *and* outbound IP traffic.) While some people will debate the need to block IP traffic while war driving, others would prefer to not gain a Dynamic Host Configuration Protocol (DHCP) IP address while passing through a network. This minimizes the risk of leaving a trail of their MAC address if the DHCP server is logging DHCP lease transactions.

What Network Information Can I Discover from a War Drive?

Surprisingly, it can be amazingly easy to create a profile on the target network using the information gathered in a war drive. Company information, identification, and details of the wired network are only a few of the items we will discuss.

If you are not using a personal firewall to block IP traffic, you may obtain or identify an IP address from an internal DHCP server. This IP address can be very handy in determining the size of the wired network. Were you handed a public IP address or a private IP address? (For more on this topic, see the sidebar.) How large is the subnet mask on this IP address? Does it specify a small network or a larger supernet?

If you were handed a private 192.168.x.x/24 IP address, the network could turn out to be small (under or around 250 hosts). If the private IP address is in the 10.x.x.x/8 or 172.16.x.x/16 range, odds are that the network you uncovered is tied back into a larger enterprise.

If you were handed a nonprivate IP address, some additional information like the upstream provider can be gained. Domain Name System (DNS) lookups against this IP address can tell you who provides Internet service to this network. The forward DNS name might give you a clue like companyXYZ-rtr0.upstream .net, or could be as visible as xxx.xxx.xxx.xxx-company.com.

Additionally, you may be able to answer the corporate network/private net-work question by looking at the upstream provider. A private circuit to the ISP (like a T1 or DS3) could lean the evidence towards a company connection, while private or small office/home office (SOHO) networks could connect via a digital subscriber line (DSL) or a cable modem uplink.

Regardless of the IP address or subnet information, standard network dis-covery tools can be deployed to map out the boundaries and contents of the wireless/wired network. One such tool is Nmap. Nmap is a full-featured network discovery tool that can be used to "scan" a user-defined scope of IP addresses and report back on how many devices are in operation, the type of devices in opera-tion, and what operating system the host is running. Nmap will also show the Transmission Control Protocol (TCP) or User Datagram Protocol (UDP) ports that are open and waiting for incoming connections. (For more details on Nmap, visit their Web site at www.insecure.org/nmap. Be sure to check out Chapter 9 in this book for a real-time demonstration of Nmap.)

Corporate identifiers might also be found in the information the AP passes back to your AP mapping software. An example would be where the company name was used for the SSID of the wireless network. (From a security standpoint, this is a *bad* idea. A good WLAN designer should be able to create a naming con-vention that does not hand out this sort of information!) Another example would be where specific contact information (name/location/internal phone number) is placed in the AP's configuration. (This information can also be commonly gained by the Simple Network Management Protocol [SNMP] when scanning the AP.)

Can War Driving Be Detected?

Recently published reports of war driving have given estimates that less that 20 percent of the networks discovered have WEP encryption enabled. Although WEP can be circumvented, this low figure seems to indicate a lack of due diligence given to the deployment of WLANs. It might be difficult to believe that the people who have left such glaring security holes in place could be auditing the efforts of those who are war driving. It is possible, taking hints from the recent "HoneyNet" projects, but these efforts would be few and extremely uncommon. With each device connecting to the network having a MAC address (Wireless personal digital assistants [PDAs], laptops, desktops, servers, switches, routers, and so on), a typical network could contain hundreds of MAC addresses. Although some of the high-end network management software like HP OpenView and CiscoWorks will monitor MAC addresses on a network and report on new entries, they are expensive and require specific configuration for this feature. To manually maintain such a state table would be a very daunting task.

War driving could also be detected by auditing DHCP logs. If your network's DHCP server logs all DHCP requests, the requesting MAC's address, and the IP addresses assigned to them, filters could be created to show the entry of foreign MAC addresses. This security measure poses its own challenges as employees could purchase their own wireless-capable devices and bring them in to work.

Another way war driving could be detected is through the examination of the AP's log files. Most commercial-grade APs have the capability to log events to a syslog server or forward alerts to a SNMP-trap server. Depending on how the AP is configured to log events, it is possible it could record the insertion of a wireless MAC, the authentication/association request to the AP, and the success/failure of those requests.

Again, with the large number of deployed WLANs lacking configuration beyond what is implemented right out of the box, it is doubtful your war driving will make any notation on a target network's radar.

Stealing User Devices

In the early days of network security, when there was no Internet through which to attack, hackers would often attempt to walk into businesses or military locations in order to steal crypto boxes known to use fixed or private key encryption. Connecting that legitimate and trusted box to the network turned into a simple workaround of tough security measures.

The same techniques can work just as easily today. If an attacker simply steals a wireless device containing ID or access information, it could allow an unauthorized user to pose as a legitimate employee.

A recent report by the Gartner Group stated that the most common places where laptop or PDA theft occurred were at airports (security checkpoints, ticket counters, and curbside check-ins) and hotels (restrooms, meeting rooms, and registration areas). With the increased implementation of wireless networks in the corporate space, odds are increasing that the stolen laptop could not only include a wireless network interface card (NIC), but also contain information that could be useful in breaking into the WLAN.

What Are the Benefits of Device Theft?

The computer insurance firm Safeware states that they find the main reason for laptop theft is the high resale value of the laptop itself. With a quick format of the hard drive, and the application of an Operating System, the laptop can fetch a tidy sum of money at a computer swap meet, convention, or pawnshop.

While a petty thief will only see the dollar value of the physical hardware, the sophisticated thief will understand that the data contained on the hard drive is far more valuable than the actual laptop. The information contained with financial spreadsheets, confidential e-mail, business plans, or legal documents could cost a company millions of dollars to re-create or recover if that information was leaked to a competitor or to the news media. The Gartner Group also suggested that up to 15 percent of stolen laptops are taken by criminals intent on selling the data.

Can the information found on the stolen device lead to a compromised WLAN? Absolutely! Let's take a look at a scenario in which the theft of a device has been carried out for the purpose of gaining entry on a specific WLAN.

For starters, we will assume that a company has been targeted for intrusion, and that specific WLAN-capable devices (like company laptops) are being watched for theft opportunities. With one turn of the head, or a short walk to the water cooler, a laptop could be in the possession of the thief. Now, using tools found on the Internet, a sophisticated hacker could recover from the device its owner's domain information, including their user ID and password.

Next, the laptop owner's e-mail address, server information, and password can be captured and recorded. Finding the SSID for the wireless network will also prove to be simple, as most wireless client programs store them unencrypted in the Windows registry. All that remains to be found is the WEP key for the corporate WLAN. Depending on the wireless card's vendor, exploits exist to pull this information from where it is encrypted within a Windows registry key and crack it as well.

The odds are also high that if MAC filtering is occurring, the MAC address of the wireless device has been considered "trusted" and will be allowed to authenticate/associate with APs on the WLAN. Armed with this information, gaining access to the WLAN and the attached resources becomes trivial.

MAC Filtering

In order to fully discuss the advantages and disadvantages of MAC filtering, let's have a short review on what a MAC address is. The term "MAC" stands for Media Access Control, and forms the lower layer in the Data-Link layer of the OSI model. The purpose of the MAC sub-layer is to present a uniform interface between the physical networking media (copper/fiber/radio frequency) and the Logical Link Control portion of the Data-Link layer. These two layers are found onboard a NIC, whether integrated into a device or used as an add-on (PCI card or PCMCIA card).

What Is a MAC Address?

In order to facilitate delivery of network traffic, the MAC layer is assigned a unique address, which is programmed into the NIC at the time of manufacture. The operating system will associate an IP address with this MAC address, which allows the device to participate in an IP network. Since no other NIC in the world should have the same MAC address, it is easy to see why it could be a secure way to equate a specific user with the MAC address on his or her machine.

Now, let's look at an actual MAC address. For example, my laptop has a MAC address of 00-00-86-4C-75-48. The first three octets are called the organizationally unique identifier (OUI). The Institute of Electrical and Electronic Engineers controls these OUIs and assigns them to companies as needed. If you look up the 00-00-86 OUI on the IEEE's Web site (http://standards.ieee.org/regauth/oui/index.shtml), it will state that the manufacturer of this NIC is the 3Com Corporation.

Corporations can own several OUIs, and often acquire additional OUIs when they purchase other companies. For example, when Cisco purchased Aironet Wireless Communications in 1999, they added the 00-40-96 OUI to the many others they have.

Some other OUIs you could see on your WLAN might be:

- 00-02-2D – Agere Communications (previously known as ORiNOCO)
- 00-10-E7 – Breezecom
- 00-E0-03 – Nokia Wireless
- 00-04-5A – Linksys

The remaining three octets in a MAC address are usually burned into the NIC during manufacture, thus assuring that duplicate addresses will not exist on a network. I say "usually" because there are some exceptions to this rule. For example, in some redundancy situations, one NIC on a machine is able to assume the MAC address of the other NIC if the primary NIC fails. Some early 802.11 PCMCIA cards also had the ability to change their MAC address. Although not necessarily easy to do, changing the MAC address gives a user the ability to spoof the MAC address of another PCMCIA card. This could be used to circumvent MAC filtering or be employed in a denial of service (DoS) attack against a specific user.

Where in the Authentication/Association Process Does MAC Filtering Occur?

When a wireless device wants to connect to a WLAN, it goes though a two-part process called Authentication and Authorization. After both have been completed, the device is allowed access to the WLAN.

As mentioned earlier, when a wireless device is attempting to connect to a WLAN, it sends an authentication request to the AP (see Figure 6.4). This request will contain the SSID of the target network, or a null value if connecting to an open system. The AP will grant or deny authentication based on this string. Following a successful authentication, the requesting device will attempt to associate with the AP. It is at this point in time that MAC filtering plays its role. Depending on the AP vendor and administrative setup of the AP, MAC filtering either allows only the specified MAC addresses—blocking the rest, or it allows all MAC addresses—blocking specifically noted MACs. If the MAC address is allowed, the requesting device is allowed to associate with the AP.

Figure 6.4 MAC Filtering

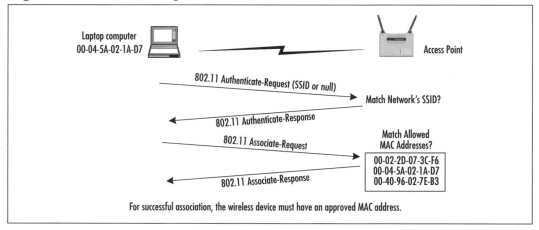

Determining MAC Filtering Is Enabled

The easiest way to determine if a device has failed the association process due to MAC filtering is through the use of a protocol analyzer, like Sniffer Pro or AiroPeek. The difficulty here is that other factors besides MAC filtering could prevent association from occurring. RADIUS or 802.1x authentication, or an incorrect WEP key could also prevent this. These of course are costly mechanisms commonly seen in large corporate environments. Due to the costs involved with setting up the higher forms of non–AP-based authentication, most small businesses or home installations will use MAC filtering to limit access (if they use anything at all).

MAC Spoofing

If you discover that your MAC address is not allowed to associate with the Access Point, don't give up! There are other ways into the network besides the front door!

First off, just because you can't associate with the AP doesn't mean you can't sit there and passively watch the traffic. With 802.11b protocol analysis software, your laptop can see all the other stations' communication with any AP within range. Since the MAC addresses of the other stations are transmitted in clear text, it should be easy to start compiling a list of the MAC addresses allowed on the network.

Some early runs of 802.11 PCMCIA cards had the ability to modify their MAC addresses. Depending on the card and the level of firmware, the method to change your MAC address may vary. There are sites on the Internet that can give you more specific information on altering these parameters.

Once you have modified the MAC address, you should be able to associate it with the AP. Keep in mind however, that if the device bearing the MAC address you have stolen is still operating on the network, you will not be able to use your device. To allow the operation of two duplicate MAC addresses will break ARP tables and will attract a level of attention to your activities that is undesirable. The advanced hacker we are discussing would realize this. In attempts to subvert the security mechanisms, traffic would be monitored to sufficiently pattern the intended victim whose MAC address and identification are to be forged in order to avoid detection.

Bypassing Advanced Security Mechanisms

Due to the lack of general knowledge regarding WLANS, many first-time implementers of wireless networks fail to deploy their new network properly. Without considering the security implications, APs are deployed inside the network firewall as if they were an ordinary piece of network equipment. By not treating an AP the same way as another Remote Access Server, administrators have instantly negated one of their first, and best, lines of defense.

Due to the industry acceptance of the 802.11b standard, it is incredibly easy to roll out wireless services to the office or corporate network. All that is necessary is to plug in the AP, make a few configuration tweaks, and you are up and running. This ease of implementation easily lends to the potential downfall of your WLAN. Recent news has stated that nearly 40 percent of wireless LANs surveyed had yet to change their configuration from the factory-default.

One of the most common mistakes is not altering the network's SSID on the AP. It is widely known that "tsunami" is the default SSID for Cisco's wireless products, and the "Linksys" SSID for Linksys equipment makes identification easy.

Another default in need of change is the access control on the Access Point. Many APs can be configured through SNMP, Telnet, or an unencrypted Hypertext Transfer Protocol (HTTP) session. The Telnet capability can be disabled, passwords can be added to the SNMP configuration, and access to the Web front-end should be tightly controlled. Administrative passwords also add a layer of access control.

Although access control is mentioned last, it should really top the to-do list when you are planning to deploy a WLAN. You need to create a network design that will best address your users' accessibility needs without compromising the integrity of your network. Consider running the wired side of your WLAN on a different virtual LAN (VLAN) and routing that traffic to an authenticating firewall before the traffic is allowed into your production network. In this manner, even if a device is able to spoof a MAC address, and get past all your other measures, the device will be prompted for an additional password in order to gain entry into the part of the network where the attacker really wants to go.

Notes from the Underground…

Access Point Defaults

An extensive list of vendor-specific defaults has been compiled and is available for download at www.wi2600.org/mediawhore/nf0/wireless/ssid_defaults. This list not only covers the default SSIDs for specific gear, it also outlines vendor-default WEP keys and passwords.

Firewalls

In networking terms, a firewall is a machine connected to at least two different portions of a network whose sole purpose is to determine what sort of traffic will be allowed between the networks connected to the firewall. Through the use of rules and access filters, the firewall will check all incoming and/or outgoing network traffic to see if it meets the requirements necessary to pass through the firewall to the network on the other side.

Filtering by IP Address

The first line of defense your firewall has to offer relates to the access it will allow to the network if a user's IP address falls with certain ranges. In particular scenarios, a company may want to allow wireless access to a certain limited set of resources. Since the DHCP server can specify the range of IP addresses to assign to the wireless devices, it would be easy to create a firewall rule set to grant or deny access based on IP address.

More often than not, however, wireless users will expect to have the same amount of access to network resources as they would from their desks. This is a great boost for the hacker! This means that even if a firewall is between the

Access Point and the rest of the network, the odds are in the hacker's favor that the firewall will only limit minor activities. The rest of the network is still open and waiting to be discovered and exploited.

In order to properly limit a network's risk exposure, the security policy must state that wireless users are not guaranteed full and complete network access. While firewalls are a good thing to have on a network, if not properly implemented, they are as worthless as if not having one at all.

Filtering by Port

Port filtering is like filtering access based on IP addresses except it is more granular in nature. Instead of granting access to all services a server may offer, a port filter will specify a range of allowed ports on a specific IP address. This can be very useful in limiting the types of traffic that can be carried over the WLAN.

For example, the decision could be made that only Secure Shall (SSH) connections to Unix hosts are allowed over the WLAN. The port filter would allow TCP transmissions over port 22, and would block all port 23 (Telnet) communications. Another example would be that HTTP traffic would be allowed to specific hosts within the network. The firewall rule set would specify the exact hosts allowed and that only traffic being carried over port 80 would be allowed.

A design consideration here would be to add a Web proxy server into your WLAN. This proxy server would operate on a specific port (not 80) and all HTTP-related traffic would have to pass through the proxy before it would be handed off to the destination server. While the inclusion of proxy servers can assist in the cleaning up of your Web-related traffic, they also run the risk of introducing latency into your network. Since they inspect every packet handed them, these systems need to be sitting on a beefy server in order to avoid user complaints about a slow network.

There are limitations to the effectiveness of port filtering. The majority of these shortcomings fall along the lines of application usage. If your company has a wide range of applications that require communications across numerous ports, it might be counter-productive to punch holes in your firewall for these applications. The answer to this scenario would fall under the lines of network access policy. The wireless policy might state that not all network services would be available to wireless users.

What Happens Now?

The addition of firewall filtering by IP address and port will add a greater level of granularity to your access controls. However, you cannot base your network security model on firewall filtering alone. The addition and/or modification of rule sets require manual changes, and because they are time consuming, they are pushed to the bottom of the to-do list. Sometimes, rule sets are left in the configuration long after the need for them has passed. These types of manual delays can decrease the effectiveness of your firewall. Using these sorts of holes (unintentionally left open), an attacker can gain access to areas you never intended.

IP and port filtering, while limiting the majority of potential traffic on your LAN, present one enormous downside—they place the brunt of security on the end server. For example, even if you have a firewall rule that only allows port 80 (HTTP) traffic to a specific host, the balance of security rests upon that host's ability to fend off malicious attacks carried on port 80. Keeping the server secure places an enormous amount of responsibility on the administrator to ensure that all relevant security patches have been applied. Doing so will prevent this host from being compromised and serving as a jumping off spot for further attacks against the network.

Exploiting Insiders

By far, the easiest way to gain entry into a network is with the assistance of someone who already has access to the network. In many cases, disgruntled employees provide assistance to an outsider or a former worker in attempting to circumvent access controls.

Another form of insider exploitation is *social engineering*. Quite simply, social engineering is the art of extracting the information you desire from a person or persons without them necessarily knowing they gave it to you. It could be as simple as a phone call to the help desk asking for a password or an IP address of a machine. Social engineering attacks are the trademark sign of a truly skilled attacker. Even a sophisticated intruder would not want to waste the time and energy to perform an attack on a network and risk being detected, when a simple means of obtaining the information is available through unsecured human interactions.

What Is at Stake?

Results from network penetration-testing returns the same result time and again: passwords are the number one item on an attacker's mind. With that password, an intruder can gain access to confidential e-mail, log in to file servers, and if the level of authority is great enough, create new accounts on the network.

There are two ways to discover the value of a user's password, complete disclosure and a password reset. Complete disclosure is exactly what it sounds like—the intruder is told exactly what the password is. A password reset is where the attacker is able to get a user's password reset to a certain value. This value can be critically important, as it may be consistent with other users who have had their passwords reset recently. If an attacker can build a theory that passwords are being reset according to a scheme like "passwordmonthday," it can lend significant help in hacking into other accounts. This method, while typically having a greater success rate in achieving access, does have some drawbacks. Sooner or later, the employee will discover that his/her password no longer works and will contact the help desk for another password reset. At such time, the attacker will be locked out of the account or network.

Another weak point that can be leveraged into WLAN access is old WEP keys. Some older Access Points do not have a mechanism to remotely change their WEP key. Not only is there hassle involved with logging in to every Access Point to change the WEP key, but re-keying the wireless client devices must also be addressed. Due to the amount of effort required to accomplish these changes, some WLANs still have the same WEP key they had six months ago. If a person can be located that remembers an old WEP key, the odds are high that the same key is still in use. Unchanged keys mean the hacker can walk away from the trail he left two months ago, and come back later to exploit the vulnerability he intended originally. It also allows the hacker to pattern your security policy for future hacking endeavors.

Social Engineering Targets

In order to gain access, the intruder needs to have vital information about the target network. Typically, the first stop is the help desk. Posing as a clueless worker in need of assistance, they will ask seemingly innocuous questions. Due to lack of proper training on PCs and computer equipment—especially in light of the rapid advances in technology, help desk personnel are trained to assist the end-user in any capacity. If strong password-changing or account creation policies are not in place and enforced, help desk personnel will prove to be unwitting accomplices to an intruder.

Another source of information for a "social engineer" are contractors or temporary workers. Due to their limited involvement with the rest of the staff, they might not be able to know if a person is supposed to be asking the sort of questions a social engineer will ask. Even more dangerous, they certainly won't be up to speed on the organization's current security policy.

Another group of helpful souls in the cross hairs of the social engineer are office administrators or secretaries. Due to their proximity to important people, these employees are in constant contact with information that might not be readily shared with the rest of the office staff. A good social engineer might befriend one of them, possibly interact with them in a nonbusiness scenario, and slowly attempt to gain the information necessary to launch a network-based attack.

Installing Rogue Access Points

The trick of installing a rogue device into a network is not new to security, and the nature of wireless has created the opportunity for an attacker to install a rogue or unauthorized mobile station in close proximity to the network.

By definition, if an Access Point has been deployed on a network without the direct consent or knowledge of the IT staff, and without IT control, responsibility, or oversight, it is a rogue Access Point.

As the cost of APs decreases, it becomes more trivial to purchase them and surreptitiously place them on a wired LAN. Many corporations are having to deal with this issue as more and more of their employees are wanting to take their laptops into meeting areas and work outside of their desk areas.

For an intruder, placing a rogue AP into a WLAN provides an easy way of capturing network traffic, WEP keys, and other authentication information.

Where Is the Best Location for a Rogue AP?

By this time, an attacker has narrowed his scope to a company that has already deployed their WLAN. Due to the high number of wireless users and the authentication schemes that can be captured, there is a direct advantage in using a rogue AP instead of just "sniffing" the packets traversing the WLAN.

The attacker will probably attempt to place a rogue AP close to where the wireless traffic is occurring. Some planning is involved here, as he would not want to place the AP too close to another legitimate Access Point. To do so would cause a large amount of reassociations, which could draw undue attention to the fact that a new AP is in the area.

Using a site surveying tool like NetStumbler, the attacker would measure the signal strength from the other APs in the area. Using this as a guide, the rogue AP would ideally be positioned in a location equidistant between the legitimate APs. This would ensure that the wireless devices could reauthenticate and reassociate with the legitimate APs once the rogue AP had captured their information. This location could be in an area that while providing good reception would not be discovered by the casual onlooker. External antennas and excessively trailing power cables would only accentuate the position of the rogue device, and would be avoided.

Configuring the Rogue AP

Once the AP was in place, the attacker would set the SSID of the AP to the one currently in place by the legitimate APs. (This information would have been discovered through the use of NetStumbler or a wireless sniffer.)

If this WLAN were using WEP encryption, a conscientious attacker would have discovered the key through some of the methods explained earlier in the chapter. Having the rogue AP carry the same WEP key lends a good deal of credibility to the attack, and could prevent the rogue device from immediate discovery.

Risks Created by a Rogue AP

Now that the rogue AP is in place, the stage is set for several different kinds of attacks on the network. First off, the person running the rogue AP could capture and analyze the network traffic that passes through it. From discovering confidential e-mail to gathering passwords, a serious threat of exposure exists. The rogue AP could also be used for a DoS attack. By placing the rogue AP on the same RF channel as a legitimate AP, the rogue AP could cause a level of interference that could seriously degrade the performance of the WLAN. Due to the interference, the wireless devices would spend the majority of their time retransmitting, and not passing packets.

Are Rogue APs Detectable?

With the obvious risk of exposing confidential information due to the inclusion of a rogue AP, it is important to detect and remove them from your WLAN. The ease of detecting a rogue AP depends on the sophistication of the intruder. While a casual attacker might just throw an AP out on the WLAN without a good deal of forethought, a sophisticated attacker would have configured the rogue AP to be as close to a legitimate AP as possible.

The easiest way to discover rogue APs would be through the use of NetStumbler. However, this would only be true if the rogue AP was deployed as an open system. If it were deployed as a closed system, it would avoid detection through this manner.

Another way to detect rogue APs is through a systematic search of the MAC addresses on the LAN. The resulting list of MAC addresses can be compared to known Access Point OUIs. While this will not detect rogue APs occurring outside your LAN, it can find those that have been employee-deployed.

Yet another way to detect and remove rogue Access Points is by deploying 802.1x authentication throughout your WLAN. Unlike RADIUS authentication that only authenticates the end-user, 802.1x will also require the Access Point to authenticate itself back to the central server. This solution is not without fault, as a rogue AP could be used to capture 802.1x transactions and enable the intruder to analyze them for potential playback.

Exploiting VPNs

While VPNs are increasingly being touted as a secure solution for remote access, they still present a number of weaknesses, such as session hijacking, that can be exploited by an attacker. The use of VPNs on wireless networks may give the appearance of increasing the amount of data integrity, but unless properly implemented, it can also widen those security gaps.

This is especially true when speaking of VPNs established for telecommuters or employees who take their laptops home. Due to the lack of controlled supervision during the VPN client installation, most VPN deployments end up with incorrect drivers or other misconfigurations.

A skilled attacker could use these issues to his advantage. By utilizing a misconfigured or incorrectly installed VPN client, the VPN session could be remotely hijacked. With the hacker now in control of the VPN connection, he is able to probe the network on the far end of the VPN tunnel.

Session hijacking is not the only way to gain control of a user's VPN connection. If a user is connecting to a VPN over the WLAN, a protocol analyzer could capture all packets related to the building of the VPN session. This data could be played back on a future attack or analyzed to see if vital information could be determined (VPN server IP address, possible username/password pairs).

Another method to get into a target VPN is to steal the VPN username/password pair from the target computer. This can be accomplished through the introduction of a keystroke logger hidden in a piece of software or Trojan. While the keystroke logger would report back everything the target user types, the real items the hacker is interested in are user IDs and passwords.

Summary

In this chapter, we have covered a broad range of ways to get around the basic security mechanisms found on 802.11b networks. We have seen that while the tools needed to mount an attack on a WLAN are available, a certain amount of planning is necessary to ensure that the intrusion will be successful when it is attempted. We have also looked into the practice commonly referred to as "war driving," and how by locating open system APs a large amount of information about the network the target WLAN is connected to can be revealed.

After validating the existence of the wireless network, we looked at ways of inserting a computer on that network, including using software to crack WEP, bypassing MAC filtering, and exploiting internal employees through the use of social engineering. We even went so far as to discuss the theft of devices belonging to that target network.

In the next chapter, we will discuss monitoring of the wireless network, including topics like intrusion detection and the some benefits you can expect from it.

Solutions Fast Track

Planning and Preparations

☑ In preparation for intrusion, a hacker will have to discover if a wireless network exists, as well as determine the boundaries of the wireless network. The necessary equipment includes a computer, an PCMCIA-based 802.11b radio, an antenna, and software.

☑ Windows users can use NetStumbler, which discovers *open networks*, or Ethernet sniffing programs like Network Associates' Sniffer Wireless or WildPacket's AiroPeek for the discovery of *closed networks*. Many Unix-based wireless network discovery tools exist, the most notable being Ethereal.

☑ *Open systems* or *open networks* accepts incoming connections if the end-device is looking for a wireless network with an "empty value" SSID. APs of a *closed network* ignore the "empty value" SSID beacons; programs like NetStumbler will not be able to ascertain the existence of that WLAN.

Exploiting WEP

☑ Exploiting the Wired Equivalent Privacy (WEP) standard is possible due to the reuse of weak initialization vectors.

☑ A static WEP key on an Access Point (AP) opens the door for future exploitation of past known keys.

☑ Cisco and Funk Software have released Access Control servers that support continual WEP re-keying, thus eliminating a static WEP key scenario.

War Driving

☑ War driving can only discover wireless local area networks (WLANs) that are operating as "open systems."

☑ War driving can be detected, but only if a large amount of effort is made.

☑ A good deal of the discovered information can be leveraged into potential attacks against the AP.

Stealing User Devices

☑ A petty thief will see the dollar value of the physical hardware, and a sophisticated thief will understand that the data contained on the hard drive is far more valuable.

☑ The e-mail address, server information, and password can be captured and recorded from a stolen laptop. Next, it is possible to obtain the SSID and the WEP key for the corporate WLAN.

MAC Filtering

☑ Media Access Control (MAC) filtering is effective against casual attackers.

☑ MAC filtering can be circumvented by changing the MAC address on the client device.

☑ It is difficult to determine if the lack of association is due to MAC filtering or other reasons like an incorrect WEP key.

Bypassing Advanced Security Mechanisms

- ☑ Treat an AP the same way as another Remote Access Server.

- ☑ Change the AP's default settings: alter the network's SSID and change the access control. The Telnet capability can be disabled, passwords can be added to the SNMP configuration, and access to the Web front-end should be tightly controlled.

- ☑ The addition of firewall filtering by IP address and port will add a greater level of granularity to your access controls.

- ☑ Firewalls are only feasible if a strong security policy states that wireless devices will not have the same level of service as wired devices.

- ☑ Port filtering or proxying certain ports can prevent "drive-by spamming," or prohibit certain protocols altogether (like Telnet).

Exploiting Insiders

- ☑ The easiest way to gain entry into a network is with the assistance of someone who already has access to the network, often through social engineering.

- ☑ Gaining passwords is a common goal of social engineers. Discovering old WEP keys is another.

Installing Rogue Access Points

- ☑ If an Access Point has been deployed on a network without the direct consent or knowledge of the IT staff, and without IT control, responsibility, or oversight, it is a *rogue Access Point*.

- ☑ Placing a rogue AP into a WLAN, ideally positioned in a location equidistant between the legitimate APs, provides an easy way of capturing network traffic, WEP keys, and other authentication information.

- ☑ Some strategies for detecting a rogue AP include the use of NetStumbler, systematic searches of the MAC addresses on the LAN, or by deploying 802.1x authentication throughout your WLAN.

Exploiting VPNs

☑ If a user is connecting to a VPN over the WLAN, a protocol analyzer could capture all packets related to the building of the VPN session. This data could be played back on a future attack or analyzed to see if vital information could be determined, such as VPN server IP address, or possible username/password pairs.

Frequently Asked Questions

The following Frequently Asked Questions, answered by the authors of this book, are designed to both measure your understanding of the concepts presented in this chapter and to assist you with real-life implementation of these concepts. To have your questions about this chapter answered by the author, browse to **www.syngress.com/solutions** and click on the **"Ask the Author"** form.

Q: Where can I get an 802.11 protocol analyzer?

A: Network Associates and WildPackets both sell 802.11 protocol analyzers. Ethereal is an open source alternative, but requires a certain amount of configuration in order to work with a specific wireless card.

Q: Is a spectrum analyzer necessary to detect closed networks?

A: No, a 802.11 protocol analyzer will show traffic from closed networks. The real benefit from a spectrum analyzer is to pinpoint the location of potential interference to the WLAN.

Q: Is 128-bit WEP more secure than 64-bit WEP?

A: Not really. This is because the WEP vulnerability has more to do with the 24-bit initialization vector than the actual size of the WEP key.

Q: If I am a home user, can I assume that if I use MAC filtering and WEP, that my network is secure?

A: You can make the assumption that your home network is more secure than if it did not utilize these safeguards. However, as shown in this chapter, these methods can be circumvented to allow for intrusion.

Q: Where can I find more information on WEP vulnerabilities?

A: Besides being one of the sources who brought WEP vulnerabilities to light, www.isaac.cs.berkeley.edu has links to other Web sites that cover WEP insecurities.

Chapter 7

Monitoring and Intrusion Detection

Solutions in this chapter:

- **Designing for Detection**

- **Defensive Monitoring Considerations**

- **Intrusion Detection Strategies**

- **Conducting Vulnerability Assessments**

- **Incident Response and Handling**

- **Conducting Site Surveys for Rogue Access Points**

☑ Summary

☑ Solutions Fast Track

☑ Frequently Asked Questions

Introduction

Network monitoring and intrusion detection have become an integral part of network security. The monitoring of your network becomes even more important when introducing wireless access, because you have added a new, openly available entry point into your network. Security guards patrol your building at night. Even a small business, if intent on retaining control of its assets, has some form of security system in place—as should your network. Monitoring and intrusion detection are your security patrol, and become the eyes and ears of your network, alerting you to potential vulnerabilities, and intrusion attempts. Designing secure wireless networks will rely on many of the standard security tools and techniques but will also utilize some new tools.

In this chapter, you'll learn about the planning and deployment issues that must be addressed early on in order to make monitoring and intrusion detection most effective when the system is fully operational.

You'll also learn how to take advantage of current intrusion principles, tools, and techniques in order to maximize security of your wireless network. Specialized wireless tools such as NetStumbler and AirSnort will also be used to provide a better overall picture of your wireless security.

Intrusion Prevention (IP) systems may offer an additional layer to detection. We'll discuss the pros and cons of their use, and their relationship to conventional intrusion detection. You'll also learn how to respond to incidents and intrusions on a wireless network, as well as conduct site surveys to identify the existence of rogue Access Points (APs).

Designing for Detection

In this section, we will discuss how to design a wireless network with an emphasis on monitoring, focusing on the choice of equipment, physical layout and radio interference. The decision-making involved in the design, deployment, and installation of a wireless local area network (WLAN), combined with the choice of product vendor, can play a key role in later efforts to monitor the network for intrusions. *Designing for detection* occurs when you build a network with monitoring and intrusion detection principles in mind from the start. For example, when a bank is built, many of the security features, such as the vault security modules, closed circuit cameras, and the alarm are part of the initial design. Retrofitting these into a building would be much more expensive and difficult than including them in the beginning. The same idea is true with a network. Designing your network for detection, having made the decisions about monitoring strategies and the infrastructure to support them, will save you time and money in the long run.

If you've followed the design and configuration advice given in this book, you should be able to identify certain false alarms. Knowledge of your building's layout and physical obstacles, as discussed earlier, will strengthen your ability to identify red herrings. Additionally, understanding sources of radio interference and having an idea of the limits of your network signal can also help avoid potential headaches from false alarms and misleading responses when patrolling the network for intruders. Keeping these points in mind, laying out your wireless network for the most appropriate detection should be no problem.

Starting with a Closed Network

The choice of vendor for your wireless gear can dramatically alter the visible footprint of your wireless network. After an Access Point is installed, it will begin emitting broadcasts, announcing, among other things, its Service Set Identifier (SSID). This is a very useful function for clients to be able to connect to your network. It makes discovery and initial client configuration very easy, and quick. The ease of contact, however, has some security implications. The easily available nature of the network is not only available for your intended users, but for anyone else with a wireless card. The easier any system is to find, the easier it is to exploit.

In order to counteract some of the troubles with openly available and easily discoverable wireless networks, some vendors have developed a system known as closed network. With closed network functionality enabled, the wireless AP no longer broadcasts its SSID to the world; rather it waits for a client to connect with the proper SSID and channel settings. This certainly makes the network more difficult to find, as programs such as NetStumbler and dstumbler will not see it. The network is now much more secure, because it is much more difficult for an attacker to compromise a network he or she can't see. The potential disadvantage, however, is that clients must now know the SSID and settings of your network in advance in order to connect. This process can be difficult for some users, as card configuration will be required. From a security standpoint, however, a closed network system is the ideal foundation from which to begin designing a more secure wireless network solution. A closed network-capable AP is recommended for all but those who wish to have an openly available wireless network (in such a scenario, security concerns are generally not primary).

Ruling Out Environmental Obstacles

Another important design consideration is the physical layout. A knowledge of the obstacles you are designing around is vital for determining the number of APs that will be required to provide adequate coverage for your wireless network. Many installations have suffered from administrators failing to take notice of trees, indoor waterfalls, and even the layout and construction materials of the building. Features such as large indoor fountains and even translucent glass walls can be a barrier to proper signal path. Fixing a broken network is much more of a burden than making sure everything is set up properly from the beginning. Before starting, learn as much as you can about the building in which you're planning to deploy. If the building is concrete with a steel frame, the 802.11 signal will be much more limited than if it were passing through a wood/drywall frame building. When placing the initial 802.11 AP, design from the inside-out. Place the AP toward the center of your user base and take advantage of the fact that the signal will radiate outwards. The goal of this placement is to provide the best quality of signal to your users, while limiting the amount and strength of the signal that passes outside of your walls. Remember, potential attackers will be looking for a signal from your network, and the weaker the signal is when it leaves your premises, the less likely an attacker can safely snoop on your network. *Safely*, in this case, means that an attacker doesn't need to worry about being seen in an unusual place with a laptop. For example, an attacker sitting in your lobby with a wireless card is suspicious, but, someone sipping coffee in a coffee shop with their laptop isn't. Of course, signal strength alone isn't a security measure, but is part of a whole secure security package you will want to have built into your wireless network.

The second physical consideration that should be kept in mind when designing a wireless network is the building floor plan. Using the inside-out method of AP placement, place the AP as far from possible from external windows and doors. If the building layout is a square, with cubicles in all directions, place the AP in the center. If the building is a set of long corridors and rooms, then it will be best to experiment with placement. Try putting the APs at different locations, and then scout the location with NetStumbler or other tools to determine where the signal is strongest, and whether or not it can be seen from outside of your facility. We'll talk more about using NetStumbler and other site evaluation tools a bit later.

Another consideration should be your neighbors. In most environments, there will be other companies or businesses operating nearby. Either from the floors above, below, or right next door, your signal may be visible. If you have competitors, this may be something which you wish to avoid, because they will be able to join your network, and potentially exploit it. Close proximity means that an attacker could easily and discreetly begin deciphering your wireless encryption keys. Proper placement and testing of your APs before deployment can help you gain a better understanding of your availability to those around you.

SECURITY ALERT

Remember that good design requires patience and testing. Avoid at all costs the temptation to design around obstacles simply by throwing more APs at the situation, or increasing the signal strength. While providing more signal and availability, this potentially dangerous scenario adds more points of entry to your network, and can increase your chance of compromise.

Ruling Out Interference

Thought should also be given to whether or not there are external or internal sources of radio interference present in your building. Potential problems can come from microwave ovens, 2.4GHz wireless phones, wireless video security monitors, and other 802.11b wireless networks. If these are present in large numbers in your environment, it may be necessary to do some experimentation with AP placement and settings to see which combination will provide the most available access. We'll discuss interference in more detail in the next section, but be aware that these devices may create holes, or weaken your range. Having properly identified these sources and potential problems can help you diagnose future problems, and realize that an outage may not necessarily be an attacker but rather a hungry employee warming lunch.

Defensive Monitoring Considerations

Monitoring wireless networks for intrusion attempts requires attention to some newer details, which many security administrators have not encountered in the past. The use of radio for networking introduces new territory for security administrators to consider. Issues such as signal strength, distortion by buildings and fixtures, interferences from local and remote sources, and the mobility of users are some of these new monitoring challenges not found in the wired world. Any attempt to develop an intrusion detection regime must take into account these new concepts. Security administrators must make themselves familiar with radio technology and the direct impact the environment will have on networks using these technologies.

Security monitoring is something that should be built into your initial wireless installation. Many devices have logging capabilities and these should be fully utilized in order to provide the most comprehensive overall picture possible of what is happening on your network. Firewalls, routers, internal Web servers, Dynamic Host Configuration Protocol (DHCP) servers, and even some wireless APs will provide log files, which should be stored and reviewed frequently. Simply collecting the logs isn't enough; they should be thoroughly reviewed by security administrators. This is something that should be built into every security procedures guide, but is often overlooked. A firewall log is worthless if it's never reviewed! Having numerous methods and devices in place to review traffic and usage on your network will provide critical insight into any type of attack, either potential or realized.

Availability and Connectivity

Obviously the most important things in building and operating a wireless network are availability and connectivity. A wireless network that users cannot connect to, while very secure, is completely useless. Interference, signal strength and denial of service (DoS) attacks can all dramatically affect your availability. In the past, for an attacker to perform a denial of service attack against your internal network, they would have needed to gain access to it, not always a trivial task. Now, however, an attacker with a grudge against your organization needs only to know that a wireless network is present in order to attack. We'll discuss the possibilities of denial of service attacks later in this section. Even if the network has been designed securely, simply the fact that the network is radio-based means these issues must be considered.

Interference and Noise

Identifying potential sources of interference during the design phase can help you identify potentially malicious sources of interference within your environment once you undertake your monitoring activities.

For example, during one wireless deployment, we were experiencing a major denial of service in one group. Users in one group were either unable to connect to the AP at all, or suffered from diminished bandwidth. It was suspected there was a potentially malicious source of activity somewhere, but after reviewing our initial design notes about the installation, we remembered a kitchen near these users. At the time of deployment, there was no known source of interference in the kitchen, but upon investigating further, we discovered the group had just installed a new commercial grade, high wattage microwave oven. As you can see, when deploying a wireless network, it's important to explore all possible solutions of interference before suspecting foul play. If your organization uses noncellular wireless phones, or any other type of wireless devices, be certain you check whether or not they are operating in the 2.4GHz spectrum. While some devices like telephones won't spark a complete outage, they can cause intermittent problems with connections. Other devices like wireless video monitors can cause serious conflicts, and should be avoided at all costs. Identified potential problems early can be very useful when monitoring for interference and noise in your wireless network environment.

It should be noted that some administrators may have few, if any, problems with microwave ovens, phones, or other wireless devices, and tests have been performed on the World Wide Web supporting this. A simple Web search for microwave ovens and 802.11b will give you plenty of information. However, do realize that while some have had few problems, this is no guarantee you will be similarly blessed. Instead, be thorough. Having an idea of potential problems can save you time identifying later connectivity issues.

As mentioned earlier, knowledge of your neighbors is a good idea when building a wireless network. If you are both running a wireless network with similar settings, you will be competing on the same space with your networks, which is sure to cause interference problems. Given this, it's best to monitor what your neighbors are doing at all times to avoid such problems. Notice that conflicts of this kind are generally inadvertent. Nevertheless, similar situations can be used to create a denial of service, which we'll discuss later.

Signal Strength

From a monitoring standpoint, signal strength is one of the more critical factors to consider. First, it is important to monitor your signal regularly in order to know the extent to which it is available. Multiple APs will require multiple investigations in order to gain a complete picture of what a site looks like externally. Site auditing discovery tools should be used to see how far your signal is traveling. It will travel much farther than most manufacturer claims, so prepare to be surprised. If the signal is adequate for your usage, and you'd like to attempt to limit it, some APs will allow you to fine-tune the signal strength. If your AP supports this feature, experiment with it to provide the best balance between internal and external availability.

Whether you can fine-tune your signal strength or not, during initial design you should have noted points externally where the signal was available. Special attention should have been paid to problematic areas, such as cafes, roadways or parking lots. These areas are problematic because it is difficult, or impossible to determine whether or not an attacker is looking at your wireless network specifically. When monitoring, those areas should be routinely investigated for potential problems. If you are facing an intrusion, knowledge of places like these, with accessibility to your network could help lead you to your attacker.

Detecting a Denial of Service

Monitoring the wireless network for potential denial of service attacks should be part of your security regime. Surveying the network, checking for decreases in signal strength, unauthorized APs, and unknown Media Access Control (MAC) addresses, are all ways to be proactive about denial of service.

Denial of service attacks can be incredibly destructive. Often times, however, their severity is overlooked because a DoS attack doesn't directly put classified data at risk. While this attitude may be acceptable at certain organizations, at others it can cost a tremendous amount of money both in lack of employee productivity and lost customer revenue. One only needs to look back at the DoS attacks conducted in February 2000 against several major E-commerce companies to realize the threat from such attacks.

On an Internet level, this type of attack can be devastating, but at the wireless networking level, they may not be as severe. The largest possible loss could come from lost employee productivity. The availability of a wired alternative can help mitigate the risks from a wireless DoS, but as networking moves toward the future, and away from wires, this may become less of a possibility.

As mentioned earlier, the radio-based nature of 802.11b makes it more susceptible to denial of service. In the wired world, an attacker generally needed access to your internal network in order to cause a DoS outage. Since many wireless installations offer instant access into this network, it can be much easier for an attacker to get in and start shutting things down. There are two main ways an attacker can conduct a DoS against your wireless LAN. The first method would be fairly traditional. They would connect to the network, and simply start blasting packets to any of your internal machines—perhaps your DNS servers or one of your routers. Either scenario is likely to cause connectivity outages on the network. A second method of denying service to wireless LANs wouldn't even require a wireless LAN card, but rather just a knowledge of how the technology works. An attacker with a device known to cause interference could place it in the path of your wireless network. This is a very crude, but potentially effective method of performing a DoS attack. A third way to conduct a DoS against a wireless LAN is similar to the scenario we've just discussed, but requires a wireless AP. In this scenario, an attacker would configure a wireless AP to mimic the settings on your AP, but not connect the AP to the network. Therefore, users connecting to this AP would not be able to communicate on the LAN. And, if this AP were placed in an area with many of your users, since their cards are generally configured to connect to the strongest signal, the settings would match, making detection potentially difficult. A good way to save yourself from this scenario is to identify the MAC addresses of all your wireless APs, and then routinely do surveys for any nonmatching APs. This type of situation closely mirrors what we will discuss later when talking about rogue APs.

Monitoring for Performance

Keeping an eye on the performance of your network is always a good idea. Knowing your typical baseline usage, the types of traffic that travel on your network, as well as the odd traffic patterns that might occur will not only help you keep an eye on capacity, but clue you in to potential intrusions. This type of monitoring is generally part of a good security regime in the wired world, but should be adopted to cover traffic on your wireless network as well.

Knowing the Baseline

Knowing the baseline usage that your network generally sees can help you identify potential problems. Over time, you should be watching the network to get an idea of how busy it gets throughout the day. Monitoring baseline performance will give you a good idea of your current capacity, and help provide you with a valuable picture of how your network generally operates. Let's say, for example, your network generally sees its peak usage at 9AM at which point it generally sees a load of 45 percent. Then, in monitoring your performance logs you notice usage peaks at 3AM with much higher bandwidth consumed—you have an anomaly that should be investigated. Additionally, if, when monitoring, you find that massive amounts of bandwidth are being consumed, and you only have four or five users with minimal usage needs, this should be a red flag as well. A common attack motive for intruders is to gain access to bandwidth.

Monitoring Tools of the Trade

There are many performance-monitoring tools, with diverse prices and levels of functionality. Commercially available tools such as Hewlett-Packard's OpenView have great amounts of market share. OpenView can be configured to watch just about any aspect of your network, your servers, bandwidth, and even traffic usage patters. It is a very powerful tool that is also customizable and can be made to monitor just about anything imaginable. Being a solution designed for enterprise type organizations, it does come with a hefty price tag, but is generally considered one of the best monitoring tools available. There are some downsides to OpenView, however. It isn't security friendly, in that it requires the use of the User Datagram Protocol (UDP), which is something that is sometimes not allowed through firewalls due to the fact that it is a connectionless protocol. Connectionless protocols do not allow firewalls to verify that all transmissions are requested by the initiating party. In other words, there is no connection handshake like with the Transport Control Protocol (TCP). OpenView also has some problems working in a Network Address Translation (NAT) environment. Implementing OpenView into a secure environment can also be a real challenge, and may require some security requirement sacrifices. Proceed with caution.

If you are looking for something with a lower price tag, and potentially easier integration, SNIPS (formerly known as NOCOL) is an excellent monitoring package. It is very flexible in what it can do, but one particularly useful function is that it can be used to watch your Ethernet bandwidth. Watching bandwidth, as mentioned earlier, is a good idea because it can help you spot potential excess usage. SNIPS can also be configured to generate alarms when bandwidth reaches a certain level above what is considered normal use in your environment. Notification of this kind could alert you early to network intrusion, and when combined with specially designed detection software can be a very powerful combination. The screenshot in Figure 7.1 shows the different alert levels SNIPS features, and how they are sorted.

Another excellent tool for watching bandwidth on your network is called EtherApe. It provides an excellent graphical view of what bandwidth is being consumed, and where. With breakdowns by IP or MAC address, and protocol classifications, it is one tool that should be explored. It is freely available at http://etherape.sourceforge.net. For example, if you were detecting great slowdowns on your network, and you needed to quickly see what was consuming your resources, start EtherApe. It listens to your network and identifies traffic, protocols, and network load. Additionally, it traces the source and destination of the traffic, and provides a nice visual picture of the network. It's a great tool for identifying problems with the network, and can assist in explaining bandwidth and traffic issues to nontechnical people. Figure 7.2 shows EtherApe in action, illustrating how the traffic is displayed, graphically. The hosts are presented in a ring, with connections shown as lines drawn between them. The more intense the traffic, the larger the connection lines. Traffic can also be sorted by color, which makes it instantly easier to distinguish between types.

Figure 7.1 SNIPS: A Freely Available Monitoring Package

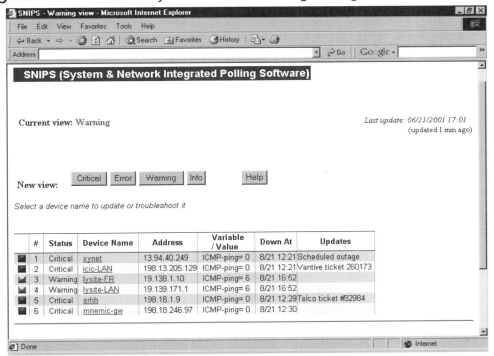

Intrusion Detection Strategies

Until now, we've primarily discussed monitoring in how it relates to intrusion detection, but there's more to an overall intrusion detection installation than monitoring alone. Monitoring can help you spot problems in your network, as well as identify performance problems, but watching every second of traffic that passes through your network, manually searching for attacks, would be impossible. This is why we need specialized network intrusion detection software. This software inspects all network traffic, looking for potential attacks and intrusions by comparing it to a predefined list of attack strings, known as *signatures*. In this section, we will look at different intrusion detection strategies and the role monitoring plays. We'll learn about different strategies designed for wireless networks, which must take into account the nature of the attacks unique to the medium. These include a lack of centralized control, lack of a defined perimeter, the susceptibility to hijacking and spoofing, the use of rogue APs, and a number of other features that intrusion detection systems were not designed to accommodate. Only a combination of factors we've discussed earlier, such as good initial design and monitoring, can be combined with traditional intrusion detection software to provide an overall effective package.

Figure 7.2 EtherApe for Linux

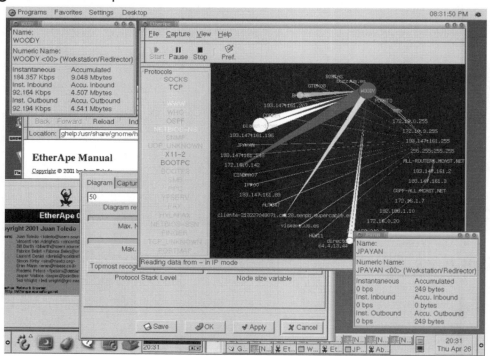

Integrated Security Monitoring

As discussed earlier, having monitoring built in to your network will help the security process evolve seamlessly. Take advantage of built-in logging-on network devices such as firewalls, DHCP servers, routers, and even certain wireless APs. Information gathered from these sources can help make sense of alerts generated from other intrusion detection sources, and will help augment data collected for incidents. Additionally, these logs should help you to manually spot unauthorized traffic and MAC addresses on your network.

Tools & Traps…

Beware of the Auto-responding Tools!

When designing your intrusion detection system, you will likely come across a breed of tools, sometimes known as *Intrusion Prevention Systems*. These systems are designed to automatically respond to incidents. One popular package is called PortSentry. It will, upon detection of a port scan, launch a script to react. Common reactions include dropping the route to the host that has scanned you, or adding firewall rules to block it. While this does provide instant protection from the host that's scanning you, and might seem like a great idea at first, it creates a very dangerous denial of service potential. Using a technique known as IP spoofing, an attacker who realizes PortSentry is being used can send bogus packets that appear to be valid port scans to your host. Your host will, of course, see the scan and react, thinking the address that its coming from is something important to you, such as your DNS server, or your upstream router. Now, network connectivity to your host is seriously limited. If you do decide to use auto-responsive tools, make sure you are careful to set them up in ways that can't be used against you.

Watching for Unauthorized Traffic and Protocols

As a security or network administrator, it is generally a good idea to continuously monitor the traffic passing over your network. It can give you an idea of the network load, and more importantly, you can get an idea of what kinds of protocols are commonly used. For most corporate networks, you are likely to see SMTP (e-mail), DNS lookups, Telnet or SSH, and, of course, Web traffic. There is also a good chance if you are using Hewlett-Packard printers, there will be JetDirect traffic on port 9100. If you have Microsoft products such as Exchange server, look for traffic on a number of other ports, with connections to or from your mail servers. After several sample viewings of network traffic, you should start to notice some patterns as to what is considered normal usage. It is from these samples that you can start looking for other unknown and possibly problematic traffic. IRC, Gnutella, or heavy FTP traffic can be a sign that your network is being used maliciously. If this is the case, you should be able to track the traffic back to its source, and try to identify who is using the offending piece of software. There are many Gnutella clients today, and it has become the most heavily used peer-to-peer networking system available. It is advised you become familiar with a few Gnutella clients, so they can be quickly identified and dealt with. BearShare, Gnotella, and LimeWire are some of the more popular ones. LimeWire, shown in Figure 7.3, provides an easy-to-use interface for Gnutella and offers lots of information about clients. Another point of caution about peer-to-peer client software should be the fact that it is often bundled with spyware—software which shares information about the user and their computer, often without their knowledge.

Figure 7.3 LimeWire: A Popular Gnutella Peer-to-peer File Sharing Program

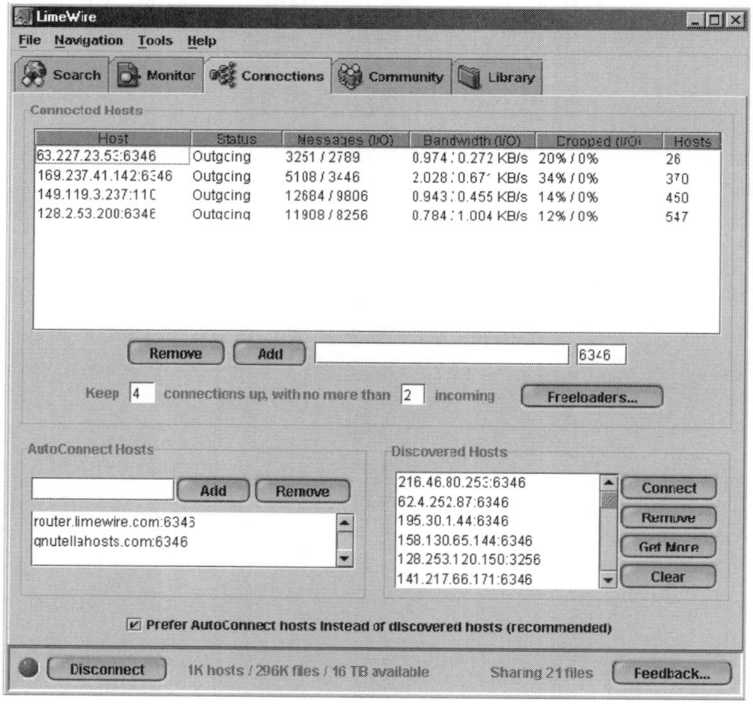

Within your security policy, you should have defined which types of applications are not considered acceptable for use in your environment. It is advisable to ban peer-to-peer networking software like Napster, Gnutella, and Kazaa. Constant monitoring is essential because the list grows larger each day and current policies may not prohibit the latest peer-to-peer software. Aside from possibly wasting company bandwidth, these tools allow others on the Internet to view and transfer files from a shared directory. It is very easy to misconfigure this software to share an entire hard drive. If shared, any other user on the peer-to-peer network would potentially have access to password files, e-mail files, or anything else that resides on the hard disk. This is more common than one would expect. Try a search on a peer-to-peer network for a sensitive file name like archive.pst, and you might be surprised by what you find.

Internet Relay Chat (IRC) traffic can also be a sign that something fishy is happening on your network. There are legitimate uses for IRC on an internal network. It makes a great team meeting forum for large groups separated by distances, or for those who require a common real-time chat forum. It should be kept in mind though that attackers commonly use IRC to share information or illegally copied software. If you are using IRC on your network, make sure you have a listing of your authorized IRC servers, and inspect IRC traffic to insure it is originating from one of those hosts. Anything else should be treated as suspect. If you aren't using IRC on your network, any IRC traffic (generally found on TCP port 6666 or 6667) should be treated as suspect.

A good way to automate this kind of scanning is generally available in intrusion detection packages. Snort, the freely available IDS has a signature file that identifies Gnutella, Napster, IRC, and other such types of traffic. Network Flight Recorder has similar filters, and supports a filter writing language that is incredibly flexible in its applications. We'll discuss some of the IDS packages a bit later in this chapter.

Unauthorized MAC Addresses

MAC address filtering is a great idea for wireless networks. It will only allow wireless cards with specified MAC addresses to communicate on the network. Some APs have this capability built in, but if yours doesn't, DHCP software can often be configured to do the same. This could be a major headache for a large organization, because there could simply be too many users to keep track of all of the MAC addresses. One possible way around this is to agree upon the same vendor for all of your wireless products. Each wireless card vendor has an assigned OUI or organizationally unique identifier, which makes up the first part of an Ethernet card's MAC address. So, if you chose Lucent wireless cards, you could immediately identify anything that wasn't a Lucent card just by noting the first part of the MAC address. This type of system could be likened to a company uniform. If everyone wore orange shirts to work, someone with a blue shirt would be easily spotted. This is not foolproof, however. An attacker with the same brand of wireless card would slide thorough unnoticed. In a more complicated vein, it is possible for attackers to spoof their MAC addresses, meaning they can override the wireless network card's MAC address. A system based solely on vendor OUIs alone wouldn't provide much protection, but it can make some intrusions much easier to identify.

Popular Monitoring Products

The number of available intrusion detection packages has increased dramatically in the past few years. There are two main types of intrusion detection software: host-based and network-based. Host-based intrusion detection is generally founded on the idea of monitoring a system for changes to its file system. It doesn't generally inspect network traffic. For that functionality, you'll need a network intrusion detection system (IDS), which looks specifically at network traffic, and will be our focus for this section.

Signature files are what most Intrusion Detection Systems use to identify attacks. Therefore, an IDS is generally only as good as its signature files. Using just a small snippet from an attack, the IDS compares packets from captured traffic to the signature file, searching for the specified attack string. If there's a match, an alert is triggered. This is why it's important to have control and flexibility with your signature files. When spotting new attacks, time is always of the essence. New attacks occur daily, and the ability to add your own signature files to your IDS sensor can save you the wait for a vendor to release a new signature file. Another thing to keep in mind with signature files is that, if they are written too generically, false alarms will become the norm. The downfall of any IDS system, false alarms can desensitize administrators to warnings, thus allowing attacks to sneak through—a perfect real-life example of "crying wolf."

Of all of the commercially available IDS products, one of the most flexible and adaptable is Network Flight Recorder, from NFR Security. Its sensors are run from a CD-ROM based on an OpenBSD kernel. Its greatest flexibility comes with the specially developed N-Code system for filter writing. N-Code can be used to grab any type of packet and dissect it to the most minimal of levels, then log the output. This is particularly useful when searching for attack strings, but can also be used to identify unknown network protocols, or to learn how certain software communicates over the network. Having the ability to write your own filters can be very helpful as well. For example, if your company has a specially developed piece of software, and you would like to identify its usage and make sure it isn't being utilized outside your network, a filter could be written to identify traffic from that specific program—a task which would be impossible with a hard-coded signature file system. Another excellent use of N-Code is in developing custom attack signatures. We'll discuss why having custom signatures can be important in the next section. NFR also supports the use of multiple sensors distributed throughout an environment, with a central logging and management server. Configurations and N-Code additions are done via a GUI, through a Windows-based program. Changes are centrally done, then pushed out to all remote sensors, eliminating the need to manually update each remote machine. This can be a huge timesaver in big environments.

A free alternative to NFR is a program called Snort, which is an excellent and freely available tool (downloadable from www.snort.org). Snort is a powerful and lightweight IDS sensor that also makes a great packet sniffer. Using a signature file or rule set (essentially a text file with certain parameters to watch the traffic it is inspecting), it generates alerts to a text file or database. We'll take a more in-depth look at writing rules in the next section. Snort has a large community of developers, so it is continually being updated to stay current with the latest changes in security. It is also now more able to deal with tools like Stick and Snot, which were designed to fool IDS sensors. One potential downside to Snort, however, is that because it is freeware, the group that writes it does not offer technical support. For home or small business use this might not be a problem, but for larger companies who require support when using Snort, a company called Silicon Defense offers commercial support and also sells a hardware, ready-to-go Snort sensor.

Signatures

It isn't uncommon for a sophisticated attacker to know the signature files of common IDS sensors, and use that knowledge to confuse the system. For a very simplistic example of this, let's say a particular attack contains the string "Hacked by hAx0r." A default filter might therefore search specifically for the string "hAx0r." Countering, an attacker with knowledge of the default signature files could send benign packets to your network containing only the string "hAx0r." This technically wouldn't be an attack, but it could fool the IDS. By sending a large series of packets all with "hAx0r" in them, the sensor could become overwhelmed, generating alerts for each packet, and causing a flurry of activity. An attacker could use this to their advantage in one of two ways. They could either swamp the IDS with so many packets it can't log them any more, or they could swamp it with alerts in order to hide a real attack. Either strategy spells trouble.

A custom signature could be defined to look for "by hAx0r," therefore defeating this type of attack strategy. Again, this scenario is a very simplistic example of custom signature writing. In reality, there is much more in the way of actual analysis of attacks and attack strings that must be done. Simple signatures can be very easy to write or modify, but the more complex the attack, the more difficult it is to write the signature. The best way to learn how to write signatures is to investigate already written ones included with the system. In the case of NFR, there are many N-Code examples that ship with the software, and many more can be found on the Web. A comprehensive N-Code guide is also available, which gives a detailed explanation of all the features and abilities of N-Code.

Snort, on the other hand, as we earlier described, just uses a text file with rules. A sample rule file for snort looks like this:

```
alert tcp $HOME_NET 21 -> !$HOME_NET any (msg:"FTP-bad-login";flags:PA;
    content:"530 Login incorrect";)
alert tcp !$HOME_NET any -> $HOME_NET 21 (msg:"FTP-shosts";flags:PA;
    content:".shosts";)
alert tcp !$HOME_NET any -> $HOME_NET 21 (msg:"FTP-user-root";flags:PA;
    content:"user root |0d|";)
alert tcp !$HOME_NET any -> $HOME_NET 21 (msg:"FTP-user-warez";flags:PA;
    content:"user warez |0d|";)
alert tcp !$HOME_NET any -> $HOME_NET 21 (msg:"IDS213 - FTP-Password
    Retrieval"; content:"passwd"; flags: AP;)
alert icmp !$HOME_NET any -> $HOME_NET any (msg:"IDS118 - MISC-
    Traceroute ICMP";ttl:1;itype:8;)
```

From this example, the format is easily readable. To create a simple signature, one only needs to specify the port number, an alert string, which is written to the file, and a search string, which is compared to the packets being inspected. As an example, we'll write a rule to search for Xmas tree scans, or a port-scan where strange packets are sent with the FIN, PSH, and URG TCP flags set. Most port scanning software, like Nmap will perform these scans. To begin, we can run some test Xmas tree scans just to watch what happens. Using a packet sniffer like Snort or Ethereal, we can see exactly which flags are set in our scan. Once we have that information gathered, the next step is to actually write the rule. So, our sample rule looks like this:

```
alert tcp !$HOME_NET any -> $HOME_NET any (msg:"SCAN
    FullXMASScan";flags: FPU;)
```

All alert rules start with the word "alert." The next three fields tell Snort to look for Transmission Control Protocol (TCP) packets coming from outside of our network on any port. The other side of the arrow specifies the destination of the traffic. In this case, it is set to anything defined as our home network, on any port. Next, we set our message, which is logged to the alerts file. It's generally a good idea to make the message as descriptive as possible, so you know what you're logging. The final two parts of the rule are where we fill in the information gathered from our sniffer. We know that the TCP flags were set to FPU, so we enter that in the flags field. This way, from start to finish the rule reads "make an alert if there is any TCP packet that comes from outside of our network, on any port, to anywhere on our home network, on any port with the flags FPU." Try reading through some of the rules listed previously and see if they begin to make sense. The first rule would read "Make an alert if anything on our network tries to connect to an FTP server outside of our network, and fails." Snort rules are fairly straightforward to read and write. For more complex rules, and a better definition of all the features that can be included with Snort rule writing, see the Snort project's home page.

Damage & Defense…

Keep Your Signatures Up to Date!

Most IDS sensors work by comparing traffic to a predefined list of signatures. When a match is found, an alert is triggered. This system has worked well in the past, but a new type of tool has been developed to mimic authentic signatures. One common tool is called Stick, and can be used to generate thousands of "attacks" per second, all from spoofed IP addresses. An attacker could use this to cause a denial of service to your IDS sensors, or to provide cover for his or her specific attack to your network. Some IDS vendors claim to now be able to distinguish between these fake attacks and real ones. Nevertheless, proceed with caution. And don't forget to update your signatures often!

Conducting Vulnerability Assessments

Earlier in the book, we discussed the importance of vulnerability assessment in order to make initial design decisions. Using the same principles as mentioned earlier, reassessments are an essential part of determining the current status of your network security. Being aware of changes in your network is one of the keys to detecting problems. Performing this kind of an assessment on a wireless network will be a fairly new exercise for most administrators. There are a number of new challenges that will arise from a radio transmission-based network, such as the mobility of clients and the lack of network boundaries.

When beginning a wireless vulnerability assessment, it's important to identify the extent of the network signal. This is where tools like NetStumbler, and the ORiNOCO client software will be very handy, because they will alert you to the presence of wireless connectivity. A good place to start the assessment is near the wireless AP. Start the monitoring software and then slowly walk away from the AP, checking the signal strength and availability as you move. Check out the entire perimeter of your area to make note of signal strength, taking special notice of the strong and weak points. Once you have a good idea about the signal internally, try connecting to your network from outside your facility. Parking lots, sidewalks, any nearby cafes, and even floors above and below yours should be investigated to analyze the extent of your signal. Anyplace where the signal is seen should be noted as a potential trouble area, and scrutinized in the future. If your signal is available far outside your premises, it might be a good idea to rethink the locations of your APs. If you can see your network, so can an attacker. Try to lower the signal strength of your AP by either moving it or making adjustments to its software, if possible. If limiting signal strength isn't an option, more emphasis should be placed on constant monitoring, as well as looking into other security devices.

If you have a signal from your network, externally, you'll now want to look at the visibility of your network resources from your wireless network. A good security design would isolate the wireless AP from the rest of the network, treating it as an untrusted device. However, more often than not, the AP is placed on the network with everything else, giving attackers full view of all resources. Generally, the first step an attacker takes is to gain an IP address. This is generally done via DHCP, which works by assigning an IP address to anyone who asks. Once an IP address has been handed out, the attacker becomes part of the network. They can now start looking around on the network just joined. In conducting a vulnerability assessment, become the attacker, and follow these steps to try to discover network resources. The next step is to perform a ping scan, or a connectivity test for the network, to see what else on the network is alive and responding to pings. Using Nmap, one of the best scanning tools available, a ping scan is performed like this:

```
# nmap -sP 10.10.0.1-15


Starting nmap V. 2.54BETA7 ( www.insecure.org/nmap/ )
Host  (10.10.0.1) appears to be up.
Host  (10.10.0.5) appears to be up.
Nmap run completed — 15 IP addresses (2 hosts up) scanned
    in 1 second
#
```

With this scan, we've checked all the hosts from 10.10.0.1 through 10.10.0.15 to see if they respond to a ping. From this, we gain a list of available hosts, which is essentially a Yellow Page listing of potentially vulnerable machines. In this case, .1 and .5 answered. This means they are currently active on the network. The next step is to see what the machines are, and what they run, so an exploit can be found to compromise them. An OS detection can also be done with Nmap like this:

```
# nmap -sS -O 10.10.0.1


Starting nmap V. 2.54BETA7 ( www.insecure.org/nmap/ )
Interesting ports on  (10.10.0.1):
(The 1530 ports scanned but not shown below are in state:
    closed)
Port          State         Service
22/tcp        open          ssh
25/tcp        open          smtp
53/tcp        open          domain
110/tcp       open          pop-3


TCP Sequence Prediction: Class=random positive increments
                         Difficulty=71574 (Worthy
                             challenge)
```

```
Remote operating system guess: OpenBSD 2.6-2.7

Nmap run completed — 1 IP address (1 host up) scanned in
    34 seconds
#
```

With this information, we now know that there is a machine with OpenBSD v2.6 or 2.7, running the services listed. We could now go and look for possible remote exploits that would allow us to gain access to this machine. If this were a real attack, this machine could have been compromised, giving the attacker a foothold into your wired network, and access to the rest of your network as well.

Snooping is another angle to consider when performing your vulnerability assessment. It can be every bit as dangerous as the outright compromising of machines. If confidential data or internal company secrets are being sent via wireless connection, it is possible for an attacker to capture that data. While 802.11b does support the Wired Equivalent Privacy (WEP) encryption scheme, it has been cracked, and can be unlocked via AirSnort or WEPcrack. These programs use the WEP weakness described by Scott Fluhrer, Itsik Mantin, and Adi Shamir in their paper "Weaknesses in the Key Scheduling Algorithm of RC4," which can be found at numerous Internet sites by searching for either the authors' or the paper's name. WEP does make it more difficult for an attacker to steal your secrets by adding one more obstacle: time. In some cases, it could take up to a week for an attacker to break your encryption. However, the busier the network, the faster the key will be discovered. To insure the best data privacy protection, have all wireless users connect to the internal network through a virtual private network (VPN) tunnel.

There are many opportunities for an attacker to gain access to a wireless network, simply because of their radio-based nature. After performing a vulnerability analysis, you should be able to spot some potential weaknesses in your security infrastructure. With these weakness identified, you can develop a plan of action to either strengthen your defenses, or increase your monitoring. Both are recommended.

Incident Response and Handling

Incidents happen. If your company has a network connection, there will eventually be some sort of incident. Therefore, an incident response and handling procedure is a critical component when it comes to protecting your network. This policy should be the definitive guide on how to handle any and all security incidents on your network. It should be clearly written and easy to understand, with steps on how to determine the level of severity of any incident. Let's take, for example, wireless intrusion attempts on two different networks, one without a good incident response policy, and one with more thorough policies in place.

Imagine one company without a formal security policy. As the company's network was built, the emphasis was placed on superior deployment, speed, and availability. While the network matured, and wireless access was added, there was little done in the way of documentation—they simply didn't afford it the time. There was still no security policy in place after adding wireless access, and no particular plans for how to handle an incident. Several weeks after deploying their companywide wireless network, the network administrators began to receive complaints of poor performance across the network. They investigated, based on what the various network administrators deemed necessary at that time. It was eventually concluded that perhaps one of the wireless Access Points was not functioning properly, and so they replaced it. After several more weeks, law enforcement officials visited the company—it seemed that a number of denial of service attacks had been originating from the company's network. Having had no formal security policy or incident handling process, the company was unable to cooperate with the officials, and could not produce any substantial evidence. Without this evidence, investigators could not locate the culprit. Not only was the company unable to help with the investigation, they had no idea they had even been attacked, nor did they know to what extent their internal data had been compromised. This left them with many more hours of work, rebuilding their network and servers, than if they had taken the time at the beginning to create a security and incident handling policy.

Next, imagine another company, one that attempted to balance performance and security considerations, and noticed some suspicious activity on their network from within their internal network. Through routine monitoring, the administrators detected some unusual traffic on the network. So, when their IDS sent an alarm message, they were ready to investigate. Within their security policy, guidelines as to how to handle the incidents were clearly detailed. The administrators had forms and checklists already prepared, so they were immediately able to start sleuthing. Using a number of steps outlined in their policy, they were able to determine that the traffic was coming from one of their wireless APs. They found this to be strange, as policy dictated that all APs were to have been configured with WEP. Further investigation found that this particular AP was mistakenly configured to allow non-WEP encrypted traffic.

In this case, having a good policy in place, the administrators were quickly able to track down the problem's source, and determine the cause. They were then able to systematically identify and reconfigure the problem Access Point.

Having an incident response policy is one thing, but the additional complexity posed by a wireless network introduces new challenges with forensics and information gathering. Let's investigate some of those new challenges, and consider some suggestions on how to contend with them.

Policies and Procedures

Wireless networking makes it easy for anyone to poke a gaping hole in any network, despite security measures. Simply putting a wireless AP on the internal network of the most secure network in the world would instantly bypass all security, and could make it vulnerable to anyone with a $100 wireless access card. It is for that reason that a provision to ban the unauthorized placement of any kind of wireless device should be drafted into a company's policy. This should be made to cover not just wireless APs, but the cards themselves. A user connected to your internal network could potentially be connected to an insecure wireless network, and bridging between the two interfaces on that machine would be very simple. The consequences of this to your network could be detrimental. Enforcing this policy can be difficult, however, as some popular laptop makers, such as Toshiba, have imbedded wireless access cards in their new notebooks. It should be considered a very severe infraction to place a wireless AP on the network—possibly one of the most severe—due to the level of risk involved. Having a wireless access card should also be treated seriously. Though this poses less of a risk than the AP, it should still be classified accordingly. Excellent sample policies are available on the SANS Web site at www.sans.org/newlook/resources/policies/policies.htm.

Reactive Measures

Knowing how to react to an incident is always a question of balance. On one hand, it would be tempting to close everything down and pull the plug on the whole network. That would certainly give you ample time to investigate the incident without further risk of compromise, but it would make your systems unavailable to your users. Some balance must be reached. When dealing with a wireless network compromise, it might be a good idea to disable wireless access until you can identify the entry point for the intrusion. Since wireless access is more of a luxury than a crucial business need, this may be possible. Of course, in organizations where wireless is critical, this isn't feasible. In either case, the WEP keys should be immediately changed, and if WEP isn't enabled, it should be. This will lock out the attacker for a limited time, hopefully giving you more of an opportunity to deal properly with the intrusion. In a secure and well-designed network (something which will be discussed later in this book), the scenario of a user joining a wireless network and immediately compromising it isn't as likely because more safeguards are in effect. If your network has been compromised through its wireless network, it's probably time to take some additional security measures.

While your network has been locked down, or at least had new keys installed, make sure to gather evidence of the intrusion. If the attacker was just passively listening to the network, there will be little evidence available, and not much taken as a result. However, if there were compromises into other network machines, it is critical to follow your company security policy guidelines to properly document the intrusion and preserve the evidence for the proper authorities. As mentioned in the introduction, covering how to handle evidence collection and performing forensics on a hacked machine is a book of its own!

Reporting

A wireless intrusion should be reported in the same manner as any other type of intrusion or incident. In most cases though, a wireless intrusion can be more severe, and difficult to document. Reporting a serious intrusion is a key part of maintaining a responsible approach to security. This is where a complete logging and monitoring system with IDS will be very useful. Having gathered and examined all log files from security devices; try to gain an understanding of the severity of the intrusion. Were any of the machines successfully attacked? From where were the attacks originating? If you suspect a machine was compromised, shut it down immediately, running as few commands as possible. Unless you really know what you are doing, and are familiar with computer forensics, the evidence should be turned over to investigators or forensics experts. The reason for this is that attackers will generally install a rootkit or backdoor system in a machine. These often feature booby traps, which can run and destroy critical information on the server. The primary places for booby traps like these are in the shutdown scripts, so it is possible you will have to unplug the machine, rather than use a script to power it down. Once that has been done, it's best to make two copies of the infected machine's disk for evidence purposes. If the authorities have been notified and will be handling the case, they will ask for the evidence, which should now be properly preserved for further forensics and investigation.

Cleanup

Cleaning up after an incident can pose a huge challenge to an organization. Once the level and extent of the intrusion has been determined, and the proper evidence gathered, one can begin rebuilding network resources. Generally, servers can be rebuilt from tape backup, but in some cases it may be necessary to start again from scratch. This is the type of decision that should be made after determining the extent of the intrusion. It is critical that when restoring from tape, you don't restore a tape of the system, post-intrusion—the same problems and intrusion will still exist. Some administrators feel there is no need to rebuild an infected machine, but simply to patch the security hole that allowed the intrusion. This is a particularly bad idea, because of the problem we mentioned with backdoors. The most advisable solution is to begin from scratch, or a known-to-be-safe backup. From there, the machines should be updated with the latest verified patches from the vendor.

Assuming the compromise did come from a wireless source, the wireless network should be re-examined. It may be difficult to determine exactly which AP was used for the compromise, but if you have an AP in a location that makes it easily accessible externally, you should probably consider moving it.

Prevention

As we've emphasized throughout this chapter, the best way to prevent an attack to your wireless network is to be secure from the start. This means designing a secure installation, maintaining firewalls and server logs, and continually patrolling your network for possible points of attack.

A secure wireless network is one which takes as many precautions as possible. Combining a properly secured AP with a firewall will provide a minimum level of security. Several steps that can be taken to help secure the network are adding a VPN to provide data privacy protection to your network. This is a critical step for organizations that require their data not be captured or altered in transmission. Isolation of network APs by a firewall is another often-overlooked step which should be implemented. Finally, simply making sure that WEP is enabled and enforced in all of your wireless APs can be just enough of a deterrent to save you from an intrusion. This may sound like quite a bit of extra work, which it is, but in order to remain secure, precautions must be taken. Building secure wireless networks isn't impossible, and will be discussed in more detail in other chapters in this book.

Conducting Site Surveys for Rogue Access Points

Even if you don't have a wireless network installed, it's a good idea to perform scans of your area for wireless traffic. The low cost and ease of setup makes installing unauthorized or rogue APs very appealing. Whether installed by well-intentioned users of your own network, or by malicious outsiders, making sure you routinely patrol for any wireless activity on your network is a sound idea.

In this section, we'll discuss some strategies for surveying your network and tracking down rogue wireless APs. Using tools like the ORiNOCO Client Manager and NetStumbler we'll describe how to locate unauthorized wireless access at your network site, and instruct you in how to see your network as an attacker would.

The Rogue Placement

There are really quite a few scenarios in which a rogue AP could be placed on the network. In this section, we'll take a look at two scenarios, one done without any bad intentions, and one placed by an attacker hoping to gain access to a network.

The Well-intentioned Employee

The first situation involves a well-meaning employee. This person has been looking at advertisements at computer shops that feature low cost wireless network equipment, and having just purchased a wireless networking installation for home, wants to bring that convenience to work. Believing that having a wireless network available for the other employees will provide a great service, this employee goes to the shop and brings back the $150 wireless AP on sale that particular week. After carefully following the instructions from the manufacturer, the AP is made available, and the user announces the availability of the AP to fellow employees. Wanting the configuration to be as simple as possible, the well-intentioned employee has configured the AP not to require a preconfigured SSID string, allowing anyone to connect to it. This now provides the freedom to other department employees to roam about freely with their wireless cards. Note that none of this was done with authorization, because the user had no idea of the security implications involved. As we've discussed earlier, this now provides an open point of entry to anyone within range of the signal.

Scenarios such as this demonstrate the need to educate users as to the dangers of adding wireless APs to the network. Visual demonstrations or real-world examples assist in providing powerful explanations detailing the repercussions of this kind of security breach. It should also be made known that there exists within the company security policy a provision banning any kind of wireless networking.

The Social Engineer

A determined attacker will stop at nothing to compromise a network, and the availability and low cost of wireless networking equipment has made this task slightly easier. In this scenario, an attacker who has either taken a position at your company as a nightly custodian or has managed to "social engineer" their way into your office space will place a rogue AP.

One often-overlooked possibility for intrusion comes from an attacker posing as a nightly custodian, or one that has officially obtained that position. Night custodial staff often have unsupervised access to many areas of an office space, and as such are in the position to place a rogue wireless AP. Given time to survey the surroundings and find an inconspicuous location for an AP, this type of attacker can establish an entry point into your network for later access. In this kind of situation, an attacker may try to disguise their AP both physically, and from the network side. If there are other wireless APs present in your environment, the attacker may choose to use the same vendor, and SSID naming schema, making it all the more necessary to keep listings of the MAC addresses of all your authorized wireless APs. Another possibility is that an attacker will enable WEP encryption on their AP, ensuring that only they are able to access it at a later date. Attackers often tend to feel very territorial towards their targets.

A similar scenario to this involves a technique known as social engineering. This generally involves representing oneself as someone else. A good way to social engineer a situation is to first know some inside information about the organization which you are targeting. If it's a large company, they may have a published org-chart which will have important names that the social engineer can quote from to seem legitimate. Other sources for names include the company's Web site and press releases. In one example, during a vulnerability assessment for a fairly large firm, we were generally unable to find easy access to the network, so we employed a social engineering tactic. Posing as a vendor replacing hardware, we were able to gain access to the Accounting department and were able to place an AP in the most suitable location we could find: a VP's hard-wall office, overlooking the parking garage across the street. With this AP in place, we were successfully able to demonstrate both the need for education about the dangers of social engineering, and the need for tightened security on the company's internal network.

Tracking Rogue Access Points

If after conducting a vulnerability assessment or site audit, you've spotted an AP that should not be present, it's time to begin tracking it down. It may be that your assessment found quite a few APs, in fact. In a city office environment this is to be expected, don't worry. There's a better than average chance that many organizations around yours are using wireless access, and their APs are showing up on your scan. Nevertheless, they should all be investigated. A clever attacker could give their AP on your network the name of a neighboring business.

Investigating APs can be a tricky proposition. Perhaps the first step is to try to rule out all those who aren't likely to be in your location. This can be done with signal testing tools like NetStumbler, or LinkManager from ORiNOCO. Signals that appear to be weak are less likely to be coming from your direct area. For example, let's say we're looking for an AP called *buzzoff* that turned up on our NetStumbler site survey.

In Figure 7.4, we can see on our NetStumbler screen that two APs have been spotted. The AP called covechannel has a pretty weak signal, when it's even visible, so it's probably not nearby, though we may want to check it again later. Instead, we'll look at buzzoff, because it's showing a very strong signal. A very useful tool for investigating signal strength is the ORiNOCO Site Monitor, which comes bundled with the ORiNOCO Client Manager. Bringing up the client manager software and clicking on the **Advanced** tab will reveal the Site Monitor option. In this example, the Site Monitor software reveals that the signal for buzzoff is still fairly weak.

From the information we've seen in Figure 7.5, it looks like we're still a bit far from the AP. The signal isn't all that strong, and that's not terribly surprising since we've just started looking. Now we need to find this AP. The signal is strong enough to assume that it's probably somewhere nearby, so we'll start walking around until we get a stronger signal. At this point, finding the AP becomes a lot like the children's game, "Hot and Cold." When we move out of range, the AP's signal becomes weaker or "cold," so we move back in until the signal strengthens. This process can be time-consuming and slow, but with patience you'll be able to close in on the signal (as seen in Figure 7.6).

With a signal this strong, we're very close to the AP. At this point, it's time for the grunt work of the physical search. Knowing where all the LAN jacks are is helpful, because the AP will be plugged into one. It wouldn't be much of a threat otherwise. So, by systematically checking all possible LAN connections, we are able to locate this rogue AP sitting on top of an employee's computer. In this particular instance, it appears we have found an AP that falls under the "well-intentioned employee" scenario. Though, since we don't know for sure that it was the employee who placed it there, the AP should be handled very carefully.

Figure 7.4 Network Stumbler: We've Found a Few Interesting APs

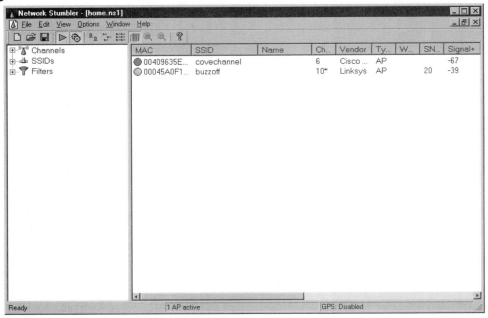

Figure 7.5 ORiNOCO Site Monitor: Looks Like We're Not too Close Yet

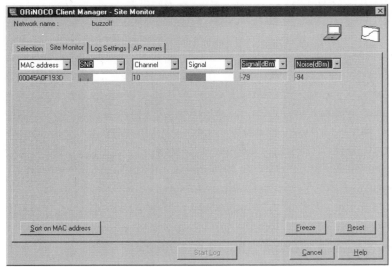

Figure 7.6 ORiNOCO Site Monitor: A Much Stronger Signal—We're Almost There

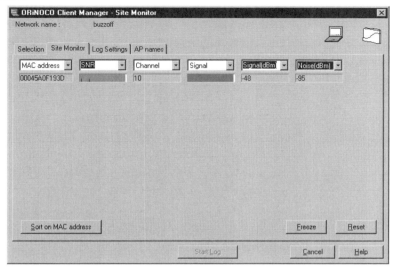

With the AP found, it would also be advisable to conduct more audits of system machines to see if there were any break-ins during the time the rogue AP was available. To do this, refer to the monitoring section earlier, and start watching traffic patterns on your network to see if anything out of the ordinary pops up. Another good area to watch is the CPU load average on machines around the network. A machine with an extraordinarily high load could be easily explained, but it could also be a warning sign.

Summary

In this chapter, we've introduced some of the concepts of intrusion detection and monitoring, and discussed how they pertain to wireless networking. Beginning with the initial design for a wireless network, we've focused on the fact that security is a process that requires planning and activity, rather than just a product shrink-wrapped at the computer store. Through proper investigation of our site, we can build a wireless network in which we are aware of potential problems before they occur. Examples of this are noting potential sources of interference, and knowing which physical structures may be a barrier to the network.

After designing the network, we discussed the importance of monitoring. Using a combination of software designed for monitoring and the logs from our security devices, we can gain a valuable picture of how the network is supposed to look, and from there deduce potential problems as they occur. Knowing that the network is under a much heavier load can be a sign of an intrusion. Along with monitoring, dedicated intrusion detection software should be used in order to watch for specific attacks to the network. The software, using signature files that can be customized to look for specific attacks, will generate alerts when it finds a signature match in the traffic.

From there, we moved on to discussing how to conduct a vulnerability assessment. This is important to do regularly because it can help you learn to see your wireless network as an attacker does, hopefully before they do. Spotting problems early on can save time and money that would be wasted dealing with an intrusion.

Intrusions do happen, and adding a wireless network without proper security definitely increases that risk. That is why it is critical to have a security policy in place that not only prohibits the use of unauthorized wireless equipment, but also educates users to the dangers of doing so. Updating the security policy to handle wireless issues is key to maintaining a secure network in today's environment. However, should an intrusion occur through the wireless network, we discussed a few strategies on how to deal with the incident itself, and then how to contend with the cleanup afterward. We didn't delve into the realm of the actual computer forensics, however. That is a very complex and involved field of security, and is definitely a book of its own. Should you be interested in learning more about forensics, there are a number of excellent manuals available on the Internet that deal specifically with the forensics of Unix and Windows systems.

Lastly, we dealt with rogue Access Points (APs), possibly one of the greatest new threats to network security. Rogue APs can be placed by an attacker seeking access to your network, or placed by a well-meaning employee, trying to provide a new service. Either way, they offer attackers a direct and anonymous line into the heart of your network. After conducting a routine site audit, in our example, we discovered a rogue AP and tracked it down using a combination of the ORiNOCO Site Monitor and the NetStumbler tool. Once it was found, we handled it very carefully, in order to uncover where it came from, and why.

Intrusion detection and monitoring are one of the key building blocks in designing a secure network. Being familiar with the operations of your network, and knowing how to spot problems can be a huge benefit when an attack occurs. Proper intrusion detection software, monitored by a conscious administrator, as well as a combination of other security devices such as virtual private networks (VPNs) and firewalls, can be the key to maintaining a secure and functional wireless network.

Solutions Fast Track

Designing for Detection

☑ Get the right equipment from the start. Make sure all of the features you need, or will need, are available from the start.

☑ Know your environment. Identify potential physical barriers and possible sources of interference.

☑ If possible, integrate security monitoring and intrusion detection in your network from its inception.

Defensive Monitoring Considerations

☑ Define your wireless network boundaries, and monitor to know if they're being exceeded.

☑ Limit signal strength to contain your network.

☑ Make a list of all authorized wireless Access Points (APs) in your environment. Knowing what's there can help you immediately identify rogue APs.

Intrusion Detection Strategies

☑ Watch for unauthorized traffic on your network. Odd traffic can be a warning sign.

☑ Choose an intrusion detection software that best suits the needs of your environment. Make sure it supports customizable and updateable signatures.

☑ Keep your signature files current. Whether modifying them yourself, or downloading updates from the manufacturer, make sure this step isn't forgotten.

Conducting Vulnerability Assessments

☑ Use tools like NetStumbler and various client software to measure the strength of your 802.11b signal.

☑ Identify weaknesses in your wireless and wired security infrastructure.

☑ Use the findings to know where to fortify your defenses.

☑ Increase monitoring of potential trouble spots.

Incident Response and Handling

☑ If you already have a standard incident response policy, make updates to it to reflect new potential wireless incidents.

☑ Great incident response policy templates can be found on the Internet.

☑ While updating the policy for wireless activity, take the opportunity to review the policy in its entirety, and make changes where necessary to stay current. An out-of-date incident response policy can be as damaging as not having one at all.

Conducting Site Surveys for Rogue Access Points

☑ The threat is real, so be prepared. Have a notebook computer handy to use specifically for scanning networks.

☑ Conduct walkthroughs of your premises regularly, even if you don't have a wireless network.

☑ Keep a list of all authorized APs. Remember, Rogue APs aren't necessarily only placed by attackers. A well-meaning employee can install APs as well.

Frequently Asked Questions

The following Frequently Asked Questions, answered by the authors of this book, are designed to both measure your understanding of the concepts presented in this chapter and to assist you with real-life implementation of these concepts. To have your questions about this chapter answered by the author, browse to **www.syngress.com/solutions** and click on the **"Ask the Author"** form.

Q: I already have a wireless network installed, without any of the monitoring or intrusion detection you've mentioned. What can I do from here?

A: It's never too late to start. If you already have a network in place, start from the design phase anyway, and follow the steps we've listed. Adding to a currently in-production wireless network doesn't have to be difficult.

Q: I don't really think I know enough about security to perform a proper vulnerability assessment. What should I do?

A: You can always try. That's the best way to learn. However, until you're more comfortable, consider hiring an outside security vendor to perform a network vulnerability analysis for you. Even if you do know what you're doing, a second set of eyes on something can always be beneficial.

Q: I've bought an IDS system that says it is host-based. How can I make it start seeing the network traffic like you described in this chapter?

A: You can't. Host-based intrusion detection software is very different from network IDS. It mainly looks at the file system of the server on which it is installed, notices any changes to that system, and generates an alert from there. To watch the traffic, you need to look specifically for a network-based intrusion detection system.

Q: I can see a ton of APs from my office. How can I tell if any of them are on my network?

A: The first way would be to check the signal strength. If you're getting a faint signal that only appears intermittently, chances are it's not in your area. If you detect a strong signal, you can attempt to join the network and see if it assigns you an address from your network. Additionally, you could look at some of the traffic on the network to determine if it's yours, but that may introduce some legality questions, and is definitely not advised.

Q: I've found a rogue AP on my network. Now what?

A: First, start by determining who placed it. Was it an employee or an outside party? If it appears to be the work of an employee, question them about it to find out how long it has been present. The longer it has been around, the more likely an intrusion has taken place. In the case of it being put there by an attacker, handle it very carefully, and if necessary, be prepared to hand it over to the authorities. Also, consider having a professional system audit to see if any machines have been compromised.

Chapter 8

Auditing

Solutions covered in this chapter:

- **Designing and Planning a Successful Audit**
- **Defining Standards**
- **Performing the Audit**
- **Analyzing Audit Data**
- **Generating Audit Reports**

☑ Summary

☑ Solutions Fast Track

☑ Frequently Asked Questions

Introduction

Auditing is by far the most overlooked activity when deploying any technology system or application. In contrast, audits are the most fundamental tools used for establishing a baseline and understanding how a system behaves after it has been installed.

In this chapter, you'll learn about the fundamental principles of security auditing. While our discussions will consider industry "best practices" and commonly used standards employed in auditing wireless networks, the base methodology applied when auditing other systems is similar. The guidelines provided in this chapter are generally applicable to most wireless networks. You may choose to add or remove auditing components to fit your own specific environment and systems.

Lastly, our hope is you will learn that auditing is an activity that should be performed continuously over the lifetime of a wireless network system. Doing an audit once will not guarantee a system will perform as advertised in perpetuity. Systems are constantly being stretched and expanded to meet the ever-changing roles of an organization. Audits will ensure that as new features and functionalities are added, they do not inversely affect the system.

Designing and Planning a Successful Audit

What specifically is an audit? An audit is a methodology used to test systems or components against predefined standards of operation or industry accepted best practices. Audits provide a means of assessing accountability and establishing metrics through performance measurements.

Audits have authority, in that the auditors are bound to an accepted auditing charter that specifies their roles, responsibilities, accountabilities, and access to information rights. Charters are defined by professional organizations and auditing groups. When ratified by management, they provide a means of authority with a clear chain of command. While audit groups operate within organizations, they are generally a distinct function within the organization that operates with a unique set of responsibility and accountability. This means that the auditing team can have the liberty to openly audit systems without the fear of reprisals from the mainstream corporate management.

Audits are performed in accordance to prespecified and preapproved plans. These plans provide the objective, scope and sampling size of the audit, along with detailed tasks and procedures to be performed during each phase of the audit. Audit plans provide guidance on budget and resource allocations, audit evidence handling, analysis, and report writing. They also indicate the risks involved in being able to meet auditing objectives such as staffing, equipment and auditing tool limitations, sampling size, and other factors that can impact the impartiality and accuracy of the audit.

Audits can be performed in a number of ways. Most audits consist of an interview portion and a technical analysis function. The interviews tend to be one-on-one or small intimate group interviews of users, administrators, and management and can last from less than an hour to a full day or longer. The technical analysis involves both verification and testing of systems and resources using hands-on and automated auditing tools.

Types of Audits

There can be as many types of audits as there are operational standards. Some standards define the behavior of a resource under certain conditions, while other standards will define the security elements used to safeguard a system. The type of audit performed on any given system or application depends of the level or type of verification that is required to be ascertained for that system. In general, audits are performed to:

- Assess risk
- Measure a system's operation against expectations
- Measure a system's policy compliance
- Verify change management
- Assess damage

Assessing Risk

The old cliché of "information is power" is probably the most applicable reason why audits are performed on wireless networks. With few people truly familiar with all of the individual components and how each of them operate, audits are important tools which can be used to understand how the overall wireless system behaves and how it interacts with other network components, as well as devices emitting radio signals.

Information systems and network technologies have always been at risk of malicious attacks, configuration errors, disasters and user error. Wireless networks are just as, if not more, prone to these same threats. The fact is that we have reached a level of confidence in the overall security and operation expected from some of our existing systems, based on many years or even decades of experience. Wireless technologies are new, and as such, present an unknown challenge.

Wireless network risk assessments involve determining the likelihood of each potential threat as it pertains to operations of the system. They can be used by management and technical staff to understand the factors which may impact operations. This information can then be used to provide clear guidance regarding the development of policies directing the implementation and use of components.

Typically, risk assessment involves:

■ Determining the likelihood of a specific threat based on historical information and the real-world experience of experts, administrators, and other technical staff

■ Ranking each threat from least likely to most likely

■ Determining the value and criticality of each resource based on use and impact to day-to-day operations, including revenue loss, customers resentment, and so on

■ Developing cost-effective methods for mitigating risk

■ Documenting an action plan which addresses risk

There are several methods used for determining risk. In general, they each use elements of quantitative and qualitative analysis. The insurance and banking industries have developed extensive models and case studies providing detailed quantitative analysis of many types of risk, while other groups provide more qualitative studies on risk. In the end, the method used for determining risk is dependent on the level of detail required for each assessment.

One of the additional benefits of performing a threat-risk assessment audit is that it can be used as a source document in the establishment of funding for activities relating to security functionality and equipment upgrades.

Risk assessments are an integral part of wireless network management. They provide the basis for what is referred to as the *assessment and audit chain* (see Figure 8.1). Risk assessments are used to assist in defining and implementing policies. They are also used to promote awareness regarding the special needs and circumstances of wireless network deployments. Lastly, they provide the baseline for establishing auditing and monitoring functions.

Figure 8.1 A Risk Assessment and Audit Chain

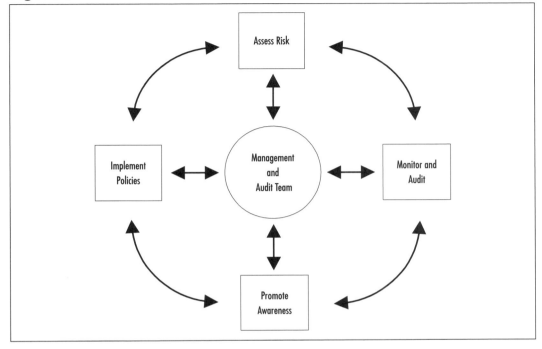

Measuring System Operation

Audits are also used to measure a system's operations. This is effective in helping to determine the capability requirements for a resource, and to verify that a system is meeting its operational targets.

When audits are employed for this purpose, they can provide metrics on how the users are utilizing a system, what the performance levels are for various operations, and what the overall system behavior and user experience is. The audit information can be used for building business cases and justifying the upgrade of components. They can also be used to verify that a system is meeting the advertised vendor specifications and load target.

In wireless networks, it is important to audit system operation to ensure performance expectations are met. Metrics on access speeds, roaming, and zone of coverage are some of the factors that need to be investigated.

Measuring System Compliance

Audits are most often used to determine a systems' overall compliance to existing policies and procedures. In this scenario, the auditors would verify that systems are deployed, managed and used according to the predefined rules.

This can help identify deficient policies and procedures along with enforcement issues. The results of a system compliance audit are generally used to update existing policies and procedures, and powers of authority.

In wireless networks, system compliance audits are generally used to ensure that installations meet a minimum requirement, that system use is for approved users and applications, and that prescribed security functionality is effectively used to protect the system resources.

Verify Change Management

Audits are also used to ensure a smooth transition during change management. These audits verify that new components operate within specified operational and functionality guidelines and that existing data and applications are not negatively impacted.

Change management audits provide the information required to make decisions for keeping a newly integrated system, or for rolling back to previous components. They provide an authoritative document that minimum specifications were met during the installation.

In wireless networks, change management audits are used to ensure that the new systems are not disruptive to existing installations and that applications and functionalities meet a minimum requirement.

Assessing Damage

Lastly, audits can be an effective means of assessing the damage that has occurred to a system or installation due to a malicious attack, system failure, or other disaster. Typically damage audits revolve around three major areas of assessment:

- Physical damage audits
- Logical damage audits
- Impact audits

Physical damage audits deal primarily with the physical aspect of a system or component. In the case of a fire, flood, or other disaster, an assessment is performed over the affected components along the environment around the components, for existing damage and potential threats. With wireless networks, auditors would verify the components making up base stations, transmission towers, APs, and others to determine if devices need to be repaired or replaced.

Logical damage audits are used to determine the level of system penetration an attacker reached before being identified and stopped. These audits are used to assess the systems that were exposed in terms of data access and data loss. They are also used to determine if foreign elements such as applications, viruses, or Trojans were introduced, or if other threats exist on the system that could be attacked in a similar fashion.

Impact audits provide data on the resulting state of the system and its users. They can also be used to determine what the impact of the damage is to partners, customers, and other interest groups. The impact can consist of both tangible and intangible costs, perceptions, and loyalty issues.

When to Perform an Audit

While audits can be performed at anytime during the lifetime of a system, they generally occur as follows (see Figure 8.2):

- At system launch
- In accordance with a particular schedule
- In maintenance windows
- During unplanned emergencies

Figure 8.2 When to Perform Audits

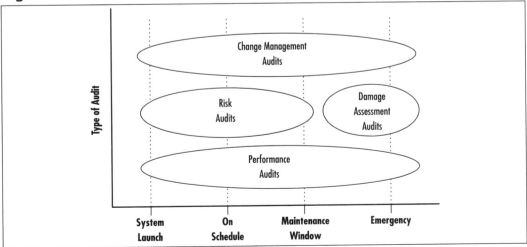

At System Launch

Audits are often performed on systems prior to launch, and as they are first launched. Audits performed prior to launch generally consist of *risk audits*, while audits performed at system launch usually are combinations of *performance audits* and *change management audits*.

These audits are used to document system characteristics, operational performance, and other factors impacting the new system and its relationship with other existing infrastructures. It is very typical to have a *risk assessment audit* performed when a new wireless networking technology is about to be introduced within an existing environment. It can help quantify the special environmental and security specifications for the deployment. Upon introduction, the wireless network is then subject to verification against the expected performance and functionality specifications.

On Schedule

Scheduled audits are the most routine audits performed. They are generally repeated on a bi-annual or annual basis. These consist of *compliance audits*, which for the most part are used to ensure system operations have maintained at least the minimum level of functionality and security as dictated by the policies governing the resource. In general, they fall into the following categories (see Figure 8.3):

- Host audits (every 12–24 months)
- Component audits (every 12–24 months)
- Network audits (every 12 months)
- Critical system audits (every 6 months)

In wireless network deployments, scheduled audits ensure that systems are up to date and incorporate the latest software, firmware, and other supporting application releases. They also ensure that installations were not modified since the last audit to support unauthorized functions or applications.

Maintenance Window

Maintenance window audits are often the most critical audits. While related to the wireless network system launch audits, they are generally used to verify new components that are installed within an existing system, or when a change occurs to the baseline system. *Wireless network system audits* and *wireless network change management audits* are usually performed in the wireless network maintenance window audit.

Figure 8.3 Scheduled Audit Timing

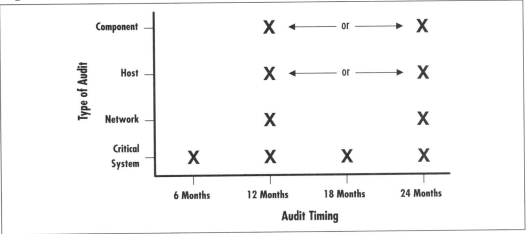

With the maintenance window audit, activities are focused on ensuring the continuing operation and functionality support post maintenance.

Unplanned Emergency Audits

Unplanned emergency audits generally involve *risk assessment audits* and *damage assessment audits*. They are used to define and quantify the state of a system post incident. While they are unplanned with regards to timing, they should not be considered "unplannable" from an activity perspective.

With care and diligence, unplanned emergency wireless network audit guidelines can be specified to meet most types of emergencies including disasters, attacks, and other incidents. Guidelines should be specified to address the types of assessment audits to be performed based on the criticality of each resource. They should also specify the order of the assessment audits, staffing expectations, and other resource requirements.

Auditing Activities

Wireless network audits consist of several stages where different resources or tools are needed to perform a specific activity. These activities generally fall into six categories:

- Audit Planning
- Audit Information Gathering
- Audit Information Analysis and Report Generation
- Audit Report Presentation
- Post-audit Review
- Next Steps

Audit Planning

Audit planning consists of all the activities required to prepare for an audit. It involves the reviewing the auditing charter to determine its applicability to the specific type of audit to be performed, reviewing existing policy and procedure documents, reviewing component documentation, writing and reviewing auditing checklists, and submitting the audit plan for approval.

Generally speaking the audit planning activity for a typical wireless network deployment represents between 20 percent and 25 percent of the overall audit schedule. This timeline can be compressed if audits are performed using existing audit plans and methodologies.

Audit Information Gathering

The *audit information gathering phase* consists of performing user, administrator, and management interviews, performing wireless network system and wireless network application checks using hands-on and automated auditing tools, and obtaining or generating documentation on the configuration and management of the system being audited.

The audit information gathering phase for a typical wireless network deployment usually represents between 20 to 25 percent of the overall audit schedule but can vary based on scope, number of systems, policies, and personnel to be reviewed.

Audit Information Analysis and Report Generation

The *audit information analysis and report generation phase* consists of all the activities involved in performing the actual audit based on information gathered in the previous phase.

It involves reviewing existing wireless network policies, procedures, and configurations against accepted policies, industry best practices and other guidelines.

It also involves reviewing the output of automated tools, benchmark tests, and other systems analysis. Additionally, it can include revisiting specific wireless network facilities, individuals, or other audited components for clarification on specific issues, or to perform additional auditing tests.

The last element of this phase involves writing a comprehensive and detailed analysis and review of the audited resource. It represents the results of the audit, notes key findings, identifies ways to address the major issues and offers guidance for future audit work.

This phase is often the most intensive in an audit in terms of time and resource commitment and can represent between 25 and 35 percent of the overall auditing activity.

Audit Report Presentation

The *audit report presentation* is the phase when the final report is presented to management or the group that requested the audit. Wireless network audit reports are usually formally presented with a short slide-deck review of the key findings, recommendations, and other comments. It also specifies the suggested audit period for the follow-up audit.

The audit report review process may take several weeks or months, at which point a second presentation may be in order to clarify or discuss specific aspects of the overall report. This process takes up between 5 and 10 percent of the overall audit schedule.

Post-audit Review

The *post-audit review* is the last stage of an audit. At this point in the wireless network audit process, the auditing team should review the entire audit process to generate lessons learned, identify key areas of success, as well as where improvement needs to be addressed.

The team also reviews the findings to determine methodology or other component applicability to other audits. Overall this phase represents between 5 and 10 percent of the overall auditing schedule.

Next Steps

While technically not an auditing activity per se, the "Next Steps" phase is an activity that is performed by management or the group who requested the audit after the audit has been completed. In a sense, it is the actual end result or goal of the audit.

The Next Steps phase is usually associated with the launch of new initiatives within an organization to address the follow-on work as it relates to updating systems, policies, and procedures to address the key findings of the audit report. This can be very involved and may at times represent a drastic shift in the way wireless network systems are implemented or managed.

Elements of the Next Steps phase are typical of traditional projects or program initiatives in that they list the personnel responsible for establishing a prioritized action plan, the action items that will address each issue, and the timeline for the completion of each task. It may also list a timeline for the next scheduled wireless network verification audit or post-Next Steps audit.

Auditing Tools

Audits run the entire spectrum, depending on the type being performed. These can range from simple system and quality assurance audits questionnaires to technical audits involving the design and integration of specialized auditing tools.

In all cases, one of the most critical elements of auditing is selecting the tools to be used to perform an audit and verifying its operation and compliance to the policies or environment being assessed. A number of tools are available to audit wireless networks, which can be categorized into two groups:

- Auditing interview tools
- Technical auditing tools

Auditing Interview Tools

Audit interview tools generally consist of questionnaires, spreadsheets, and matrix tables intended to provide the basis for audit discussion. When effectively used, they provide a means for the persons being interviewed to offer information on the state of the wireless systems, attribute applicability values to policies and procedures, and provide other relevant information on the wireless network being audited.

The documentation process can be performed using tape recorders, but laptop computers with documentation programs are generally more effective and less intrusive. Whenever interviewing someone, it is important to inform them that their opinion will be kept confidential and will be incorporated anonymously with that of all other interviewed personnel within the report.

Technical Auditing Tools

Many technical auditing tools are available for the Microsoft platforms, as well as for Linux, Unix, and other operating systems. Some of these include wireless network scanners, password crackers, protocol analyzers, and more.

Many security product vendors, including Intrusion.com, ISS, Computer Associates, IBM and others offer scanning products geared to the wireless network deployments. These tools typically assess the state of specific wireless network components such as session ID and encryption.

Shareware and Freeware applications and scanning products are also available from the many Linux user groups. They generally offer specific capabilities that in some cases are not offered by the mainstream vendors. While they are often very effective in addressing specific wireless environments, it should be noted that support is not always available for all platforms and vendors.

Regular auditing tool training should be enforced so that auditors can be comfortable with the full operations of each tool. The main benefit of this is that a thorough understanding of the capabilities and limitations of each of the reports generated by the auditing tools will yield to a more effective and precise audit.

Two of the leading factors in selecting an auditing platform include mobility and security.

Typically, laptops are used due to their portability, power, and security profile. Often, organizations will have dedicated machines used exclusively to stage wireless audits. This ensures configurations are not changed between audits and that the platform is not subject to other elements.

The auditing platforms are generally configured for dual-boot or multiple operating systems operation to support various auditing tools and user configurations. Often times, older, more stable, and well-documented operating systems with understood patches and capabilities are chosen for the Windows, Linux, and Unix platforms.

In all cases, the auditing platforms have extraordinary security features implemented that include strong passwords, file encryption, specialized wireless and network card drivers, virus protection, and other intrusion detection systems.

Some configurations include additional specialized tools such as compilers and various development or database tools. These can be effective when auditing systems for unexpected application calls and other end user scenarios.

Securing Auditing Tools

Whenever using wireless network auditing tools, care should be taken to verify they are original and have not been tampered with. With these tools, you will be building your evidence to describe conditions which may or may not be viewed favorably by management or by the groups supporting the wireless network components being audited. Without the assurance that these tools are providing an accurate account of the environment, the data captured is useless and cannot be used to back any recommendation.

The discrediting of the audit data or methodology used to obtain it is by far the most effective means of invalidating a wireless network audit report. Therefore, take time to ensure your wireless auditing tools are operating.

Some auditors rely on the reinstallation of tools from a known controlled medium at the beginning of each audit to ensure no transient agent has been introduced that could alter the findings. Others rely on verifying the digital signatures generated by the auditing application. The use of one method over another is generally based on personal preference.

Critical Auditing Success Factors

The success and effectiveness of wireless network audits depends on the level of involvement and support the audit team has from senior management. Without senior management buy-in, audits are relegated to a low-level duty cycle and will be performed on a "when I feel like it" basis. Without proper senior management support, Audit teams can feel the crunch of limited resource allotments. This can slow down the audit process whereby the final report and findings can be obsolete before they are published.

The second critical auditing success factor consists of determining the focus points for the audits. It is impossible to verify all the elements that make up a wireless network, and as such, an appropriately sized sample needs to be established. With focused attention, a scope can be defined which details the various elements to be included within the audit.

After the focus points and scope are defined comes the definition of processes and procedures for use within the audit. Within this framework, it is possible to define a process that effectively surface-probes scope elements and identifies possible deficiencies as potential targets for future auditing activities.

Audits can be viewed by some system administrators and technical experts as very personal challenges to their integrity and technical abilities. It is important to involve these resources early on within the audit process. Insist on having them participate in the planning of the audit. Wireless deployments can be very complicated and may involve expertise that is not readily available from within the auditor pool. Drawing on the knowledge base of these groups is essential in ensuring that all the critical system and personnel elements were considered for inclusion in the audit.

Business units and technology groups supporting wireless network deployments need to be held responsible for their audits. These groups live with the wireless technologies and are going to be the benefactors of the audit information. They will also be involved in the follow-up work necessary to address recommendations. Auditors can only perform successful audits on wireless systems they can access and verify. Again, as with system administrators and technology experts, business units and technology support groups need to feel they are part of the solution and that the successful and satisfactory completion of the audit depends on their involvement.

Lastly, the most important critical auditing success factor is developing efficient documentation methodologies and mechanisms used for the storage and sharing of auditing data. Often times, many sites will be assessed and many individuals will be interviewed during wireless networking audits. With clear summary reports, data analysis can be performed easily and efficiently. It is far more difficult and costly to the credibility of an auditing team to redo an audit or spend hours or days reinterpreting data than it is to implement and use effective document and data management techniques.

Defining Standards

Choosing which auditing standard to adopt, as well as the methodology and tools to use requires a good understanding of security, operational and user guidelines, policies, and procedures. It is worthwhile to take a look at what each of these are and what they represent in the auditing scheme of things.

Standards

Standards are defined by standards bodies, governments, and professional organizations, who act as a group authority on specific implementations and technologies. Standards generally specify the operations applicable to a given environment employing methodologies that can be used to address particular issues.

Standards can vary regarding specificity. Some are open to interpretation by equipment vendors and implementers, while others provide thorough definitions of each of the elements used in a system.

Many standards exist, and are important because they provide a framework for operation. A listing of government organizations, standards bodies, and baseline auditing procedures are provided in the "Auditing Standards and Best Practices" section found later in this chapter.

Guidelines

Guidelines provide direction in the application of standards and methodologies. They are often used to define default settings or configurations applicable to implementing a standard.

Some wireless network auditing guidelines are very specific, while others are open to interpretation. In the latter case, an understanding of the best practices supported by the issuing body can yield more appropriate implementations. In all cases, professional judgment and due care should be taken before choosing a specific implementation. Critical decisions should also be documented to support variances where they occur.

Best Practices

Best practices are a loose amalgam of anecdotal and day-to-day experiences that result in a list of generalized rules for the configuration and installation of systems. They are typically developed by professional organizations, enterprises, user groups, and special interest groups.

Wireless auditing best practices are generally used in reference to the application of guidelines, and often address specific implementations or environments. Best practices are specified when standards are not available or applicable.

Policies

Policies are mandated specifications or operations and are defined by professional organizations, enterprises, user groups, and special interest groups. As such, they provide specifications for the operations of systems and delineate roles and responsibilities.

Policies can be used in conjunction with security specifications, quality-of-service metrics, and other implementation parameters to define the operations of an environment.

Procedures

Procedures involve the day-to-day operations of a service or component. They provide detailed information on the roles and responsibilities of individuals and processes.

Auditing, Security Standards, and Best Practices

While there are several audit and security standards issued by government, industry, and professional associations, very few exist that specifically address wireless networks. In many cases, these basic standards provide a good start and can be adapted to other wireless environment. Some of these organizations and standards include:

Information Systems Audit and Control Association – ISACA The Information Systems Audit and Control Association provides IT governance, as well as control and assurance information. It provides certification for the CISA (Certified Information Systems Auditor) designation and develops information systems auditing and control standards. (www.isaca.org/)

International Information Systems Security Certification Consortium – (ISC)^2 The International Information Systems Security Certification Consortium provides a code of ethics, a common body of knowledge on information security, and certifies industry professionals through the Certified Information Systems Security Professional (CISSP) and System Security Certified Practitioner (SSCP) designations. (www.isc2.org)

American Institute of Certified Public Accountants – AICPA The American Institute of Certified Public Accountants provides a code of ethics, resource information, and has issued Statement on Auditing Standards (SAS) documentation. The SAS documents provide guidance for independent auditors using generally accepted auditing standards. (www.aicpa.org)

Information Systems Security Association – ISSA The Information Systems Security Association is an international organization of information security professionals and practitioners that provides a code of ethics, education forums, and publications on security matters to its members. (www.issa.org)

Computer Security Institute (CSI) The Computer Security Institute is a membership organization that provides training and awareness information on encryption, intrusion management, the Internet, firewalls, and Windows systems, among others. It issues a security newsletter, quarterly Journal, Buyers Guide, surveys and reports on topics that include computer crime and information security program assessment. (www.gocsi.com)

Computer Operations Audit and Security Technology (COAST) Computer Operations Audit and Security Technology is a university research laboratory that investigates computer security issues through the Computer Sciences Department at Purdue University. It works in conjunction with major corporations and government agencies to address the security requirements of legacy systems. (www.cerias.purdue.edu/coast/coast.html)

ITAudit.org ITAudit.org is a Web resource that provides a reference library and discussion forums to auditors and IT auditors on information technology. It is sponsored by The Institute of Internal Auditors (IIA). (www.itaudit.org)

The Institute of Internal Auditors – IIA The Institute of Internal Auditors is a membership organization that provides certification, guidance, education, and research to members who perform internal audits, governance, and internal control and IT audits. (www.theiia.org)

Forum of Incident Response and Security Teams (FIRST) The Forum of Incident Response and Security Teams is a round-table that brings together incident response teams from corporate, government, and academic fields. Its goal is to encourage cooperation and coordination in incident investigations and promote the information exchange between members and other groups. (www.first.org)

International Organization for Standards – ISO The International Standards Organization provides over 13,000 international standards for business, government, and society through the network of national standards institutes from over 140 countries around the world. (www.iso.org)

It has published several auditing- and IT security-related standards, guidelines, and codes of practice. Some of these include:

- **ISO/IEC TR 13335 Information Technology:** Guidelines for the management of IT security

- **ISO/IEC 15408 Information Technology:** Security techniques – Evaluation criteria for IT security

- **ISO/IEC 17799:2000 Information Technology:** Code of practice for information security management

Internet Engineering Task Force – IETF The Internet Engineering Task Force is an international community concerned with the evolution of the Internet. Its contributors include corporate, government, industry, academic, and other interested parties. Working groups are established that issue standards and guidance in the forms of Request for Comments (RFCs). (www.ietf.org)

The IETF has issued several security handbooks and guidance on security matters. RFC 1244 Site Security Policy Handbook Working Group (SSPHWG) was developed by the IETF Security Area and User Services Area and provides information on security policies and procedures, policy violations, and incident response, among other topics. It is not an Internet standard.

U.S. Government Auditing Standards The United States Government has issued several standards on the operation and use of information systems within the government. These include the Rainbow Series of documents. (www.radium.ncsc.mil/tpep/library/rainbow/index.html)

The United States General Accounting Offices has issued a number of standards and policy documents on the use of information systems. While they do not specifically address the subject of auditing wireless network deployment, many provide relevant information on appropriate auditing practices, documentation, and audit data management. (www.gao.gov)

The United States National Institute of Standards and Technology (NIST) also recognizes the importance of conducting risk assessments on information resources. They have issued a number of guidance documents addressing risk assessment and computer security. (www.nist.gov)

Corporate Security Policies

As we touched on earlier, policies are mandated specifications or operations. Wireless network deployment corporate policies are defined by one or more governing bodies within an organization. These can include Legal and IS departments among others. These groups establish the benchmark for the implementation and deployment of technologies and services within their environments.

In specifics, policies list the various system resources such as servers, applications, wireless access points and wireless nodes along with who is entitled to use and administer them. They define access use rules that constitute user granted privileges. Furthermore, they specify the users rights and responsibilities, classifications of services, and minimum security provisions such as password rules, desktop configurations, and other specifications. They often include basic information for use during emergency scenarios, along with incident logging procedures.

Remember the intended audience when defining policies. Policies need to be clearly written to minimize confusion and interpretation. They must be relevant and succinct, providing the right amount of information without overwhelming the reader. Stick to policies that are directly applicable to an environment and avoid complex or misleading policies at all costs. If a policy is difficult to understand, it will be equally difficult to implement and audit.

Contrary to popular belief, it is not better to have a bad policy than no policy at all. Bad policies tend to lead to a false sense of security and often result in a more vulnerable environment. Remember, it's better to write a simple policy that can be understood and applied by everyone than to create an overly detailed policy that ends up collecting dust on a shelf.

There are times when the status quo becomes policy. These policies are often referred to as unwritten policies. Whenever possible, document all policies and perform audits based on them. Just because something is acceptable for a wired environment does not necessarily mean it is the right policy for the wireless environment.

In the end, corporate security policies are a treatment of the assessment of risk within an organization. They provide a foundation for system operation, and as such, provide the basis for performing audits.

Policies are a link on the cycle of evolution of wireless network systems. Policies need to be tested and verified against the operating environment using audits. The results of audits are provided in reports which offer recommendations.

Recommendations are then formulated into action plans for the update of deployments resulting in the update of policies. See Figure 8.4.

Figure 8.4 Audit and Policy Cycle

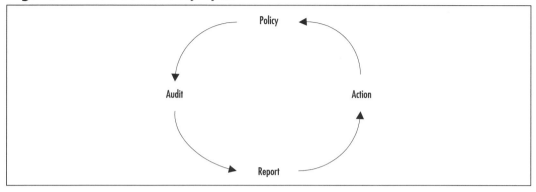

Security Alert

Every day, new ways are being devised by hackers to attack and penetrate wireless systems. Because of the Internet, this knowledge of new wireless vulnerabilities can circle the globe within seconds.

It is critical for the safeguard of our wireless networks that policies be put in place to ensure our wireless networks are not vulnerable to attacks including:

- Denial of service attacks, such as:
    - Signal jamming attacks
    - Signal flood attacks
- Information compromise attacks, such as:
    - Brute force attacks
    - Signal flood attacks
    - Viruses, Trojans, and worms
    - Insertion attacks
    - Eavesdropping, interception, and stealing of communications and conversations

Poor management and enforcement of security policies can lead to a lax security environment. Stringent policies can stifle action and lead to antiquated security measures that are not easily adaptable to mitigate new threats. A middle ground of regular policy review and enforcement audits as outlined in Figure 8.4 is one of the best ways to address changing needs.

The important thing to remember when establishing policies and policy documentation is that policies should be dynamic and adaptable. Policy documents should be considered living documents that can address changes within organizations and within the IT field.

Auditing Charters and Irregularities

Auditing is a methodology that must have clearly defined rules, regulations, and boundaries. The possibility of abuse can occur within the auditing organization if conduct is not clearly governed by standards and industry-accepted norms.

This information is usually contained within the *auditing charter*, which specifies the mandate of the auditing group and the types of actions that can be performed by individuals under the auspices of an audit. It also clearly defines the roles and responsibilities of each auditor, along with the minimum qualifications, certifications, and other training required to perform audits. It may list technology and auditing paths that specify the types of audits performed by the group and the level of seniority and experience required to perform specific audits. Lastly, it might recommend that auditors chosen for specific projects have a minimum set of competencies in order to successfully perform the audit.

While audit groups can operate as distinct functions within the organization, and generally without fear of reprisals from the mainstream corporate management, auditors cannot operate completely unbounded of authority. The auditing charter needs to define a clear path of authority and should specify the remedies used to address deviances in terms of conduct and auditing irregularities.

Auditing irregularities generally consist of three categories. These include:

- Sampling irregularities
- Biased opinions
- Fraud

Sampling Irregularities

Sampling irregularities generally refer to issues regarding the size and applicability of a selected auditing sample. This can include the geographic dispersion of a sampling group, variations in applicability, along with other sampling and statistical factors that affect the overall perception and applicability of the audit.

Sampling irregularities can also include irregularities in how auditing data was obtained, managed, and stored. These factors will reflect on the data analysis and final audit conclusions.

Biased Opinions

There are times when auditors cannot guarantee an arms length relationship with an auditing project, or when auditors have a predisposition regarding their perceptions of a system, group of people, or other constraint.

With impartiality being the hallmark of the auditor, it is critical that a means exist to facilitate the identification of conflicts of interest and other factors that can be perceived as an unbiased opinion.

Without proper regulations, issues over impartiality can impede the overall flow of the audit, the willingness of participants to provide information, and the level of access provided to systems and facilities. Overall, it can have a nefarious affect on the final audit report findings, conclusions, and recommendations.

Fraud

In their day-to-day affairs, auditors are often privy to sensitive corporate information. The code of ethics contained in the auditing charter should list a code of conduct that specifies the rules for discussing or divulging information to third parties.

On rare occasions, an auditor may be coerced into providing audit statements or audit data to third parties for personal gain. In these cases, clear delineation of fraudulent behavior needs to be addressed and documented in accordance with rules and regulations to facilitate removal and/or summons at a trial.

Establishing the Audit Scope

Part of the preplanning activities for wireless network audits involves defining the scope and depth of the audit. Surveys conducted within the organization can provide guidance on the areas that should be investigated.

Reports and statistical information provided by independent research firms, professional associations, and other sources can also be used to identify generally observed areas of concern. In general, network breaches include viruses, access abuse by users, leaks, destruction of data, and hacking, among others.

Lastly, the two largest obstacles to the successful completion of audits has to do with the budgets allocated to the task, and communications to the end users regarding their role in the wireless network auditing process. These are the two most critical elements within the wireless network *audit scope*.

Other factors which need to be assessed when establishing the scope include the technical complexity of the audit, the weakness of the audit tools, the roles and responsibilities of all those involved, proper audit staff training, and central-ized authority.

Establishing the Documentation Process

The documentation process involves establishing the guidelines used in the man-agement of audit data as it is generated, and the collation of interview responses into a document that can be used during the analysis phase of the wireless net-work audit report generation.

Safeguards need to be defined which will protect the wireless network audit report and audit data after the audit report is submitted. These include estab-lishing rules regarding the distribution and management of the audit report, as well as storage of the audit report.

Some organizations limit the distribution of the completed wireless network audit report on a need-to-know basis. Printed audit reports should be numbered and should require the signing of an acknowledgment of receipt.

An audit report storage policy should be specified in the cover of the report to ensure reports are stored in an environment that is protected from intruders, potential hazards, and disasters.

Electronic audit data and audit reports should be stored in an encrypted format in an environment that is protected from intruders, potential hazards, and disasters.

Performing the Audit

Now that preplanning activities have been completed, it is time to perform the wireless network audit. This phase of the audit represents a sampling of the overall wireless network environment for deployment correctness and applica-bility of standards, policies, procedures, and guidelines.

Auditors and Technologists

Depending on the organization and type of audit being performed, authorized auditing personnel will consist of internal employees, hired third-party consul-tants or a combination of both. Determining the ratio and mix of internal employees versus consultants should be at the sole discretion of the auditing pro-ject management office.

Generally speaking, auditing personnel consists of individuals that have an understanding of the organization or group being audited. They will also be required to attest to being in a position where they can maintain auditor independence with those involved in the audits.

With wireless network assessments, it is important to use personnel that possess, at minimum, experience auditing information systems and networks. Furthermore, it would be wise to include as part of the auditing team, individuals with experience auditing security applications and an understanding of both symmetric and asymmetric cryptographic systems.

Lastly, auditors conducting interviews should be able to communicate in a professional and effective manner with other people. They should have the ability to create an interview environment that is comfortable and open, and be able to ask questions with impartiality—that is, ask questions in a manner that does not bias the interviewed personnel answers in any direction.

Auditors should also have the ability to clearly document the results of hands-on and automated assessments and personnel interviews.

Obtaining Support from IS/IT Departments

IS and IT departments have to recognize that audits are an important part of their overall wireless network security posture. Without this belief, audits will be neglected and will rarely occur. In the cases where a clear mandate is not directed from management, individual organizations may provide limited support or no support at all. This generally results in audits that over-sample or over-represent certain factors and not others.

The most effective means of ensuring involvement is to have senior management direct budgets for the specific support of audit activities. This way, equipment and application owners will have an easier time justifying their involvement and will be in a position do develop the procedures and tools required to adequately verify the on-going operations.

It should be understood that limitations of budgets and audit activities, do not preclude effective audits. While these factors will impact the overall scope and reach of the audits, in that they will force audits to be primarily focused on specific high-risk elements, proper activity planning, tool selection, and local IT/IS department involvement can offset some of these limitations. By identifying potential security vulnerabilites, an auditor can also provide IS/IT personnel with support for their own cases to management for increased budget or resources.

Senior Management Support

Senior management support of the audit is critical, ensuring that resources are available to support the audit activities. It also sends a clear message to the overall organization that an audit should be taken seriously, and that audit findings need to be reviewed and action taken to implement appropriate changes to wireless network policies, procedures, and security controls.

Support can consist of several aspects but is most effective when it is used to determine the scope and depth of the audit, establishing priorities, allocating funds, and approving an action plan that addresses the key audit findings.

A way to obtain senior management buy-in for audits is to present credible evidence of the likelihood of threats. This report should not be a fear report, but should accurately describe the various operations that are impacted by, and have impact on, the wireless network.

Report data can be obtained from many analyst and research organizations, insurance companies, banks, and other enterprises making similar wireless deployments. The Internet has hundreds of sites that provide wireless networking and wireless security statistics, and can be an effective means of establishing a list of the top risks associated with a specific wireless deployment. Security and wireless conferences can also be a great source of data.

In the report, a clear correlation needs to be established between performing the audit and risk reduction. Cost metrics, brand impact, user and customer loyalty issues, and other factors should be used to demonstrate the value of the audit activities.

IS/IT Department Support

By far the most effective means of obtaining IS/IT department support is through establishing a clear ownership stake by each of these groups in the successful completion of the audit and in the implementation of the audit recommendations.

Individuals and targeted groups should be designated as primes that can assist in the planning, deployment and review of the audit activities. They should be part of a larger audit-user group that reports back to senior management on the audit process and provides feedback and recommendations as required.

Once the audit has been completed and a plan has been established to address the recommendations, the primes can be an effective means of communicating information to other groups operating wireless networks on the audit process and the various lessons learned. This can be an effective means of easing the tensions and concerns of groups and users who have not been through the audit process.

Gathering Data

Now that the audit preplanning activities have been completed and that senior management and IS/IT department buy-in have been established, it is time to perform the data gathering phase of the wireless audit. There are several components that make up this phase, which include:

- Interviews
- Documentation review
- Technical review

Interviews

The interview process can involve participants representing several different roles and job functions and can include wired and wireless network system administrators, wireless network users, support managers, technical architects, and other relevant functions.

Generally speaking, the interviews involve the use of anonymous questionnaires, spreadsheets, and other data capture tools. These should not be equated with the testing participants or in assessing right and wrong answers. They should be used as guides for discussions, and as data capture tools.

Interview discussions typically revolve around usage patterns, security policies and component descriptions. Participants should be asked if they are aware of the existence of any wireless network security policies, usage guidelines, or other related practices. In the case where they believe these exist, they should be asked to provide a synopsis in their own words of what each specifies.

When discussing components, interviews should also pose questions regarding the participants' understanding of the overall wireless network, the use of systems and resources, and the relative criticality of each system or component that was described.

Lastly, they should be asked about their views and perceptions of the audit and what they believe the sentiment of others are regarding the audit activities.

Document Review

The document review process can involve many sources of documentation, but for the most part will consist of:

- Wireless hardware and software documentation
- Wireless network architecture documentation
- Wireless deployment documentation
- Personnel roles and task assignments

- Wireless usage policy

- User documentation

- Administrative procedures

- Wireless networking guidelines

- Incident logs

- Disaster planning documentation

- Other documentation related to wireless networking

The primary goal of the document review is to determine the level of policy integration within the existing documentation and to identify deficiencies where policy or other information is lacking, in error, or is nonexistent.

As with any other network or infrastructure components, wireless network deployments should have plans that address what to do in the event of critical system failures and disaster scenarios. Care should be taken when reviewing these plans to ensure they are valid and that they do not circumvent other security policies.

Technical Review

Technical Reviews consist of performing analyses of wireless network and system components for adherence to established policies, procedures, guidelines, and best practices.

Technical reviews of wireless networks often involve the use of hands-on and automated tools. These can be used in the identification of wireless network weaknesses, deficiencies, configuration errors, and unapproved services and applications. They can also be used to test wireless systems for their tolerance and resiliency against known attacks.

Wireless network technical reviews allow for the verification of system logs, configuration files, system settings, release and patch levels, administrative and user accounts, application paths, and resource ownership.

They should also be used to verify existing documentation for applicability and correctness.

Analyzing Audit Data

The *audit data analysis* phase involves the review of all captured data from interviews, scans, and system documentation for compliance with accepted standards, policies, procedures and guidance.

Matrix Analysis

There are several ways of analyzing the data gathered during the audit. One of the more efficient methods is to create policy, security, and issues tables that denote the current state of compliance of various sites and technologies.

Matrices and score cards are effective in providing a quick review of the level of compliance to policies at different sites or for different applications.

In the first and second examples shown in Matrix One and Two of Figure 8.5 and Figure 8.6, a rating of 1 to 5 is used to represent the level of compliance. A rating of 1 denotes noncompliance while a rating of 5 denotes full compliance. Ratings of 2, 3, and 4 would denote partial compliance with comments.

Figure 8.5 Wireless Network Audit Data Analysis Matrix One

Issue	Site A	Site B	Site C
Use of strong passwords	5	5	3
Use of VPN link encryption	5	5	1
Use of WEP encryption	5	5	5
Use of SSIDs	5	5	4
Latest OS patch release	5	5	4
Access Point physically secured	5	5	3

Figure 8.6 Wireless Network Audit Data Analysis Matrix Two

Site "A" Security Policy Compliance Review					
Security Policy	X	X	X	X	X
Who can use a resource	X	X	X	X	X
Proper use	X	X	X		
Authentication	X	X	X	X	
Administrative privileges	X	X	X	X	
User rights	X	X	X	X	X
Security logs	X	X	X	X	X

In addition to matrices, data analysis would involve written descriptions of compliance levels and deviations. This type of analysis would provide insight and backing information describing how conclusions were arrived at.

Recommendations Reports

Recommendations can be written up in several ways. Most reports use a combination of detailed written recommendations and matrices (see Figure 8.7). Recommendations are generally categorized in terms of criticality and time frame, including:

- Short-term recommendations

- Medium-term recommendations

- Long-term recommendations

Figure 8.7 Wireless Network Audit Data Recommendation Matrix

Site "A" Security Policy Compliance Review - Recommendations				
Recommendation	Criticality	Cost	Resource Requirement	Time Requirement
Integration of authentication systems	HIGH	$100,000	15	6 weeks
Security audit log implementation	HIGH	N/A	6	3 weeks
Operating system patch update	HIGH	N/A	2	4 weeks
VPN integration	MEDIUM	$250,000	4	6 weeks
User rights policy update	LOW	N/A	1	ongoing

Generating Audit Reports

Generating the final audit report is the goal of the wireless network audit. It provides the means of communicating key findings and recommendations to users, administrators and management.

It identifies the general posture and state of the wireless network and lists system, resource and documentation that have improved, stayed level, or deterred since the last audit. When deficiencies are identified, the audit report should provide suggestions for improving the position.

It should also provide an abbreviated lessons learned section, along with suggestions on the direction of future audits.

Lastly, it may be beneficial to have technical writers involved in the report writing process to ensure that the final document meets the needs of the intended reader.

The Importance of Audit Report Quality

Audit reports need to be of a high quality to ensure that those reading the report will feel confident it represents a professional and unbiased effort. Without this belief, key findings and recommendations may not be seriously considered and acted upon. As additional high-quality wireless audit reports are written, a reputation will be gained that will influence a more ready acceptance of findings.

Successful challenges demonstrating errors, inconsistencies or lack of sufficient data can greatly impact the perception and value of sections of the audit report and in some cases call into question the entire report along with the auditing methodology and the competence of the auditing staff.

The best means of safeguarding against challenges is to demonstrate that findings and recommendations are fully supported with corroborative data. This will, in effect, provide a quality control mechanism that ensures the audit reports are effective.

Writing the Audit Report

The audit reports writing process involves gathering all of the findings and recommendations generated during the analysis phase of the audit and producing a document that effectively represents the data. As such, it should represent a synopsis of the collected data into a clearly readable document. Metrics should be provided when making judgments, and findings should be backed-up with supporting facts where appropriate. Generalities and qualitative state descriptions should be avoided whenever possible.

Reports should be written with the intended audience in mind, and clear distinctions made between sections destined to be read by senior management, systems managers, technical architects, administrators, and end users.

Wireless network audit reports tend to be substantial documents and can range from 20 or 30 pages to several hundreds of pages when all the appendices and corroborative scans are included. The depth of technical detail should increase throughout the report.

Several sections constitute a wireless network audit report. They include:

- Executive summary
- Prioritized recommendations
- Main body
- Detailed recommendations
- Final conclusions
- Appendices
- Glossary

Executive Summary

This section is often the most difficult to write, and is usually the last to be completed. It should be written in a clear, concise manner that can be easily read and understood by senior management. It generally spans one to two pages and establishes the report's tone and setting.

Some of the key elements that make up the executive summary include:

- The reasons for performing the audit
- A brief overview of the audited systems and organizations
- Changes since the last audit
- A listing of significant strengths and weaknesses
- A listing of noted abnormalities
- A listing of key findings
- A listing of top recommendations

Prioritized Recommendations

The prioritized recommendations section provides a bulleted listing of major recommendations in order of priority and impact. The descriptions include information about the systems, policies, and procedures that are affected, along with suggested enhancements.

Main Body

The main body is generally regarded as the simplest part of a wireless network assessment report to write . It should be very thorough and provide introductions that explain the purpose and scope of each subsection as well as the overall importance each has relative to the overall document. It may, in some cases, provide additional reference materials used to educate the reader regarding special distinctions and applications of technologies.

This section is where the reader will obtain information on how the audit process was performed along with a listing of auditing tools used. It explains why specific components, individuals, or groups were selected and included in the audit sample.

The main body has full descriptions of findings, recommendations, and claims identified in the executive summary, and provides a detailed review of how auditors arrived at each conclusion, offering a grading system that identifies the criticality of each discovery. It should provide reasons that account for any variation between the data captured and the expected results.

Lastly, this section details and contrasts findings arrived at in the current audit with those of previous audits. It references issues and provides an assessment of the effectiveness of the resolutions should they be implemented.

The writing of the main body section of a wireless network audit report can be simplified by creating subsections specific to an area where the wireless audit was performed. Subsections may include, but are not limited to, the following:

- Wireless network deployment configuration

- Wireless network security

- Wireless host security

- End station security

- Policies, procedures, and related documentation

- Physical security

- User perceptions

- Retention, access, and security of audit data

Detailed Recommendations

The detailed recommendations section provides a listing and synopsis of all the findings identified in the main body of the wireless network audit report and provides specific recommendations to address and improve the overall posture of each identified element.

Each item in the list is matrixed into a grading system that identifies the criticality of the finding with respect to the others. It provides a means to determine the key findings and top recommendations included in the executive summary.

Final Conclusions

This section is the bridge that links the various sections of the wireless network audit report together. It provides a review of the key findings and a synopsis of the top recommendations. The final conclusion provides an overall grade or evaluation as it applies to the total system.

Appendices

This section contains the audit data that cannot fit within the main body of the report. This data may include data files, system dumps, and other supporting documentation, and may appear in either a processed or raw form depending on the applicability.

It provides a listing of all the wireless systems or components that were examined along with the output generated for each during the audit. Appendices list the appropriate operating system, security, and firmware updates that should be applied to address vulnerabilities identified on each component.

The appendices provide detailed information on the tools used to perform the audit and may include configurations. It will provide information on how audit data generated by the auditing tools was handled and stored during and after the completion of the audit process.

Lastly, the appendices will provide suggested readings relevant to wireless networking and wireless network auditing. These will consist of books, papers, analyst reports, professional associations, user groups, and Internet Web sites.

Glossary

The glossary would contain an alphabetical list of all the wireless, networking, and auditing technical terms used in the report.

Final Thoughts on Auditing

Auditing is a skill that is learned and improved upon with hands-on experience and approved training. The more audits you perform, the more thorough and efficient you will become.

There are several organizations that sponsor professional auditing certifications. You may wish to learn more by joining those that reflect your interests.

Don't be shy when auditing systems. You are there to learn how the wireless network components you are auditing have been configured *in this* environment. While you may understand how systems are typically implemented and operated at other sites, it is your duty to determine if this site has followed, and is adhering to, the specified standards, policies, procedures, guidelines, and other mandated configurations

Remember to be open and unbiased when conducting interviews. Be careful to ensure you are not leading on interviewed personnel to conclusions or "appropriate" answers.

Sample Audit Reports

Sample Management Report: Wireless Network Security Audit Report XYZ Corporation

EXECUTIVE SUMMARY

Introduction

This report, issued on <DATE>, contains the results of the wireless network security audit performed on the helpdesk departmental wireless LAN at the Corporation.

Audit Purpose

The wireless network security audit was conducted as part of the annual information systems technology review audit to identify issues and provide guidance on improving the security of wireless networks.

Background

The IS department of the Corporation is responsible for the deployment and maintenance of wireless networks across the corporation. Wireless networks are used to provide connectivity between existing centralized servers located on wired LANs and wireless roaming users.

There are currently ten wireless networks deployed within the Corporation.

(A diagram would be inserted and technical descriptions of the components would be provided in this section)

Audit Objectives

The audit objectives consisted of assessing the effectiveness of the wireless network deployment, assessing the adherence to established corporate security policies and procedures, and assessing the application of industry guidelines and best practices.

Conclusions

The audit team concluded the overall security posture of the helpdesk departmental wireless network met all the established security policy and guidance requirements.

They also concluded that a more effective means of securing the session data being communicated between the wireless nodes and the wireless Access Point is required.

Noteworthy Accomplishments

The IS department integrated the standardized user ID/password authentication system to the helpdesk departmental wireless network, thereby eliminating the need to create wireless network-specific user IDs/passwords.

This addresses the recommendation from the previous wireless network security audit performed on <DATE>.

Audit Scope and Methodology

The wireless network security audit scope was to examine the wireless network components, as well as the documentation. The audit was conducted in accordance with the the Corporation auditing standards. It included tests of the audit records and other auditing procedures considered necessary within the environment.

A preliminary review of the helpdesk departmental wireless network systems was conducted to gain an understanding of the operations and to form a basis for selecting technology and documentation targets for audit.

Sample Technical Report
Wireless Network Security Audit Report:
XYZ Corporation

Report Contents

- Risk Classification Summary
- Security Ratings
- Vulnerability Type Summary
- Vulnerability Assessment Details
- Appendix A: Risk Definitions

Risk Classification Summary

Wireless network security vulnerabilities are classified according to the level of risk they represent, as well as the likelihood that they will affect the systems. A summary of the ten main issues we discovered in relation to classes of risk is presented in Chart 1.

Chart 1 Risk Classification Summary

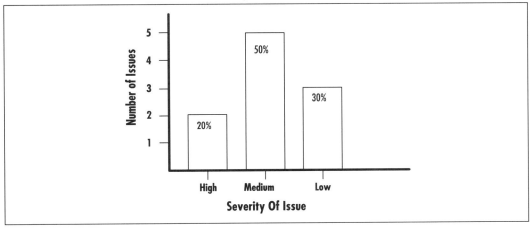

Security Rating

The comparative wireless network security rating shows the difference between the helpdesk departmental wireless network security posture and that of other wireless network deployments. See Chart 2.

Chart 2 Security Rating

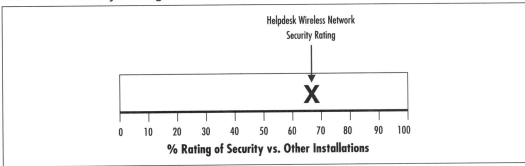

Vulnerability Type Summary

The summary provides a listing of the various issues that were reported. They are distributed across the different test categories. See Chart 3.

Chart 3 Vulnerability Summary

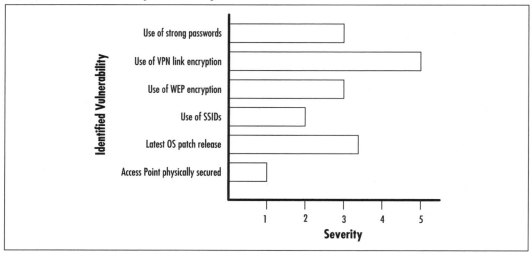

Vulnerability Assessment Details

The vulnerability assessment details provide a listing of all the vulnerabilities identified by the helpdesk wireless network.

High-risk Vulnerabilities

- List of Vulnerabilities
- Details of Vulnerabilities

Medium-risk Vulnerabilities

- List of Vulnerabilities
- Details of Vulnerabilities

Low-risk Vulnerabilities

- List of Vulnerabilities
- Details of Vulnerabilities

Ports and Services

- List of Ports and Services
- Details of Ports and Services

Other Findings

- List of Other Findings
- Details of Other Findings

Appendix A: Risk Definitions

Readers of the audit report should note that risk classifications were arrived at in accordance with the Corporation audit risk classification methodology.

High-risk Vulnerabilities   High-risk vulnerabilities represent risks that can be used to breach the security of systems or to render systems inactive such as Denial of Service attacks.

Medium-risk Vulnerabilities   Medium-risk vulnerabilities represent exposures that can be used to obtain access servers, databases, and other information stores to mount attacks using the combined resources of the compromised systems, or information gathered from these independent sources.

Low-risk Vulnerabilities   Low-risk vulnerabilities are risks that are not problems by themselves. It is possible, however, that while they do not represent significant security risks by themselves, they can be used in conjunction with other vulnerabilities to compromise a system or resource.

Summary

Audits are one of the most effective means of assessing accountability and establishing wireless network operating metrics through the use of performance measurements. This chapter provided you with practical knowledge of audits and how to conduct them within your organization.

Different types of audits can be performed to assess risk, measure a system's operation against expectations, measure a system's policy compliance, and verify change management. They can also be used for assessing damage to physical and logical components along with the overall impact to other related systems' logical and impact damage.

Wireless networks audits are generally performed at system launch, on schedule, during a maintenance window, and during unplanned emergencies.

Wireless network audits are performed in accordance with prespecified and preapproved plans which outline the objective, scope, and sampling size of the audit. This chapter reviewed each of the detailed tasks and procedures to be performed during each phase of the wireless network audit.

Professional organizations, standards bodies, and government agencies provide guidance on auditing standards and information security standards. That guidance can be used throughout all typical wireless network auditing phases, including audit planning, audit information gathering, audit information analysis and report generation, audit report presentation, post-audit review, and next steps.

Wireless audits are not just technology-oriented. There are many ways to obtain auditing information, including technology assessment using wireless network auditing tools, personnel interviews, policy and procedure reviews, and hands-on assessments of the wireless components being audited.

When using auditing tools, care needs to be taken to ensure that the tools are operating as expected and that they have not been tampered or modified in anyway prior to the audit. The audit chain of evidence is critical in establishing wireless network audit recommendations.

There are many ways you can analyze wireless network audit data using matrices and other rating systems. You can also organize the audit data information within the audit report in different ways. Audit reports are structured documents that provide a listing of short-, medium-, and long-term recommendations, within the context of an executive summary, prioritized recommendations, main body, detailed recommendations, final conclusions, appendices, and glossary.

A couple of abridged sample audit reports in this chapter provided you with general guidelines on the content, form, and details found in both executive audit reports and technical audit reports.

Wireless network audits are not one-time events but instead should be performed continuously over the lifetime of a wireless network. This ensures that as the network is stretched and expanded to meet its changing roles, new features and functionalities do not inversely affect the operation or security of the overall wireless network system.

Solutions Fast Track

Designing and Planning a Successful Audit

- ☑ Audits are a means of assessing systems against established standards of operation and industry best practices, and of establishing metrics through performance measurements.

- ☑ Audits are performed to assess risk, to measure system operation against expectations, to measure compliance to policies, to verify change management, and to assess damage.

- ☑ Audits and assessments are part of the lifecycle of systems. They are used to implement policies, as well as promote awareness, which in turn can then be reaudited and assessed, feeding the cycle again.

- ☑ Audits are typically performed at system launch, on schedule, during a maintenance window, and during unplanned emergencies.

Defining Standards

- ☑ Technology standards, which are defined by standards bodies, governments, and professional organizations, generally specify the operations applicable for a given environment, with methodologies that can be used to address specific issues.

- ☑ Some standards are open to interpretation by equipment vendors and implementers, while others provide very thorough definitions of each of the elements used in a system.

- ☑ Very few standards exist that specifically address wireless networks.

☑ Wireless network deployment corporate policies are defined by one or more governing bodies (such as the legal department) within an organization, which establish the benchmark for the implementation and deployment of technologies and services within their environments.

Performing the Audit

☑ Audits are performed in accordance with prespecified and preapproved plans.

☑ The steps involved in performing a wireless audit include audit planning, audit information gathering, audit information analysis and report generation, audit report presentation, post-audit review, and auditing next steps.

☑ There are different types of audits. Both host audits and component audits should be performed every 12 to 24 months, while network audits should be performed every 12 months. Critical system audits, on the other hand, should be performed every 6 months.

☑ Wireless network audits consist of technical and staff interviews, as well as policy and procedure reviews.

☑ Wireless audit interviewing tools include questionnaires, spreadsheets, and matrix tables.

☑ Wireless audit technical auditing tools include wireless scanners, password crackers, and protocol analyzers.

☑ Some of the critical factors in performing the audit include senior management support, determining the focus of the audits, a documented audit process, business unit and technology group involvement, and efficient and secure audit data documentation process.

☑ Wireless network audits are performed by authorized auditing personnel who have an understanding of organization, wireless technology, as well as an understanding of security.

Analyzing Audit Data

☑ The audit data analysis phase involves the review of all captured data from interviews, scans, and system documentation for compliance against accepted standards, policies, procedures, and guidance.

Generating Audit Reports

☑ When generating the wireless network audit report, auditors must ensure that the readers feel confident in the audit findings and that they can substantiate claims and address challenges to audit findings.

☑ Reports consist of several sections including:

- An executive summary which provides a succinct overview of report and key findings.

- A prioritized recommendations listing which provides bullet form descriptions of major recommendations in order of priority and impact.

- A main body which is a thorough account of the wireless network audit details and findings.

- A detailed recommendations section which lists a synopsis of all the findings identified in the main body.

- A final conclusions section that provides a review of the key findings and an overall grade or evaluation of the audited system.

- Appendices which contain the detailed audit data that did not fit within the main body.

- A glossary that lists alphabetized terms used in the audit report.

Frequently Asked Questions

The following Frequently Asked Questions, answered by the authors of this book, are designed to both measure your understanding of the concepts presented in this chapter and to assist you with real-life implementation of these concepts. To have your questions about this chapter answered by the author, browse to **www.syngress.com/solutions** and click on the **"Ask the Author"** form.

Q: I am familiar with a generalized methodology for performing wireless network audits, but are there special requirements which should be considered when assessing cellular-based data networks versus wireless LAN networks, or wireless PAN networks?

A: The basic methodology is similar for all wireless networks. While there are differences which come into play with regards to the radio transmission technologies used for each network, the most critical difference which impacts the wireless audit generally involves the policies and procedures in place to support each of the networks. They can vary vastly based on each targeted use and expected security posture.

Q: When it comes to the writing of wireless network audit reports, do standards or best practices exist regarding the overall look and presentation of the report itself?

A: Several best practice documents exist from ISACA, (ISC)[2], CSI, ISSA, AICPA, IIA, to the U.S. government and others regarding what should be contained within audit reports. Keep in mind that the report should be factual and applicable to your specific environment and audit requirements.

Chapter 9

Case Scenarios

Solutions in this chapter:

- Implementing a Non-secure Wireless Network

- Implementing an Ultra-secure WLAN

- Taking a War Drive

- Scouting your Location

- Developing a Wireless Security Checklist

☑ Summary

☑ Solutions Fast Track

☑ Frequently Asked Questions

Introduction

Building wireless networks, in principle, can be simple, but securing them demands practice. In this chapter, you'll learn how easy it is to install a wireless local area network (WLAN) straight out of the box, and full of security holes. We'll demonstrate how easy it is to take your network for granted whether the fatal flaw is failing to modify factory default settings, or ignoring the risks from untrained users. In the second part of the chapter, you will learn how to take advantage of every technical and administrative security control available to create a wireless LAN for the truly paranoid. You will learn how a war drive is conducted, and what types of equipment you will need. Next, you will step inside an attacker's shoes and see how to exploit weakness in a common wireless network scenario.

> **NOTE**
>
> *War driving* is a new term for wireless LAN discovery, and consists of traveling through a populated area searching for wireless networks. It was derived from an older term, *war dialing*, which meant using a modem to dial a large series of phone numbers in order to look for computer systems. The "war" part of both terms is a reference to the 1983 film *WarGames*.

After seeing the world through the eyes of an attacker, you'll learn the steps necessary to conduct an effective location walk-through, in order to identify the obstacles and hazards you are likely to encounter in a variety of building environments. Whether it is avoiding cordless phones or brick walls, we'll give you suggestions on how to best place your wireless Access Point (AP).

We'll also present a guide for creating a checklist to help you make sure you haven't overlooked any obvious deployment or security issues.

Remember that an unprotected wireless network is an *easy* target. If you have decided to deploy a wireless network, but don't have or don't want to part with the extra time or money to properly secure it, you may wish to reconsider. The alternative will almost surely result in more time and money wasted in rebuilding servers, not to mention costly third-party security audits.

Implementing a Non-secure Wireless Network

It's easy to build an unsecure wireless network. Continuing war driving tests and media reports are showing that in some metropolitan areas fewer than 35 percent of wireless LANs are even using Wired Equivalent Privacy (WEP). We will take you through the basics of installing a typical wireless network that pays little or no attention to security fundamentals. This should serve as an important lesson in how easy it is to get things wrong, or simply neglect the basics of security.

The easiest way to set up a wireless AP is as easy as removing it from its packaging, powering it up, and plugging it in to your local area network. You won't notice many differences; it will act the same way it did through the wire. This is the point at which a user may walk away, pleased with the new connectivity. However, having achieved one goal, connectivity, the network has now been opened up to the public, and anyone walking or driving by can freely peruse the network, as is the case in Figure 9.1.

Figure 9.1 An Out-of-the-box Unsecure Wireless Network

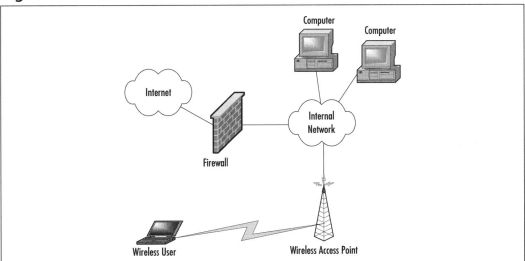

Why is this so? Many wireless APs come from the manufacturer configured with few of the built-in security mechanisms enabled. Having an AP with the default Extended Service Set Identifier (ESSID) and name make it relatively easy for potential attackers to find. The manufacturers are trying to make setup as easy as possible, so most APs also broadcast their availability and allow anyone with

any ESSID to connect. WEP comes disabled by default because the AP administrator must set the passphrase or keys. Security comes at a price; it is much easier
to just plug the AP into an existing connection on the network, without placing
it behind a firewall. From there, little work needs to be done, as the Dynamic
Host Configuration Protocol (DHCP) provides Internet Protocol (IP) addresses
for potential users.

At this point you may be thinking, "I would never do anything like that."
While that may be true, it's not necessarily true of all users on your LAN. Let's
take, for example, the following scenario where two users of a fictional company,
Ecom.com, decide to go wireless.

Having grown weary of always disconnecting their laptop machines from the
network every time they go to and from meetings and offices, they decide to
head to their local computer store and buy a wireless networking kit. With wireless APs now available for less than $200, and cards available for less than $100,
they can alleviate all of their troubles and install the AP for their whole group to
use. However, being somewhat computer knowledgeable, they realize that some
of the default settings need to be changed. They decide to change their ESSID to
something helpful like "Ecom.com webgroup," and change the name of the AP
to "5th Floor 101 First Ave." They, of course, place their AP in their office and,
for convenience purposes, it is installed next to the PC, by the window. They
resolve not to use WEP, because they don't want to help everyone configure their
client software with the passphrase or keys now required. After two hours of
work, including the trip to the shop, their new wireless network is ready for use.
They are happy. But, as the Ecom.com security administrator, should you be?

Definitely not! In fact, you should be very worried about the security of your
network. In the next section, we'll take a look at the mistakes they made, point-
by-point, and give suggestions on how to correct them. We'll also describe, on a
technical level, how to leverage this scenario into a super-secure solution.

Implementing an Ultra-secure Wireless LAN

Based on the variety of security measures and countermeasures we've already discussed in the book, we will now try to incorporate various security measures into
a typical wireless network installation, from investigating the installation site and
choosing vendors, to running monitoring and detection. We'll also look at incor-
porating a secure virtual private network (VPN) with proven security protocols
like IPSec.

We finished the previous section with the brand new wireless network created by the Ecom.com employees—a great example of a completely unsecure configuration. Using this scenario as an example, we'll take you through the following four aspects of securing a wireless network:

- Physical location and access
- AP configuration
- Secure network design
- Security policy

Physical Location and Access

The physical placement of your wireless AP is critical to its security. Two things to consider are its accessibility and its signal range. The AP should be placed in a location where it would be difficult for an attacker to modify or tamper with its settings. Even the most securely configured AP can be compromised if anyone with a USB port on their notebook can change the configuration and WEP keys. That being said, we also want to make sure your AP cannot be reconfigured via its wireless adapter. While certainly being more convenient, this functionality opens the AP up to a much greater risk of tampering. We simply won't consider any AP that has administration of this type for your secure LAN.

The other physical access concern comes with the signal strength. Wireless signals are radio signals, and these can travel through walls and windows and often at a greater distance than advertised by the manufacturer. It is important to survey your site, and place the device in a location where it will be radiating its signal outward to the users. The goal of placement is to locate the AP so the signal strength is high within your environment and weaker by the time it leaves the premises. Design it from the inside out. If the building floor layout is a square, with the users sitting around the edge, the AP should be placed in the middle where it can reach users sitting on all sides. Make sure it is also as far as possible from the windows on the outside, so the signal is considerably weaker before it leaves the building. The Ecom.com employees placed their AP near a window. Not only does that make it more difficult for users on the other side of the building to see their AP, it allows anyone on the freeway or parking lot outside of the Ecom.com office to hop on the network and begin snooping.

Configuring the AP

The next aspect of building your super-secure wireless network concerns the configuration of the AP itself. Each manufacturer's AP has a different configuration interface with different combinations of hardware and software, but the concepts involved are the same. Before plugging the device into the network, it is crucial that the default settings be changed. In your earlier example with Ecom.com, the employees managed to change a few of the default settings on their AP. However, the network remains poorly configured and unsecure.

Let's take a look at some of their configuration mistakes. While they did change the ESSID and AP name, they used bits of information that make it easier for potential attackers to pinpoint their location. Using geographical information for names is basically drawing a roadmap for an attacker to establish the best signal and location to see your AP. Listing the company name in the ESSID also gives an advantage to attackers. Though the "security through obscurity" principle isn't a recommended way to secure a network, giving an attacker more information about you than they need makes their job much easier. Instead, choose names that don't have any relevance to your company or location. Try something innocuous like colors or cartoon characters.

Ideally, however, you should have an AP that doesn't give away its ESSID so an attacker with a discovery tool like NetStumbler won't be able to see your AP. The feature, called "closed network," isn't currently available in many lower cost models.

Another setting that should be enabled is the option to force clients to only connect to the ESSID specified in your configuration. Forcing the use of your specific ESSID is just another step that can be taken to ensure that only authorized users will be accessing your network.

Changing the ESSID and disabling broadcasting are a great start, but there's still quite a bit of work left to shore up your AP. WEP should be enabled in 128-bit mode. It can be argued that WEP is insecure as we've seen in earlier chapters, but it is still an effective part of an overall security plan. With exploit tools like AirSnort, an attacker can break WEP given several hours, though it generally takes longer. Sitting in a parked car on the side of the road is inconspicuous for an hour or so, but rather impractical for longer periods. Thus this time factor acts as a deterrent, encouraging the attacker to look for an easier target.

We'll also make sure that your WEP keys are changed periodically, just in case they have been compromised. This also makes it more difficult for someone who is actively trying to discover them. The method for distributing the new keys to your users will be detailed in your security policy, which we'll discuss later.

Another feature provided by many wireless APs and the networks on which they live is the Dynamic Host Configuration Protocol, a service that is designed to assign IP addresses to new machines on a network. After receiving a broadcast request, the DHCP server assigns an IP address from a prespecified pool of addresses and also configures routing and Domain Name System (DNS) information. From a network management standpoint, DHCP provides an easy method of handing out IP addresses to those who ask. However, from a security standpoint, you have very little control over who is assigned an address. In itself, DHCP isn't necessarily a security risk. However, you're trying to make as much work as possible. Therefore, you should turn it off. Because DHCP provides an IP address and routing information, attackers would immediately be participating on your LAN segment. By requiring individual IP configuration of client cards, you can force an attacker to have to snoop out the info, costing him time, and giving you a longer opportunity to track him down. Individually assigning IP addresses also makes it much easier for you to track malicious activity because the assigned IP addresses will be tied to specific users.

Taking this one step further, some APs and routers allow filtering based on the network card's Media Access Control (MAC) address. This means that only cards with a specified list of MAC addresses are allowed to function on the wireless LAN. MAC address spoofing is possible, and under Linux it is also possible to set your own MAC address. However, this requires a more sophisticated attacker. So using a product that supports MAC filtering makes accessing and compromising the network that much more difficult.

Bear in mind though, securing the settings on the AP and enabling WEP aren't enough. As stated earlier, a determined attacker with enough time will be able to find your network and crack the WEP keys, which is why you'll need to take some additional measures in securing your wireless network, which we'll discuss next.

Designing Securely

It's not just the wireless network you should secure. Your entire company network is placed at risk when wireless APs are enabled on the LAN. An unprotected wireless AP on your network is like an unlocked door with a neon sign beckoning people to enter. You therefore need to place the APs at a location on the network where you can mitigate as much of the risk as possible. On the unsecure network set up by the Ecom.com employees, the AP was placed directly on the company network. This was certainly the quickest and cheapest way to get connected, but it leaves the network exposed to anyone with a $100 wireless card. A wireless network AP should be thought of as an untrusted device, and be placed on the network accordingly. For your super-secure wireless implementation, the AP will be placed in its own untrusted segment, which will be separated from the rest of your network by a firewall with a very strict rule set. So your clients will be connecting into an isolated network of their own, providing protection for your internal network because now an attacker won't have access to any company data even if they manage to find your network and crack the WEP.

You have now reached the crucial point of actually getting the real users to your company's internal network. Connectivity to the internal network will be provided using a virtual private network. This gives you two advantages. First, all your users will be authenticated. Since this is a super-secure scenario, we'll be using a two-factor identification system. You will ask the users for a password, and then for a number provided by a token. An example of this system is RSA's SecurID. Once properly authenticated, the users will become part of the company LAN. The second advantage provided by a VPN is confidentiality. Most commercial VPN systems today use IPSec, with strong encryption systems. This will help you make up for the weaknesses in WEP and protect data from snooping eyes.

There are many different ways to design a VPN server implementation. We're going to take a look at two of those ways, one using a single firewall, and one using a more secure dual firewall setup. Either of these would have dramatically helped the bad security situation generated when the Ecom.com users created their network.

The single firewall scenario shown in Figure 9.2 has the internal network separated from the internet by a single firewall. Internet accessible resources such as Web or mail servers will sit on the internal company network, as will the VPN server. Generally, this isn't the most secure approach to take because it means any compromise of a server will result in a compromise of the internal network. Nonetheless, such scenarios are common, and may make sense in certain instances. To construct your VPN setup, you'll need to install another network interface on your firewall. The new interface will be connected to only your wireless AP. You will write a single firewall rule to allow traffic from the wireless network to your VPN server. Nothing else will be needed or allowed.

Figure 9.2 A Single Firewall Solution

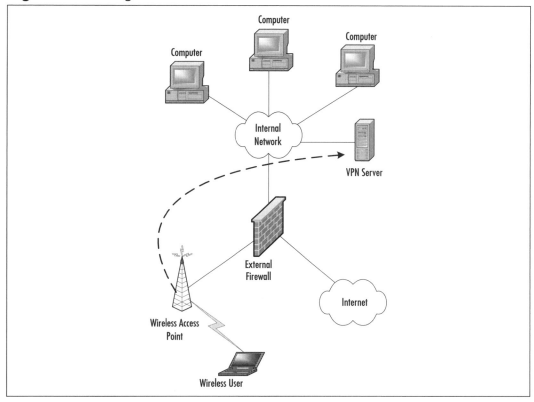

The single firewall solution does meet your authentication and encryption needs, but it's still not ideal because the security of your internal network relies heavily on the security of the VPN server. If there was a flaw in the software that allowed an attacker to compromise the machine, they would have direct access to any machine on the internal network. For your super-secure wireless network, you're going to put your VPN server in a *Demilitarized Zone* (DMZ) network. A DMZ is a network added between a protected network and an external one in order to provide an additional layer of security. In Figure 9.3 you can see that your network now has two firewalls, one protecting the internal network, and one facing the Internet. Between the two is the your DMZ, where your VPN server will live. The addition of the wireless network will be handled exactly as it was in the single firewall case. A new network interface will be added to the external Internet-facing firewall. A new network will be created to host the wireless AP and clients, and traffic will only be allowed to the VPN server in the

DMZ. In this instance, a compromise of your VPN server doesn't give the attacker the advantage of having compromised an internal machine, just an empty DMZ. You never want to let external connections have direct connectivity to your internal machines. On the other hand, it's also a good idea to proxy all outbound connections as well. This just makes it more difficult for an attacker, once in, to get back out again.

Figure 9.3 A More Secure, Dual-firewall Solution

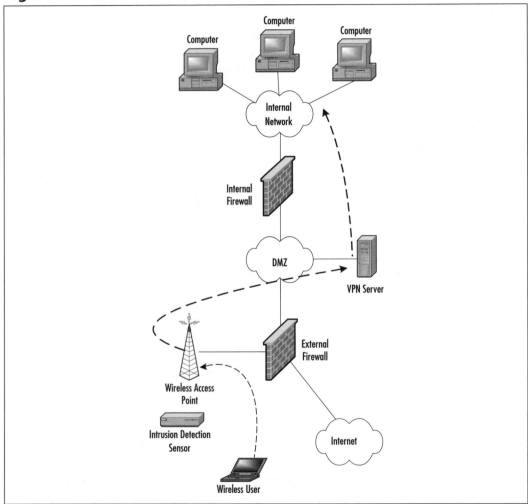

Before throwing the switch on your newly designed secure network, you should consider adding some type of intrusion detection system (IDS). After all, it is important for you to know what's going on in your new wireless network. You should place a sensor for your corporate-wide intrusion detection system on the same segment where the wireless AP lives. This will help to alert you to any potential threats that may occur. Should an attacker gain access, and attempt to scan other users, you will be given adequate warning of the abuse. You'll also know if the attacker is scanning your firewalls. This kind of activity would mean that your WEP keys have been compromised, so you'll know immediately to change them. Proper maintenance of your IDS calls for your alert logs to be read frequently. Often times IDS are ignored after deployment, completely removing any effectiveness they bring. An unread alert and activity log is the same as not having a sensor at all. This is a practice that should also extend to your firewall logs. You'll want to make sure you keep a critical eye on the firewall logs related to your new wireless bubble. One final thing to consider when configuring your secure network is your client machines. In this scenario, your security is only as good as your users. While connected to the wireless network, the users machines are vulnerable to any other machines on that network. As you've seen earlier, you can never be certain who may show up on the network, so a potential attacker could compromise a client machine, install snooping software, and still gain access to the internal network. For your super-secure wireless LAN, we'll show you how to make sure all your client PCs have installed some kind of personal firewall software, such as Zone Labs' ZoneAlarm Pro or Tiny's Personal Firewall.

Securing by Policy

With your secure network in place, you're almost ready to flip the switch and open it up for the users. You just need to update the company's security. The security policy should be considered a living document in every organization and should be easily adaptable and continually updated. You need to include provisions banning the placement of wireless APs on the internal company network. This type of offense should be classified as one of the most serious violations, because it is one of the most difficult to prevent and is potentially very damaging. As the popularity of wireless networking increases, it is important that security considerations are taken into account throughout the company, particularly given the fact that they are not usually included in the manufacturer's marketing. You also need to explain to the users why this is such a risk. A strong security policy, and good user education could have saved Ecom.com from the disaster that may come from their users' unsafe AP deployment.

In the case study, you make a point of educating all users about how placing the AP on the company network compromises security/integrity. Utilizing real-world comparisons, you can illustrate this with wireless setups, where your network is now being broadcast like a radio station, to which anyone can tune in. If necessary, you can also use the exploit tools mentioned earlier to perform a demonstration of this.

Another process that should be detailed in your security policy is the method of updating WEP keys on user workstations. There are many ways to do this. Whether by manually updating each workstation, sending keys via encrypted e-mail, or via regular mail, a process should be selected and documented.

With your AP secured, firewalls in place, and your security policy updated, you're on the way to having a secure wireless network installation. This does not mean the network is inviolable, but it does mean you've identified and attempted to minimize as many of the risks as possible. However, the measures discussed so far all work together, and also need to be constantly updated. Neglecting one aspect of security provides chinks in the amour that a determined attacker can exploit to gain a foothold into your network, so it's critical you be vigilant in maintaining your new network. Some attackers can be very determined, and as you'll see in the next section, they're always looking for new targets. Don't let it be your network!

Taking a War Drive

This section will take you through the eye-opening process of conducting a real war drive, including choosing your equipment, war driving your target locations, remaining inconspicuous, interpreting the results, and identifying obvious weaknesses.

Most media depictions of "war driving" are written from a white hat perspective, meaning that most articles and information simply depict the informing of an unsuspecting public of the potential dangers of wireless networking. Many of these reports only give a general indication of the risks involved. They fail to mention the specific risks concerned with open APs. We're going to take a different approach and follow through the dangers to explore what a malicious attacker can do to your network once they have found your AP. In this section, we are therefore going to conduct a war drive from the perspective of a black hat.

You'll start by gearing up for a war drive through San Francisco, and then, using the data you find, you'll choose a target, search for vulnerabilities in what you are able to access, and take a look at some possible uses an intruder might have for your network. In this scenario, you should hopefully see just how easy it is for a malicious party to take full advantage of an improperly secured LAN.

Since you'll be mobile, the size, weight and amount of your equipment are important. To start with, you'll use a sub-notebook computer, such as the Sony PictureBook or the Fujitsu LifeBook P series. These machines are small, light, and have good battery life. In a pinch, they can be quickly stashed in a backpack or under a car seat—something important for your black hat to remain inconspicuous. Technically, however, any notebook computer capable of supporting a wireless LAN card can be used.

You'll also need a wireless PCMCIA card. Choosing the right one for your needs can be a bit tricky, as manufacturers don't tend to include in their documentation "Great for 802.11b hacking" labeling on the packages. Of the two chipsets you should consider, Hermes and PRISM2, each offers different advantages. You'll first need a card with a hermes-compatible chipset in order to find the APs and detect whether or not they're using WEP. The most common card for this purpose is the ORiNOCO Gold card, which also supports the use of external antennas, important for your AP discovery. However, it doesn't support promiscuous mode, which means you can't use it to sniff packets. For that functionality, you'll need a card with a PRISM2 chipset. As of this writing, the following cards have PRISM2 chipsets, and will work with the available tools:

- Addtron AWP-100
- Bromax Freeport
- Compaq WL100
- D-Link DWL-650
- Linksys WPC11
- Samsung SWL2000-N
- SMC 2632W
- Z-Com XI300
- Zoom Telephonics ZoomAir 4100

This list is by no means comprehensive, so for cards not listed, be sure to check with manufacturers to determine the chipset.

Using Hermes versus PRISM2

There are several types of wireless network card chipsets, but the two chosen for your war-driving project are the hermes and PRISM2. From the end user perspective, the cards are almost identical. They have similar feature sets, the same levels of WEP, and support connection speeds of up to 11 megabits. The differences really only become apparent when using tools like NetStumbler or AirSnort. The hermes chipset supports the features in NetStumbler that allow multiple APs within range to be seen. It will also provide detailed information about each AP, including whether or not WEP is enabled. The PRISM2 chipset will also provide information about nearby APs, but, so far, has not been able to detect WEP, though one new tool claims to have that functionality. One advantage of the prism2 chipset is the promiscuous mode support, meaning that it can be used to view other packets on the wireless network. This is crucial for AirSnort because it needs to capture packets in order to break the WEP keys. Of course, if the traffic on your wireless LAN is unencrypted, an attacker can use tools like prism2dump to view the cleartext traffic. All the more reason to make sure WEP is enabled!

Once you have the cards, you'll need some software. For the ease of use, NetStumbler for Windows (www.netstumbler.com) is difficult to beat. It supports the use of the Global Positioning System (GPS) and can save settings and findings easily. It's also really easy to grab a quick screen shot for later use. dstumbler for BSD operating systems is a close second. An additional feature of dstumbler is that it will also support AP discovery using the PRISM2 chipset. You'll still need an Orinoco card in order to find WEP, however. If you're in the situation of only being able to have one card, the PRISM2 cards with dstumbler will work pretty well.

For packet sniffing, you'll need a Unix-based operating system like Linux or BSD. A number of toolkits exist under both platforms that perform a wide range of functions. One of the most comprehensive toolkits is the bsd–airtools package from Dachb0den Labs, available at www.dachb0den.com/projects/bsd–airtools.html. It requires a current BSD OS like OpenBSD, FreeBSD, or NetBSD. This toolkit contains the AirSnort package, used for cracking WEP, dstumbler, and the prism2dump wireless packet sniffer.

With these tools at your disposal, and your Windows/FreeBSD dual boot laptop, you're almost ready to go. The antenna is the last part you need to think about. Since you're trying to remain fairly inconspicuous, smaller is better. In some cities, you can find plenty without any type of external antenna. For your sample outing, the Lucent external antenna will be perfect. There are also quite a few sites on the Web that have "do-it-yourself" antenna kits, one even made with a Pringles can. These homemade antenna tend to be on the large side, however, and maneuvering around town with a laptop and a large Yagi antenna can be alarming to bystanders, and is likely to attract quite a bit of attention.

It's now time to hit the open road in search of the prime target. For your war drive in black hat mode, you will be casing the financial district of San Francisco. Like any good black hat you've done your homework and know there are many businesses that are likely to have APs in this area. Enlisting the help of a friend to drive the car, you set out on your war drive. You've mapped out an area where you're hoping to collect some APs. Heading down one of the major streets, the APs are already starting to appear on your NetStumbler screen. Making another turn onto another major street, you see even more points appear. As you sit in traffic, you're able to see which points are currently active.

According to what you see in Figure 9.4, there are four APs that are currently active, but only one showing a strong signal. Drive one more block and see what you find—take a look at Figure 9.5.

Figure 9.4 Four Visible APs from Your War Drive

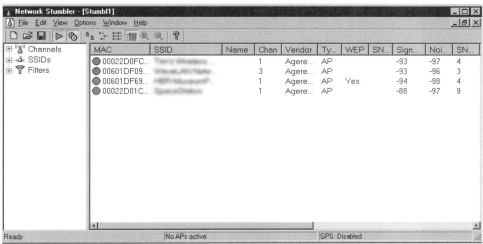

Figure 9.5 Doubling the Number of APs Seen within Moments

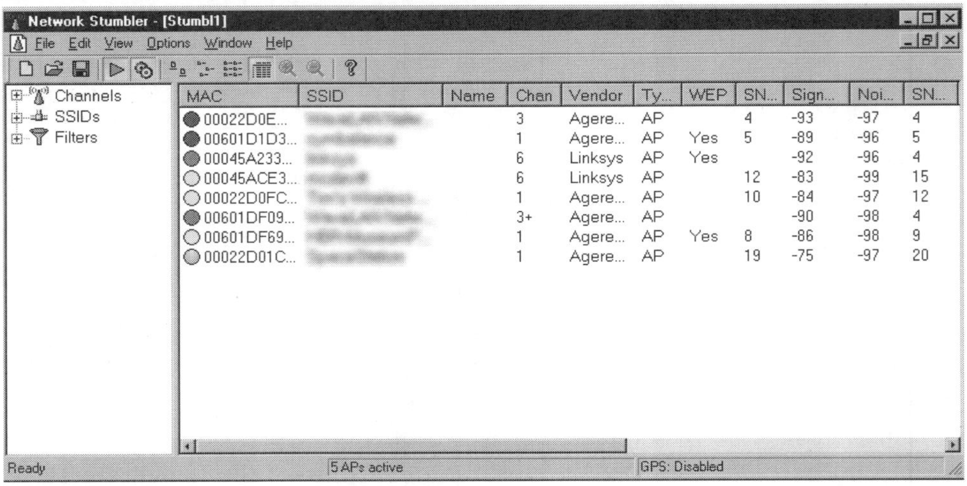

Aha! In Figure 9.5, you'll notice there are a few more APs, including one without WEP enabled, and using "linksys" as its ESSID. You'll make note of this one, and return later. One final thing to remember as a true black hat is that you're looking for a big target. Since you've driven by a well-known brokerage firm, and several APs have appeared, consider that your prime target. But first, you might as well go after some of the "low hanging fruit," meaning APs with strong signals and no WEP enabled. The "linksys" AP happens to be near a sandwich shop, which is where you should set up your surveillance operations. Using Windows, you can quickly pull up a DHCP address from the "linksys" network, and within minutes you're able to surf the Web. This network has no outbound proxies or restrictions for its users. Now, being that you've assumed the role of a black hat, let's see what can be done with your newly found connectivity. The first step is to get to know the machines and the network around you. Using the IP and routing information provided by the DHCP server, you can take a look around the network to find other active hosts with a tool called Nmap.

```
C:\WINNT\NMAP-NT> nmap-nt.exe -sP -v 10.10.0.1-15

Starting nmap V. 2.53 SP1 by ryan@eeye.com
based on nmap by fyodor@insecure.org  ( www.insecure.org /nmap/ )
Host  (10.10.0.1) appears to be up.
Host  (10.10.0.2) appears to be up.
```

```
Host  (10.10.0.3) appears to be up.
Host  (10.10.0.4) appears to be down.
Host  (10.10.0.5) appears to be up.
Host  (10.10.0.6) appears to be up.
Host  (10.10.0.7) appears to be up.
Host  (10.10.0.8) appears to be down.
Host  (10.10.0.9) appears to be up.
Host  (10.10.0.10) appears to be up.
Host  (10.10.0.11) appears to be up.
Host  (10.10.0.12) appears to be up.
Host  (10.10.0.13) appears to be up.
```

Judging from the output, there are ten other hosts on this network responding to your ping scan. You now have a list of machines that are alive. Check and see what services are running on these machines, and find out which operating system they're using. Choose one at random, say, 10.10.0.11. Using Nmap, run a SYN scan against the host. A SYN scan sends only TCP packets with the SYN flag set. In the past, this was a good way to fool IDS systems. Today, most IDS systems can easily identify syn, ack, fin, and other types of scans. Some will even label an attack as an *nmap scan*. There are always ways to get around being detected by an IDS, but most will require more time than you, as a war driver, are willing to spend.

```
C:\WINNT\NMAP-NT> nmap-nt.exe -sS -O 10.10.0.11

Interesting ports on (10.10.0.11):

(The 1492 ports scanned but not shown below are in state:
    closed)
Port        State       Service
7/tcp       open        echo
9/tcp       open        discard
13/tcp      open        daytime
19/tcp      open        chargen
21/tcp      open        ftp
23/tcp      open        telnet
25/tcp      open        smtp
37/tcp      open        time
79/tcp      open        finger
111/tcp     open        sunrpc
```

```
512/tcp      open        exec

513/tcp      open        login

514/tcp      open        shell

515/tcp      open        printer

540/tcp      open        uucp

587/tcp      open        submission

665/tcp      open        unknown

898/tcp      open        unknown

4045/tcp     open        lockd

6112/tcp     open        dtspc

7100/tcp     open        font-service

32771/tcp    open        sometimes-rpc5

32772/tcp    open        sometimes-rpc7

32773/tcp    open        sometimes-rpc9

32774/tcp    open        sometimes-rpc11

32775/tcp    open        sometimes-rpc13

32776/tcp    open        sometimes-rpc15

32777/tcp    open        sometimes-rpc17

32778/tcp    open        sometimes-rpc19

32779/tcp    open        sometimes-rpc21

32780/tcp    open        sometimes-rpc23


TCP Sequence Prediction: Class=random positive increments

                        Difficulty=37949 (Worthy

                              challenge)


Remote operating system guess: Sun Solaris 2.6


Nmap run completed — 1 IP address (1 host up) scanned in 7

    seconds
```

The output of the scan against this machine is good news for a black hat. According to the OS guess, this machine is running Solaris 2.6, and judging by the number of services running, it is a default installation. Black hats know that there are many exploits against services running on unpatched Solaris servers, and so it is very easy to compile and run one of these to have administrative access on this machine. After running another Nmap scan on a Windows host, you've managed to locate a machine that happens to be sharing its "C" drive. A quick search for ⋆.pst, finds that the user is sharing their archive.pst file, one of the best sources for digging up passwords and other information about the network. Within an hour, there's a very good chance that a black hat would be able to have control of most of this network. You could also install some sniffing toolkits, like dnsiff, to start pulling passwords, e-mail, files, and URLs from this network. Let this serve as a lesson on how important it is to keep servers updated and patched, and not to put 802.11b wireless APs on an internal network! Simple intrusions of this kind, though, can be thwarted, most of the time, by simply making sure that 128-bit WEP is installed. Think of it as if you're simply locking your doors. Your house may not be burglar-proof, but it is much more difficult to rob with the doors bolted.

Now that you've managed to find and theoretically compromise one network, you're ready for a bigger challenge. Looking back at your NetStumbler output, it looks like you may have found an AP in the area around the brokerage firm that you passed and noted earlier. There are a number of active points at this location, all with WEP. We'll select the one called "financial-5," since the others have names like "atoz," "strider," and "gandalf." The name "financial-5" sounds like something that might be worth your while, so it's time to boot into BSD and start cracking. Finding a spot at a café, get started with the program AirSnort, a tool based on the theoretical Fluhrer, Mantin, and Shamir attack. In order to actually break the 128-bit WEP running on this AP, you'll need to collect quite a bit of data, usually between 100MB and 1GB—or about 1500 "interesting" packets. This AP seems to be really active, being that you've already logged 19 interesting packets since starting the tool. Nevertheless, it's going to take a while to capture 1500 packets, even though this appears to be a fairly busy network. Sitting at a café for hours on end isn't terribly practical, but if an attacker were really determined to crack this network, a great vantage point for overnight and multiple-day surveillance can be had at the hotel across the street for $175 per night. If you were to proceed with this exercise, you'd check into the hotel and wait to crack the WEP keys, which could take most of the night or longer, depending on traffic slowdowns. The point is, however, that it *can* be done, and as in the previous example, the intruder would once again have a foothold into your network. The point at which the WEP keys are cracked is the point at which your network can no longer be trusted. A sophisticated attacker (and many script-kiddies) will immediately, upon compromise of a machine, make themselves another entry point into that machine. Tools like Back Orifice 2000 for Windows or any number of remote access programs under Unix will let an attacker control a machine from any location—wireless cards no longer needed!

Hopefully, by now, you're starting to see that taking the security of your wireless APs seriously is critical. Even the slightest lapse in control can lead to a tremendous compromise of your network, costing considerable money and man-hours. Being vigilant in maintaining the strictest security regarding APs, and, as we'll discuss in the next section, doing periodical audits will help save headaches in the end.

Scouting Your Location

Scouting out the location can be a fun but challenging part of building a wireless network. There are many factors that need to be addressed, such as the building design, its layout, construction materials, location, and so on. In this section, we will look at some common design factors, and then do a sample installation in a location that is, mildly put, difficult for wireless networks.

Building the perfect wireless setup for each environment is likely to be a trial and error situation. Every situation will be different. Many modern buildings are constructed from concrete or steel, neither of which is ideal for passing 802.11 signals. However, as we saw in earlier sections, this can work in your favor because it will help contain your signal. When looking at your building, here is a list of potential obstacles that should be avoided.

- Solid concrete walls, or reinforced walls

- Steel beams, girders, or other steel framework

- Water features like fountains or waterfalls

- Elevator shafts or stairwells

- Interference from kitchen microwave ovens or cordless phones

- Signals from other wireless networks, possibly from neighboring buildings

In deciding where to place APs, it is important to take a look at the entire floor plan of your office space. The general principle is to design from the inside out. Place the APs at the center of your user-base and the signal will broadcast outward. Remember to keep the APs away from windows. After all, you don't want to serve people in your parking lot!

After placing APs, it will be necessary to see exactly where the signal is traveling and to monitor its strength. Many wireless card makers provide signal strength monitors with their driver software. If not, NetStumbler, which you used in the previous section, can be used for this purpose. Travel all around your location, taking note of how strong or weak the signal is in certain areas, then do the same from the street or parking lot. One factor that is often forgotten is the multidirectional nature of 802.11 signals—it is possible that floors above and below yours will be able to see your signal. If a competitor's office space is near yours, you should seriously consider implementing the ultra-secure 802.11 signal mentioned earlier. In this case, you ensure that even if someone were to crack your WEP, they would just be decrypting IPSec encrypted packets. Also, take note of nearby hotels or coffee shops for this same reason.

Installing in Difficult Situations

Not every installation is going to be as simple as a simple rectangular floor plan with an obvious place to put an AP. Building architects and engineers rarely, if ever, consider 802.11 usage and security when designing! One such difficult building, which we'll use as an example of a nightmare wireless installation, can be seen in Figure 9.6.

Figure 9.6 The Nightmare Wireless Installation

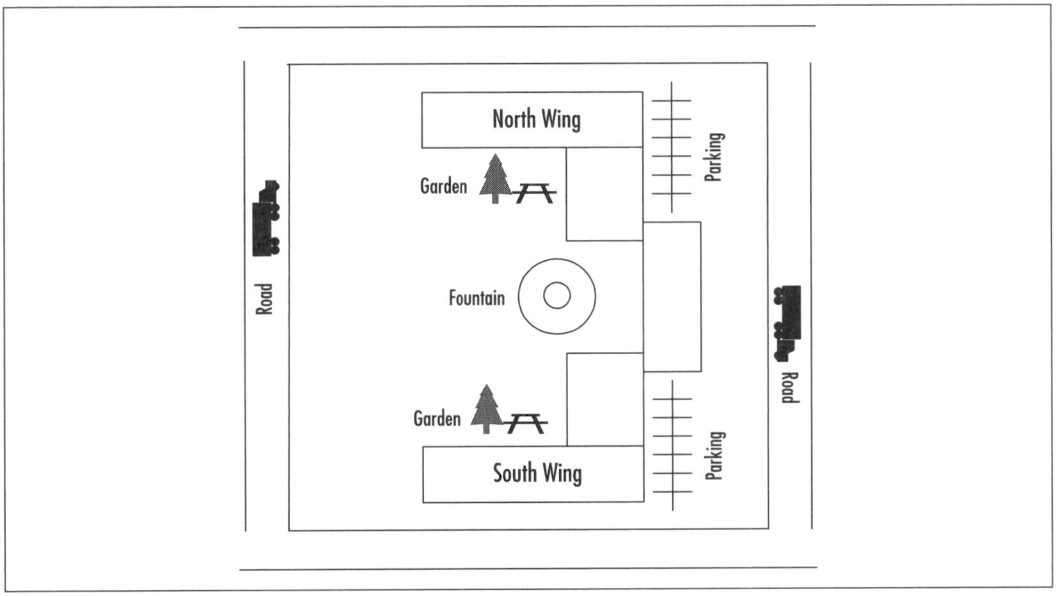

In this example, the building has been constructed in a snake-shaped layout, with roads and parking lots on all sides. The exterior of the building is all glass, and between the north and south wings is a park with a large water fountain. To make things more difficult, the wireless intercom system may be using the 2.4GHz spectrum, the same as 802.11b. The walls between offices are made of dense textured concrete, over a steel frame. Given this scenario, you certainly have your work cut out for you.

The first step in planning the wireless setup in this example is to consider where wireless connectivity is needed. The owners would like to be able to roam with their wireless devices. As the walls are made of thick concrete and steel, you'll need multiple APs, because the signal won't be able to travel through the walls, as it normally might. The only saving grace with this particular building is that instead of the users all having separate offices, there are office regions, with open floor plans. You should make use of this by placing APs in the center of each of these rooms. This adds considerably to the expense of the project.

You would normally be able to pass the signal from the north wing to the south wing, through the park. However, since the 802.11 signal can be disturbed by the fountain, you'll have to go around by snaking a wireless LAN through the hallways.

The wireless intercom in the building will also require your attention. Any wireless product is a potential problem, as many of them share 802.11b's 2.4GHz frequency. If this building were using a 2.4GHz system, you would need to test your wireless AP in a number of different configurations on different channels. While it is possible for devices using the same frequency range as 802.11b to cause problems, they are generally low bandwidth enough to be able to be designed around. Devices such as cordless phones and voice-only intercom systems may not interfere with the wireless LAN. However, the onsite day care center's video baby monitors, which consume quite a bit of bandwidth, are more likely to cause disturbances. You will need to run tests to see if there is any interference.

Finally, you need to make sure you're operating this wireless solution as securely as possible. You already know that the signal will escape the building since its exterior is entirely glass. This could be a problem for you because there are busy roads on all sides of the office complex. You must therefore insist that this particular wireless LAN be built using the strictest security specifications, like those mentioned in the ultra-secure model in a previous section of this chapter. With these measures in place, even if you have people making attempts at your network, you can feel reasonably secure.

This scenario detailed a setup that was quite difficult to secure. The architecture required the use of more hardware, thus adding to the expense. You also had to take into consideration the fact that the signal was visible from outside the building, and you therefore needed a more detailed security design. The best way to figure out the proper solution for your environment is to experiment with different placements of APs. Build a suitable security solution based on the signal strength, the classification of the data, and the general paranoia of your company. In the end, it is important to realize that this is a wireless solution, and by definition, your network is now accessible from outside of your premises. It is critical to realize that more than good placement and planning will be necessary to keep your network secure.

Developing a Wireless Security Checklist

If you feel like you're ready to start building your new wireless network, this section will help prepare you. Presented as three scenarios of varying security levels, read over each and choose the level you feel is appropriate for your installation. Following the steps listed with each security level will help give you an idea of the type of equipment and planning that will be necessary.

Minimum Security

Objective: The objective of a minimum security wireless access installation is to provide a minimal level of security for a home office or small company. Since a fairly determined attacker with plenty of time can compromise this type of system, it is not recommended for sensitive or confidential data.

1. Determine your requirements. Get an idea of the number of users, the type of environment you are working in, the amount of bandwidth you expect to consume, and define what you classify as your minimum security standards.

2. Scout your locations. Knowledge of your building layout and the location of your user base should assist you in finding suitable AP placements.

3. Decide which AP to get. Make certain it supports 128-bit encryption. If you have some additional money to spend, find one that also supports the closed network functionality.

4. Enable WEP, change your SSID, and alter the configuration of the AP, based on the suggestions provided in the earlier sections.

5. Install WEP keys on the client workstations, and update your security policy to determine proper key distribution methods.

6. Test your system for vulnerabilities before going live. As described in the previous sections, war drive your location and try to see it as an attacker would.

7. Enjoy minimally secured wireless access, but realize that an attacker, given the motivation and enough time, can break this network with commonly available tools.

Moderate Security

A moderate security solution is a good choice for a larger company who wishes to have a wireless LAN with tighter access controls. It also assumes that the 128-bit encryption found in WEP will be sufficient to protect company data. This means that an attacker may still be able to view data on the wireless network. This solution is not recommended if it is crucial that a third party never intercept data.

1. Determine your requirements. Get an idea of the number of users, the type of environment you are working in, the amount of bandwidth you expect to consume, and define what you classify as your minimum security standards.

2. Scout out your location. Through trial and error, and using the preceding text as a guide, determine the best placement of your AP. Avoid windows and doorways.

3. Shop around for an AP. For moderate security, find one that supports MAC address filtering. This means that only predetermined MAC addresses will be able to participate on the network. This tightens the access controls down to a specific set of cards and also provides better logging capabilities, now that cards can be traced to specific users. If it's not possible to find one that supports MAC filtering, configure your DHCP server to only assign IPs based on the MAC address. Additionally it is important to make sure the AP has 128-bit WEP and supports the closed network functionality.

4. Enable WEP, change your SSID, and alter the configuration of the AP, based on the suggestions provided in the earlier sections.

5. Install client WEP keys, and update the security policy to provide for a secure method of key distribution.

6. Test your system for vulnerabilities before going live. As described in the previous sections, war drive your location and try to see it as an attacker would.

7. You're ready to go. Realize that this solution requires considerable determination for an attacker to breach since the AP isn't advertising itself, it supports MAC filtering, and it's using WEP. It's not unbreakable, but it certainly isn't an easy target.

Optimal Security

The objective behind optimal security is to provide the best possible protection for your wireless LAN. This type of scenario would be useful for larger companies, financial institutions, or any company that must guarantee with all possible certainty that the data is not compromised.

1. Determine your requirements. Get an idea of the number of users, the type of environment you are working in, the amount of bandwidth you expect to consume, and define what you classify as your minimum security standards.

2. Scout out your location. Through trial and error, and using the previous text as a guide, decide the best placement of your AP. Placement is critical in the optimal security model. Make certain that the AP is placed in a tamper proof location, and make certain to avoid windows. Do your homework, and scout the location to know the distances your signal travels.

3. Find the best wireless AP. It's critical that 128-bit WEP and closed network functionality are supported. It's also a generally good idea that it support MAC filtering, though in particularly large installations this can be a real headache, due to the size of the user base.

4. Rewrite all of the default settings. Using the tips provided in the earlier section, make sure you are using a new SSID, password, have disabled the SSID broadcasting, and that WEP is enabled. This is also a good time to enable MAC address filtering and protocol filtering.

5. Build your network. For this installation you'll need to place your AP behind its own firewall. This is also the time to begin investigating intrusion detection packages, if you haven't already standardized on one.

6. Install and configure your VPN server. Decide exactly where on your network this will live. Ideally, it should be placed in the DMZ network.

7. Install client WEP keys, and update the security policy to provide for a secure method of key distribution.

8. Test your system for vulnerabilities before going live. As described in the previous sections, war drive your location and try to see it as an attacker would.

9. Consider hiring an outside security group to perform vulnerability testing against your network. Even if you think you've done it all correctly, it's always a good idea to have independent verification.

10. Enjoy your wireless network, knowing that you've done many things to make it difficult to compromise. This is not to say that it is impossible to breach, but that it would be very difficult using known attack methodology. The work isn't completely over at this stage however, monitoring of the firewall and intrusion detection are a must!

Summary

This chapter examined an unsecured wireless network built by frustrated users as a starting point to discuss how to fix many of the mistakes commonly made in such an undertaking. Changing the passwords, ESSID and enabling some of the built-in security mechanisms such as 128-bit WEP start you down the path towards a better wireless network. The addition of a VPN server is used to provide a better form of encryption, making up for the weaknesses of WEP. Intrusion detection provides a set of watchful eyes to help you know if someone is trying to take advantage of your network. We also discussed the importance of proper placement of the wireless AP, and described several situations on proper and improper placement. The key concepts of placement are to design from the inside out, meaning place the AP at the center of your user base, while also trying to avoid broadcasting your signal out of your windows.

Having gone on a sample war drive from the standpoint of an attacker, you saw how easily a poorly guarded wireless network can be exploited. Using tools like NetStumbler or dstumbler you were able to find quite a few APs in a big city. From there, a black hat could choose the ones not using WEP, and start exploring them. As for the ones that were using WEP, it was discussed that with time and motivation, you could decrypt the packets and start watching the data.

Next, you built a wireless network in a very challenging location. The design of the building was perhaps one of the least conducive for wireless networking. The thick concrete walls made it difficult to pass the signal from the inside out, and the glass siding offered us no barrier to shield the signal from the outside. By using a combination of proper AP placement and leveraging, the super-secure VPN setup discussed earlier, a solution was decided on that not only worked well, but was generally secure.

For optimal security, one might follow these steps: determine your requirements, classifying your minimum security standards; scout your locations; find the best wireless AP (it is critical that 128-bit WEP and closed network functionality are supported—it is also a generally good idea that it support MAC filtering); scout out your location to decide the best placement of your AP; rewrite all of the default settings (make sure you are using a new SSID and password, have disabled the SSID broadcasting and that WEP is enabled); build your network, placing your AP behind its own firewall and investigating intrusion detection packages; install and configure your VPN server, ideally in the DMZ network; install client WEP keys; and finally, test your system for vulnerabilities before going live. With these tips, and trying different combinations of solutions, the most ideal, secure wireless network is within reach.

Solutions Fast Track

Implementing a Non-secure Wireless Network

☑ Continuing war driving tests and media reports show that in some metropolitan areas fewer than 35 percent of wireless local area networks (WLANs) are even using Wired Equivalent Privacy (WEP).

☑ Setting up a wireless Access Point (AP) is as easy as removing it from its packaging, powering it up, and plugging it in to your local area network. The network has now been opened up to the public, and anyone walking or driving by can freely peruse the network.

☑ The manufacturers try to make setup as easy as possible, so most APs broadcast their availability and allow anyone with any Extended Service Set Identifier (ESSID) to connect. WEP comes disabled by default because the AP administrator must set the passphrase or keys.

Implementing an Ultra-secure WLAN

☑ Make sure that your AP allows you to change ESSID, passwords, and supports 128-bit WEP.

☑ If possible, find an AP that supports the "closed network" functionality, meaning that it doesn't broadcast your ESSID.

☑ Be certain that the AP you buy supports flash upgrades. This will be useful for the manufacturer when it comes time to add new functionality and fix problems with the firmware.

☑ Isolate the AP and regulate access from its network into your internal network.

☑ Conduct audits of your network using NetStumbler or other wireless scanning tools to make sure others aren't enabling unauthorized APs.

☑ Update security policy to reflect the dangers of an unsecured wireless network.

Taking a War Drive

☑ Get to know the tools of the trade. Learn how to use NetStumbler, dstumble, AirSnort, and other tools.

☑ Use other open networks as leverage to convince others of the dangers of an open wireless network.

☑ Be certain you don't exploit or use networks that you find with NetStumbler. Seeing the networks is one thing, but joining and using network resources is another.

Scouting Your Location

☑ Know your environment. Research the construction of your building and design appropriately.

☑ Make a list of potentially problematic structures or sources of interference and try to work around them.

☑ Test, test, test. In order to build the perfect installation, lots of testing will be necessary.

Developing a Wireless Security Checklist

☑ Patch machines on your internal network. Vendors generally have updates posted on their Web sites. If a server hasn't been patched in the past six months, there's a very good chance it's vulnerable.

☑ Even if you have no plans to implement a wireless solution, you never know when a wireless AP may be added to your network. Taking a proactive approach to security machines can save time and money in the long run.

☑ Consider an intrusion detection system (IDS) on your internal network to clue you in to scanning. Being scanned on your internal network should set off some really loud alarms.

Frequently Asked Questions

The following Frequently Asked Questions, answered by the authors of this book, are designed to both measure your understanding of the concepts presented in this chapter and to assist you with real-life implementation of these concepts. To have your questions about this chapter answered by the author, browse to **www.syngress.com/solutions** and click on the **"Ask the Author"** form.

Q: Do I really need to install a VPN just to use a wireless network?

A: For home use? Probably not. For company use? The answer to that is based around the industry you work in, and the sensitivity of the data you're trying to secure. If your company is just using the company network to look at Internet sites, probably not. However, if you're involved in banking or health care, your clients' personal data will need to be protected, as required by local and federal laws. Consult a lawyer for clarification on the requirements for data security in your specific industry.

Q: Won't enabling all of these security features like WEP and a VPN bring performance to a halt?

A: Having the safeguards will bring with them slight performance degradation, but generally nothing too serious or noticeable. However, isn't keeping your data secure more important than a marginal slowdown?

Q: Is one type of AP or VPN better than another?

A: Some APs are very similar in their offerings, the same can be said for VPNs. Different scenarios need different solutions. The case studies we've discussed in this chapter have been as non-vendor specific as possible, and can be built, in most cases, regardless of which kind of hardware is used. For AP security, consider some of the security features we've discussed. Consult with the different vendors and choose the solution that best suits your wireless and security needs.

Q: Several hours to break WEP sounds like a lot to me, and therefore seems pretty impractical. So, isn't WEP enough to secure my wireless network?

A: Well, it's been said that nothing can stop a determined attacker. However, will WEP help stop opportunistic intrusions? Yes, most likely it will. However, if someone is *really* determined to break into your network, you'll need the extra security measures discussed here.

Q: I really like the idea behind the super-secure firewall case study, but it sounds very expensive. Is there any way to do something like that without spending a fortune?

A: That depends on several factors. One of the first to consider is the design of your current network. Which firewalls are you currently using? What type of licensing scheme do you have? If the hardware is there, adding a new network card to the firewall may be allowed in the licensing of your firewall software. If you're using a firewall product from a hardware vendor like Cisco, this may be more difficult. Of course, if nothing has been built yet, or you're willing to switch, there are many very good open source firewall products available for free. OpenBSD provides an excellent packet filtering firewall software with its distribution. If you're interested in proxy-based firewall systems, Zorp is a great choice, and runs under Linux.

Hack Proofing Your Wireless Network Fast Track

This Appendix will provide you with a quick, yet comprehensive, review of the most important concepts covered in this book.

❖ Chapter 1: The Wireless Challenge

Wireless Technology Overview

☑ Wireless technologies today come in several forms and offer a multitude of solutions applicable to generally one of two wireless networking camps: cellular-based and wireless LANs.

☑ Cellular-based wireless data solutions are solutions that use the existing cell phone and pager communications networks to transmit data.

☑ Wireless LAN solutions are solutions that provide wireless connectivity over a coverage area between 10 and 100 meters. These provide the capabilities necessary to support the two-way data communications of typical corporate or home desktop computers

☑ Open source code does not necessarily have to be free. For example, companies such as Red Hat and Caldera sell their products, which are based on the open source Linux kernel.

☑ Convergence within devices will be the norm over the next two years.

☑ While the majority of cellular-based wireless traffic today mainly consists of voice, it is estimated that by the end of 2003 nearly 35 to −40 percent of cellular-based wireless traffic will be data.

☑ Information appliances will have a big impact on wireless network deployments

☑ Information appliances are single purpose devices that are portable, easy to use, and provide a specific set of capabilities relevant to their function.

☑ Information appliance shipments will outnumber PC shipments this year.

Understanding the Promise of Wireless

☑ Corporate applications of wireless will consist of: Corporate Communications, Customer Service, Telemetry, and Field Service

☑ New wireless services will allow for a single point of contact that roams with the user.

☑ New context (time and location) sensitive applications will revolutionize the way we interact with data.

Chapter 1 Continued

Understanding the Benefits of Wireless

☑ New end user applications and services are being developed to provide businesses and consumers alike with advanced data access and manipulation

☑ The main benefits of wireless integration will fall primarily into five major categories: convenience, affordability, speed, aesthetics, and productivity.

Facing the Reality of Wireless Today

☑ Fraud remains a big issue.

☑ New more powerful and intelligent devices will provide additional options for attackers.

☑ The WAP standard is a moving target and still has many issues to overcome.

☑ WEP is limited and has many known security flaws.

☑ General wireless security posture: the majority of devices employ weak user authentication and poor encryption. Two-factor authentication, enhanced cryptography, and biometrics are necessary

Examining the Wireless Standards

☑ Cellular-based wireless networking technologies and solutions are categorized into three main groups: 2G Circuit Switched Cellular Wireless Networks, 2.5G Packed Data Overlay Cellular Wireless Networks, and 3G Packet Switched Cellular Wireless Networks.

☑ 3G will provide three generalized data networking throughputs to meet the specific needs of mobile users: High Mobility, Full Mobility, and Limited Mobility.

☑ High Mobility: High Mobility use is intended for generalized roaming outside urban areas in which the users are traveling at speeds in excess of 120 kilometers per hour. This category of use will provide the end user with up to 144 Kbps of data throughput.

☑ Full Mobility: Full Mobility use is intended for generalized roaming within urban areas in which the user is traveling at speeds below 120 kilometers per hour. This category of use will provide the end user with up to 384 Kbps of data throughput.

Chapter 1 Continued

- ☑ Limited Mobility: Limited Mobility use is intended for limited roaming or near stationary users traveling at 10 kilometers per hour or less. This category of use will provide the end user with up to 2 Mbps of data throughput when indoors and stationary.

- ☑ There are four largely competing commercial wireless LAN solutions available: 802.11 WLAN (Wireless Local Area Network), HomeRF, 802.15 WPAN (Wireless Personal Area Network) based on Bluetooth, and 802.16 WMAN (Wireless Metropolitan Area Network).

- ☑ The 802.11 standard provides a common standardized Media Access Control layer (MAC) that is similar to 802.3 Ethernet (CMSA/CA). It supports TCP/IP, UDP/IP, IPX, NETBEUI and so on, and has a Virtual Collision Detection VCD option. It also supports encrypted communications using WEP encryption. There are still many issues being worked on by the standards bodies, including support for voice and multimedia, QoS specifications, intervendor interoperability, distributed systems, and roaming.

- ☑ HomeRF is based on existing standards like TCP/IP and DECT. It is a solution aimed at the home wireless LAN market, and supports data, voice, and streaming multimedia.

- ☑ The 802.15 WPAN standard is based on Bluetooth, and provides a network interface for devices located within a personal area. It supports both voice and data traffic. 802.15 WPAN Task Groups are investigating issues including interoperability with other technologies.

- ☑ The 802.16 WMAN standard addresses support of broadband wireless solutions to enterprises, small businesses, and homes. Several working group streams are investigating solutions for licensed and unlicensed frequencies.

❖ Chapter 2: A Security Primer

Understanding Security Fundamentals and Principles of Protection

- ☑ "The Big Three" tenets of security are: *confidentiality*, *integrity*, and *availability*.

- ☑ Requirements needed to implement the principles of protection include proper authentication of authorized users through a system that provides for a clear identification of the users via tested non-repudiation techniques.

Chapter 2 Continued

☑ Logging or system accounting can be used by internal or external auditors to assure that the system is functioning and being utilized in accordance to defined standards and policies.

☑ Logging can also be the first place to look for evidence should an attack does occur. Ensure that logging is going to a trusted third-party site that cannot be accessed by personnel and resources being logged.

☑ These tools are essential to protecting the privacy of customer, partner, or trade secret information.

☑ Encryption has provided many tools for the implementation of these security fundamentals.

☑ Encryption is not the definitive solution to security problems. There is still a possibility that a known secret key could be stolen, or that one of the parties utilizing encryption could be tricked or forced into performing the activity, which would be seen as a valid cryptographic operation as the system has no knowledge of any collusion involved in the generation of the request.

Reviewing the Role of Policy

☑ Once basic fundamentals and principles are understood, then through the creation of policies and standards an organization or entity is able to clearly define how to design, implement, and monitor their infrastructure securely.

☑ Policies must have direct support and sign-in by the executive management of any organization.

☑ A properly mitigated risk should reduce the impact of the threat as well as the likelihood that that threat will occur.

☑ A clear and well-defined classification and labeling system is key to the identification of resources being protected.

☑ Information classification techniques also provide a method by which the items being classified can then have the proper policy or standards placed around them depending on the level or importance, as well as the risk associated with each identified item.

☑ Some organizations are required by their own regulations to have clear and well defined standards and policies.

Chapter 2 Continued

Recognizing Accepted Security and Privacy Standards

☑ Basic policies are based on years of research by the security community and have generated many security standards and legal documents that attempt to protect a company's information.

☑ Some standards provide methods of evaluating and reporting on targets being reviewed for security risks, as well as classifying the systems or resources of an entity.

☑ There are many government policies and regulations that have been enacted to protect the citizens' personal non-public information.

☑ Many businesses that utilize electronic record keeping fall under federal regulation when it comes to providing proper policy and protection of their information. Some of these industries include health care companies, financial services, insurance services, and video stores.

☑ Governments have accepted that Internet communications are going to occur within their own borders as well as internationally. Acts such as the E-Sign act were created to authorize electronic communications, and have activities that occur online have the same legal representation as if they had taken place first-hand.

☑ Many businesses that may not be regulated can also be required under civil liability law to have proper security policies and controls that protect their information.

Addressing Common Risks and Threats

☑ By examining the common threats to both wired and wireless networks, we are able to see how a solid understanding in the basics of security principles allows us to fully assess the risks associated with using wireless and other technologies.

☑ Threats can come from simple design issues, where multiple devices utilize the same setup, or intentional denial of service attacks which can result in the corruption or loss of data.

☑ Not all threats are caused by malicious users. They can also be caused by a conflict of similar resources, such as with 802.11b networks and cordless telephones.

Chapter 2 Continued

☑ With wireless networks going beyond the border of your office or home, chances are greater that your actions might be monitored by a third party.

☑ Unless your organization has clear and well-defined policies and guidelines you might find yourself in legal or business situations where your data is either compromised, lost, or disrupted. Without a clear plan of action that identifies what is important in certain scenarios, you will not be able to address situations as they occur.

❖ Chapter 3: Wireless Network Architecture and Design

Fixed Wireless Technologies

☑ In a fixed wireless network, both transmitter and receiver are at fixed locations, as opposed to mobile. The network uses utility power (AC). It can be point-to-point or point-to-multipoint, and may use licensed or unlicensed spectrums.

☑ Fixed wireless usually involves line-of-sight technology, which can be a disadvantage.

☑ The *fresnel* zone of a signal is the zone around the signal path that must be clear of reflective surfaces and clear from obstruction, to avoid absorption and reduction of the signal energy. *Multipath reflection* or interference happens when radio signals reflect off surfaces such as water or buildings in the fresnel zone, creating a condition where the same signal arrives at different times.

☑ Fixed wireless includes Wireless Local Loop technologies, Multichannel Multipoint Distribution Service (MMDS) and Local Multipoint Distribution Service (LMDS), and also Point-to-Point Microwave.

Developing WLANs through the 802.11 Architecture

☑ The North American wireless local area network (WLAN) standard is 802.11, set by the Institute of Electrical and Electronics Engineers (IEEE); HiperLAN is the European WLAN standard.

Chapter 3 Continued

☑ The three physical layer options for 802.11 are infrared (IR) baseband PHY and two radio frequency (RF) PHYs. The RF physical layer is comprised of Frequency Hopping Spread Spectrum (FHSS) and Direct Sequence Spread Spectrum (DSSS) in the 2.4 GHz band.

☑ WLAN technologies are not line-of-sight technologies.

☑ The standard has evolved through various initiatives from 802.11b, to 802.11a, which provides up to five times the bandwidth capacity of 802.11b—now, accompanying the every growing demand for multimedia services is the development of 802.11e.

☑ 802.11b provides 11 Mbps raw data rate in the 2.4 GHz transmission spectrum.

☑ 802.11a provides 25 to 54 Mbps raw data rate in the 5 GHz transmission spectrum.

☑ HiperLAN type 1 provides up to 20 Mbps raw data rate in the 5 GHz transmission spectrum.

☑ HiperLAN type 2 provides up to 54 Mbps raw data rate and QOS in the 5 GHz spectrum.

☑ The IEEE 802.11 standard provides three ways to provide a greater amount of security for the data that travels over the WLAN: use of the 802.11 Service Set Identifier (SSID); authentication by the Access Point (AP) against a list of MAC addresses; use of Wired Equivalent Privacy (WEP) encryption.

Developing WPANs through the 802.15 Architecture

☑ Wireless personal area networks (WPANs) are networks that occupy the space surrounding an individual or device, typically involving a 10m radius. This is referred to as a personal operating space (POS). WPANs relate to the 802.15 standard.

☑ WPANs are characterized by short transmission ranges.

☑ Bluetooth is a WPAN technology that operates in the 2.4 GHz spectrum with a raw bit rate of 1 Mbps at a range of 10 meters. It is not a line-of-sight technology. Bluetooth may interfere with existing 802.11 technologies in that spectrum.

Chapter 3 Continued

☑ HomeRF is similar to Bluetooth but targeted exclusively at the home market. HomeRF provides up to 10 Mbps raw data rate with SWAP 2.0.

Mobile Wireless Technologies

☑ Mobile wireless technology is basic cell phone technology; it is not a line-of-sight technology. The United States has generally progressed along the Code Division Multiple Access (CDMA) path, with Europe following the Global System for Mobile Communications (GSM) path.

☑ Emerging technologies are known in terms of *generations*: 1G refers to analog transmission of voice; 2G refers to digital transmission of voice; 2.5G refers to digital transmission of voice and limited bandwidth data; 3G refers to digital transmission of multimedia at broadband speeds (voice, video, and data).

☑ The Wireless Application Protocol (WAP) has been implemented by many of the carriers today as the specification for wireless content delivery. WAP is a nonproprietary specification that offers a standard method to access Internet-based content and services from wireless devices such as mobile phones and PDAs.

☑ The Global System for Mobile Communications (GSM) is an international standard for voice and data transmission over a wireless phone. A user can place an identification card called a Subscriber Identity Module (SIM) in the wireless device, and the device will take on the personal configurations and information of that user (telephone number, home system, and billing information).

Optical Wireless Technologies

☑ Optical wireless is a line-of-sight technology in the infrared (optical) portion of the spread spectrum. It is also referred to as free space optics (FSO), open air photonics, or infrared broadband.

☑ Optical wireless data rates and maximum distance capabilities are affected by visibility conditions, and by weather conditions such as fog and rain.

☑ Optical wireless has very high data rates over short distances (1.25 Gbps to 350 meters). Full duplex transmission provides additional bandwidth capabilities. The raw data rate available is up to a 3.75 kilometer distance with 10 Mbps.

Chapter 3 Continued

☑ There are no interference or licensing issues with optical wireless, and its data rate and distance capabilities are continuously expanding with technology advances.

Exploring the Design Process

☑ The design process consists of six major phases: preliminary investigation, analysis, preliminary design, detailed design, implementation, and documentation.

☑ In the early phases of the design process, the goal is to determine the cause or impetus for change. As a result, you'll want to understand the existing network as well as the applications and processes that the network is supporting.

☑ Because access to your wireless network takes place "over the air" between the client PC and the wireless Access Point, the point of entry for a wireless network segment is critical in order to maintain the integrity of the overall network.

☑ PC mobility should be factored into your design as well as your network costs. Unlike a wired network, users may require network access from multiple locations or continuous presence on the network between locations.

Creating the Design Methodology

☑ The NEM is broken down into several categories and stages; the category presented in this chapter is based on the execution and control category, for a service provider methodology. The execution and control category is broken down into planning, architecture, design, implementation, and operations.

☑ The planning phase contains several steps that are responsible for gathering all information and documenting initial ideas regarding the design. The plan consists mostly of documenting and conducting research about the needs of the client, which produces documents outlining competitive practices, gap analysis, and risk analysis.

Chapter 3 Continued

☑ The architecture phase is responsible for taking the results of the planning phase and marrying them with the business objectives or client goals. The architecture is a high-level conceptual design. At the conclusion of the architecture phase, a high-level topology, a high-level physical design, a high-level operating model, and a collocation architecture will be documented for the client.

☑ The design phase takes the architecture and makes it reality. It identifies specific details necessary to implement the new design and is intended to provide all information necessary to create the new network, in the form of a detailed topology, detailed physical design, detailed operations design, and maintenance plan.

Understanding Wireless Network Attributes from a Design Perspective

☑ It is important to take into account signal characteristics unique to wireless technologies from several design perspectives. For example, power consumption and operating system efficiency are two attributes that should be considered when planning applications and services over wireless LAN technologies.

☑ Spatial density is a key wireless attribute to focus on when planning your network due to network congestion and bandwidth contention.

❖ Chapter 4: Common Attacks and Vulnerabilities

The Weaknesses in WEP

☑ Wired Equivalent Privacy (WEP) is only optional for implementers of 802.11 equipment.

☑ The design of WEP initialization vector (IV) is weak and allows for identification of secret keys.

☑ Many implementers of WEP reset the IV each time the machine cycles, allowing for easier identification of secret key

Chapter 4 Continued

- ☑ IEEE knew early on in the development of 802.11 that there was a weakness in the IV used in WEP.

- ☑ Cyclic redundancy checks (CRCs) used to "protect" data only ensure that data was transmitted properly. Clever attackers are able to modify packets and still have valid CRCs.

- ☑ RC4, used as the stream cipher in WEP, has weak keys in the first 256 bytes of data. No implementations correct for this flaw.

- ☑ The seed used for WEP is simply the combination of the secret key and IV, and the IV is broadcast in cleartext, making it easier for attackers to deduce the secret key used in encryption.

- ☑ WEP either supports no keys or a shared key management system. Any stronger key management system need to be deployed by the consumer and very few products support external key management systems.

Conducting Reconnaissance

- ☑ The first popular software to identify wireless networks was NetStumbler.

- ☑ NetStumbler discovered wireless Access Points (APs) set up to broadcast network information to anyone listening.

- ☑ The APs broadcast information includes much information that can often be used to deduce the WEP key if encryption is activated.

- ☑ More than 50 percent of these networks have been identified as being non-encrypted.

- ☑ If the WEP key is not the system default. or is easily deduced from the secure set identifier (SSID) or the network name, several programs exist to exploit the weaknesses within WEP to identify the secret key.

- ☑ An attacker can send e-mail or other messages to the wireless networks through their wired/Internet connection to introduce additional known plaintext, making it easier to deduce the secret key.

- ☑ An attacker can either sit outside the wireless network or install remote APs using the small computers available today.

- ☑ High-tech attackers can use malware to gain access to secret key or other authentication information stored on users' machines.

Chapter 4 Continued

Sniffing, Interception, and Eavesdropping

☑ Electronic eavesdropping, or *sniffing*, is passive and undetectable to intrusion detection devices.

☑ Tools to sniff networks are available for Windows (such as Ethereal and AiroPeek) and UNIX (such as tcpdump and ngrep).

☑ Sniffing traffic allows attackers to identify additional resources that can be compromised.

☑ Even encrypted networks have been shown to disclose vital information in cleartext, such as the network name, that can be received by attackers sniffing the wireless local area network (LAN).

☑ Any authentication information that is broadcast can often be simply replayed to services requiring authentication (NT Domain, WEP Authentication, and so on) to access resources.

☑ The use of virtual private networks, Secure Sockets Layer (SSL), and Secure Shell (SSH) helps protect against wireless interception.

Spoofing and Unauthorized Access

☑ Due to the design of the Transmission Control Protocol/Internet Protocol (TCP/IP), there is little that can be done to prevent Media Access Control/IP (MAC/IP) address spoofing.

☑ Only through static definition of MAC address tables can this type of attack be prevented, however. due to significant overhead in management. this is rarely implemented.

☑ Only through diligent logging and monitoring of those logs can address spoofing attacks be identified.

☑ Wireless network authentication can be easily spoofed by simply replaying another node's authentication back to the AP when attempting to connect to the network.

☑ Many wireless equipment providers allow for end–users to redefine the MAC address within their cards through the configuration utilities that come with the equipment.

Chapter 4 Continued

☑   External two-factor authentication such as RADIUS or SecurID should be implemented to additionally restrict access requiring strong authentication to access the wireless resources.

Network Hijacking and Modification

☑   Due to the design of TCP/IP, some spoof attacks allow for attackers to hijack or take over network connections established for other resources on the wireless network.

☑   If an attacker hijacks the AP, then all traffic from the wireless network gets routed through the attacker, so they are then able to identify passwords and other information other users are attempting to use on valid network hosts.

☑   Many users are easily susceptible to these man-in-the-middle attacks, often entering their authentication information even after receiving many notifications that SSL or other keys are not what they should be.

☑   Rogue APs can assist the attacker by allowing remote access from wired or wireless networks.

☑   These attacks are often overlooked as just faults in the user's machine, allowing attackers to continue hijacking connections with little fear of being noticed.

Denial of Service and Flooding Attacks

☑   Many wireless networks within a small space can easily cause network disruptions and even denial of service (DoS) for valid network users.

☑   If an attacker hijacks the AP and does not pass traffic on to the proper destination, then all users of the network will be unable to use the network.

☑   Flooding the wireless network with transmissions can also prevent other devices from utilizing the resources, making the wireless network inaccessible to valid network users.

☑   Wireless attackers can utilize strong and directional antennas to attack the wireless network from a great distance.

Chapter 4 Continued

☑ An attacker who has access to the wired network can flood the wireless AP with more traffic than it can handle, preventing wireless users from accessing the wired network.

☑ Many new wireless products utilize the same wireless frequencies as 802.11 networks. A simple cordless telephone could create a DoS situation for the network more easily than any of the above mentioned techniques.

The Introduction of Malware

☑ Attackers are taking the search for access information directly to end users.

☑ Using exploits in users' systems, custom crafted applications can access Registry or other storage points to gain the WEP key and send it back to the attacker.

☑ New exploits are available every day for all end-user platforms.

☑ Malware attacks are already happening against Internet users.

☑ Even if the information is encrypted, it is often encrypted weakly, allowing for the attacker to quickly pull the cleartext information out.

☑ Keeping your software up to date and knowing where these exploits might come from (Web browser, e-mail, server services running when they shouldn't, and so on) is the only protection available.

Stealing User Devices

☑ Criminals have learned the value of the information contained in electronic devices.

☑ Notebook computers are smaller to run with than a bank vault!

☑ By obtaining just your wireless network card, an attacker would now have access to a valid MAC address used in your wireless network.

☑ When equipment is stolen, end users often do not think that the thief was after the data on the machine; instead they tend to believe that the thief was only after the machine itself.

☑ Your security policy should contain plans for dealing with authentication information stolen along with the theft of a machine.

❖ Chapter 5: Wireless Security Countermeasures

Revisiting Policy

- ☑ Policy is the set of rules that governs the management, use, implementation, and interaction of corporate assets. These assets include human resources, intellectual capital, hardware, software, networks and infrastructure, and data.

- ☑ Resources must be easily accessible for trusted users, while barriers are maintained for untrusted users.

- ☑ Policy must reflect changes in corporate structure. If policy fails to comply with reorganization, it will be as effective as last year's virus definitions against this year's virus.

- ☑ Wireless local area networks (WLANs) are an "edge" technology. Policy should reflect a standard consistent with end users attempting to gain access to network resources from the "edge."

Analyzing the Threat

- ☑ Analyzing the threat is the first step in securing any network.

- ☑ Recognize what threat, vulnerability, and risk mean as they pertain to securing your network.

- ☑ Identify assets and assign risk.

- ☑ Identify potential intruders and begin to formulate a mitigation plan.

Designing and Deploying a Secure Network

- ☑ Alter the defaults!

- ☑ Treat the Access Point (AP) like a Remote Access Server (RAS).

- ☑ Specify Internet Protocol (IP) ranges that are earmarked for the WLAN only.

- ☑ Use the highest-rated, supported security feature available on your AP.

- ☑ Consider the fact that using an antenna in a benefit for both the authorized and the intruder.

Chapter 5 Continued

☑ Apply consistent authorization rules across the edge of the network for all users.

☑ Deploy hardware where it is not easily tampered with.

Implementing WEP

☑ To protect against some rudimentary attacks that insert known text into the stream to attempt to reveal the key stream, Wired Equivalent Privacy (WEP) incorporates a check sum in each frame. Any frame not found to be valid through the check sum is discarded.

☑ Used on its own, WEP does not provide adequate WLAN security.

☑ WEP has to be implemented on every client as well as every AP to be effective.

☑ WEP keys are user definable and unlimited. You do not have to use predefined keys, and you can and should change them often.

☑ Implement the strongest version of WEP available and keep abreast of the latest upgrades to the standards.

Filtering MACs

☑ Apply Media Access Control (MAC) filters as a first line of defense. Each MAC address to be used on the WLAN should be recorded and configured on the AP for permission to access the network.

☑ Log failures and review the logs to determine if someone is attempting to breach security.

Filtering Protocols

☑ Filtering protocols is a relatively effective method for restricting WLAN users from attempting Simple Network Management Protocol (SNMP) access to the wireless devices to alter configurations, and for preventing the use of large Internet Control Message Protocol (ICMP) packets and other such protocols that can be used as Denial of Service (DoS) agents.

☑ Filter all the appropriate protocols and addresses to maintain control of the data traversing your network.

Chapter 5 Continued

Using Closed Systems and Networks

☑ Ease of capture of Radio frequency (RF) traffic can be overcome by preventing the broadcast of the Secure Set Identifier (SSID) to the world from the AP.

☑ Close the network to prevent null association whenever possible.

☑ Distribute the necessary client configuration information to WLAN users securely.

Allotting IPs

☑ Determine which method of allotting IPs best suits your organization: static or dynamically assigned addresses. Static addresses prevent a hacker from automatically being dealt an IP, where dynamic addresses ease the use of the WLAN with respect to already daunting administrative tasks.

☑ Static IP ranges make hackers have to guess what your subnet is for WLAN.

Using VPNs

☑ Use virtual private network (VPN) services where appropriate. They are the single most secure method of remote access available.

☑ Some APs (like Colubris Networks and Nokia) have built in VPNs for ease of implementation.

Securing Users

☑ Educate your users as to the risk associated with the uses of WLANs and the need for agreement in security policy. They are your single largest point of failure in your security model.

☑ Include the users in the process for the best information upon which to base decisions.

☑ Enforce the policies to the extent that it remains productive.

❖ Chapter 6: Circumventing Security Measures

Planning and Preparations

☑ In preparation for intrusion, a hacker will have to discover if a wireless network exists, as well as determine the boundaries of the wireless network. The necessary equipment includes a computer, an PCMCIA-based 802.11b radio, an antenna, and software.

☑ Windows users can use NetStumbler, which discovers *open networks*, or Ethernet sniffing programs like Network Associates' Sniffer Wireless or WildPacket's AiroPeek for the discovery of *closed networks*. Many Unix-based wireless network discovery tools exist, the most notable being Ethereal.

☑ *Open systems* or *open networks* accepts incoming connections if the end-device is looking for a wireless network with an "empty value" SSID. APs of a *closed network* ignore the "empty value" SSID beacons; programs like NetStumbler will not be able to ascertain the existence of that WLAN.

Exploiting WEP

☑ Exploiting the Wired Equivalent Privacy (WEP) standard is possible due to the reuse of weak initialization vectors.

☑ A static WEP key on an Access Point (AP) opens the door for future exploitation of past known keys.

☑ Cisco and Funk Software have released Access Control servers that support continual WEP re-keying, thus eliminating a static WEP key scenario.

War Driving

☑ War driving can only discover wireless local area networks (WLANs) that are operating as "open systems."

☑ War driving can be detected, but only if a large amount of effort is made.

☑ A good deal of the discovered information can be leveraged into potential attacks against the AP.

Chapter 6 Continued

Stealing User Devices

- ☑ A petty thief will see the dollar value of the physical hardware, and a sophisticated thief will understand that the data contained on the hard drive is far more valuable.

- ☑ The e-mail address, server information, and password can be captured and recorded from a stolen laptop. Next, it is possible to obtain the SSID and the WEP key for the corporate WLAN.

MAC Filtering

- ☑ Media Access Control (MAC) filtering is effective against casual attackers.

- ☑ MAC filtering can be circumvented by changing the MAC address on the client device.

- ☑ It is difficult to determine if the lack of association is due to MAC filtering or other reasons like an incorrect WEP key.

Bypassing Advanced Security Mechanisms

- ☑ Treat an AP the same way as another Remote Access Server.

- ☑ Change the AP's default settings: alter the network's SSID and change the access control. The Telnet capability can be disabled, passwords can be added to the SNMP configuration, and access to the Web front-end should be tightly controlled.

- ☑ The addition of firewall filtering by IP address and port will add a greater level of granularity to your access controls.

- ☑ Firewalls are only feasible if a strong security policy states that wireless devices will not have the same level of service as wired devices.

- ☑ Port filtering or proxying certain ports can prevent "drive-by spamming," or prohibit certain protocols altogether (like Telnet).

Exploiting Insiders

- ☑ The easiest way to gain entry into a network is with the assistance of someone who already has access to the network, often through social engineering.

Chapter 6 Continued

☑ Gaining passwords is a common goal of social engineers. Discovering old WEP keys is another.

Installing Rogue Access Points

☑ If an Access Point has been deployed on a network without the direct consent or knowledge of the IT staff, and without IT control, responsibility, or oversight, it is a *rogue Access Point*.

☑ Placing a rogue AP into a WLAN, ideally positioned in a location equidistant between the legitimate APs, provides an easy way of capturing network traffic, WEP keys, and other authentication information.

☑ Some strategies for detecting a rogue AP include the use of NetStumbler, systematic searches of the MAC addresses on the LAN, or by deploying 802.1x authentication throughout your WLAN.

Exploiting VPNs

☑ If a user is connecting to a VPN over the WLAN, a protocol analyzer could capture all packets related to the building of the VPN session. This data could be played back on a future attack or analyzed to see if vital information could be determined, such as VPN server IP address, or possible username/password pairs.

❖ Chapter 7: Monitoring and Intrusion Detection

Designing for Detection

☑ Get the right equipment from the start. Make sure all of the features you need, or will need, are available from the start.

☑ Know your environment. Identify potential physical barriers and possible sources of interference.

☑ If possible, integrate security monitoring and intrusion detection in your network from its inception.

Chapter 7 Continued

Defensive Monitoring Considerations

☑   Define your wireless network boundaries, and monitor to know if they're being exceeded.

☑   Limit signal strength to contain your network.

☑   Make a list of all authorized wireless Access Points (APs) in your environment. Knowing what's there can help you immediately identify rogue APs.

Intrusion Detection Strategies

☑   Watch for unauthorized traffic on your network. Odd traffic can be a warning sign.

☑   Choose an intrusion detection software that best suits the needs of your environment. Make sure it supports customizable and updateable signatures.

☑   Keep your signature files current. Whether modifying them yourself, or downloading updates from the manufacturer, make sure this step isn't forgotten.

Conducting Vulnerability Assessments

☑   Use tools like NetStumbler and various client software to measure the strength of your 802.11b signal.

☑   Identify weaknesses in your wireless and wired security infrastructure.

☑   Use the findings to know where to fortify your defenses.

☑   Increase monitoring of potential trouble spots.

Incident Response and Handling

☑   If you already have a standard incident response policy, make updates to it to reflect new potential wireless incidents.

☑   Great incident response policy templates can be found on the Internet.

☑   While updating the policy for wireless activity, take the opportunity to review the policy in its entirety, and make changes where necessary to stay current. An out-of-date incident response policy can be as damaging as not having one at all.

Chapter 7 Continued

Conducting Site Surveys for Rogue Access Points

☑ The threat is real, so be prepared. Have a notebook computer handy to use specifically for scanning networks.

☑ Conduct walkthroughs of your premises regularly, even if you don't have a wireless network.

☑ Keep a list of all authorized APs. Remember, Rogue APs aren't necessarily only placed by attackers. A well-meaning employee can install APs as well.

❖ Chapter 8: Auditing

Designing and Planning a Successful Audit

☑ Audits are a means of assessing systems against established standards of operation and industry best practices, and of establishing metrics through performance measurements.

☑ Audits are performed to assess risk, to measure system operation against expectations, to measure compliance to policies, to verify change management, and to assess damage.

☑ Audits and assessments are part of the lifecycle of systems. They are used to implement policies, as well as promote awareness, which in turn can then be reaudited and assessed, feeding the cycle again.

☑ Audits are typically performed at system launch, on schedule, during a maintenance window, and during unplanned emergencies.

Defining Standards

☑ Technology standards, which are defined by standards bodies, governments, and professional organizations, generally specify the operations applicable for a given environment, with methodologies that can be used to address specific issues.

☑ Some standards are open to interpretation by equipment vendors and implementers, while others provide very thorough definitions of each of the elements used in a system.

☑ Very few standards exist that specifically address wireless networks.

Chapter 8 Continued

☑ Wireless network deployment corporate policies are defined by one or more governing bodies (such as the legal department) within an organization, which establish the benchmark for the implementation and deployment of technologies and services within their environments.

Performing the Audit

☑ Audits are performed in accordance with prespecified and preapproved plans.

☑ The steps involved in performing a wireless audit include audit planning, audit information gathering, audit information analysis and report generation, audit report presentation, post-audit review, and auditing next steps.

☑ There are different types of audits. Both host audits and component audits should be performed every 12 to 24 months, while network audits should be performed every 12 months. Critical system audits, on the other hand, should be performed every 6 months.

☑ Wireless network audits consist of technical and staff interviews, as well as policy and procedure reviews.

☑ Wireless audit interviewing tools include questionnaires, spreadsheets, and matrix tables.

☑ Wireless audit technical auditing tools include wireless scanners, password crackers, and protocol analyzers.

☑ Some of the critical factors in performing the audit include senior management support, determining the focus of the audits, a documented audit process, business unit and technology group involvement, and efficient and secure audit data documentation process.

☑ Wireless network audits are performed by authorized auditing personnel who have an understanding of organization, wireless technology, as well as an understanding of security.

Analyzing Audit Data

☑ The audit data analysis phase involves the review of all captured data from interviews, scans, and system documentation for compliance against accepted standards, policies, procedures, and guidance.

Chapter 8 Continued

Generating Audit Reports

☑   When generating the wireless network audit report, auditors must ensure that the readers feel confident in the audit findings and that they can substantiate claims and address challenges to audit findings.

☑   Reports consist of several sections including:

- An executive summary which provides a succinct overview of report and key findings.

- A prioritized recommendations listing which provides bullet form descriptions of major recommendations in order of priority and impact.

- A main body which is a thorough account of the wireless network audit details and findings.

- A detailed recommendations section which lists a synopsis of all the findings identified in the main body.

- A final conclusions section that provides a review of the key findings and an overall grade or evaluation of the audited system.

- Appendices which contain the detailed audit data that did not fit within the main body.

- A glossary that lists alphabetized terms used in the audit report.

❖ Chapter 9: Case Scenarios

Implementing a Non-secure Wireless Network

☑   Continuing war driving tests and media reports show that in some metropolitan areas fewer than 35 percent of wireless local area networks (WLANs) are even using Wired Equivalent Privacy (WEP).

☑   Setting up a wireless Access Point (AP) is as easy as removing it from its packaging, powering it up, and plugging it in to your local area network. The network has now been opened up to the public, and anyone walking or driving by can freely peruse the network.

☑   The manufacturers try to make setup as easy as possible, so most APs broadcast their availability and allow anyone with any Extended Service Set

Chapter 9 Continued

Identifier (ESSID) to connect. WEP comes disabled by default because the AP administrator must set the passphrase or keys.

Implementing an Ultra-secure WLAN

☑ Make sure that your AP allows you to change ESSID, passwords, and supports 128-bit WEP.

☑ If possible, find an AP that supports the "closed network" functionality, meaning that it doesn't broadcast your ESSID.

☑ Be certain that the AP you buy supports flash upgrades. This will be useful for the manufacturer when it comes time to add new functionality and fix problems with the firmware.

☑ Isolate the AP and regulate access from its network into your internal network.

☑ Conduct audits of your network using NetStumbler or other wireless scanning tools to make sure others aren't enabling unauthorized APs.

☑ Update security policy to reflect the dangers of an unsecured wireless network.

Taking a War Drive

☑ Get to know the tools of the trade. Learn how to use NetStumbler, dstumble, AirSnort, and other tools.

☑ Use other open networks as leverage to convince others of the dangers of an open wireless network.

☑ Be certain you don't exploit or use networks that you find with NetStumbler. Seeing the networks is one thing, but joining and using network resources is another.

Scouting Your Location

☑ Know your environment. Research the construction of your building and design appropriately.

☑ Make a list of potentially problematic structures or sources of interference and try to work around them.

Chapter 9 Continued

☑ Test, test, test. In order to build the perfect installation, lots of testing will be necessary.

Developing a Wireless Security Checklist

☑ Patch machines on your internal network. Vendors generally have updates posted on their Web sites. If a server hasn't been patched in the past six months, there's a very good chance it's vulnerable.

☑ Even if you have no plans to implement a wireless solution, you never know when a wireless AP may be added to your network. Taking a proactive approach to security machines can save time and money in the long run.

☑ Consider an intrusion detection system (IDS) on your internal network to clue you in to scanning. Being scanned on your internal network should set off some really loud alarms.

Index

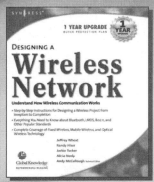

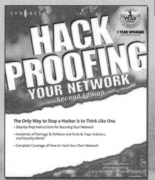